# SIREN FEASTS

Cheese, wine, honey and olive oil – four of Greece's most familiar contributions to culinary culture – were already well known four thousand years ago. Remains of beehives and of cheeses have been found under the volcanic ash of the Santorini eruption of 1627 BC. Over the millennia, Greek food has diversified and absorbed neighbouring traditions, yet retained its own distinctive character.

*Siren Feasts* is the first scholarly social history of food and gastronomy in Greece. It traces this unbroken tradition of fine food and wine from classical times, through Rome and medieval Europe, to what we eat and drink today. The focus is on the Classical, Hellenistic and Roman periods. Andrew Dalby shows how an understanding of the food and gastronomy of ancient Greece provides a useful background to reading Greek comedy and lyric poetry. His innovative study also includes discussion of the first specialist writers on food, such as Archestratus and Philoxenus.

*Siren Feasts* is comprehensively illustrated, and source material is quoted in English throughout. It is invaluable and engaging reading for all students and teachers of Greek history, and anyone who is interested in the gastronomic tradition of Greece.

**Andrew Dalby** trained as a classicist and linguist and is now Librarian of the London Goodenough Trust for Overseas Graduates. He is the winner of the 1996 Sophie Coe Prize in Food History.

*Frontispiece* Heracles as a dinner guest of Eurytius of Oechalia and his four sons. Heracles is a suitor for their sister Iole, who serves him. The young Iphitus gazes at Heracles (right), whose marriage request he alone favours. In a later encounter, unaware of Iphitus' support, Heracles will kill him. The tragedy is told in a single icon. Corinthian *kratér* in the Louvre, no. E635 (see also Figures 18 and 21)

# SIREN FEASTS

## A history of food and gastronomy in Greece

*Andrew Dalby*

London and New York

First published 1996
by Routledge
11 New Fetter Lane, London EC4P 4EE

Simultaneously published in the USA and Canada
by Routledge
29 West 35th Street, New York, NY 10001

First published in paperback 1997

Phototypeset in Garamond by Intype, London
Printed and bound in Great Britain by
Biddles Ltd, Guildford & King's Lynn

*British Library Cataloguing in Publication Data*
A catalogue record for this book is available from the British Library

*Library of Congress Cataloguing in Publication Data*
A catalogue record for this book is available from the Library of Congress

ISBN 0–415–11620–1 (hbk)
ISBN 0–415–15657–2 (pbk)

To the Greek climate we owe the development of Taste.
J. J. Winckelmann, *Gedanken über die Nachahmung der griechischen Werke in der Malerei und Bildhauerkunst*, 1755

# CONTENTS

*List of figures*   ix
*Preface*   xi
*Acknowledgements*   xv

1 THE WAY THESE PEOPLE SACRIFICE   1

## Part I   The prehistoric Aegean

2 THE GARDENS OF ALCINOUS   33

## Part II   Food and gastronomy of the classical Aegean

3 DIVINE INVENTIONS   57

4 IN THE FEASTS OF THE LYDIANS   93

5 SICILIAN TABLES   113

## Part III   Food and gastronomy of the post-classical Aegean

6 LEMONS OF THE HESPERIDES   133

7 STRYMONIAN EELS   152

8 THE IMPERIAL SYNTHESIS   168

## Part IV   The Byzantine and later Aegean

9 BISCUITS FROM BYZANTIUM   187

*Notes*   212
*Bibliography*   267
*Index of ancient and medieval sources*   287
*Greek index*   297
*General index*   310

# FIGURES

Frontispiece   Heracles as dinner guest of Eurytius of Oechalia and
his four sons                                                                    ii

1 A waitress is slapped by a diner as she spills wine over him            8
2 Classical funerary relief depicting (as often) the dead man reclining
   at a meal, attended by his household                                    16
3 After the *sympósion* a reveller captures a musician                     19
4 *Kápparis*: the caper bush, whose pickled buds were Phryne's
   earliest stock-in-trade                                                 26
5 Satyr and woman, from a sixth-century BC vase found at Istria, an
   early Greek colony on the Black Sea coast                               30
6 Threshing lentils: Alonnisos, about 1970                                 41
7 Two wild fruits of the Aegean region: (a) *kránon*, cornel (cornelian
   cherry); (b) *lotós* or *palíouros*, hackberry (nettle wood)            44
8 *Sykon* and *sykalís*: fig and blackcap ('fig-pecker') redrawn from a
   Roman wall-painting from Boscotrecase, Campania                         54
9 *Attagâs*: the francolin, observed on Samos in the eighteenth
   century, but said now to have disappeared from Greece                   64
10 *Glaûkos*, a prized fish but not firmly identified                      69
11 *Orphôs*: the grouper or mérou, modern Greek *rofós*, Turkish *orfoz*   70
12 *Skáros*: parrot wrasse was one of the gourmet treats of the Roman
   Empire, though less sought after at other times                        71
13 *Khéme leiá* or simply *leiá*                                           73
14 *Téthyon*: not an oyster – not even in the *Iliad* – but a sea-squirt, a
   delicacy still appreciated in Provence: an ancient recipe is supplied
   by Xenocrates                                                           74
15 Two greens: (a) *adráphaxys*, orach; and (b), nowadays much more
   commonly used, spinach (modern Greek *spanákia*)                        84
16 A silphium plant, the traditional type of Cyrene, here paired with
   the horseman sometimes seen on the gold coins of the city              87
17 *Magydaris*, the plant that so closely resembled silphium,
   flourishing on Rhodes                                                   88

18 Heracles as dinner guest of Eurytius of Oechalia and his children   94
19 Drinking party in a vineyard   98
20 A waiter dips wine from a *kratér*   102
21 Behind Heracles' couch, at Eurytius' feast, wine stands in a *kratér* and meat is prepared for dinner   112
22 Red mullet have pride of place among the catch at a small harbour just south of Miletus on the Turkish shore of the Aegean – just as they did around 360 BC when Archestratus visited the place   117
23 *Aphye*: the anchovy, *engraulís*   120
24 Fruit as a punning coin type   126
25 The *agorá* at Ephesus   129
26 Fruit and vegetables in the modern covered market at Bodrum (Halicarnassus)   134
27 *Melánthion* and *kyminon aithiopikón*: the local substitute, love-in-a-mist, and the Indian spice plant, nigella   139
28 Hecamede mixes *kykeón* for the white-bearded Nestor   151
29 Drunkenness in the later stages of a *sympósion*   155
30 A flute-player oblivious to her audience's inebriation   170
31 Preparing a meal on the beach: Alonnisos, about 1930   183
32 Honeycombs on sale in the spice market of Istanbul   191
33 Pierre Belon, sensitive observer of early Ottoman Greece and of Venetian Crete   194
34 *Orkhís, satyrídion*: the bulbs of Orchis mascula are the favoured constituent of *salep*   202
35 The coffee shop, *kafeneío*, a traditional masculine preserve which thus serves one or two functions of the ancient *sympósion*   206
36 The Easter lamb: Alonnisos, about 1980   208
37 A sixteenth-century sherbet-vendor   210

# PREFACE

This is the book that I wanted to have beside me when I began to study the social history of Greece. The food and entertainment of the classical Aegean are rich fields for research, endlessly fascinating in themselves, indispensable background for all who study the ancient world, important to anthropologists and to students of later Mediterranean history; yet no one in this century has set out to guide others to what is known and to provide a starting-point for further research.

Beginning with an exploration of the dining and drinking of the classical Aegean, we shall gradually expand the enquiry to earlier and later times, concentrating on two questions. What did Greeks eat? How did gastronomy and food writing develop among them?

It is a big subject. The sources of information are disparate, and no specialist commands them all. I begin from the classical written evidence. But in reading modern papers on aspects of classical social life, one soon becomes aware that their authors could be led astray by mistaken assumptions as to what went before and what came after: that is one reason why the plan of this work includes a second chapter on the food of the prehistoric Aegean and a last chapter sketching some Byzantine and modern developments.

On some of the topics that are dealt with here, every modern scholar seems to have written something. Others, such as the development of Greek gastronomy and gastronomic writing, have scarcely been touched. The level of detail, and the closeness of argument, in the present book must therefore vary. I may be thought to have spent too long on the food writers and authors of recipe books. The reason is that reliable information about them cannot be found conveniently gathered elsewhere.

The references given in the end notes (pp. 212–66) are limited in number and carefully selected. I have tried to keep in mind the needs of readers in other fields equally with those whose main interest is Greek history and literature. Both kinds of references, those to ancient texts and to modern scholarship, will, I hope, be useful to both kinds of readers.

From the huge modern literature on Greek social history, and on the history and archaeology of food, references are generally given here only to recent outlines or definitive treatments. In these, as a rule, full bibliographies will usually be found. References have also been given to some modern commentaries on classical texts, in cases where the editor has usefully brought together parallel passages and thus assisted the study of a particular word or aspect of behaviour. For full details of works cited, see the bibliography (pp. 267–86).

References to ancient texts are, wherever possible, to standard text divisions to be found in most modern editions and translations: some guidance will be found in the index of ancient and medieval sources (pp. 287–96). With the availability of the Thesaurus Linguae Graecae on CD-ROM, classicists will soon no longer need or expect in works of this kind exhaustive references to the use of a particular word. My aim is to save readers' time by selecting those references that will help to put a topic in context or otherwise assist its understanding.

Since Athenaeus' *Deipnosophists* remains the largest fund of source material on the subject and will be more accessible to many readers than the expensive standard editions of fragmentary authors, a reference – in square brackets – has been given to the *Deipnosophists* whenever a cited text can be found there. These citations follow the standard reference system for Athenaeus, the page numbers of Casaubon's 1597 edition: Casaubon's page numbers are repeated in the margins of nearly every subsequent edition. As there is a great difference between the coherence and reliability of the full text (which survives for most of books 3 to 15, as will be explained in Chapter 8) and of the late Byzantine epitome, the distinction is here signalled by citing the former as 'Athenaeus' and the latter as '*Epitome*'.

Those who use the English translation of Athenaeus' *Deipnosophists* by C. B. Gulick in the Loeb Classical Library text of Athenaeus (Cambridge, Mass.: Harvard University Press, 1927–41), and indeed those who use English translations of other texts cited, will often find that their translators' views on points of detail differ from mine. The translation of classical Greek texts is not an exact science. The many points of uncertainty signalled in the course of the present work help to show why. I have generally tried to translate quoted texts just as they appear in the manuscripts, if the manuscript text will bear a meaning, for modern conjectures have (to say the least) uncertain status as evidence.

The Greek index (pp. 297–309) serves as a supplement to the text. Under most names of foodstuffs, in the Greek index, will be found the scientific Latin term for the plant or animal concerned. English, modern Greek and Turkish equivalents have also been given where possible.

In this book I have not tried to convert ancient lists of ingredients, or cookery instructions, into recipes for modern use. For this see *The classical cookbook* by Sally Grainger and myself (British Museum Publications, forthcoming)!

The transliteration of Greek that is adopted here retains the accents (tonal accent in classical Greek, word stress in later forms of the language) because of their special importance in word history.

Italics have not been used for botanical names, as is customary, in order to distinguish them clearly from classical Latin names.

# ACKNOWLEDGEMENTS

I must first acknowledge the help of an ancient author. With all his digressions, for which modern scholars in so many fields are grateful, Athenaeus in the *Deipnosophists* put together a record of researches very similar in intention to mine. I hope the more explicit and obtrusive structure necessary in what is intended to serve as a handbook does not destroy the fascination of the subject on which he and I have worked.

I have had the advantage of seeing most of the papers which will by now have appeared in *Food in antiquity* (Exeter University Press), 1995, a volume which carries forward the study of many topics discussed here: I am grateful to the editor, John Wilkins, for letting me see them in proof.

Begun simply as a leisure activity, the work that follows became the first half of my Ph.D thesis (Birkbeck College, University of London, 1992). I am grateful to Jane Rowlandson, who supervised it; to Lin Foxhall and Robin Osborne, who examined it; to Gerald and Valerie Mars, Feyzi Halici and Harlan Walker, under whose respective auspices some of this work was presented to the London Food Seminar, the International Food Congress and the Oxford Food Symposium; and to Alan Davidson, who published my first notes on Philoxenus and Hippolochus and has also allowed me to reproduce illustrations by Soun Vannithone and others that were originally made for his *Mediterranean seafood* (Penguin). I want to thank Caroline Davidson and Richard Stoneman without whom this book might well not have been published; Joanne Snooks, Vicky Peters and Sarah Conibear, whose hard work has brought it nearer the heart's desire; and Maureen, Elizabeth and Rachel, who have lived with it as well as with me for all this time.

I am grateful to the following for permission to reproduce copyright illustrations: Alan Davidson (Figures 11, 13, 14 and 23); Rena Salaman (Figures 6, 31, 35 and 36); Professor R. B. Barlow (Figures 22, 25 and 26); Agence Photographique, Réunion des Musées Nationaux (frontispiece and Figures 3, 18, 20, 21, 28 and 30); Ashmolean Museum (Figure 19); the Master and Fellows of Corpus Christi College, Cambridge (Figure 29); the Martin von Wagner-Museum, Universität Würzburg (Figure 1; photo: K. Oehrlein); and Spink & Co (Figures 16 and 24).

# 1

# THE WAY THESE PEOPLE
# SACRIFICE[1]

The food and gastronomy of Greece are part of the background to the history of the country, a history that demands the attention of all who are interested in the sources of their own civilisation. Greek gastronomy is also the direct ancestor of the much better known food culture of Rome. Thus it stands at the origin of much in modern European food and cuisine.

This book tells two stories in parallel. It is a history of the foods that have belonged to the Greek menu; it also explores how traditions of cookery and food appreciation developed, for the first time in Europe and with very little precedent anywhere in the world, in the special environment of the Aegean shores.

Little will be said here of political history. The appearance of new foods and new methods of cookery has usually nothing to do with politics but much to do with trade; it usually comes from the interchange of peoples and ideas. We shall see that many foods now well known in Greece and Turkey have a history in the region longer than either the Turks or the Greeks themselves.

It is necessary to set the scene by saying something of the social context in which these foods were eaten. This can most easily be done by sketching the meals and entertainments of classical Athens, the best known and best recorded of all ancient Greek societies. The best known – yet in spite of the wealth of classical literature, some aspects of the private life of classical Athens are anything but clear.

We can begin from an important, quite newly available, literary source of the end of the fourth century BC. Before the rediscovery of Menander's *Bad-Tempered Man* there was not one extended description of a family meal in the literature of classical Greece: the earliest otherwise, four centuries later and of questionable realism, is the one in Dio Chrysostom's *Euboean Oration*. The study of this Athenian comedy therefore brings about a small revolution in modern views of Athenian family life – and it entails the reinterpretation of some literary evidence that has long been known.

The 'New Comedy' of Athens has in the past been all too unfamiliar.

1

Not one complete play was transmitted from Byzantine to later European scholarship. Moreover, the original nature of the genre was effectively obscured, for later readers, by the gradually developing imitations of it that have successively charmed audiences in republican Rome, in Renaissance and in modern Europe. With twentieth-century discoveries of papyri, the known corpus of plays of Menander, the greatest playwright of the New Comedy, has been growing.[2]

At the centre of our study are the personal, individual, domestic and family contexts of Greek food. This perspective will in itself result in some surprises. Little will be said here of dinner at the town hall; little of dinners of clubs or brotherhoods. The real importance of such events in classical daily life is hard to grasp, for we know little of them except that they occurred. We shall see something of dinner at a *hetairá*'s, a 'courtesan's'; we shall see something of *parásitoi*, a concept sadly confused by dramatists and by the antiquarians of the Roman Empire.

We highlight not the commonwealth of citizens but the well-defended private house. And the reality visible through Athenian authors' depiction of their own contemporary experience is less hospitable and more defensive than might be assumed. Athenians locked their house doors (Demosthenes, *Against Euergus and Mnesibulus* 35–8) and locked the tower that formed the 'women's quarters', the *gynaikonîtis*, of a country farm (ibid. 53–5). The locked doors of Athens were opened on the householder's orders. To force them open, most particularly in his absence, was a shocking act. At least one Athenian, appealed to by his neighbour's slaves to help deal with burglars, 'did not think it right [to enter] when the householder was not there' (ibid. 60).[3] These doors were opened to his family, of course. They were opened to his friends, his 'equals', when they came to dine and to drink. They were also opened to some who had something to offer in exchange for their food, the dancer, the musician, the prostitute, the poet, the philosopher, the joker, the flatterer.

## THE UNEQUAL FEAST

In Menander's *Bad-Tempered Man* a festive day in the life of a whole family is to be enacted – the central sacrifice and feast are to be imagined just out of view. But one half of this domestic life is passed over almost in silence. The mother of the hero, Sostratus, is not named; she apparently speaks briefly two or three times, though that is far from certain. Speaking or not, she crosses the stage from the Athens road to the central shrine and is lost to the audience's sight. Her daughter may or may not be with her.[4] The 'bad-tempered man''s daughter speaks once from her doorway: she is not named. The least anonymous women in the play are two slaves. One has a speaking part, but even she is not named until very late in the action (931). Another, silent, comes in for a male slave's abuse: 'she's good for nothing except screwing – and blaming me when we're caught' (461–3).

The silence that veils almost all the women's activities, and even their names, does not impugn the realism of the play. There is plenty of evidence that many Athenian women's lives were secluded from the observation of strange men, so that a plaintiff, complaining of trespass, could speak of intrusion on 'my sister and my nieces, who had had such a modest life that they were shy of being seen even by relations' (Lysias, *Against Simon* 6). They went outdoors rather seldom, and if outdoors they were not to be 'seen', still less accosted, by men.[5] Moreover, they were publicly named by their relationship to a man and not by their own personal names: 'A woman who goes out of the house ought to be at the stage of life at which those who meet her do not ask whose wife but whose mother she is', not, at all events, what her own name is (Hypereides fragment 205 [Stobaeus, *Florilegium* 74.33]).[6] So it is that we hear something of Sostratus' mother and his sister; but we see them only briefly, and cannot be sure of their names. Athenian plays, like nearly all Athenian literary works, were dialogues among men: male depictions of a male world.[7]

Women melt into the background of the *Bad-Tempered Man*. But if we dare to focus on this background, there is much to be seen. The centre of the day is a sacrifice at a country shrine of the god Pan, a sacrifice naturally followed by an open-air meal and jollity. For Greek sacrifice, not unlike feast days in many other religious systems, was at the same time a religious observance, an occasion for enjoyment and an opportunity for meat-eating. An acid comment on this by the eponymous bad-tempered man, Cnemon, happened to be known from a quotation by Athenaeus before the full text of the play was rediscovered: 'The way these vandals sacrifice! They bring couches, wine-jars – not for the gods, for themselves. . . . They offer the gods the tail-end and the gall-bladder, the bits you can't eat, and gobble the rest themselves' (Menander, *Bad-Tempered Man* 447–53). Editors of Athenaeus and of the fragments of comedy, unable to understand or believe that the circumstances were essentially those of a picnic, in printing this fragment had customarily removed the reference to the fetching in of couches.[8]

Every detail of this sacrifice – when it was to take place, where and to whom, what was to be sacrificed – all these decisions are in the dialogue explicitly attributed to women and slaves in spite of the women's near invisibility. Such decisions are clearly central to a household's life: they also involve considerable expense (in the purchase of a whole sheep, in the hire of a cook, and no doubt in arrangements to be made at the shrine). The sacrifice itself takes place, to no one's apparent concern, before the free men of the house have put in an appearance. Sostratus and his father are content to turn up late and eat their lunch. One is not surprised, then, to find that Callippides (who must make the formal decision) is the last to hear of Sostratus' hopes of a wedding, long after the slaves and the women know all about it.

Let us retrace the leisurely progress of the fictional sacrifice and meal. Sostratus' mother, unusually enthusiastic for the kind of piety that entailed country sacrifices, had decided on the event and its location after a dream.[9] The family slave Getas had been sent to hire the indispensable *mágeiros* 'sacrificer-cook' – and presumably to select the sheep. Sicon (the *mágeiros*) and Getas arrive first at the shrine:

> 'Getas, boy, you're a long way behind.'
> 'Those blasted women fastened up four donkey-loads for me to carry.'
> 'There's a big group coming, then. I can't count the rugs you're carrying. Put them here.'
> 'Yes, if she has a dream about Pan of Paeania, we're off there straight away, you know, off to a sacrifice.'
> 'Someone's had a dream, eh? Who?'
> 'The mistress! She saw Pan, here, putting our young master Sostratus in chains and telling him to get digging – in this very field. That's why we're sacrificing, so that the bad omen will turn to good.'
> 'Pick this stuff up again and take it in. We'll put the mats in place inside and get the other things ready. Nothing's to hold up the sacrifice once they arrive.'
>
> (401–21, abridged)

An interlude allows Getas to say, when his mistress (Sostratus' mother) arrives with daughter and maid (430–9):

> 'We've been sitting waiting for an age.'
> 'Is everything ready for us?'
> 'Of course. The old sheep can't wait for you. Nearly died already, poor thing. Well, come in. Get the baskets ready, the water-jugs, the incense-cakes. . . .'

The sheep must thereupon be slaughtered, though the event goes unnoticed. The dramatist now compresses time drastically. Sostratus appears and is told by Getas:

> 'We've just sacrificed, and we're making your lunch.'
> 'Is mother here?'
> 'Been here for ages.'
> 'Father?'
> 'Expected. Go on in.'

Sostratus invites his new friend Gorgias, and Gorgias' slave, to join him, and Gorgias accepts (619). An interlude follows. At last Callippides, the head of the household, arrives (775):

'I'm probably too late. They'll have scoffed the mutton and be away
in the countryside.'
'Poseidon! He's ravenous. Shall we ask him now?'
'Let him have lunch first. That'll soften him.'
'Now then, Sostratus. Have you lunched?'
'There's some left for you, father.'

These comings and goings are skilfully interwoven as a backdrop to the
main plot (Sostratus' falling in love with the bad-tempered Cnemon's
daughter), but they can hardly be used as evidence for social history
without examining their overall realism. It is necessary to the plot that
Callippides should arrive late; Sostratus, by the one really unlikely coincidence in the play – or rather, thanks to the arrangements of the god Pan
– turns up just when he is expected though he had not even known the
location of the sacrifice. But the salient point is that both of them were
expected to arrive long after the women. The women came later than
expected too, but they were certainly expected to arrive after the single
slave and the *mágeiros* who had appeared first to prepare the scene. It
seems reasonable to conclude that such staggered arrivals, for a family
sacrifice, would not be wholly abnormal, otherwise Menander would have
offered more in the way of motivation or excuses.

## SEPARATE CIRCLES

When did the women eat? So little is said that is relevant to the question
in any other classical Athenian context that one is reduced to making the
most of a single meagre hint. Gorgias, invited by Sostratus to the sacrificial
meal, answers that he must see to his mother first. There is no dramatic
reason to delay Gorgias' presence at the shrine; hence this seems to be a
piece of realism. So why, since Gorgias's slave could be invited to eat,
could his mother not be invited too (616–19)? Women lunched with other
women, after all.[10] The best answer is that the women are by now supposed
to have finished their meal: they arrived earlier than the men, were present
at the sacrifice and ate straight afterwards. The women's meal was *followed*
by the men's – itself staggered, but only because Callippides was late –
and it would have been impossible to invite Gorgias' mother to the men's
meal. Thus Getas can say (568–70) with the advantage of recent observation
that the women would not dream of sharing their meal: they had then just
eaten, and without any guests.

The hypothesis that the women's meal and the men's meal were separate
can now be set against other Athenian evidence on men, women and their
food.[11] This demands careful interpretation. 'Married women do not go
out to dinners with their husbands, nor do they care to dine with men of
other families' (Isaeus, *On Pyrrhus' Estate* 14): this remark by a litigant

forms part of a demonstration that a certain Phile was promiscuous. One could read it as evidence that respectable women did not eat outside their own households. The most convincing interpretation, however, is that family festivity could involve both men and women, but that the sexes formed separate groups, sometimes with different timetables. The separateness appears most clearly from a quotation from Euangelus' *Unveiled* in which the bride's father reminds the cook: 'I told you, four tables for the women and six for the men' (Euangelus 1 [Athenaeus 644d]). This is said to be a late text, of the third or even the second century BC. But already towards the end of the *Bad-Tempered Man*, when all has been resolved, Sostratus can say to his father:

> 'There must be a good drink for us now, dad, and an all-night wake for the women.'
> 'I know better – the women'll drink, and we'll be kept awake all night!'
>
> (855–9)

All-night festivity really was particularly associated with women.[12] Indeed, it is central to the plot of Menander's *Arbitrators* that the flute-girl Habrotonon attended the Tauropolia, a women's all-night festival, with a party of respectable women and played to accompany the girls' dancing (451–85). But whether or not the women's celebrations on the present occasion were expected to last all night, the picture of festivities for the two sexes going on side by side is finally confirmed by Sicon's boast at the very end of the *Bad-Tempered Man*:

> 'Up there I got ready a symposium for the men. . . . [Getas] spread a semicircle of rugs on the ground, I did the tables: that's my proper job[13] . . . I'm a *mágeiros*, remember . . . and someone tipped bearded old *Eúios*[14] into a deep jug, mixed with the streams of the Nymphs [water], and drank toasts with the men in their ring, and another with the women; and it was like pouring it into sand.'
>
> (940–9)

## THE OFFICIATORS

Those who constructed the menu of a meal, and who put it into effect, considered another set of demands besides those of the host and his guests. They themselves were also participants. Hence Sicon can promise Getas, 'I'll feed you properly today!' (423–4), and a cook no doubt made the same promise to himself. The unreasonably large number and size of meat and fish dishes at Athenian dinners described in dramatic and other poetry, as in similar descriptions from other times and places, make sense only if it is considered that there were others in the household, even beyond host,

6

guest, waiters and cooks, who also had to be fed. On occasion these others laid claim to the best of the food, as did the mother of one dutiful courtesan who was entertaining a rival:

> Gnathaena was once at dinner at Dexithea's, and Dexithea was putting almost all the dishes aside for her mother.
> 'By Artemis, woman', said Gnathaena, 'if I'd known this would happen I'd have had dinner with your mother, not with you!'[15]
>
> (Machon [Athenaeus 580c])

Like Penelope and her maids, perhaps, who cleared up in Odysseus' house after the men had had their meal, and like the womenfolk of the trans-humant Sarakatsani of modern times,[16] those of the household would more normally have had to make do with what was left uneaten. No wonder Getas, in the *Bad-Tempered Man*, disliked the idea of unexpected guests:

> 'What did you say? You're going to go off and invite some people in to lunch? Bring three thousand as far as I'm concerned. I always knew there wouldn't be a taste for me: how could there be? Bring them all. . . .'
>
> (563–7)

Female household slaves, whether or not required to wait at dinner, evidently might share in the enjoyment. Sicon reports the end of the same celebrations thus: 'And one of the maidservants, sodden [with wine], shading the bloom of her youthful face, broke into dancing steps, hesitating and trembling with shyness, and another joined hands with her and danced' (950–3). In a less idyllic context, Antiphon's speech, *On a Case of Poisoning* (1.14–20), tells the story of a slave concubine, frightened of being sold into prostitution, accompanying her owner from Athens to Piraeus for a sacrifice to Zeus, and putting what she thought was a love philtre in his wine after the sacrificial meal. But few texts allow us to picture the involvement of domestics in their masters' celebrations: slaves, like women of the household, were generally neither heard nor seen.

What of the entertainment, the musicians and dancers and indeed the prostitutes to be found especially at men's drinking parties? No surviving anecdote suggests any interest in whether they ate, or indeed whether they spoke. This applies equally to the erotic dancers of Xenophon's *Symposium* (2.1) – not a word of dialogue is given to them, nor does any character in the dialogue address them, though their act is the centre of prolonged discussion – and to the servant girl Lais, later to become a famous *hetairá*, brought by Apelles to a drinking party (Polemon [Athenaeus 588c]). Yet, hardly aware of the fact, men did see them eat. Why else should the typical foods linked to women, in one allusion after another, be the very foods that men chewed with wine at a symposium such as eggs, nuts, roasted pulses and fruit? Why should it be hinted, by one comic playwright after

*Figure 1* A waitress is slapped by a diner as she spills wine over him. Athenian red-figure cup of the mid-fifth century in the Martin von Wagner-Museum, Würzburg, no. L483

another, that women liked to drink neat wine? For it was at the moment of the libation of neat wine, when the main business of eating was already over and all there was to eat was dessert, that women were admitted to a men's drinking party.[17]

Service at purely domestic meals might well be the duty of a female slave or of a wife, and one recalls Aristotle's remark that 'the poor, having no slaves, must use their wives and children as servants' (*Politics* 1323a4). But the evidence leads firmly towards the conclusion that at any wider or more formal celebration involving men, the servants were male slaves of the host household, even when the entertainment took place elsewhere.[18] When there was a sacrifice to be undertaken, and meat to be eaten, they worked as a rule with a hired *mágeiros*.[19] For a modest household giving an unaccustomed party, two additional hands might well not be enough. A comedy *mágeiros* therefore could expect to be told 'how many tables you're going to set, how many women there are [the right kind of answer to these questions is given in the fragment by Euangelus already quoted], what time dinner will be, if I'm to bring along a *trapezopoiós*, if you've enough crockery in the house, if the oven's indoors' and so on (Menander, *Samian Woman* 287–92). It was not only crockery that could be hired. So could the *trapezopoiós* himself, the 'table-maker', 'who will wash the dishes, prepare the lamps, make libations [etc.]' as another comedy fragment conveniently specifies (Antiphanes 150 [Athenaeus 170d]).[20] If there was to be no *trapezopoiós*, the same work was shared between *mágeiros* and domestics.

It is worth considering what was the status, for the time being, of those who served at meals. Were they as subordinate as in the modern stereotype of a slave or scullion? Or were they as proud and mighty as in the Athenian comedy stereotype of a learned, professional, boastful cook?[21] We can find our way to an answer if we examine the relations between *mágeiros*, domestics and patron in surviving comedy dialogues. The cook is naturally respectful to his temporary employer even while delivering a lecture on nutrition, addressing him as 'father' and showing no resentment at his abrupt interruptions. No less clearly the cook claims seniority over domestics, who must for the occasion work to his direction, so that Sicon addresses Getas as 'boy' (i.e. 'slave'). But there is a certain balance and a certain negotiation between cook and slave, for the skills and knowledge of both were required to avoid mishaps for which both could be blamed; it was not always true that 'when the cook gets it wrong, the flute-player's slapped' (Eubulus 60 [Athenaeus 381a]). And it might well have been the household slave, rather than his master, who had gone to the appropriate section of the market to hire the cook. It does not matter here whether the typical Athenian *mágeiros* was Athenian-born or foreign, slave or free. Why did it matter so much to Athenaeus (658e–662d) and the commentators on whom he drew? It puzzled them precisely because their own stereotype of classical Athens could hardly accommodate slaves who went to market to hire free men.

In the work of cooking, the *mágeiros* gave the orders. In the act of sacrifice his role was central.[22] 'No one has injured a *mágeiros* and got away with it: our trade is somehow sacred. You can do what you like to a *trapezopoiós*', said Sicon in the *Bad-Tempered Man* (644–7).[23] One must not, of course, assume that sacrifice could not be carried out without a *mágeiros*. At Eumaeus' farm, and elsewhere in the epics, and in the wilds of Euboea in post-classical times, no *mágeiros* was needed.[24] Nor was he needed anywhere, strictly, for any householder could carry out the ritual of sacrifice inseparable from the eating of fresh meat. In towns, however, circumstances became different. An animal for sacrifice would probably have to be bought: it might well not be wholly consumed and the remaining meat could best be sold at market.[25] The *mágeiros* was the man to deal with both ends of this transaction as well as to look after the messy business in the middle.

The *mágeiros* himself chose the *trapezopoiós* if one was wanted: this and many other clues show that he watched over the whole presentation of the meal. In the Euangelus fragment, for example, instructions about the tables are given to the same interlocutor, surely a *mágeiros*, as instructions about the food. A host sometimes inclined to leave these details to others. In Plato's *Symposium*, at any rate, 'Agathon' boasts of keeping his hands off:

> 'Well, boys, bring the rest of us our meal. Set things out entirely as you please, since there is no one supervising you – a thing I have never done – imagine you have invited myself and the others to dinner, and serve so as to win our praise.'
>
> (Plato, *Symposium* 175b)

Circumstances would probably often dictate, as they did in the background to the *Bad-Tempered Man*, that the particular animal to be sacrificed, the animal that would provide fresh meat, would be selected by the *mágeiros*, or by slave and *mágeiros* together: but many a comedy exchange demonstrates how tight a negotiation between host and cook (if not sometimes between guest and cook) decided the choice of fish and the completed menu.

One knew in advance if one wanted a cook. Entertainment was not necessarily so completely planned. At one extreme was the host who arranged everything. Circumstances might then alter. In Plato's *Symposium* (176e) guests wish to talk seriously, and Socrates suggests: 'I think we should tell the flute-girl[26] (who had just arrived) to go away and play to herself, or – if she prefers – to the women inside.' The proposal is pertinent because they could not simply send the flute-girl home: she had been hired by their host, so must now be given some job to do even if it was only to 'play to herself'. By contrast an embarrassing host sketched in Theophrastus' *Characters* (20.10), not having cared to commit himself to the expense in advance, offers to send out to the brothel for a girl if his guests say the word. In between lay a market for touts who looked for signs of feasting and drinking and called to offer the services of their performers, apparently earning free food and drink for themselves into the bargain. Such was Stratocles, 'master of the rout', who provided two whores at the *Attic Dinner* described by Matron [Athenaeus 134d–137c]. Such was the unnamed Syracusan proprietor of the two entertainers at the *Symposium* narrated by Xenophon (2.1):

> When the tables had been taken away and they had poured a libation and sung a *paián* 'hymn', a Syracusan joined the revel. He had a good flute girl and a dancing girl who could do acrobatics and a very pretty boy who played the lyre and danced very well, and he made money by exhibiting them like a sideshow.

These touts were not so very different, after all, from the men who lived by providing entertainment themselves at dinner, like the *gelotopoiós*, 'joker' described by Xenophon in the same narrative (1.11–15):

> Philippus the joker knocked at the door and told the servant to announce . . . that he had come with all the equipment needed to eat someone else's meal. . . .
>
> 'Lie down, then', said Callias, 'my guests are full up with serious-ness, as you see, but perhaps rather short of humour.'
>
> As they ate Philippus tried to make a joke – to do the job that he was always invited to dinner to do. There were no laughs, and he was clearly upset. A bit later he tried another joke. They did not laugh at that either, so he stopped eating and lay there with his head covered. . . . 'If laughter has vanished from the Earth, my business is ruined. The reason I have been invited to dinners is to make the guests cheerful by laughing at me. Why would anyone invite me now?'[27]

Philippus and his fellow *gelotopoioí* have evidently something in common with the *parásitoi*,[28] 'fellow-eaters', who appear to have gone in for flattery and self-mockery more than for conscious humour. Athenaeus collected a mass of information on *parásitoi* in fourth- and third-century BC Athens, one of whose distinguishing features, as with the habitual beggar and errand-runner of the *Odyssey* (18.6), is that 'the young men' had a nickname for them.[29] Good-looking *parásitoi* – defined as diners-out at someone else's expense – who had no identifiable entertain-ment skills to offer might be suspected of paying for their meals with sexual services.[30] But a *parásitos* was, quite simply, one who ate with another without the ability or intention to return the invitation: thus a well-intentioned parent can say 'Melesias, here, and I dine together, and the youngsters *parasiteî* with us' (Plato, *Laches* 179c), meaning no more than that they are privileged to share their fathers' meal. The really powerful, such as the monarchs of fourth-century Macedonia and the later Greek world, were reputed to dine surrounded by *kólakes*, 'toadies', parasites who offered flattery as their meal-ticket.[31]

Slaves for sale, and men and women looking for work, were to be found in the *agorá*, 'market-place' and were bought or hired there. Cooks, for example, were hired in the section called *mageireîon*, or so a later source asserts.[32] It is probably right to assume that in some neighbouring district one found dancing-girls and flute-girls for hire. A comedy slave, at any rate, claimed to have been sent into town to find both cook and flute-girl for a country banquet.

## MEAL TIMES AND EATING PLACES

Families often must have eaten at home, but only the briefest descriptions are to be found. If sacrificing and eating fresh meat, families might eat at shrines: this is the kind of meal with which we began, and here the *Bad-Tempered Man* is the principal source of evidence. Men formed dining clubs which could assume political importance: evidence for them comes from historical sources and occasional inscriptions, but there is no full description of such a dinner.[33] The state acted as celebrant at general religious festivals and as host for entertainments at the town hall, the *prytaneîon*; *phratríai*, 'brotherhoods' of citizens, also held communal meals. There is evidence from inscriptions as well as literature for such events, but no descriptions.[34] Workers, soldiers and those engaged in some communal activities ate away from home, these 'working' meals sometimes being provided for them. There is external evidence, but scarcely anything in the way of a description, of such meals.[35] Travellers who could not call on acquaintances had to eat at inns. Some members of a household spent the whole day away from home, taking food with them if there was to be no communal ration. Xenophon, for example, observed that it is improper for a man to spend his days at home.[36] Women, household slaves and children then certainly ate independently of their menfolk. Women lunched with one another, as we have seen, though respectable women did not go out to dinner in the evening.

Meal times are variable, but a midday meal was usually called *áriston*, 'lunch' – this is what Callippides was late for – and an evening meal *deîpnon*, 'dinner'. The latter was perhaps typically the biggest meal of the day, and for some the only meal.[37]

Families who were sacrificing, especially if celebrating such an event as a betrothal or wedding, but on other occasions too, invited guests to their meal. Men of the socially approved age – one could be thought too young to court a *hetairá* or keep a concubine and too old to woo a boy[38] – pursued courtship by entertaining. Men entertained male guests at home, and might also celebrate some public achievement, athletic or political, with a sacrificial dinner or a party for friends. *Hetairaí*, and other women not of the proper status to be citizens' wives, might be guests at such entertainments, at home or at a shrine. These were evening and night activities: a dinner might become a drinking party, a *pótos*, or one more elaborate and organised, a *sympósion*, or a dinner or drinking party might lead, by way of the riotous revelry of a *kómos*, to another elsewhere, or to the serenading of a lover, with the aim of being admitted for supper and further drinking. These varieties of revelry are the subject of several well-known, lengthy narratives. But dinner parties and drinking parties were surely (in Athens as in most societies) less ubiquitous than their frequent occurrence in memoirs and fiction would suggest: they are certainly seldom mentioned in the forensic speeches.[39]

Overall the emphasis of surviving evidence is probably thoroughly misleading. Public and municipal entertainment, the subject of many recent studies, is not a concern of this book. But even on the domestic level there were meals that were suitable subjects for literature – men's entertainments, largely – and meals that were not. *Private*, family meals and 'working' meals are almost absent both from literature and from documents.[40]

When no strange men were in the house, women need not retreat to 'women's quarters': they could lunch at leisure, indoors or in a courtyard.[41] But the classical Athenian house, and the conviviality within it, were very inaccessible to the uninvited visitor. Women at home were invisible to law-abiding outsiders.[42] House doors were commonly locked, and interiors divided into several rooms. One of these was the *andrón*, the 'dining room' (etymologically 'men's room'): it was in this room, customarily, that men entertained others to meals and drinking parties at home. Its ground plan was laid out to accommodate a certain number of couches around the walls. *Andrônes* can be recognised archaeologically by the location of the door (always off-centre), by the length of the walls (so many couch lengths plus one couch width) and often by floor details recognisably linked to the intended placing of couches and tables. They were one-purpose rooms, more clearly so than any other room in normal houses; how frequently they were used is quite unknown. Women of respectable Athenian households did not come into contact with male guests and had no reason to enter the *andrón* when it was in use. In all the narratives of men's dinners and *sympósia* from the fifth and fourth centuries there is not one certain indication of the presence of a woman of the household, and there are several explicit signs that they were elsewhere.

Similar rooms to these *andrônes* are found in certain municipal buildings, which are thus identified as *prytaneîa* – places for municipal eating – and in buildings at shrines.[43] But many country shrines had no buildings, and certainly vase-paintings suggest that open air meals, otherwise resembling meals in dining rooms, were quite imaginable; a few literary references, scattered in time and place, and one or two paintings from Pompeii, imply that an awning (often translated 'tent') might be a regular amenity.[44]

The high Greek dining couch was a specialised piece of furniture. It is a standard feature of vase-paintings of banquets and must have been standard in the purpose-built dining rooms just described. On the vase-paintings, with few exceptions, the rule is one diner per couch: a second person on a couch will be a woman (or occasionally a beardless young man) often offering the male diner some more or less intimate service or performing it. But not all lived in such style as to own a house with a room dedicated to dining; not all could have afforded to own all those couches. The less well-off, when they entertained, are perhaps more likely than the rich to

13

have done so at shrines, and to have taken rugs and cushions with them, as depicted in the *Bad-Tempered Man*. The fashion for dining on high couches, when there was a large number of diners, was possibly never as widespread as the vase-paintings would encourage us to imagine. Many may have continued to sit to eat, as they must have done municipally in the *thólos*, the 'round house' at Athens.[45] The much more informal arrangement of dining in a semicircle, *stibás*, outdoors or indoors and sometimes on a raised dais, can be discerned in a number of texts of the classical period and was certainly the usual rule later.[46]

At any rate, some – sometimes – reclined on couches to eat and drink. The first suggestion of it in literature comes from Alcman (19 [Athenaeus 111a]) in seventh-century Sparta: 'seven couches and as many tables crowned with poppy-seed bread, with linseed bread and sesame bread and, for the girls, buckets full of honey sweets', yet even by the later fifth century the custom of reclining was not quite taken for granted. One remembered, from Homer, that heroes had sat to eat. In comedy and satyr play the contrast between reclining and sitting, the play of class and etiquette, was an excellent source of humour. 'Recline and let us drink, and make a test of it at once: are you the better, or am I?' said Heracles as slave to Syleus his purchaser (Euripides fragment 691),[47] and there is clowning in Aristophanes' *Wasps* when an unpolished father is taught to recline by his more fashionable son.[48]

Thus we know that at Athenian dinner parties the guests were limited in number. It is easy to count the couches that would fit in the purpose-built dining rooms of Attica and indeed of other Greek towns, whether private, municipal or religious: that was exactly how the size of a reception room was customarily measured. Seven couches was a common size; five to eleven couches was the usual range, or in other words hardly more than twenty participants – though admittedly there was a sixth-century fifteen-couch room at Megara and a fifth-century seventeen-couch room in the Propylaea at Athens.[49] The intimate scale was part of the nature of Greek dining and entertainment, and was built in architecturally, for in the larger of known dining rooms the layout would have produced the effect of two to four groups dining or drinking simultaneously.[50] A fourth-century poet confirms the picture: 'Philoxenus . . . describes the following kind of preparations for dinner: "A pair of boys brought in a shiny table for us, and another for others, and others brought another, until they filled the room"' (Philoxenus b.1–2 [Athenaeus 146f]). At Athens there was at one time a legal limit on private parties of thirty guests. The only larger gatherings there were open-air public festivities, for example, the sacrifices, accompanied by feasting in the *agorá*, that were offered by the general Chares after a victory in 353 BC.[51] Hellenistic monarchs were more lavish: dining rooms in the Macedonian palace at Vergina accommodated up to thirty-one couches, while Alexander the Great travelled Asia with a hundred-couch dining tent.[52]

## EATING AT HOME

We have accepted that on family occasions men and women celebrated in separate circles. It is highly pertinent that the sexes were separated during Christian worship until recently in Greece, as in some other countries (and *yinekonítis*, originally 'women's quarters', is the name of the women's part of the church, as already noted by Du Cange (1688)). But discussions of the segregation of the sexes in ancient Greece tend to stumble over the domestic life of the poor. In a one-room house, without slaves, can such rules exist? That they can is best shown by way of a modern parallel. J. K. Campbell reported of the Sarakatsani shepherds of northern Greece:

> Even in the extended family household husband and wife do not eat together. The men eat first, the women of the household afterwards. No portion of a cooked dish (*prosfái*) is set aside for the women, who must satisfy themselves with whatever is left by the men; this is often very little. . . . Only sometimes in the intimacy of the elementary family may the husband, wife, and children sit and eat together.[53]

The meagre ancient Athenian evidence is quite conformable to this. A householder might normally eat in the women's quarters of his own house when without guests (the idea of permitting a male dining companion to enter the women's quarters could be compared to sacrilege).[54] There he would expect to be waited on, whether by a slave or by his wife: 'And the little woman says nice things to me, brings me a barley-puff, sits down beside me and goes, "Have some of this! Try a bit of this!" I enjoy all that' (Aristophanes, *Wasps* 610–12).[55]

This is all very clearly visible on funerary reliefs, on which a reclining man attended by a seated woman may be in turn attended by standing children and slaves. This iconographic commonplace, to be found in Greece from the seventh century BC and so suggesting that the fashion of reclining at meals goes back to the time of the Homeric epics even though there is no hint of it in the texts of those poems, has antecedents and analogues elsewhere in the eastern Mediterranean.[56] In these reliefs the central figure is always a man – and one notes that the dead man himself was regarded as the 'host' of his own funeral banquet, at least in a later view – while a woman, in what appear to be analogous memorials to women, was pictured seated at her own tomb, a female attendant offering food on a platter.[57]

Such scenes were somehow private; they scarcely ever intrude into literature. We see a shadow of them, before the classical period, in Odysseus' intimate last meal with Calypso:

15

*Figure 2* Classical funerary relief depicting (as often) the dead man reclining at a meal, attended by his household. *Source*: from Pitton de Tournefort 1717

They came to the hollow cave, the goddess and the man together. Well, he was sitting there on the chair from which Hermes had got up, and the *nymphe* put out every food for him, to eat and drink, that mortal men eat; she was sitting facing godlike Odysseus, and house-girls put out ambrosia and nectar for her; and they set their hands to the food laid out ready.

(Odyssey 5.194–9)

We see a reflection of them, too, in a domestic dinner described in a much later text, *Lucius or the Ass* (2).

## *SYMPÓSION* AND SERENADE

We have seen in a quotation from Xenophon's *Symposium* that at a certain moment the tables were taken away, a libation was offered and a *paián* sung. This moment was widely accepted as marking the division between dinner and drinking party. A scene from the comic playwright Plato's *Laconians* (71 [Athenaeus 665b–c]) makes all clear:

'Have the men finished their dinner already?'
'Almost all.'
'Very good. Why don't you run and bring out the tables? I'll go and get the water.'
'I'll sweep the floor. After I've poured their libations I'll set up the *kóttabos*. The girl had better have the flutes at hand and be warming them up ready. Now go in and pour the perfume for them, Egyptian

and iris, and then I'll give each of the guests a wreath. Somebody
make up some fresh-mixed wine.'
'It's mixed.'
'Put the incense. . . .'[58]
'There's been a libation and they're getting on with the drinking.
They've sung a *skólion*. The *kóttabos* is coming out. Some little girl
with flutes is playing a Carian tune for the drinkers: I saw another
with a harp, and she was singing an Ionic song to it.'

*Sympósia*, the formal drinking parties that appear to have played such a
large role in the intellectual life of Athens, were occasions for masculine
enjoyment – and for sexual pursuit outside marriage. There are vase-
paintings of all-women *sympósia*,[59] but these paintings (in which the women
are naked) have come under reasonable suspicion of being male fantasies.
If Socrates' suggestion about the flute-girl, quoted on p. 10, was seriously
meant, he was not suggesting that a female *sympósion*, parallel to the men's,
was taking place in his host's women's quarters; rather he was assuming
that his host's own womenfolk, respectably tucked away, might welcome
musical entertainment similar to that enjoyed by men.

The *sympósion* itself was wholly comparable to the classical literature in
which it figured so ubiquitously. Both were conversations among friends,
as was clear to the Socrates of a later anecdote:

> When Aristophanes presented the *Clouds*, scurrilously abusing Socra-
> tes, a neighbour asked him:
> 'Aren't you angry at being satirised in that way?'
> 'No, I'm not', he said. 'The theatre is a *sympósion*, and I am [taking
> my turn as] the butt.'
> (*Bringing Up Children* [traditionally attributed to Plutarch] 10c)

In the rounded entertainment that was an Athenian *sympósion* the wine
was only one feature. Music was contributed by flute-players, harpists and
others, or by the singing of the guests. Poetry, lyric, elegiac, perhaps epic,
was likely to be recited at *sympósia*. Some was written for no other
purpose, including the *skólia*, 'drinking songs', of which an anonymous
collection survives from classical times; and we recall again the *paián* sung
at the commencement of the *sympósion* described by Xenophon. The recital
of verse could take the form of a competition: and there were other party
games, including the ever-popular *kóttabos*, illustrated on so many vase-
paintings, at which with a flick of wine from a not quite empty cup one
tried to dislodge a precariously balanced target.[60]

The wine was, however, a principal feature: wine that, after the initial
libation, was mixed with water in proportions decided by the host to
ensure the desired inexorable progress of inebriation in his guests. For
the release of inhibitions that goes with drunkenness was the aim of the

*sympósion*. Here behaviour, though it obeyed rules, did not obey the same rules as outside. Criticisms, insults, satire, dangerous political opinions were neutralised by the laughter of the moment and (one hoped) the forgetfulness of the following day.

The release of inhibitions embraced sex as well as other human concerns. The drinking parties depicted on Athenian vases of the sixth and fifth centuries may be intended as pictures to laugh at, as programmes for imitation or as documents of objective reality; whichever of these purposes may be uppermost in the artists' minds, they have shown us that sexual acts were easily imaginable as part of the festivity of a drinking party, and the literary evidence does not gainsay it. 'Bring water, bring wine, boy, bring us flowery wreaths, and I will throw a punch at Eros' (Anacreon 51 [*Epitome* 782a]).

Depending on circumstances, waiters and other domestics might find themselves precariously spectators. Here a comic Dionysus angrily imagines a continuing exchange of roles, his slave Xanthias as master, himself as attendant:

> 'Yes, wouldn't it be funny if my boy Xanthias was lolling about on Milesian rugs, screwing a dancing-girl, and suddenly wanted the po, and I was just watching him and getting a hard on, and he noticed me, the villain, and took a swipe at my jaw and knocked my front teeth out?'

> (Aristophanes, *Frogs* 541–8)

If the festivities went on all night, attendants might find more opportunities for participation, or so a witness claimed at the prosecution of Neaera:

> Chionides and Euthetion testify that they were invited by Chabrias to dinner at Cape Colias to celebrate his win in the chariot race, and saw Phrynion (here present) at dinner there with the defendant Neaera; they themselves and Phrynion and Neaera fell asleep there, and they observed men getting up during the night to go to Neaera, including some of the waiters, who were Chabrias' slaves.

> (Apollodorus, *Against Neaera* 34)

There are many varieties of revelry. For every anecdote of an all-night *sympósion* there is a matching story of a *kômos*, of nocturnal wanderings that begin at one revel and end at another. Late in the night in which Agathon had celebrated his tragedy's success with a dinner and *sympósion*, in Plato's fictionalised narrative,

> there was a knocking at the outer door, very noisy, as if it were *komastaí*: a flute-girl could be heard.
> 'Go and see, boys', said Agathon, 'and if it is anyone we like invite them in. If not, say that we have finished drinking already.'

*Figure 3* After the *sympósion* a reveller captures a musician. Athenian red-figure cup of mid-fifth century in the Louvre, no. G13

A little later they heard the voice of Alcibiades in the yard, very drunk and shouting out, 'Where's Agathon? Take me to Agathon!'

He was helped in by the flute-girl and some of his other cronies. He stood at the door crowned with a thick wreath of ivy and violets, with a great many ribbons dangling over his head, and said:

'Greetings, gentlemen. Will you take as fellow-drinker a man who is already very drunk indeed? Or shall we just put a garland on Agathon, our reason for coming, and go away?'

(Plato, *Symposium* 212c–e)

The *kômos* was so far removed from the decencies of daily life that it was customarily depicted on vases in the metaphor of a dance of Silenus and his Satyrs, tipsy, ithyphallic and slightly uglier than any drunken human. But, whether or not the komasts were as drunk as they seemed, they had a destination: a house where celebrations were in progress, a friend's house, a lover's house, a *hetairá*'s house.[61] If locked out, as Alcibiades might have been, they had at any rate drawn attention to love or desire

19

or friendship or admiration by a method that was shocking yet socially sanctioned. But they might be admitted. The flirting between Alcibiades and Socrates, which ensued at Plato's *Symposium*, is a mirror-image of the goings-on at the suppers and *sympósia* hosted by courtesans, *hetairaí*, to which tipsy but thoughtful serenaders had brought all the good wine and good food that could be desired.[62]

## BEYOND ATHENS

The picture that can be drawn of dining and festivity in other classical Greek cities is by no means so complete as the Athenian. Athenians were, however, sufficiently impressed by the contrast between their own way of life and that of the Spartans to describe the latter relatively fully. The evidence is not straightforward, however. We can read satire on Sparta and its ways, from a city that was always Sparta's rival and frequently its enemy; also we can read strong praise, from Plato and Xenophon, philosophers and moralists whose admiration for Spartan discipline and education was almost unbounded. A fictional Spartan speaks:

> Still, I think the lawgiver at Sparta was right to enjoin the avoidance of pleasures.... The custom that makes men fall deepest into great pleasures and improprieties and into all foolishness, this has been ejected by our law from every part of the country: neither in the fields, nor in the towns that the Spartiates control, will you see a *sympósion* and all that goes with it to incite men to pleasure. There is not a man who would not punish with the greatest severity a drunken reveller; he would not get away even if a festival of Dionysus were his excuse – like the time when I saw [drunken revellers] on carts in your country [Athens], while at Taras, our own colony, I watched the whole city getting drunk at the Dionysia. There is none of that with us.
>
> (Plato, *Laws* 636e–637c)

The full citizens, the Spartiates, were above over-indulgence in food and drink, or so it was claimed.[63] But the principal difference in this field between Sparta and Athens was that whereas the communal or municipal dining of Athenians seems (to judge from surviving literature) to have been of little importance, male Spartiates dined in common all the time.[64] Where and in what circumstances their womenfolk ate, no one knows. Communal meals, *syssítia*, were by no means unique to Sparta. Cretan cities, close to Sparta in dialect, were also close in social customs and there too men ate communally:

> 'The Cretans sit to eat', says Pyrgion in *Cretan Customs* III. He adds that orphans are served food without sauces; that the youngest men

stand and serve the rest; and that after pouring a libation to the gods in silence they apportion the waiting food among all. They allot to sons sitting at the feet of their fathers' chairs half as much as is served to the men; orphans have an equal share, but they receive each of the proper foods unmixed with sauces. There used to be guest chairs, and a third table, on the right as one entered the *andreîon* 'men's house': this they called 'strangers' table', or 'of Zeus of Strangers'.[65]

(Athenaeus 143e)

Outlandish though they seemed to other Greeks (hence their attribution to a 'lawgiver'), from our perspective the customs of Sparta can be seen to belong to the same spectrum as those of Athens. Athenians, like Spartans, had fixed opinions on dining together, on equal contribution to hospitality, on the separation of the sexes, on the ages at which boys began to dine as men. Spartans, like Athenians, celebrated religious occasions with food, drink, music and dance, as we know not only from the early poetry of Alcman but also from descriptions of what were evidently well-established festivals dating from the classical period or soon after it.[66]

But every Greek city was different from every other in government, in laws, in religious observance and in other customs. Sacrifice and food preparation were naturally a major source of income at places of pilgrimage and festival. Delians were nicknamed *eleodytai*, 'table-divers', and the later comic playwright Criton characterised Delos as a paradise for parasites.[67] Elis, where Olympia stood, was said to be the origin of a school of cooks.[68] Distinctions in food behaviour are among the most quickly noticed of all social peculiarities. Greeks noticed such differences among themselves: the women of Miletus, for example, who 'are not to share food with their husbands nor to call their own husbands by name' (Herodotus, *Histories* 1.146.3).

They also noticed how they were differentiated from other peoples – from 'barbarians' – by food customs, food choices and food avoidances. Herodotus was told that after sacrifice in Egyptian temples the animal's head would be cut off, cursed and if there was a market at hand with Greek traders, sold to them. If there was not, it would be thrown in the river (ibid. 2.39.4). Galen, in the second century AD, wrote superciliously of 'grubs and hedgehogs and other creatures that the people of Egypt and some others eat' (*On the Properties of Foods* 3.2.1). Greeks themselves admitted to few food avoidances,[69] though they considered dolphins sacred,[70] were doubtful of turtle and tortoise,[71] seldom ate dog and very seldom horse. Of animals that were eaten at all, nearly all parts were considered acceptable food: in other words, economical sacrifices offered very little of the animal to the gods, who had to be content with such unpalatable portions as 'the tail-end and the gall-bladder, the bits you can't eat' (Menander, *Bad-Tempered Man* 452). Some Greeks, though not all, ate brain; Pythagoras, it was later said, included heart among his odd list of forbidden foods.[72]

Finally Greeks began to notice how food, and food customs, changed over time. The Homeric epics, already classics in fifth- and fourth-century Greece, demonstrated this point, for they (it was universally accepted) told of the Greeks' own ancestors, the 'heroes', who did not recline but sat to eat, and who seldom if ever ate boiled meat or fish. It was soon realised that Greek societies had changed even within fully historical times. Many of the most interesting observations in the *Deipnosophists* of Athenaeus concern changing customs and the attempt to explain them.

## THE CLASSICAL MENU

We do not know the menu (except for mutton) at the family sacrifice imagined in Menander's *Bad-Tempered Man*. But we are told the menu of a typical Amphidromia (a baby's naming day, five or ten days after birth):

> The custom is to bake slices of Chersonese cheese, to fry cabbage gleaming with oil, to stew some fat mutton chops, to pluck wood-pigeons and thrushes along with chaffinches, to nibble little cuttlefish along with squids, to swing and beat many an [octopus] tentacle, and to drink many a warming cup.[73]
>
> (Ephippus 3 [Athenaeus 370d])

Beginning with this we may outline the regular pattern of meals of the classical Aegean in preparation for the greater detail of later chapters.

Lentils, barley and wheat formed the staple foods (*sîtos*: 'food, staple food, army food supply') of classical Greece: the lentils as soup, the barley as a mash or biscuit, the wheat as loaves, though both of the cereals could also be prepared as gruel or porridge. In addition to the older traditional forms in which these staples were eaten, sweet cakes multiplied in classical menus. Wheat, as we shall see, did not grow well in most parts of Greece and was the most expensive and the most unreliable of the three staples. Lentils and barley had been known in Greece even earlier than wheat: they were available almost everywhere. While wheat and barley together provided the staple at banquets, lentils and other pulses had a more homely connotation.

With these staples were eaten (as *ópson*, 'what one eats with bread': the English term 'relish' has been widely adopted as a convenient equivalent) vegetables, cheese, eggs, fish (fresh, salted or dried), and less frequently meat. In classical Greece the fresh meat of domestic animals formed a sacrifice, butchered with appropriate religious ritual. But the eating of meat once sacrificed, including the eating of offal and sausages, required no further ceremony.[74] The domestic animals that were most commonly eaten – sheep, goats and pigs – had a long prehistory in Greece. Small and large game birds supplemented the native domesticated quail and the domestic fowl whose arrival will be chronicled on p. 65. Cheese (in Greece normally sheep's and goats' milk cheese) had long been made. The number of species of vegetables in use had gradually grown. The number of species of fish that were exploited no doubt remained fairly constant once deep-sea fishing had become a common practice: it had, as we shall see (p. 38), a very long history.

To this structure, when meals were at their most elaborate, there were many supplements. Appetisers, not different in kind from the usual relishes but selected from those that had the most piquant flavour, preceded the meal. Wreaths and perfumes were distributed among guests as they gathered.

After the meal, wine, *oînos*, was drunk, a single taste of unmixed wine at the moment of the libation, followed by plenty of wine mixed with water.[75] Now clean tables – 'second tables' – were brought, on which cakes, sweets, nuts and fresh and dried fruit were served to accompany the wine. These delicacies were called *tragémata*, 'what one chews alongside wine' (a convenient translation is 'dessert'). The three constituents of a proper Greek meal were *sîtos*, *ópson* and *oînos*.[76]

One of the two most important changes in the diet of Greece since early neolithic times has been the introduction of wine: it has for at least the last three millennia been the customary drink of the country, often heavily diluted with water. The other has been the cultivation and regular use of olives. Wild forms of both grape and olive were found and probably used earlier in Greece, but the newly cultivated grape and olive of later prehistoric times were of enormous potential importance to the diet. Both provided cooking media and flavourings, the olive with its oil, the grape with its juice both unfermented and fermented into wine. It is a challenging hint of conservatism at the centre of the menu that grape, wine and olive were not visibly present in the main course of a classical Greek meal. Whatever the use of olive oil in cooking, and as a medium for sauces, olives themselves were eaten only before the meal as an appetiser. Whatever the use of must and wine in cooking, wine was served to diners only after they had eaten, and raisins also appeared then, with the second tables. And in general the lists of *propómata*, 'appetisers',[77] and of *tragémata* that can be extracted from the writings of comic poets and dieticians alike show a readiness to innovate that was not nearly so evident with the staple diet and its chief accompaniments in the main course.

Meat was eaten 'less frequently'. How frequently is 'less frequently'? The balance is difficult to judge. The medieval Greek traveller Nicander Nucius (16) considered the English to be 'meat-eaters, insatiable for flesh'. Although the evidence is not strong, it is likely that vegetables, fish and perhaps cheese, and not meat, accompanied the majority of meals in Greece for many millennia. Two pieces of semantic history are relevant here.

*Opson* and its diminutive *opsárion* at first meant 'relish; what one eats with bread': by later classical times these words had come to mean specifically 'fish', as indeed does their modern derivative *psári*, showing that fish was in some sense, or for some speakers, the definitive 'relish'.[78] A growing importance for cheese in post-classical times is similarly signalled by a similar semantic change. The meaning of *prosphágion*, the post-classical word for 'relish', has narrowed to 'cheese',[79] though it is still used in some modern dialects in the more general sense.

## FOOD OF NECESSITY AND FOOD OF CHOICE[80]

Although the fact is not well documented at any particular time or place within the ancient Greek world, it does not admit of serious doubt that the diet of the poor-but-not-quite-destitute was cereal accompanied by relish, like that of the better off, but the relish was severely limited, essentially to the green and root vegetables. Examples must be drawn from very early and very late literature, but it will be seen that the picture varies little.

The *Iliad* and *Odyssey* are not helpful on this question: the poorest host depicted there, Eumaeus, is, as a pig-farmer, well placed to offer a meaty meal. Hesiod, roughly contemporary with the two epics, is more informative with his references to the edible wild golden thistle and to the honey and acorns that the forest supplies to foragers. He does not mention bread alongside his mallow and asphodel, but elsewhere his ploughman's meal was essentially bread.[81]

Hesiod also repeats what was evidently a proverb, listing two important stand-bys: 'There is great usefulness in mallow and asphodel' (Hesiod, *Works and Days* 41). This line aroused a lot of interest among later Greek authors, who sometimes quoted it with a reminder that Epimenides, a legendary sage of picturesquely austere habits, counted mallow and asphodel as his *álimon* and *ádipson*, his prophylactics against hunger and thirst.[82] Mallow remained well known: Theophrastus, at the end of the fourth century, listed it as a vegetable that needed cooking, it was familiar to Galen and to Byzantine authors, and it is said still to be eaten in Greece in times of shortage. On rich tables it was a garnish or wrapping for portions of meat.[83]

Asphodel, too, was still important in the fourth century BC: Theophrastus describes its versatility, the stalk being fried, the seed roasted, the root chopped and eaten with figs. But although Pliny, in the first century AD, says the same, he is merely copying Theophrastus; Galen, an independent author not much after Pliny's time, thought asphodel was of very little use. And while Galen at least knew that asphodel (like lupins) had to be cooked to get rid of its bitterness, Aulus Gellius' symposiasts admit doubt as to what plant it was; it had become so obscure, so merely literary, that

Plutarch's fictionalised sage and tyrant, Periander, could call it *glykys*, 'sweet'.[84]

Mallow and asphodel are the best documented poor men's foods among green vegetables and roots; among pulses, lupins are spoken of most often. Poisonous when raw (indeed, so Theophrastus says, not eaten raw by any animal)[85] lupins were apparently often cooked for human food. The importance in a subsistence diet of this and other wild and semi-wild pulses is sufficiently indicated, perhaps, by Galen's anecdote:

> I know a young fellow, a medical student in Alexandria, who had nothing else as relish for four years but fenugreek, calavance, *ôkhros* and lupin. Sometimes he managed to get Memphis oil and greens and a bit of fruit, the kinds that are eaten raw: he had no access even to a [cooking] fire. He was healthy, all through those years, and his physical state was no worse at the end than at the beginning. He ate them with *gáros*, of course, sometimes just adding oil to the *gáros*, sometimes wine, or again vinegar; but at times (the lupins for example) just with salt.[86]

Theophrastus and Galen both have much to say of lupins, Galen calling them 'versatile'.[87] A play by Diphilus indicates that they were sold by the roadside in fourth-century BC Athens: the speaker is a brothel-keeper – so says a marginal note in the *Epitome of Athenaeus* – who pretends to be looking for a less stressful line of business than his own. The merchandise that would suit him, 'roses, radishes, lupins, caked olives' (87 [*Epitome* 55d]), are meant to sound hardly worth the trouble of a serious entrepreneur, collected by those who might hope to eke out their own subsistence diet by selling what others would not trouble with or what they themselves had gathered; like the capers that Phryne used to gather and sell before she became a successful *hetaírá*; almost as bad as the bitter vetch that, according to Demosthenes, it was a sign of bad times to see on sale at the roadside and the chervil that in Andocides' mind was bracketed with the charcoal-burners who had taken refuge in Athens when the Spartans were ravaging Attica.[88]

Vignettes of the life of poverty are to be found in surviving fragments of Athenian comedy:[89] poverty soon to be relieved, perhaps, in a recognition-scene or a profitable marriage alliance, though the sequelae in these cases are no longer known. If cereal is mentioned, it will be barley (not that the rich despised barley in the form of *mâza*). Pulses feature strongly, including the less attractive kinds just such as in Galen's anecdote; also mushrooms, nuts, wild pears, cicadas, snails. If there was any money it would go on cheap wine and dried figs.

The move across the poverty line into real destitution had two landmarks. One was the inability even to afford cereal: 'The beggar had no bread and yet bought cheese!' was the proverb (*Mantissa Proverbiorum*

*Figure 4 Kápparis*: the caper bush, whose pickled buds were Phryne's earliest stock-in-trade. *Source*: from G. Hegi's *Illustrierte Flora von Mittel-Europa* (Vienna, 1912)

26).[90] The second was heavy reliance on food gathered from the wild, so that, in Aristophanes' *Wealth* (298), 'wild vegetables and beggar's bag' are the attributes of the Cyclops, pictured there as a resourceless nomad.[91]

Not far above the poverty line, it seems, was the lifestyle considered by the fourth and third centuries as 'properly Athenian', as appropriate for the old-fashioned citizen and the old-fashioned city festival. The best thyme grew wild on Mount Hymettus and was sold, again, by the roadside, and thyme typified simple, old-fashioned Athens. A comedy slave speaks of 'eating the same thyme as my master', and the later commentators filled in some of the implications: 'That is, sharing the same poverty. Thyme is a kind of cheap plant' (Aristophanes, *Wealth* 253 and scholia).[92] In the early third century Hippolochus [Athenaeus 130d] pretended that the diet of Lynceus, his correspondent in Athens, a student of Theophrastus at the time (but also a gourmet), would be limited to 'thyme and rocket and those nice bread rolls'.

The differences between poverty and tradition are easily summarised. The old-fashioned citizen and the old-fashioned city festival could afford bread and cheese and oil and wine,[93] and tended to require a little meat.[94] The bread trade was no doubt central to many cities' concerns, but certainly in the late fifth century Athens was especially noted for its bread industry.[95]

As wealth and display increased, meat increased. In Athens the typical lover's gift was a hare: an appropriate gift from a proud huntsman in a territory where there was little else to hunt. Huntsmen themselves, when in open country, made do meanwhile with bread, cheese and vegetables.[96] Just as in the meals of Homeric heroes, bread and meat are depicted (in so far as anything recognisable is depicted) on the tables at the solemn dining scenes on the earliest Athenian black-figure pottery. Salt meat was the proper relish at the annual dinner at the Lyceum in Athens, and to have served salt fish earned the cook a whipping.[97]

Meanwhile, in a city like Athens, surrounded at no great distance by coastlines and the natural market for several fishing harbours, it would be unnatural if fish were not served at rich men's dinners. And while the rich landowner could always continue, Homerically, to enjoy his meat, produce of his farms and even of his own hunting, fish was a luxury that could be made available in most Greek cities on a rather more general basis. To fishermen themselves and to the inhabitants of fishing harbours fresh fish must have been available fairly liberally (indeed they might get little else to eat). Dried, smoked or salt fish had probably a long history, as we shall see (pp. 40, 75–6). It seems less likely that any kind of a market in fresh fish in non-coastal cities developed early: where was the market, until the time when a proportion of inhabitants had no land to farm, yet something to exchange for fish?

As far as Athens is concerned, this time came during the fifth century, with the beginnings of a monetary economy, the wealth of 'empire', the concentration of trade and the building work associated with Pericles: ' "Because of the greatness of our city all [kinds of] things are supplied to it from the whole world: so it is that we can take proprietorial pleasure in enjoying other people's produce no less than our own." '[98] Whatever may be conjectured for the earlier period, certainly from the middle of the fifth century onwards Athens was the kind of city that needed an active food market, and there is plenty of evidence that *eis toùs ikhthyas* and *eis toûpsa* were significant subdivisions of it, representing a vigorous trade in seafood.[99] In Athens, then, a growing demand for purchasable *ópsa*, a demand that the fish trade was best able to satisfy, naturally came with the growth of an urban trading and artisan population. The leisure and the desire to take an interest in food were the prerogative of this same new group (of its more spectacularly successsful members, at any rate): since they were not primarily landowners, the food concerned was bought on the market, and it was naturally fish. Nothing is more striking than the difference between the commonplaces of gastronomic literature in Greece and in Rome. While Roman poets were to boast of their farms and their fresh produce, Greeks wrote of the fish they bought at market and the prices they paid.

This section of the Athenian population was too well-off to have to rely on the cheapest of foods, not well-established enough to rely on the produce of their own lands, too leisured to have to spend all their time scraping a living, not leisured enough to delegate every aspect of entertaining. Not surprisingly, these Athenians concerned comedy authors. Very many of their audience were among them. And they no doubt shaded into the class of 'hangers-on', of 'parasites', of 'flatterers' of the really rich (for that is one way to develop a business), whether these hangers-on were nearly rich[100] or almost poor.[101]

In this Athens was not exceptional among Greek cities, though it was exeptionally big and prosperous. The fourth-century gourmet Archestratus helps to make this clear. Forty-eight of the surviving passages from Archestratus' poem are about fish, and only eleven are on other topics. This preponderance could have more than one cause, but it is surely a sign that fish outweighed other delicacies in the diet of Archestratus.[102] In his time there were many Greek cities that had vigorous food markets, and fish rather than meat was evidently the luxury food that was available for purchase, just as in the Athens on whose fish trade we have been speculating. Gastronomy grew in Greek cities as the fresh fish market grew: they went together, and they cannot be separated from the spread of urban households with an income derived from business rather than land. It is no coincidence if Sparta lacked all three, a business population, a market for fish, an enthusiasm for the 'Life of Pleasure'. In Athens the phenomenon is no doubt traceable to the mid-fifth century, but is most evident in the literature of the fourth. Gastronomy – and in Athens it was most audibly the gastronomy of seafood – accompanies the appearance of new wealth and disposable income.

How general was interest in the arts of cookery? History has to begin from sources. For a study of gastronomy in Greek society, that of Athens in particular, in the fourth century BC the sources are in a way remarkably good, and, what is more, many of them are conveniently threaded on the skewer of Athenaeus. As several twentieth-century scholars have shown, one could hardly wish to know more of the role of the cook in Athenian Middle Comedy (that is, early and mid-fourth-century comedy), of the cook's place in society of the time as Middle and New Comedy depicts it, and of the fascination for food shown by the characters, and presumably by the authors, and presumably by a good part of the audience of these plays.

## HIDDEN MEANINGS

At any meal the food and drink serve more purposes than simple nourishment. Hospitality cements friendships;[103] a toast can seal love.[104] But in the play by Euangelus from which a quotation has already been given, the generosity of the wedding arrangements is cleverly shown up as hollow by the host's final instruction to the cook:

'We want it to be a famous wedding. Don't take instructions from anyone else; I'll supervise and tell you everything.... Last point: height of tables to be three cubits, so that a guest has to reach up if he wants to get something.'

(Euangelus 1 [Athenaeus 644d])

So the diners were not to have too much encouragement to eat what was set out on the tables! Just such a host is outlined as one of Theophrastus' *Characters* (22.4) – a miser who counts on selling the surplus meat at his daughter's wedding, and makes sure to hire waiters who have already had their own dinner. But the very fact that others *looked* for signs of parsimony demonstrates that the rather public circumstance of a wedding, perhaps a modest household's single most significant portrayal of itself to the community, could easily tempt over-spending.[105] And the food and drink that, to other kinds of entertainment, were brought by guests themselves may also be considered as much symbols – of generosity, of relative wealth – as items to join the menu.[106] Even complaints of poor cooking need not be what they seem: they can be excuses not to pay the cook (Diphilus 42 [Athenaeus 291f]). And the fifth-century dramatist Pherecrates was ready to suggest in satirical hexameters that invitations to a sacrificial meal were issued for the pride of having issued them rather than in the hope that they would be taken up:

If one of us as celebrant invites another to dinner we are angry if he comes and frown at his presence and want him to go away as soon as possible; and somehow aware of this he puts his sandals on; and one of the company says 'Off already? Won't you drink with me? Won't you take those sandals off?' and the celebrant is angry with the questioner and quotes the elegiac verse, 'Don't detain any against his will: don't wake a sleeper, Simonides!'[107]

(162 [Athenaeus 364b])

The gods of Greece, too, attached importance to our subject. They

29

*Figure 5* Satyr and woman, from a sixth-century BC vase found at Istria, an early Greek colony on the Black Sea coast

partook of all three parts of a meal: of the meat, at least of those parts of the sacrifice that were less attractive to humans; of the wine, some drops of which in its neat state were spilt for them in a libation; of the cereal, sprinkled on their meat and sometimes sacrificed to them in the form of cakes. So it is natural that the specialist in the preparation of meat and vegetables for men had been at the same time the specialist in animal sacrifice, and philosophers might well name his skill the *mageirikè tékhne*, the 'cook-sacrificer's art'.

But in truth, as gastronomy advanced, it left the gods behind. A long distance trade in wine was irrelevant to them, for no one suggested that they preferred one named wine to another in their libations; yet the wine trade grew. Side-dishes, fancy sauces and careful preparation of chosen cuts of meat and fish were irrelevant to them, yet from a human point of view this was the centre of the cook's art, and he came to call it not *mageiriké* but *opsartytiké*, the secular art of cooking relishes. And the cakes and sprinkled barley that were offered to the gods were irrelevant to men, who could not eat them: yet the arts of making bread and cakes for men saw rapid development, bread-making as an industry of mass production, cake-making as a craft perhaps parallel to *opsartytiké*.

In this book Greek meals and Greek gastronomy are studied in their human context. Gods and symbols can provide an explanation for many things: here we concentrate on the concrete and worldly contexts of human behaviour.

# Part I

# THE PREHISTORIC AEGEAN

# 2

# THE GARDENS OF ALCINOUS[1]

'I live in clear-seen Ithaca. There is a mountain on it, steep Neriton
with tossing leaves. Around it islands, many of them, live very close
to one another, Dulichion and Same and wooded Zacynthos. It lies
land-bound, highest of all in the salt [sea], towards the dark, the
others further off towards the dawn and the sun; rough, but a good
parent.'

*Odyssey* 9.21–8

## GREECE AND ITS NEIGHBOURS

There are no satisfactory borders between Greek and neighbouring lands;
if there were, Greeks have not been inclined to draw them. The area of
study in this book is not separated off by land, but joined by sea. The
peninsulas of central and southern Greece, the islands to their west and
east and the coasts of the Aegean, are defined for travellers by sea journeys
that are short and easy in good weather, land journeys that are slow and
relatively difficult. These conditions define the field of the enquiry.

Sea travel was a practice adopted in very early times in Greece. By
40,000 BC Cephallenia was inhabited, and although the sea level was much
lower then, it could only have been reached after a sea voyage. By 9000
BC the obsidian of Melos was used at mainland sites. Frequent sea travel
has linked Greece intimately with its neighbours: northwards with the
Balkans, from which well-defined land routes reach the river mouths and
harbours of the north Aegean coast; eastwards with Anatolia, similarly
penetrated by the river valleys that descend to the eastern Aegean; north-
eastwards the Black Sea coasts; south-eastwards Syria, Palestine and
north Africa; westwards Italy and Sicily, all linked with Greece by exten-
sions of Aegean and coastal sea routes.

These routes are echoed in cultural continuities: the holy places, the
place-names and the myths that linked western Anatolia with the Greek
peninsula and with Italy and Sicily; the high civilisation, the luxuries and
practices of luxury, the literary and scientific ideas that belonged to the

Levant; the many forms of social and political organisation that made up an ever-changing continuum from Crete northwards to Epirus, Macedonia and beyond.

Yet Greece has been a country of migrations, of mixed populations and from time to time of inter-ethnic rivalry and warfare. Recent nationalism has ensured that most of the inhabitants of Greece speak Greek and that most of the inhabitants of Turkey speak Turkish, but this belies the complexity of their ancestry and history. Albanian and Aromunian are in rapid decline as languages of central and southern Greece. Turkish was recently widely spoken in Greece and Greek was common in coastal parts of Turkey. Both, as languages of empire, were adopted by the speakers of other languages now forgotten in the region, for example, by the Slavs who occupied much of peninsular Greece in the early Middle Ages.

Turkish, the language of conquerors from central Asia, has been spoken on the Aegean coasts for less than a millennium. Albanian speakers have migrated southwards at various times from the south-western Balkans. Aromunian, a group of dialects very close to standard Romanian, is the remaining sign of Roman dominance in the Balkans two thousand years ago. Greek came earlier: but when? It is at present impossible to trace languages and peoples back to that point with any certainty. In the first millennium BC Greek speakers lived in most of peninsular Greece, in the Aegean islands and on the northern and eastern shores of the Aegean. It has been argued (most recently in Drews's 1988 book) that the language came to the region about 1700 BC with conquering horsemen; but it has also been argued, in Colin Renfrew's *Archaeology and Language* of 1987, that it descends directly from the language of the Thessalian farmers of 7000 BC, who, by this argument, traced their speech and their parentage, as well as the origin of their animals and crops, to south-eastern Anatolia.

These theories – and there are several others – involve much wider questions, particularly that of the date and the original home of the postulated 'proto-Indo-European' from which Greek descends, as do many of the other languages of Europe and southern Asia. In investigating the history of food in the Aegean region, one must keep in mind the complexity of these topics. Peoples, languages and ways of life need have no simple correspondences. The Vlachs, speaking Aromunian, and the Sarakatsani, speaking Greek, are the most recent transhumant pastoralists of Greece. Through what chain of peoples did the skills and traditions of their way of life pass to them from the transhumant pastoralists who probably followed similar routes at the same times of year in 5000 or in 10,000 BC?[2]

## PREHISTORIC SETTLEMENTS AND ENVIRONMENTS

Excavated prehistoric settlements are the source of most of what is known of the way of life of the inhabitants of the Aegean lands before the beginnings there of written literature and history. The early archaeologists often found remains of plants and animals among the ruins and potsherds. Such finds may be said to have begun with the store of beans and peas at Minoan Knossos, excavated in 1878.[3] It is only in the last thirty years that a few sites have been explored more systematically for animal and plant remains and that the results have been given microscopic analysis and statistical evaluation. And now chromosome studies, alongside more traditional botanical and archaeological methods, contribute to the search for the ancestry of modern cultivated plants. Meanwhile, archaeologists and anthropologists continue to attempt to relate finds to possible patterns of behaviour.

The oldest human find in Greece, far distant from any contemporary ones in Europe or Asia, is the skull from Petralona cave in Chalcidice, well over a hundred thousand years old. But evidence on the food of the human population of Greece starts later than this. The last ice age, known to archaeologists as the Würm glaciation, reached its peak around 25,000 BC. The Aegean was never ice-bound, but its climate will have been cooler and drier than today. Before, during and after this ice age people were certainly living in mainland Greece from Elis and Arcadia northwards. Before 7000 BC the fullest information as to food comes from Frankhthi, a north-west facing cave close to the shore of the southern Argolid. Frankhthi is unique among Aegean sites of this early period – and it is still quite unusual even in a wider geographical frame – because here are found remains not only of animals, but also of plants that were of interest to its inhabitants. There are also three excavated rock shelters in Epirus: Asprokhaliko, relatively low-lying and sheltered from the north, Kastritsa and Klithi, much higher and north-facing. And there was a riverside camp on the Thessalian plain, Argissa Magoula.

There are other sites, too. But the sample is a poor one: what were then seaside meadows, around much of Greece, are now a good four hundred feet below sea level and in their inaccessible soil, no doubt, is much evidence of human activity. For example, it is known from finds of Melian obsidian – at Frankhthi from 9000 BC, elsewhere later – that people went to the island of Melos, but no early sign of their presence is to be found on Melos now.[4]

Frankhthi's second unique feature, unique so far at least, is that it spans the pre-7000 millennia (late Palaeolithic or Mesolithic period) and the post-7000 period. In the later period, however, information from Frankhthi is supplemented by that from Lerna near Argos. But on present evidence southern Greece remained sparsely populated between about 7000 and

2000 BC. By contrast, on the plains of Macedonia and, most notably, Thessaly, new settlements grew and multiplied. Some of them have provided evidence of food. They include Prodromos, Sitagri and Nea Nikomedia in Macedonia, Argissa Magoula, Sufli, Marmariani, Dimini and Sesklo in Thessaly, the last two sites being close to modern Volo. Knossos on Crete was colonised at the very beginning of the period. Little is known of early inhabitants of the east coast of the Aegean and still less of their food.

Again the sample is poor. It is useful that Balkan and Anatolian sites, further from the Aegean shores but not dissimilar in ecology to the northern and eastern Aegean, provide some complementary evidence, notably Hacilar in Turkey and Chevdar and Kazanluk in Bulgaria.

In southern and central Greece, Crete and the southern Cyclades, there was striking development after 2100 BC, culminating in the palaces of Knossos, Mycenae and Pylos with their storerooms and their archives. Evidence about food comes from excavations at Knossos and Aghia Triada on Crete, from Tiryns in the northern Peloponnese and also from two places destroyed by the eruption of Thera in 1628 BC, Therasia and Akrotiri.[5] For the first time, written records complement archaeology. The Linear B archives of Knossos, Pylos and Mycenae list produce of interest to contemporary stock-takers or accountants, saying all too little, sadly, of the society that lay behind the records. Further north there are useful finds from Marmariani in Thessaly and at the second- and first-millennium BC settlement of Kastanas in south-western Thrace.[6]

## THE EARLIEST CLUES

The small and widely scattered communities that lived in Greece between about 50,000 and 10,000 BC left discarded bones as evidence of the meat they ate: archaeologists still face the challenge of showing that they also used plant foods, and, if so, which. In later prehistoric times, traces of food storage can help to identify some of the plants that were of the greatest interest to humans, but even in Russia and the Levant food storage has not been confirmed until towards the end of this period and in Greece the evidence of it is first found later still.[7]

Gradual changes are evident in the range of animal species used for food. Did people simply eat all that was available or were they discovering new tastes, new preferences? What is clear is that climate, flora and fauna actually underwent massive changes during this long period.

The earliest finds at Thessalian sites, such as Argissa Magoula where people lived between 50,000 and 30,000 BC, include bones of rhinoceros, hippopotamus and elephant, and also of the European wild ass, still a favoured food in classical Greece. At Asprokhaliko, used from about 40,000 to about 10,000 BC, animal bones from the earliest period include bear and deer. And among the discards of the early inhabitants of Frankhthi cave in the Argolid, about 20,000 to 15,000 BC, the bones of red deer and wild ass abound. There were also wild ox, wild pig, hare and ibex – the European wild goat. The hare was to be the best-known game animal of the more settled parts of Greece in historical times.[8]

The rhinoceros, hippopotamus and elephant disappeared from Greece. But all the other animals identified, even bear, were still food for later inhabitants of the Aegean.

There are cut-marks on the animal bones at Frankhthi, but apparently no sign that they had been burnt or boiled. Other hypotheses are possible, but we may risk the deduction that they are the bones of animals that were food for the human users of the cave, food that was eaten raw or dried but not cooked.

## THE BEGINNINGS OF SPECIALISATION

Inhabitants of Greece would move on to a more concentrated exploitation of food sources, and, in gradual and almost imperceptible stages, to the control of them. By 11,000 to 6000 BC foraging had, for some, become a surprisingly specialised activity considering the variety of available foods. The same kind of specialisation has been observed elsewhere in Europe at about this period.

Some sites were occupied seasonally. Perhaps they were the typical ones. Used again and again for hundreds or thousands of years, they were ideally placed for one single food source. The rock shelter at Klithi, for example, used about 10,500 to 8000 BC, is too high in the mountains of Epirus to be habitable throughout the year but is close to one of the few likely ibex migration routes in the region. Although most bone fragments found here were too small for identification, ibex and chamois made up nineteen-twentieths of what could be identified; deer, ass and small mammals were surely available, but were scarcely used. Similar and even earlier is the case of Kastritsa cave, some way to the south, also suitable for summer use only, and used between about 20,000 and 11,400 BC. Here at least four-fifths of identified bones were red deer. It is interesting that one modern seasonal migration route of the transhumant Sarakatsani shepherds passes both Kastritsa and Asprohaliko. If these cave sites were the seasonal homes of early nomadic groups, how comparable was their way of life to that of their modern transhumant successors?

There have been excavations, too, at Sidari cave, at what is now a holiday resort on the north coast of Corfu, which was then joined to the mainland. This site was used seasonally about 6500 BC by collectors of cockles.

Frankhthi cave, apparently reoccupied about 11,000 BC after long disuse, was used in a different way. It was inhabited all the year round: at any rate the shellfish found there had been collected all through the year, as the pattern of their rings makes clear. But at Frankhthi, too, archaeologists found signs of concentration on one food at a time.

At first it was snails. Now there may be a lot of snail shells at Frankhthi around 10,700 BC not because they were Frankhthi's flavour of the century but just because the archaeologists happened on the spot where all the snail shells, over quite a long period, were thrown away; but the continuing place of snails in the Greek diet is quite clear. Doumas, one of the excavators of Minoan Akrotiri, observes that snails were eaten there before the Thera eruption and suggests that they were 'imported from Crete as a luxury item'.[9] They were still eaten in classical times.

At Frankhthi the apparent glut of snails is followed by a period when red deer seem to predominate again. Then, after 7000 BC, a great many tunny bones are found, a really novel and exciting development to which we shall return (p. 40).

But Frankhthi was not so specialised a site as the rock shelters of Epirus. In addition to these assiduously gathered foodstuffs, many others were collected and prepared at Frankhthi through this period. Animals hunted there included wild pig, fox and hare. The horn-shells and tritons appear to have been Frankhthi's favourite edible shellfish: they also were also well known later.

How were the meats used by these early communities prepared? At Klithi 'the bone surface is often stained black and sometimes carries a thin calcite skin. . . . Many cut marks can still be identified. . . . Many of the bones, especially small fragments, are burnt'.[10] At Frankhthi by this time bones were burnt, and even small bones were broken. We can suggest that great trouble was taken to extract marrow and that meat was roasted on the bone – the earliest sign in Greece of the use of fire in preparing food, though the first exploitation of fire had actually come at a much earlier period in human history.

## THE EARLIEST PLANT FOODS

Frankhthi also provides the earliest evidence in Greece of human interest in plant foods. Soon after 10,000 BC two wild kinds of nuts were being gathered there. One was almond, the wild almond that is still found nowadays from Central Asia to Turkey and is poisonous if eaten raw in quantity (there is no sign before the classical period of sweet, domesticated almonds in Greece). The second nut found at Frankhthi was a small relative of the pistachio, such as lentisk or terebinth, also found at later sites and used and stored at Akrotiri before the Thera eruption. The nuts of these species continue to turn up at later prehistoric sites in Greece and were still eaten by Greeks of historical times; indeed, they can be found in modern Near Eastern markets.[11]

The first fruit known to have been used by humans in Greece was a species of pear. Pyrus spinosa is the wild pear of south-eastern Europe: its fruits can be eaten fresh but are better when cooked or dried. This thorny wild pear was later planted not for its fruit so much as for its use in a defensive hedge. It is the *ákherdos* with which Eumaeus' farm is fortified in the *Odyssey* (14.10).[12]

Two wild relatives of later domesticated pulses, native to Greece, were being collected at Frankhthi by 10,000 BC. One was a lentil: Zohary and Hopf suggest Lens nigricans. The other was one of the Vicia species, something close to the bitter vetch of later Greek agriculture: among other possibilities, bird vetch, Vicia cracca, was collected from the wild for food in later Greece and has occasionally been cultivated. Somewhat later than these, wild peas were collected by about 8000 BC. They were probably Pisum sativum subsp. elatius: it was the humile subspecies of the Near East that was to be domesticated as the garden pea, but the elatius subspecies has been familiar, and has been used in the Balkans in later times. Barley and oats were also collected at Frankhthi. It is sometimes said that barley is native to the Near East and not to Greece, but the finds at Frankhthi suggest that its habitat stretches further west than was thought.

It now seems likely enough that barley and these pulses were being not only collected but actually encouraged, if not cultivated, in Greece before 7000 BC.[13] How were they used? Probably as human food. Grains and pulses, when not eaten fresh, could have been cracked or crushed and baked in the form of cakes in the ashes of the same fires that roasted Frankhthi's meat; and eventually they could have been milled, for the first fragment of a milling stone from Frankhthi is also dated to the seventh millennium.

Barley, so much more reliable in the Greek climate than wheat, has in all later periods been crucial to food and survival. But we cannot at present tell the relative importance of meat, fish, grains, pulses, fruits and other plants in diet of people such as those of Frankhthi in the eighth millennium BC. There is as yet no evidence of food storage. Anthropological parallels suggest that we cannot assume any single dietary staple, and that the importance of meat should not be exaggerated, though bones present themselves more obtrusively to the archaeologist's attention.[14]

## CONTACT AND CHANGE

People travelled by land and sea, for whatever purpose: if they had not travelled they could not have observed the migration routes of ibex and tunny. The seeming rapidity of some changes, therefore, and the wholesale adoption of various specialised hunting and gathering activities, ought to be no great surprise. Cultural change was catalysed by travel and by contact between groups.[15] One cannot tell what most often passed between them: information on food sources and how to use them, or human individuals – by agreement or by capture – or animals and seeds.

There need be no surprise, certainly, that tunny are the first fish for which one finds evidence of heavy exploitation: travelling in such great shoals, they were, so to speak, asking to be caught.[16] But where were Frankhthi's tunny trapped? Van Andel and Runnels take it that the people of Frankhthi had to make very long voyages for their prey.[17] Sea levels, however, have changed since then; the same authors themselves provide maps to show the huge effect of these changes on the Greek coastline. Sea currents and plankton concentrations have changed too. We can hardly know for sure what routes the tunny of the seventh millennium BC followed through the Aegean on their annual migration, and so we cannot really know where Frankhthi's tunny were caught. Yet there may be a clue in the fact that Melian obsidian, already known there for two millennia, became more common at Frankhthi about the same time that tunny did. Melos was always an island: regular sea voyages were certainly being made.

What happened to all the tunny that were taken back to Frankhthi after what must have been concentrated spells of trapping during specific short seasons? What happened to the ibex and chamois meat of which the group using the Klithi rock shelter must, once or twice a year, have had far too much to eat? Nothing is known about long-distance transport of foods. But the very existence of specialisation on this scale argues that the hard-won food was not simply used or wasted while it was fresh: that most of the tunny at Frankhthi and the ibex and chamois culled at Klithi was cut from the bone and dried for later consumption. One cannot say whether it was destined to be eaten by some other group or by the hunters, nor whether those at Klithi stayed at Klithi till they had finished their meat, or took it with them to some other site. But tools and ornaments, or the materials for them, certainly did travel surprising distances.[18] At Klithi, high in the mountains of Epirus, were found seashells of Dentalium and of Cyclope neritea; also red deer teeth, drilled for a necklace, identical to others that were found at Kastritsa. Just as these valuable commodities travelled, so foodstuffs, if it were worthwhile, could have travelled too.

## EARLY AGRICULTURE

Some time before 6000 BC sheep farming and the growing of two kinds of hulled wheat, emmer and einkorn, spread through Greece and south-eastern Europe. All three came ultimately from the Near East, where they had been known for several millennia. Domesticated sheep existed in western Iran by around 9000 BC. Emmer is found, in a wild form, in remains at human habitation sites in Palestine dating well before 15,000 BC, and the signs of cultivation and selection can be seen at a Syrian site of 9000 BC. Wild einkorn was used in Syria by 10,000 BC and cultivated forms existed by 7000 BC in Syria, Turkey and Iran. Since all three new foods appear at sites of the Greek peninsula slightly earlier than in eastern

*Figure 6* Threshing lentils: Alonnisos, about 1970. *Photo*: Rena Salaman

Macedonia or Thrace, it has been suggested that they were brought to Greece by sea.

At about the same time as these new foods we find new, domesticated varieties of some that were already known in Greece in a local wild form. It seems fair to conclude that the practices involved in cultivating them, along with seeds of the preferred varieties, came to Greece from the east as did sheep and wheat.

One important novelty is the domesticated goat. It was once suggested that the domestication of goats took place first in south-eastern Europe from the wild ibex, but it is now thought that the domesticated goats that became common in Greece at the same time as sheep are, like them, of Near Eastern origin.[19] Cultivated peas, lentils and barley, the latter in both two-row and six-row races, also appear in Greece now. These had all been grown earlier in the Near East. Peas, Pisum sativum subsp. humile, were gathered in Iraq, Turkey and Syria by 8000 BC; lentils ancestral to the cultivated kind were used in Syria by 10,000 BC, and huge quantities of evidently cultivated lentils come from Yiftah'el in Israel, and are dated to about 7800 BC. Barley, like emmer, was gathered from the wild in Palestine well before 15,000 BC and Syrian finds from 8500 BC onwards show definite signs of cultivation.

But with three further innovations of around 7000 BC, south-eastern influence, if it occurred at all, may have been on the level of ideas only.

41

Bitter vetch, Vicia ervilia, seems to be native to central Turkey and was being gathered there by 8000 BC; it was perhaps from Turkey that this pulse spread, as a cultivated plant, to Greece and Bulgaria. Toxic until the seeds are soaked, it has never become really popular elsewhere.[20] And it may be from local wild species that cattle and pigs were now domesticated in Greece, though domesticated cattle have been found almost as early from Çatal Hüyük in southern Turkey, and not much later from the Levant. Domesticated pigs appeared in Greece hardly later than in Iraq and they probably represent the domestication of wild pigs of south-eastern Europe. Until modern times, as iconographical evidence confirms, the domestic pigs of Europe were 'small, skinny and hairy'.[21]

These changes appear, certainly from a modern perspective, to have swept Greece within a surprisingly short time, in spite of the very different patterns of habitation in different districts. At Frankhthi, for example, without any indication of a break in habitation, some time before 6000 BC sheep and emmer quite suddenly come to dominate the archaeological record, einkorn increasing more slowly. The people of Thessaly and western Macedonia, meanwhile, besides being perhaps the earliest local domesticators of cattle, were enthusiastic growers of lentils, barley, emmer and einkorn, or so the evidence from Argissa Magoula and Nea Nikomedia suggests. It is just at this time, too, that settlers of unknown origin began to live at Knossos. These earliest known inhabitants of Crete grew barley and emmer, and were apparently the first farmers in the Aegean to use a new free-threshing kind of wheat. They kept sheep, goats, pigs and cows, which, together with wheat and barley, they must have brought with them to Crete by sea.

## THE NEOLITHIC DIET

From animal bones archaeozoologists can identify not only species but age. Thus we can begin to characterise the animal husbandry of this distant period.[22] Earliest 'kill-off patterns' suggest that the majority of stock was slaughtered as soon as it had reached full size, or nearly so. This system would maximise meat production, not milk production. That is perhaps not enough to show, as Sherratt argued with his so-called 'secondary products revolution', that people around the Aegean did not use milk, cheese and other animal by-products till about 3000 BC.[23] After all, wool was used far earlier at Frankhthi; and, on the other hand, the same pattern of herd management, coexisting with the production of cheese, is implied in a classical text, a comedy fragment by Antiphanes (21 [Athenaeus 402d]):

'What meat would you most like to eat?'
'The most economical. The kind of sheep that has no wool or cheese
– I mean a lamb, my friend. The kind of goat that doesn't make

cheese, a kid. The full-grown ones give so much profit that I can put up with eating this poor stuff.'[24]

The speaker is hypocritically giving economy as an excuse for eating the best meat: we can contrast with him Eumaeus, in the *Odyssey* (14.80–1), apologising to his as-yet-unrecognised master for the wastefulness of eating sucking-pig.

At any rate, at some unknown date the human use of cows', goats' and sheep's milk became customary, though there is no earlier Greek evidence for the fact than is provided by the early second-millennium Cretan seals that show men leading goats and carrying what appear to be milk churns. Cheese is suggested by the finding of what seem to be cheese strainers: Thessalian ones are dated around 3000 BC; strainers also come from Crete, Melos and several Cycladic islands as well as further mainland sites dated to the second millennium.[25] A strange grey substance found in the excavation of Therasia a century ago is supposed to have been cheese itself. In most of the Aegean region it is, of course, goats' milk and sheep's milk, and cheeses made from them, that are significant.

In the seventh and sixth millennia, as in later times, people continued to fish and to gather shellfish. Pike and what were probably carp bones were found at neolithic Sitagri. Later oysters are said to have been among the grave goods in a beehive tomb at Mycenae; sea-urchins, tritons, limpets and other shellfish were part of the diet of seventeenth-century BC Akrotiri. A widely-reproduced wall-painting from the same site shows a naked youth with a catch of dolphin-fish, *Coryphaena hippurus*. We have to assume that many other fish were caught and eaten.[26]

Now and later people collected wild fruits and nuts. Lentisk or terebinth, bitter almond and wild pear continue to appear in sites of this period. Acorns are often found: the range of their uses – certainly including their use as human food – can easily be overlooked. Cornels, wild figs, danewort and sloes, or some similar wild relative of the plum, were being gathered at Sesklo, Prodromos, Nea Nikomedia and Sitagri; blackberry and arbutus (tree-strawberry) seeds were found at neolithic Lerna; wild apple seeds come from Akhillion.[27] Of these fruits, all but wild figs and danewort are still listed in the second century AD, among those that were collected for food from the wild (Galen, *On the Properties of Foods* 2.38). As the cultivated fig spread, wild figs would no longer be an interesting food. Wild grapes were being collected at Sesklo, and later at Sitagri. Although not yet found at Aegean sites, we may add tentatively to the list hazelnuts, known from about 5500 BC at Anzabegovo in northern Macedonia,[28] strawberries and hackberries from about the same date at Hacilar in inland western Turkey and walnuts from Kazanluk in Bulgaria around 5000 BC.

Hunting continued too. Wild pig, deer, ibex and hare were evidently hunted as they had been before; hare was available even to the inhabitants

(a)                                                    (b)

*Figure 7* Two wild fruits of the Aegean region: (a) *kránon*, cornel (cornelian cherry); (b) *lotós* or *palíouros*, hackberry (nettle wood). *Source*: from G. Hegi's *Illustrierte Flora von Mittel-Europa* (Vienna, 1912)

of Thera. Ducks and geese were certainly eaten in neolithic Thessaly and Macedonia and in later Hissarlik, although we do not know whether duck and goose eggs were eaten too. Many other smaller birds probably provided food: their bones do not survive well, and the smallest of them can be and are eaten whole, so evidence will never be plentiful. The earliest relevant evidence is of pigeon sacrifices from bronze age Cephallenia and Mycenae. In later Greece, after all, sacrifices served also as food. Partridge, peacock and pheasant occur in Minoan paintings and seals.[29]

But in spite of all this it is important to note the change of emphasis from the foraging and gardening of the earliest period to a more concentrated agriculture. At the settlements that have been found, admittedly few, barley, wheat and lentils were (to judge by quantities recovered) the staples of the diet, while the major sources of meat were sheep, goats, pigs and rather less plentiful cattle.

Around 6000 BC new cooking methods became available. The appearance of pottery in Greece about that time marks the serious possibility of cooking by boiling. Peoples without the knowledge of pottery have been observed to boil food in wicker baskets sealed with clay, but there is no positive evidence that this was done in pre-neolithic Greece. In the course of the sixth millennium, too, are found the first ovens for parching grain: the earliest known is at Nea Nikomedia in Macedonia, before 5500 BC. Soon afterwards, perhaps as a result of chance discovery or experiment with parching ovens, came the development of clay ovens for baking bread. The earliest sites at which these have been found are neolithic Dimini and Sesklo in Thessaly and Sitagri in Macedonia.

Boiling should have permitted the fuller use of animal foods. As Athenaeus observed, 'no one roasts an ox foot' (*Epitome* 25e); alluding to the ox foot that was thrown at Odysseus (*Odyssey* 20.299), the aside was meant to prove that the boiling of food was practised in heroic times. From the neolithic period, then, date the long-forgotten ancestors of the 'black broth' of Sparta and other such homely stews or soups of the fifth and fourth centuries BC. Boiling also made possible the invention – as far as Greece is concerned – of those favourite, cheap and practical foods of later times, gruel, porridge and pulse soup.

Wheat, perhaps at first prepared in rough cakes or gruels like barley, was in historic times the bread grain *par excellence*, and may have been so ever since the first clay ovens came into use; it may have been so even before, for bread too can be baked in ashes.

## EXPERIMENT AND CHANGE

In the varied and infertile terrain of Greece, as population grew, each district has had to find its balance by trial and error. After millennial experimentation or indecision, reflected chiefly in differing proportions of species among the plant and animal remains at excavated settlement sites,[30] it was emmer that became the most popular cereal in the wide plains of Thessaly and Macedonia, as wheat still is; barley did better, and still does, in the dry and rocky districts of central and southern Greece and the Aegean islands. 'Wheat grows in heavy soil, barley in light soil' became the accepted wisdom (Plutarch, *Moralia* 915e).[31] Pigs and dogs were kept by farmers in both north and south. At most sites sheep and goats eventually predominated over cattle. Archaeologists often have difficulty telling sheep from goats, and so it is often uncertain which of the two were most popular. Both, probably, will have moved from winter pastures in the lowlands to summer pastures in the mountains, their seasonal migrations, under human control, perhaps being modelled on those of the ibex. In this period no upland settlement sites are known, but regular transhumance, on routes resembling those of the modern Vlachs, is suggested by one telling fact. Most of the stone tools used at Nea Nikomedia came from the Pindus mountains, far off to the south-west near modern Konitsa, a well-known modern summer pasture centre.

There was lengthy experiment with pulses, bringing some newly introduced species to eventual significance. The lentil remained a staple; well before historical times, however, the pea became less common. Its place was taken by a succession of novelties including the grass pea, Lathyrus sativus. This was possibly first domesticated in Greece or Bulgaria where, from the seventh millennium onwards, it is found at several sites, notably Prodromos, in great quantities. There are also some finds of closely related species:[32] Lathyrus aphaca, L. cicera and L. ochrus have certainly been used in later Greece, though perhaps not so much cultivated as gathered from the wild. Later came chickpea and broad bean. Chickpea was one of the major cultivated plants of the early neolithic Near East, but it was established in Thessaly only around 4000 BC. The first certain finds of cultivated broad bean in the region, at Kastanas and Lerna, are dated to the third millennium BC, paralleling those from other parts of the Mediterranean, and it is not yet clear where, and from what wild ancestor, the broad bean was domesticated.

Not long after the arrival of emmer and einkorn we find the first remains of the free-threshing kind of wheat, Triticum turgidum, ancestral to compactum and durum wheats, that developed from emmer in cultivation and is recognisable at sites in Turkey and Syria dated to about 7000 BC.[33] The settlement at Knossos, already mentioned (p. 42), was the first in the Aegean to use this free-threshing wheat. It remained popular there; yet although from now onwards grains are found at Thessalian and Macedonian sites alongside emmer, the compactum and durum wheats (classical *pyrós*) never took emmer's place as principal wheat variety of mainland Greece. Indeed, emmer and einkorn are still grown in south-eastern Europe and Anatolia today.[34]

Meanwhile, after some coexistence of two-row and six-row barley, the more productive six-row variety appears to have been the only one grown after 3500 BC.[35] There were other cereals. Broomcorn millet had been domesticated, perhaps in the neighbourhood of the Caucasus, around 5000 BC, and spread from there in cultivation to Iran, to northern China and to central Europe. It was never a popular or widespread crop in Greece, but reached as far south as Kastanas and Assiros in Macedonia at the middle of the second millennium (there had been a much earlier experiment with it in Thessaly). Also from Kastanas come sparser finds of foxtail millet, Setaria italica, classical *élymos*, *melíne*, the early cereal staple of northern China, domesticated there about 6500 BC: this was a recent introduction to Europe across the Asian steppes.

## THE ROOTS OF GASTRONOMY

From a modern, necessarily foreshortened perspective, the new foods of around 7000 BC and the new methods of preparation that came to Greece around 6000 BC do certainly group themselves as a pair of 'neolithic revolutions'. Although the foods, and methods, known earlier remained significant, the cultivated wheat and barley and the domesticated animals of the later period soon came to predominate in the diet of those whose lifestyles have so far been traced archaeologically.

Yet the food of Greece was not affected so drastically by this revolution as was that of some other regions. Our survey of the classical food repertoire will show the importance of fish, of shellfish and of wild green herbs, whose use began in the very earliest period and was in essence unaffected by cultivation and domestication. And in Greece, as in all countries, the poor have had to find their food where they can. 'To these the earth gives a good living, and the oaks bear acorns[36] at their tips and bees at their hearts', said Hesiod (*Works and Days* 232–3). Hesiod here includes, as prime food available to foragers, not only the modest acorn but also, to sweeten the diet, what was surely the earliest luxury food item available in Greece. He reminds us, too, that the availability of honey did not await the practice of bee-keeping.[37]

The domestication of bees may have come relatively late. They were kept in Egypt in the late third millennium BC, but the first identified beehive of Greece comes from Akrotiri, destroyed by the eruption of Thera in 1628 BC. The find reported by Doumas is over a thousand years older than the earliest evidence of bee domestication in Greece previously known.[38]

Honey is to humans essentially a relish, a flavouring agent and a preserving agent: it is never common enough to be a dietary staple. Its introduction to the diet, whenever it came, both followed a pattern and set an example.

Honey followed the pattern of salt, which is always present in the human diet, but which, as those who live near the sea or near sources of the solid mineral will first discover, can be taken in the pure state and added to food in variable quantities with useful and pleasing results. Olives and sorbs, if eaten, customarily require salt in their preparation, but it is not known how early people discovered the effect of salting these fruits, and fish and meat. Sweeteners can be varied in flavouring just as salt can, and with analogous effects. Honey was the most prestigious sweetener in Greece of historical times, though fruit sugars, especially dried figs and date syrup, were not ignored.

Honey set the example of a product in limited supply, easy to store, desirable for its flavouring properties; essentially a luxury. This example was followed by other luxuries, not casually discovered but purposefully developed, which made their appearance in Greece in the millennia that followed the 'neolithic revolution'. Their dating is difficult and controversial.

First to be considered are grapes and wine. A sequence of grape pips of gradually increasing size comes from Sitagri, beginning roughly 4500 BC and ending about 2500 BC. This sequence in itself, taken without considering evidence from elsewhere, might suggest that the vine was being gradually domesticated locally.[39] Yet there were vines in Palestine by 3500 BC, raisins in Egypt by 2900 BC, and grape pips in southern Britain by 2600 BC;[40] the vine is not native in those places, and the pips and dried fruits that have been found there seem to be of a cultivated kind, so it appears that already by 3500 BC domestication had been completed, in some other place or places, and cultivated plants or their products were spreading elsewhere.

Vines grow wild, and wild grapes were used, across a wide belt from the western Mediterranean to the Caucasus. Wild grape pips from archaeological sites in southern France are dated to 7500 BC, in the Caucasus to 6000 BC and in Greece not much later. It is usually thought that domestication took place at the eastern end of this range, in the Caucasus or southeastern Anatolia, but other sites are possible.[41] It is perfectly possible that many growers in many places developed cultivated stocks from local wild grapes. Archaeobotanical study suggests that this is how the Crimean vineyards of the Greek colony of Chersonesus Taurica were developed around 400 BC.[42] If this is the right model, further research may begin to show to what extent growers of any one region were influenced or guided by developments elsewhere.

Grapes were a fresh or dried fruit long before they were the raw material for wine. The first Aegean evidence of grape pressing, and thus of wine-making, comes in a find of grape pips, stalks and skins together at Myrtos in Crete, dated before 2000 BC. There are similar finds from Iran before 3000 BC. Then, in the late second millennium, wine-lees are found in a jar from Mycenae; the impression of a vine leaf, on the clay seal of a jar from Meneleon near Sparta, also seems to be graphic evidence of the storage of wine. The *kratér*, the 'mixing bowl' which was an invariable accompaniment of classical Greek wine-drinking, is already named on a Linear B tablet from Mycenae (*Ue 611*), suggesting that even by 1400 BC wine was customarily mixed with water before use.[43]

If it is difficult to pin down the origin of grape cultivation, it is even less clear where and when domesticated figs developed. The seeds are tiny and it is practically impossible for archaeologists to tell wild from cultivated ones. Moreover, since farmers have always had to take account of the fact that most kinds of cultivated fig – the 'Smyrna' group of modern varieties – need wild male fig trees close at hand for pollination, they have sometimes planted wild fig cuttings conveniently close to their fig orchards: on the windward side, says Pliny (*Natural History* 15.80). Thus the present geographical range of the wild fig is no sure guide to its early habitat. At all events, people have collected figs, from France to Iran, since 8000 BC or soon after. Somewhere across this range, and most probably in the Levant, they began to select and propagate the female trees. Like grapes, figs are easily dried and then form a useful and readily transported sweet food.

Wild olives had been known, and perhaps used, in the neolithic Near East; they were native to Greece also, but there is little evidence that people used them there before 2000 BC. The early neolithic find of a wild olive stone at Sufli in Thessaly is not enough to prove that olives were in human use. Olives were cultivated in Syria, Palestine and Crete in the third millennium; the earliest find is of stones of cultivated olives from early fourth-millennium Palestine. It seems to have been not until much later that olives spread in quantity around the Aegean. The first serious Aegean evidence is in what appear to be olive presses at Cretan sites from the early second millennium onwards. Very few stones are found until the end of the second millennium, and it is at that time too that pollen samples from various sites in Greece show an increase in olive pollen.[44] Olive oil was important in the palaces of Knossos, Mycenae and Pylos not least for their perfumed oil industry, but for this wild olives were preferred.[45] At any rate, people had certainly begun to make more regular use of the olive and its oil in their diet. In contrast with the grape and the fig, cultivation has never produced an olive that is good to eat fresh.

Grape, fig and olive share a characteristic with honey. They are luxuries. This may seem an inappropriate term for items that were widely available and that certainly served to flavour the food of the poor. The important point is that these fruits and their products, which had achieved considerable economic importance in the Aegean by the early centuries of the first millennium BC, and have retained this importance to the present day, cannot be counted staples. They added relish to the diet in the form of strong flavour and alcoholic potency, and added prestige to those who possessed and distributed them. The contribution of these four foods is of a different kind from that of the cereals, the pulses and the meat whose introduction to Greece has been traced above: their arrival marks the earliest step in Aegean gastronomy.

## PREHISTORIC VEGETABLES

As ingredients in stews and soups, and as relishes eaten fresh with bread and olive oil and cheese, green and root vegetables have been essentials in the Greek diet since earliest historical times; in poorer households and simpler circumstances they have been all the more important, taking the place of unattainable meat and fish. The positive evidence for their use in prehistoric Greece is weak, but the probability that they were already important is strong, for many of the most familiar appear to have been native to southern Europe or the eastern Mediterranean coasts. Some species can be used in several different ways: it is among these, in all probability, and not through trade, that the cooks of the Aegean found their first spices.

Excluding cereals, pulses and tree fruits, the earliest plant in which people in Greece were interested (so far as present evidence goes) is a very versatile one: a coriander fruit was found in a seventh-millennium BC context in the Frankhthi cave. The plant appears to be native to the eastern Mediterranean basin, where it certainly grows wild now. But with a single isolated find one has to allow for doubt: is it a modern intrusion? Was the plant used for food? Roughly contemporary with the date ascribed to the Frankhthi specimen, fifteen fruits were discovered at Nahal Hemar cave in Israel, but this find too has been doubted. The next earliest find of this tiny fruit is in the excavation of Therasia. Not long after the date of that deposit, coriander fruits were among the supplies in Tutankhamen's tomb, about 1325 BC. By about 400 BC there is literary evidence for the use of coriander as far afield as India (Panini, *Grammar* 6.1.139). It appears from Linear B tablets that coriander was used in two forms in Mycenaean times: *ko-ri-ja-do-no*, perhaps 'coriander leaf', seems to be distinguished from the plural *ko-ri-(j)a-da-na*, perhaps 'coriander seed', which came in different measures. The same distinction may be observed in classical Greek texts; coriander is still grown in Greece both as a spice, for its tiny seed-like fruits, and as a herb for the pungent flavour of its leaves.

There is positive evidence for several more herbs in second-millennium Greece; again they are the versatile ones whose leaves may be eaten and whose seeds may be used as spices.

Mustard is the next earliest example, a bag of white mustard seeds having turned up in a bronze age context at Marmariani in Thessaly; mustard is generally listed among herbs, not spices, in classical Greek written sources (e.g. Galen, *On the Properties of Foods* 2.68.2). All other herbs for which there is early evidence from Greece happen to belong, like coriander, to the Umbelliferae family. Iron age Kastanas provides evidence of the use of celery, known also in Egypt. Fennel is identified with some confidence in Linear B texts as *ma-ra-tu-wo*. Fennel, both wild and cultivated, was much used by later Greeks as a vegetable, but there is no other prehistoric evidence for it either in Greece or elsewhere. Fouqué reported that aniseed had been found at Therasia. Aniseed is not mentioned in written sources before the time of Theophrastus, who listed it among substances used for perfumes and not grown in Europe (*Study of Plants* 9.7.3). Theophrastus was probably right, though the plant was available in the Aegean: botanists now believe that it is native to Chios and western Anatolia.[46] Dill, a herb and spice native to the Mediterranean shores, is frequently mentioned in Greek literature and its seed has been found at late second-millennium BC Kastanas. At the roughly contemporary tomb of Amenophis II of Egypt sprigs of dill are also said to have been identified.[47] Finally, Linear B tablets list quantities of *ku-mi-no*. Greeks of historical times used this name (classical *kyminon*) for cumin, classed by Theophrastus as a pot-herb, but also a source of spicy seeds widely used in cookery. This is the only plant, of the group just listed, that people must clearly have introduced to Greece, for its wild relatives are native, not to the Mediterranean, but to central Asia, according to Zohary and Hopf.[48] It was well known in the Near East in the second millennium BC, and its Greek name has Near Eastern antecedents.[49]

This, the list of green vegetables for which there is positive evidence from prehistoric Greece, makes up an odd collection. There can be no doubt that the varying chances of preservation in archaeological contexts, and the circumscribed interests of the record-keepers who wrote in Linear B, have so far kept from our knowledge the prehistoric use in Greece of such valuable plants as lettuce and cabbage. One Greek site as fruitful, or well-sifted, as Bulgarian Chevdar and Kazanluk might change the picture radically; there, dated to around 5000 BC, were found seeds of a Brassica species (turnip, cabbage or black mustard?), mallow, goosefoot, sorrel and nightshade, all known as foods in classical or modern Greece. For these and many others the first Greek evidence will come, as we shall see (pp. 83–5), in written texts of the sixth, fifth and fourth centuries BC.

But the few vegetables that *are* known from prehistoric Greece are notable not only for their versatility but also for their strong taste: each of them has a powerful effect, whether used as herb or as spice, on the flavour of the foods with which it is eaten.

## FLAVOURS AND COLOURS

Here once more, it seems, a pattern was being set. If people could experiment with food flavours by judiciously adding these useful plants, they could also try the effect of substances whose *only* contribution would be flavour or colour. Two leaves, one flower and three aromatic seeds may be listed under this heading as having been known in the prehistoric Aegean. Mint, pennyroyal and safflower are identified in Linear B records as *mi-ta*, *ka-ra-ko* and *ka-na-ko*. All three were certainly used in food in classical or later times, as we shall see, though safflower, a yellow colouring now commonly used as a substitute for saffron, might well have served as a dye for hundreds or thousands of years before anyone thought of adding it to food. The first evidence of that, anywhere in the world, is in Greek texts of about 400 BC (*Regimen* 2.45.4; Anaxandrides 42 [Athenaeus 131e]). Safflower was known in Egypt in the second millennium BC, but here again perhaps as a dye and not a food additive. Safflower oil, well known to ancient pharmacists, is now used as a cooking medium, but this is quite a modern development.

The three aromatic seeds, sesame, poppy and flax, were all being used to garnish loaves around 600 BC, when the Spartan poet Alcman happened to list them in a passage quoted by Athenaeus:

> Poppy-seed loaves are mentioned by Alcman in book V: 'Seven couches and as many tables crowned with poppy-seed bread, with flax-seed bread and sesame bread and, for the girls, buckets full of *khrysókolla*', these being a sweetmeat made of honey and flax-seed.[50]
>
> (Alcman 19 [Athenaeus 111a])

All three seeds were known in the prehistoric Aegean. Flax had arrived in Greece and the Balkans before 5000 BC, having been domesticated at least a thousand years earlier in the Levant, but the finds at prehistoric Greek sites are few and in any case the main uses of flax are not culinary. The first evidence in Greece for human interest in poppies comes from finds of seed at Kastanas and from a Cretan sculpture, both datable to the end of the second millennium, and an earlier cache of corn-poppy seeds at Thermi on Lesbos. There are earlier finds of poppy seed from western Europe, where the plant was probably first brought into cultivation. The wild ancestor of the opium poppy is native to the western shores of the Mediterranean. Poppies are useful for their narcotic latex and for their oil as well as for their aromatic seeds.

According to Linear B tablets, the palace of Mycenae had an interest in *sa-sa-ma*, sometimes abbreviated to *sa*.[51] Sesame is native to south Asia or possibly to eastern Africa.[52] At any rate it was in use in north India by around 2000 BC. There have been two unconfirmed finds of sesame from the Mediterranean before 1000 BC: it was reported among the deposits in Tutankhamen's tomb from fourteenth-century BC Egypt, and from Akrotiri on Thera, destroyed in 1628 BC.

There is a danger of assuming unjustifiably that plants now called herbs or spices were already used in food, simply because they were known. Neither the archaeological finds nor the Linear B records prove that these six were used *in cooking* in Mycenaean Greece. Substances such as these, and some of the Umbelliferae seeds discussed above (pp. 49–51), were valuable as medicines and as aromatic ingredients in perfumed oils, and that is probably why the scribes of the Linear B tablets took the trouble to list them.[53] Flax and its oil, sesame oil (if it is sesame) and poppy latex had importance quite apart from any food use. But at any rate they were available for adding to food, and one may suspect that the effect was tried.

This is the place to list two new fruits introduced to second-millennium Greece. The pomegranate was known in bronze age Crete, as is evident from pictures; seeds have been found at Tiryns. It had been grown in Palestine, is identified in Sumerian and Akkadian records in the third millennium[54] and appears in Egypt soon after 2000 BC. Wild forms are found in north-eastern Turkey, whence, presumably, it was introduced both to the Levant and to Greece, though there are also wild pomegranates in Albania and Montenegro. By late prehistoric times people in Greece also knew of musk melons, of which a few seeds survive from bronze age Tiryns – though whether an edible, sweet fruit was grown or whether it was the seeds that were eaten is unknown. Musk melons were cultivated in Mesopotamia by about 2000 BC.[55]

## PATHS AND PATTERNS OF INNOVATION

Changes in the peripherals of the diet seem to be far more readily made than changes in the staple food. Six thousand years after the introduction of wheat to Greece, older-established barley, though in an improved variety, was still the staple for most people there in the first millennium BC; and the old-fashioned ways of preparing cereal, unavoidable before ovens were built, were still widely used. Tunny, known in the Argolid at least as early as barley, was still being caught in huge quantities – perhaps from further afield – in historical times, and eaten fresh, dried and salted, a highly prestigious food to most Greeks. Yet Greeks of the fifth and fourth centuries would show enthusiasm for imported nuts, newly introduced fruit and fashionable appellations of wine.

It is in fact far more difficult and risky to establish a replacement to the staple food than to play with relishes and snacks. Barley grows reliably in Greece; wheat, though it might have seemed a more attractive crop when first introduced in the seventh millennium, too often fails there. If fifth-century Athens relied on imported wheat as heavily as is often said, this would have been as dangerous as was Ireland's later dependence on the newly introduced potato.

But, not surprisingly, human preferences match themselves to ecological constraints. It is misguided to read into early Greek literature the dislike for barley which is so clear in Roman sources: if Greeks had disliked barley they would have risked starvation. At a fashionable Athenian banquet, the fifth- and fourth-century sources suggest, the ideal was to serve wheat bread *and* barley cakes – no doubt in proportions adapted to their current availability and to the host's generosity.[56]

The narrative above follows the archaeological evidence for foodstuffs to the end of the second millennium BC. If there was, as many think, an episode of catastrophic destruction in Greece and beyond around 1300, followed by a very long period of low population and agricultural decline, it had no identifiable influence on the long-term history of foodstuffs. The catastrophe itself seems solidly based in settlement archaeology, in the layers of fire and destruction noted at so many sites. Information on what followed is more difficult to analyse. Is the apparent steep decline in numbers of settlements explained not, or not entirely, by a decline in population, as many assume, but also by a retreat to more centralised, more easily defensible sites? If the owners of homes, gardens and farms simply disappeared, the newly-introduced foodstuffs of the late prehistoric period – cumin, pomegranates – might also be expected to disappear; the complex traditions of vine and olive cultivation might suffer disastrous interruption. There is no strong evidence for any of this.[57] On the contrary, in these last prehistoric centuries, apparently after Mycenaean times but before the earliest Greek literature, a series of new foods reached the Aegean region for the first time, in particular cultivated varieties of many orchard fruits and nuts. It is a relatively confident farmer who plants orchards: a farmer who feels confident that he himself, or those for whom he cares, will still be there a decade or more later. The destruction of olive

groves was a feature of the barbarous warfare of the fifth and fourth
centuries BC, not, apparently, of the 'dark ages'.

*Figure 8 Sykon* and *sykalís*: fig and blackcap ('fig-pecker') redrawn from a Roman
wall-painting from Boscotrecase, Campania

# Part II

# FOOD AND GASTRONOMY OF THE CLASSICAL AEGEAN

# 3

# DIVINE INVENTIONS
## The classical food repertoire[1]

## THE INFORMATION AND ITS SOURCES

We can now set out to develop a picture of the commonly used foodstuffs of the archaic and classical Aegean – of the first four centuries of recorded history, 650 to 250 BC.[2] This means confronting the archaeological information of Chapter 2 with the evidence of classical Greek texts. We come face to face with the limitations, and the discontinuities, of these disparate sources.

The kind of archaeological material on which Chapter 2 relied is scarcely available for the classical period. The last years of occupation of Frankhthi and Kastanas, utterly insignificant as such sites must be called in the context of classical history, shine out like a beacon to the archaeobiologist. Very little in the way of food remains is available from excavations of classical sites. Such excavations even now concentrate on the recovery of artefacts and architecture. Admittedly there are exceptions. The excavation of Sardis, for example, brought fascinating information on food use, especially in a sacrificial context. But exceptions are few, and thus sites of the first millennia BC and AD elsewhere in the Mediterranean world can be useful as controls on the meagre Greek evidence. Examples are Pompeii in southern Italy and Stobi in the southern Balkans, both of them relatively close to Greece.[3]

Would finds from classical sites of vegetable and animal remains, especially fish remains, be more varied than those from earlier millennia? No one can say with confidence. What will become clear in these chapters is that many more foodstuffs are recorded as of use and interest in Greek literature than the prehistoric archaeology of Greece has so far brought to light. It must be remembered that some foodstuffs, by their nature or the nature of the environment, are unlikely to leave recognisable remains at any period.

Meanwhile the literary sources show an imbalance of their own. They do immediately make us aware of the use as food in Greece of far more plant and animal species than archaeology has been able to show. However, the information is selected for us, and dependent not on the skills of the researcher or on the chances of survival so much as on the knowledge, aims and prejudices of authors. Surviving classical Greek literature has a bias towards Athens, and even if more of it survived, the same bias would probably be visible. We know a great deal, therefore, of the foods that Athenians ate and liked to talk about. That last clause is all-important, and it helps to explain why some foods, certainly available in the region ever since prehistoric times and certainly in use now, are almost or entirely absent from the corpus of classical literature.

## DOMESTIC ANIMALS

For most Greeks, in most historic times, to eat meat meant, most commonly, to eat the meat of domesticated animals. Hunting provided tasty and much-appreciated food, but wild animals and birds were not sufficiently common to be a frequent element of the diet.

Among domesticated animals the three major providers of human food were certainly sheep, pig and goat. A long tradition of careful herd management with these species is implied by at least two pieces of evidence. There was a full technical vocabulary identifying animals of different ages: this was, once upon a time, recorded in the lost treatise of Aristophanes of Byzantium *Perì helikiôn, On Ages*). And an impressive range of detailed observations of signs of maturity is recorded in Aristotle's *Study of Animals* (544b12–546b14, 571b3–578a24). It is no coincidence, then, that two of the major *domesticated* animals are at the centre of sacrifice and festivity in different scenes of the *Odyssey*.

The meat of the third of them, the domesticated goat, *aíx*, is also mentioned in an aside in the *Odyssey* (17.213–4) as well as by Hesiod (*Works and Days* 591). In truth goats were possibly most significant economically as providers of cheese, but they were regularly sacrificed and eaten. Their meat was good only at certain ages or at certain times of year, having a rank taste or smell at other times, but it was considered highly nourishing,[4] and a story was told of a Theban athlete who ate little else and outperformed all his contemporaries, though they laughed at him because of the smell of his sweat (Cleitomachus of Carthage [Athenaeus 402c]), or possibly his wind.[5]

Goats are not especially prolific: kid was therefore a relative luxury, one that Hesiod's farmer could enjoy in the heat of summer (*Works and Days* 591), one that could form a *pièce de résistance* at an urban dinner party of the Athenian or the Spartan kind.[6]

The *Odyssey* episode concerning mutton is that part of the narrative of Odysseus in which, after blinding the pastoralist Cyclops, Odysseus and his men seize his sheep. They allot the ram to their leader, who in turn offers it to Zeus in vain hope of his favour. It is the ram, therefore, once

Zeus has had his share, that provides the food for that day's carousing: 'So then all day long till the sun set we sat dining on plenty of meat and fine wine, and then we went to sleep on the sea beach' (9.556–9). A sheep, *próbaton*, carried to the place of sacrifice by the cook, is the centrepiece of the picnic that is supposed to be taking place, off stage, during Menander's *Bad Tempered Man* (393–401); a sheep sacrifice is played out largely on stage, with much byplay revealing interesting detail, in Aristophanes' *Peace* (937–1126).[7]

Lamb, like kid, was in classical times a delicacy suited to an expensive dinner: suckling lamb is mentioned at least once. Philoxenus' gastronomic poem sketches several dishes in which lamb and kid were served together, both meat and offal. The two are often listed in literary and dietary menus as companions or alternatives.[8] Nicander's *Georgics* (fragment 68 [Athenaeus 126b]) offered a recipe:

> But when you prepare fresh-killed kid or lamb or even chicken as food, put some fresh wheat grains, crushed, in a deep pan, and stir up together with fragrant oil. When the stew is boiling, pour it over [the crushed wheat] and cover it with the lid, for when so treated the heavy meal swells up. Serve, just warm, with bread-spoons.

The scene in which Eumaeus sacrifices a pig, *hys*, as food for himself, his labourers and his guest, the disguised Odysseus (*Odyssey* 14.413–56), has taken the fancy of many later hearers and readers, including the authors of classical satyr play and comedy. An unnamed piece by Aeschylus (fragment 309 [Athenaeus 375d–f]) may well come from a satyr play based on this episode:

> 'I shall put this plump sucking-pig in a moist *kríbanos*:[9] what better *ópson* could a man have? . . . the piglet is white, why not? and well-singed. Stew away, and don't be afraid of the fire! . . . This piglet I have sacrificed is from the same sow that has been a nuisance to me in the house, galloping about and turning things upside down.'

The pig was indeed a sacrificial animal like the rest, at least in classical times. To judge by the sample of comedy fragments preserved by Athenaeus, pork was the commonest meat in Athenian menus. Pork was also salted: one kind of ham was named after the hedonist philosopher Aristoxenus of Cyrene.[10]

As with the other domestic animals, a series of technical terms existed to denote pigs of specified age and sex. These were carried over into culinary terminology, so that it is clear that well-grown young pigs, *délphakes*, were commonly used for food; *khoîroi* were sometimes considered too small, while sucking-pigs, *galathenoí*, were a particular delicacy.[11]

The sacrifice of an ox, *boûs*, is the centrepiece of one of the episodes of

*Odyssey* book 3 (404–73). A ritual is there described at length, beginning with the gilding of the animal's horns, proceeding with washing of hands, sprinkling of barley-meal[12] on the head of the victim, the blow with an axe downwards on the neck to kill, the lament raised by women, the cutting of the throat and collecting of the blood; then the cutting of slices from the thighs to be wrapped in a fold of fat and burnt over wood with red wine poured on, this forming the god's portion.

> But when the thighs were burnt up and they had tasted the vital parts, they cut up the rest and stuck it on spits and roasted it, holding the sharp spits in their hands. . . . So, when they had roasted the upper flesh and pulled it [from the spits], they sat and ate, and good men waited on them, pouring wine in golden cups.
>
> (*Odyssey* 3.461–72)

Whatever the reality that might lie behind the *Iliad* and *Odyssey*, beef and veal have been something of a rarity in Athens and other cities of central and southern Greece. In the literary menus of the fourth century BC beef is notable for its absence. There was none even at the wedding feast of Caranus.[13] References to it, and to beef offal, can certainly be found, but in special circumstances. Aristophanes, in *Peace* (1280), incorporates beef-eating in a passage of joky epic formulas, 'thus then they dined on the flesh of oxen, and all that stuff'; Theophilus (8 [Athenaeus 95a, 417b]) includes boiled ox feet in a list of foods representing heavy gluttony.

Aristotle in the *Study of Animals* (542a27) brackets pig and dog together as *synanthropeuómena*, 'animals symbiotic with man'. Both were eaten in classical Greece, but dog, *kyon*, was not a food of which one boasted. It is never listed in the comedy menus or in the gastronomic poetry of the fourth century. Roast dog was, however, recommended for certain diets by the author of the Hippocratic dietary text *Regimen*, puppy meat for others (79, 82). Greenewalt,[14] a propos of puppy sacrifices in sixth-century Sardis, has collected references from Greek literature to dogs as food. Dogs were 'very commonly eaten among some peoples', said Galen (*On the Properties of Foods* 3.1.11), implying that by the second century AD Greeks were no longer among them.

The domestic ass, *ónos*, was apparently sometimes eaten, though it was not a delicacy like its wild relative:

> The meat of wild asses that are healthy and young comes close to [hare]. Some people, I note, also bring to table the meat of domestic asses that are getting on in years, though it is most cacochymous, most dyspeptic, indigestible and also unpleasant to eat, like that of horses and camels, for these too are eaten by men who are asinine and camelid in mind and body.[15]
>
> (Galen, *On the Properties of Foods* 3.1.9)

Horse, *híppos*, was a very uncommon choice as food among Greeks, though its dietary qualities are assessed in *Regimen* (46). Finally, this may be the place to mention the eating of human flesh, which according to an amusing aside of Galen's was not quite so rare as might be thought:

> It is evident that the flesh of pigs and of human beings is similar, since people have eaten human flesh in place of pork without suspecting either the taste or the smell; the possibility has been discovered, before now, by unscrupulous innkeepers and others.
>
> (*On the Properties of Foods* 3.1.6)

Not only the muscle but almost every other part of the major domestic animals was tried as food in classical Greece. The 'vital parts' (*splánkhna*) of the quotation above from *Odyssey* (3.461–72) were the heart, liver and kidneys, roasted during the sacrifice, tasted by those participating and shared with the god (Aristophanes, *Birds* 518–19). Marrow might be a delicacy to eat beside wine (Pherecrates 158 [Athenaeus 653e]); we recall the orphaned boy of Andromache's lament, 'sitting on his father's knee he used to eat nothing but marrow and rich mutton fat' (*Iliad* 22.501). Tongue was again special, set aside for Hermes or as the prerogative of the officiator: 'those leaving a dinner pour a libation to [Hermes] over the tongues' (*Epitome of Athenaeus* 16b; cf. Aristophanes, *Peace* 1109). There was evidently a lively trade in sausages and white offal at the daily market at Athens: a sausage-seller is antihero of Aristophanes' *Knights*, from the text of which some details of the business can be deduced. Among domestic animals the pig is most distinguished for its versatility, for almost every part of it can be eaten. Sow's womb, now not commonly used, was thought of as a delicacy in classical times. The womb of a sow that had just miscarried was considered the best of all.[16]

## WILD ANIMALS

The hare, *lagós*, was the only wild quadruped likely to be taken by huntsmen near Athens. Naturally, then, it was highly regarded there: Xenophon's pamphlet on *Hunting* (2–8) largely concerns the pursuit of the hare. It features as a love-gift in painted courtship scenes on vases of the sixth and fifth centuries. It first occurs in comedy as one of the features of the dinner parties of the rich Callias: 'there are langoustines, skates, hares and women with swaying hips', said a character in Eupolis' *Flatterers* (174 [Athenaeus 286b]), borrowing for the last phrase a Homeric epithet originally applied to oxen. In comic menus of the fourth century the hare is one of the labels of an exclusive, expensive, intimate dinner, or rather supper.[17]

> There are many ways, many rules for the preparation of hare. This is the best, that you should bring the roast meat in and serve to

everyone while they are drinking, hot, simply sprinkled with salt, taking it from the spit while still a little rare. Do not worry if you see the ichor seeping from the meat, but eat greedily. To me the other recipes are altogether out of place, gluey sauces, too much cheese, too much oil over, as if one were cooking a weasel.

(Archestratus 57 [Athenaeus 399d])

The occasion on which hare – or birds, see pp. 63–5 – was served was one that emphasised choice and flavour rather than quantity: 'not extravagant, but neat' (Nicostratus [*Epitome* 65d]). One notes the sprinkling of chopped coriander, salt, cheese, highly-flavoured sauces, to maximise the impact of a dish that must rely on quality since it cannot be appreciated for its size. The offal and blood of hare were prepared separately, as a stew, *mímarkys*, later sources assert.[18]

Where it was available, wild boar, *kápros*, was highly appreciated: 'let the goat meat be for the boys, the wild boar you shall have for yourself and your friends', wrote a third-century gourmet (Lynceus [Athenaeus 402a]).[19] Wild goat, *aíx ágrios*, was well worth eating.[20] Wild ass, *ónagros*, was a gourmet dish:[21] presumably this still means Equus hydruntinus, now extinct. Fox, *alópex*, was also good: it was at its best at harvest time because this was when the foxes had been able to fatten themselves on grapes.[22] Red deer, *élaphos*, was easiest to catch, and tasted best, in summer, and new-born fawns, *nebrós*, were caught in the spring; roe deer, *próx*, is less talked of.[23] Even bear, *árktos*, and lion, *léon*, were eaten: bear tasted worse, needing to be boiled twice, said a later source (Galen, *On the Properties of Foods* 3.1.10). These were surely seldom met with, though the tract of Epirus between Nessus and Achelous was the one region of Europe where lions could be found,[24] and Macedonian royalty was proud of its prowess in the lion hunt.

Among the lower ranks of the animal kingdom male and female cicadas, *téttix*, *kerkópe*, were sometimes used for food, the egg-bearing females being best to eat.[25] And the snail, *kokhlías*, probably eaten before neolithic times by the inhabitants of Frankhthi cave, remained an article of diet later. Snails had a reputation as an aphrodisiac,[26] and Galen would be careful to include them in his dietary survey:

It cannot be counted as airborne or aquatic, that is clear. So if we do not deal with it among quadrupeds we shall have said nothing about the nutritional value of the snail at all. And it would not be right to leave it out, as we shall leave out grubs and hedgehogs[27] and other creatures that the people of Egypt and some others eat: none of them is going to read this book, and we are not going to eat any of their foods. But all Greeks eat snails every day. They have tough flesh, but, once cooked, are highly nourishing.

(*On the Properties of Foods* 3.2.1)

## BIRDS

Many more birds had been tried as food than would be familiar to most modern Europeans.[28] Aristotle in his studies of birds (especially *Study of Animals* 614b1–620b9) seldom mentions eating them, though he refers to the work of the bird-catchers from whom, probably, a good deal of his information came. We do learn from Aristotle that one kind of owl is 'not palatable enough to be served as food', while another 'is considered a delicacy'; that the flesh of the *képphos*, a sea-bird, perhaps the storm petrel, 'has a good odour'; and that the *askolópas* could be caught with nets in gardens. This may have been the woodcock, not common in Greece but well known in the southern Balkans.

Birds, like hare, could be spit-roasted: they made attractive, tasty dishes, for an intimate supper or *sympósion* (Archestratus 62 [Athenaeus 101c]) rather than for dinner. Their presence spoke of the discrimination and purchasing power, if not usually of the hunting prowess, of a host or donor. Just as with hare, their flavour could be enhanced with a sprinkling of cheese, oil and silphium before roasting, and a sweet sauce, *katákhysma*, poured over when the dish was served.[29] At Athens they came from the bird market (*ek tôn ornéon*), which apparently dealt in small birds both as pets and for food. There one might buy thrushes, *kíkhle*, with air blown into them to make them look plumper, blackbirds, *kópsikhos*, hung up for sale with a feather through their nostrils, chaffinches, *spínos*, strung together and sold at seven to the obol. There also, probably, Athenians bought the larks, starlings, jays, jackdaws, sparrows, siskins and blackcaps – *kórydos*, *psár*, *kítta*, *koloiós*, *strouthós*, *akanthís*, *sykalís* – that they some-times ate.[30] To this list we may add from a later source *melankóryphos*, great tit (or a similar species) and *khlorís*, greenfinch.[31]

The evidence for the availability of larks on the Athenian market is the scurrilous joke on Eucrates, nicknamed 'Lark', in Lynceus' *Reminiscences* [Athenaeus 241e]: 'Conversation turned on the high price of thrushes. Lark was there: he was supposed to have prostituted himself. "Ah", said Philoxenus the Ham-Cleaver, "I can remember the time when Lark only cost an obol." ' Not in itself strong evidence, and it does not show that larks were eaten – after all, they can be sold and kept as cage birds – but they also occur in what is certainly a list of foods, the satirical Thracian wedding breakfast in Anaxandrides (42 [Athenaeus 131f]).[32]

Equally highly regarded were larger birds, some caught in the wild, some bred in gardens, none of which, evidently, had reached the level of commonness of domestic fowl now. Quail, moorhen, goose and capon were among gifts with which a man might seduce a boy (Aristophanes, *Birds* 705–7). Pigeons, quail, geese, pheasants, mallards (*nêssa*)[33] and moor-hens (if these are *porphyríon*)[34] were bred and kept for food.

As generous egg-layers, quails, *órtyx*, were a doubly useful domesticated

*Figure 9 Attagâs*: the francolin, observed on Samos in the eighteenth century, but said now to have disappeared from Greece. *Source*: from Pitton de Tournefort 1717

animal, and certainly at the beginning of the classical period they were the farmyard bird *par excellence*.[35] Geese, *khén*, were not only domesticated,[36] they were already being force-fed – and perhaps in particular for the sake of their livers, foie gras. Two quite early references link geese with feeding in a way that seems to set them apart from other farmyard animals (*Odyssey* 19.536–7; Cratinus 49, both cited at Athenaeus 384c). This suggests that some such practice had indeed already begun. 'I have twenty geese at home, eating wheat soaked in water', says Penelope in the *Odyssey* passage, beginning to tell her dream. What better image for the rapacious suitors than unnaturally fattened geese?[37]

It seems unlikely that pheasants, already known in Minoan times and native throughout southern and central Europe, were (as Greeks always assumed) introduced to classical Greece from the eastern extremity of the Black Sea, whatever the link between their name *phasianós* and the river Phasis.[38] The domestic pigeon, *peristerá*, was apparently recognised to be, as indeed it is, the domesticated variety of the rock dove, *peleiás*.[39] Close relatives of the pigeon, likewise eaten, included wood pigeon, *phátta*, turtle dove, *trygón*,[40] and probably stock dove, *oinás*, though for the stock dove as food it is only possible to cite a late source, Aelian.[41] Other larger birds that provided food include grebe, *kolymbís*, plover, *trókhilos*, coot, *phalarís*,[42] wagtail, *kínklos*,[43] rock partridge, *pérdix*,[44] and francolin, *attagâs*. The latter is a species found in western Asia whose range apparently included the eastern Aegean in earlier centuries: Tournefort observed it on Samos.[45] There was even crane, *géranos*, 'very bad food' according to the Sicilian Epicharmus (87 [Athenaeus 338d]), and later said to require hanging for several days: two days, according to a Byzantine authority.[46]

One significant new source of animal food was introduced to Greece at the beginning of the historical period. This was the domestic fowl, *órnis*, *alektryón*, domesticated in India several millennia ago. When did it reach Greece? Some literary evidence argues for a relatively recent date. To Cratinus, in the mid-fifth century BC, the bird was 'the Persian awakener' (279 [Athenaeus 374d], and to Aristophanes 'the Persian bird' (*Birds* 485), as if it were an introduction from the east not older than Greeks' acquaintance with Persia. However, the earliest literary references are a 'return home at dawn, at the first call of the awakeners' (*Theognis* 863–4) and 'eggs of geese and of awakeners' (Epicharmus 152 [*Epitome* 57d]), both without reference to Persia. Iconographic evidence is earlier than literary, for the unmistakable figure of the cock appears on sixth-century Laconian and Rhodian vases and on Corinthian vases and metalwork of the seventh century.[47] Thus domestic hens had come to Greece before 600 BC. They were, at first, another lovers' gift, another prestigious feature of supper or *sympósion*, like hare and wild birds.[48]

## HONEY, EGGS AND MILK

The skills of bee-keeping were, by classsical times, highly developed. Here the archaeological evidence can be set beside the fairly full information given in Aristotle's *Study of Animals* (623b16–627b22). Aristotle knew, for example, that the flavour of honey, *méli*, depends partly on which flowers are available to the bees – he does not mention thyme among them – and that it was best in spring. Honey was important in cookery, and especially in confectionery, as the principal available sweetener, though dried dates, dried figs and concentrated must were sometimes alternatives. On the Athenian market honey could be bought in the form of honeycombs. Attic honey, specifically that of Mount Hymettus, was widely said to be the best.[49] Mead, *hydrómeli*, product of the fermentation of diluted honey, was later recorded by Pliny (*Natural History* 14.113) as being made in Phrygia.[50]

Quails, and later domestic hens, were kept partly for their eggs, *ôion*. These, hard- or soft-boiled, were served among desserts; egg yolk and egg white were ingredients in certain dishes. Later judges would consider the eggs of peahens and Egyptian geese, *khenalópex*, better than those of hens (*Epitome* 58b), but few would have had the opportunity to know.

Neither milk nor butter occurs among the lists of ingredients required by cooks in classical Greek comedy scenes. Milk is called for, incidentally, in only three of the Roman recipes of *Apicius*. In a pre-technological age milk, *gála*, was available as a beverage only to those who lived close to the land. Hence, in Greek literature, milk-drinking is a mark of the pastoral peoples who did not, like the Greeks themselves, live in towns.[51] Butter, *boútyron*, was also valued little by most Greeks, no doubt partly because of its limited life and low melting-point; olive oil made a much better cooking medium. 'Butter-eaters' was a term for the Thracians of the northern shore of the Aegean. The very name of the product puts it at a cultural distance: the Greeks can only have learnt of this 'cow cheese', as they strangely called it, from a people who kept cattle instead of sheep and goats, and who made butter instead of cheese with the milk.[52] But honeyed clotted cream, or some such confection, *melípekton*, made an accompaniment to roast hare or game birds.[53] Beestings, *pyós*, and a milk pudding, *khórion*, were also served as dessert.[54] Yoghurt, or something very like it, was known in classical times as *pyriáte*. Galen was surely right to identify this older term with the *oxygala* familiar in his own day, which was definitely a form of yoghurt and was eaten by some on its own, by others with honey (Galen, *On the Properties of Foods* 3.15, cf. Chapter 9).

In the *Odyssey* the dropping-in of special vocabulary for cheese-making makes it clear that cheese, *tyrós*, was a regular manufacture for farmers (9.219, 246–9; Aristotle, *Study of Animals* 522a22–b6), generally using fig sap, *opós*, as rennet. It will have been principally sheep's and goats' milk cheese. Cows' milk was recognised to be the richest. Asses' milk was too thin to make cheese. Fresh or soft cheese was sold at separate stalls, 'the green cheese', on the Athenian market; this kind of cheese was sold by weight, and, much later, fetched two-thirds the price of mature cheese. According to Galen, cheese was wrapped in *drakóntion* leaves to keep it fresh.[55] Cheese was not only simply eaten with bread, but also with honey, with figs, with olives and with green vegetables. It was often a major ingredient in cooked dishes, such as the Greek-named *tyrotarichus* known from Latin sources, and it was baked into bread as an early form of pizza.[56]

## SEAFOOD

Fish, according to literature, were a highly symbolic, highly significant and highly valued part of the diet of many classical Greeks, and they are a significant part of the modern Aegean diet too. Fish were even occasionally sacrificed (Athenaeus 297d).[57] How far back does their importance go? The answer is that the knowledge and use of these fish in Greece is older, probably millennia older, than our record of them. Very little evidence for seafood has been retrieved from prehistoric or classical Greek archaeological sites. This is because fish bones are small, hard to identify satisfactorily and perishable. We know that shellfish, tunny, pike and carp have been taken and eaten in Greece for millennia: these appear in the record because the shells of the first, and the large durable bones of the rest, were the most likely to survive and to catch the archaeologist's eye.[58]

Literature makes it clear that many more species than this were well known in early historic Greece. As a matter of fact, most fish and most shellfish are edible, and a fisherman's catch is not restricted to the species he expects or looks for or wants; other kinds of seafood, if caught, would certainly be sold and eaten. What follows is a survey, based on written evidence, of seafood taken in Greek waters, identified by name and used for food by about 250 BC.[59] The nature of the evidence actually improves the relevance of the resulting list: for the sources are not works for specialists, but for an audience whose interest in the subject was tangential. These are kinds of fish that were well known, casually referred to in literature, fish that were preferentially sold and selected for food.

We are not quite limited to literary evidence as to the species that were of interest. Probably in the late third century BC the minor Boeotian city of Acraephia erected a price list for fish, presumably with the intention of prescribing maximum prices, in the form of a stone inscription much of which survives. The text is too fragmentary for translation here: in particular many of the prices are partly illegible. Those that can be read range from *skaren*, perhaps parrot wrasse, at 8 units, to belly cuts of tuna at 26 units.[60] Identifications of fish names on the Acraephia price list are sometimes difficult, though the city is geographically not far from Athens, from which so many of the literary sources derive: in the ancient as in the modern Mediterranean, fish names varied considerably from dialect to dialect. There are other problems, too, in the identification of Greek fish names with known species. Most of the source materials can be found gathered in Thompson's *Glossary of Greek fishes* (1947).[61]

The fish in the present survey naturally range from the large and imposing to the minute: from those so small that dozens might be fried together, without anyone ever worrying what kind they were, to those big enough individually to form one of the main dishes for a well-provided dinner, and those so big that only 'steaks' would be served.[62] All had their place. For all there were approved recipes, these again the subject of lively discussion not only for the specialists but, apparently, also for the comedy audience. Shellfish, too, were familiar enough to many Greeks, even to those who did not live near the sea, since they were often pickled. But only a few kinds of shellfish are commonly mentioned in literature, just as only a few kinds are common at archaeological sites of the prehistoric Aegean.[63]

If we can judge from the comedy fragments, in classical times, in a maritime city such as Athens, a good selection of fish made up the major 'relishes' at a big dinner, and seafood played a large part among the appetisers. Meat might be in short supply or absent, making it all the more important to vary the appearance, the flavour and the texture of the fish. The choice would differ considerably with the seasons, not only because of availability but also because of variations in quality and flavour.[64]

We will begin with the largest and the fish which were less likely to be served whole. These included tunny, angler-fish, grey mullet, bluefish, pike, catfish, conger eel, dogfish, skate, ray,[65] carp, sheatfish, sturgeon, swordfish – *xiphías* – and *híppouros*, probably dolphin-fish,[66] the last of these being the species depicted in the 'fisherman fresco' of bronze age Akrotiri. 'These things the poor cannot buy: the belly of a tuna, the head of a bass or a conger,[67] or cuttlefishes, which I think even the blessed gods do not despise' (Eriphus 3 [Athenaeus 302e]). Of those just listed the four freshwater fishes are the least often met with in classical texts because of their relative unfamiliarity to Athenians. The carp, *kyprînos*, is, as we have seen, known from prehistoric finds. The pike seems best known not for its quality as food but for the comic paradox that what was called *sphyraina*, 'hammer', elsewhere had to be called *késtra*, 'bolt', in Attic. The great river fish, *glanís* and *sílouros*, catfish and sheatfish, are not favoured in gastronomic sources.[68]

Without doubt the tunny, *thynnos*, was the most important of these economically. Its annual migration was well known so far as the route lay in waters sailed by Greeks. A later author, Strabo (*Geography* 7.6.2), traces the tunny fisheries of the Black Sea coasts leading up to the huge catches made annually in the Golden Horn at Byzantium. Further catches were made at Samos, Carystus, off Sicily and off the south-western coast of Italy, where watch-towers signalled the anxiety of fishermen not to miss the harvest. Polybius knew of their passage into the open Atlantic. The rich of classical Greece were prepared to place among their main dishes, and to boast of eating, not only fresh tunny but also the salt tunny that was exported in jars from Byzantium, Sicily and southern Spain – see p. 76.[69]

Sturgeon, *antakaîos*, the speciality of the northern edge of the Black Sea, was a rarer delicacy in Greece than tunny. It also was best known in salted form (see p. 76), and a piece of sturgeon might form an appetiser rather than a main relish.[70]

The grey mullets, *kestreús*, *képhalos*, *nêstis*, are among the smaller fish in the list above, and were certainly often served whole. As with tunny, Greek had a range of terms for kinds and sizes of grey mullet, with explanatory tales to go with some of the names.[71] Grey mullet was a fine fish requiring respectful cooking (Archestratus 45 [Athenaeus 311a]). Of the angler-fish, *bátrakhos*, only the tail is worth serving as meat.[72] Bluefish (Pomatomus saltator) will serve here for a tentative identification of the *glaûkos*, a fish with which much legend was linked. Like grey mullet, it could be served whole: the head section was highly praised.[73]

The great eels were recognised as offering meat fit for gourmets: the

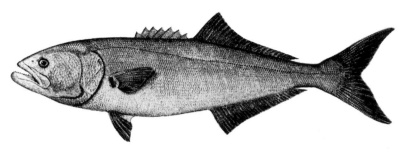

*Figure 10 Glaûkos*, a prized fish but not firmly identified. Perhaps it was the bluefish, shown here after a drawing by H. L. Todd. 'A good fish. Grill, bake or poach.' (Davidson 1981)

conger, *góngros*, was said to be best at Sicyon, while the eels, *énkhelys*, of Lake Copais in Boeotia were brought to the Athenian market and much prized. Those of the River Strymon perhaps already came to southern Greece salted, as they did in Hellenistic times. The moray, *myraina*, was rarer in Greece, though well known in Sicilian waters.[74]

We come to the cartilaginous fishes, the *selákhe* of Archestratus 46 [Athenaeus 319d] and Aristotle. Sharks and dogfish[75] had a higher reputation as food in classical Greece than they generally have now. It was for one of the sharks, *karkharías*, that Archestratus (23 [Athenaeus 310c, 163d]) gave a detailed recipe:

> In the city of Torone you must buy belly steaks of the *karkharías*; sprinkling them with cumin and not much salt you will add nothing else, dear fellow, unless maybe green olive oil. When they are done you will be serving a *trimmátion* and the steaks in it. As you fry all these steaks, a 'crew' for your cooking pot, don't mix in a splash of water with them, or wine vinegar, but just pour on oil by itself and dry cumin and aromatic herbs. Fry over embers, not putting a flame to them, and stir frequently so that they do not burn without your noticing. Not many men know this divine food or want to eat it, none of those men who have a [cowardly?] soul and are paralysed because the creature is a man-eater. But every fish likes human flesh if it can get it.

The dogfish, closely related but less fearsome, were grouped under the Greek names *galeós* (cf. *galê*, 'weasel') in the Aegean, while they were called *kyon píon*, 'fat dog', in Sicily. Different cooking methods were recommended for different cuts. Also popular as food, rightly, was the odd-shaped angel shark, correctly called a kind of *galeós* by Aristotle, a fish whose skin could be used for polishing wood[76] (hence ancient *ríne* meant both 'angel shark' and 'file').

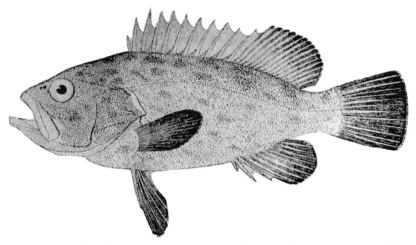

*Figure 11* Orphôs: the grouper or mérou, modern Greek *rofós*, Turkish *orfoz*.
*Source*: Davidson 1981

The terms 'skate' and 'ray', if taken to distinguish the harmless from the stinging members of the order Rajiformes,[77] correspond well enough to Greek *batís* and *nárke*, both widely appreciated, though considered by at least one gourmet to deserve the cheese and oil dressing that he reserved for the coarser kinds of fish (Archestratus 48–9 [Athenaeus 314d, 286d]) and by another to be 'as good as eating an old cloak' (Dorion [Athenaeus 337d]). In this group, too, belong the less praised *leióbatos* and *kítharos*.[78]

Fish that were normally sold and served whole make up a longer list of Greek names, one which it will be convenient to present in groups. Bass, grouper and comber (*lábrax*, *orphôs*, *pérke*) are on the borderline, like the grey mullet with which Archestratus links them. The larger specimens were evidently available as steaks but the smaller comber would be split and probably fried.[79] Though not closely related, the maigre, corb and ombrine (probably represented by Greek *khromís* and *korakînos*) may be placed alongside the bass group. *Khromís*, best in spring or summer, received praise as early as the late sixth century BC.[80]

The bonito (*amía*), a smaller relative of the tunny, occurs in many literary menus. In one of the longer surviving fragments of Epicharmus (124 [Athenaeus 276f]) it helps to characterise the good life of the mythical land of the Sirens:

'In the morning, just at dawn, we used to barbecue plump little anchovies, some baked pork, and octopus, and drink down some sweet wine with them.'
'Oh, you poor fellows!'
'Hardly a bite, you see.'

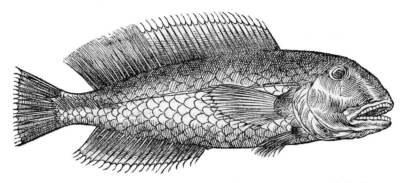

*Figure 12 Skáros*: parrot wrasse was one of the gourmet treats of the Roman Empire, though less sought after at other times. *Source*: this depiction is from Pierre Belon's *Observations* (1555)

'What a shame!'
'Then all we would have was one fat red mullet and a couple of bonitos split down the middle and wood pigeons to match and rascasses....'

The mackerel, *skómbros*, was well known too, reaching Athens salted or smoked from the direction of Byzantium, like tunny.[81]

Bream (Sparidae), numerous in the Mediterranean, were carefully distinguished by kind and quality in Greek markets. At least fourteen Greek names, of fishes eaten and talked of during the classical period, seem to belong to this family, eleven of them probably corresponding to those known in French as bogue, morme, saupe, sar, sparaillon, pagre, daurade, oblade, denté, griset and pageot.[82] The Greek names for these eleven are, respectively, *bôx*, *mórmyros*, *sálpe*, *sargós*, *spáros*, *phágros*, *khrysophrys*, *melánouros*, *synódous*, *kántharos*, *erythrînos*. The three additional Greek names, less closely identified, are *synagrís*, *hys* and *hépatos*. French has to be adopted at this point, few English names being in current use: it will be seen that several of the French names descend, by way of Latin borrowings, from the Greek. In spite of the wealth of vocabulary, the general view of these fish was that with the exception of the daurade or gilthead they were not of the highest quality; some were good only in parts and some were downright bad, though the saupe, for example, redeemed itself in late summer: 'The saupe I shall always think a bad fish: it is most palatable when the corn is reaping. Get it at Mytilene', said Archestratus (37 [Athenaeus 321e]). The master's opinion as to the season finds support both in ancient sources and in modern.[83]

Wrasses were grouped with some similar small fish in the designation *petraîa*, 'rock fish'. At least four ancient names belong to the genera

Labrus and Crenilabrus (*phykís, kóssyphos, alphestés, kíkhle*); separately identifiable, in addition, are the rainbow wrasse, *ioulís*, and the parrot wrasse, *skáros*. All were eaten, but only the last received modest praise: the parrot wrasse would one day fascinate the gourmets of Rome, for reasons difficult to comprehend.[84]

A miscellaneous group of smaller fish was also caught and eaten. The cépole, *tainía*, is notable as the subject of the only surviving recipe from Mithaecus' cookery book [Athenaeus 325f]. Weever, flying fish, garfish, gurnard, rascasse[85] (*drákon, khelidón, belóne, kókkyx, skórpios*) are occasionally listed. Scad, *saûros*, was the object of a comedy cookery lesson (Alexis 138 [Athenaeus 322c]):

> 'Do you know how to cook scad?'
> 'I will when you've told me.'
> 'Take out the gills, rinse, cut off the spines all round, split neatly and spread it out flat, whip it good and sound with silphium and cover with cheese, salt and oregano.'

Among the relatives of cod, rockling and hake were probably the kinds distinguished as *ónos* and *kallarías*.[86]

Finally we come to the smallest fish, those likely to be bought and brought to table in some numbers. Of these the only kind, probably, with a high reputation on its own account was the red mullet, *trígle*. Goby, *kobiós*, picarel, *maíne*, anchovy, *engraulís*, shad, *thríssa*, sand-smelt, *atheríne*, pilchard, *trikhís, khalkís*, sardine, *íops*, and sprat, *bembrás*, were bought as such, but the latter in particular were sometimes fried in quantity and called *bembraphye*. This dish was named after the well-respected *aphye*, typical of Athens, the small fry of several species found in the bay of Phalerum, taken fresh and fried for a very short time. 'It catches the heat and at once sizzles, like olive oil: hence the proverb, "The *aphye* saw the fire"' (Clearchus of Soli 81 [Athenaeus 285d]).[87] Fish suitable for such a dish could be called *aphyai* again, or the diminutive *aphydia*, or *hepsetoí*, 'fried'. Lists of them by Dorion [Athenaeus 285a, 300f] include little cuttlefish, squid and crabs as well as gobies, sand-smelts, little red mullets and sardines.

Flatfish were much less assiduously classified, at least in the sources available to us, than the fish dealt with so far. The sinistral flatfish may come together as *psêtta*, for which Eleusis near Athens was renowned (Lynceus [Athenaeus 330a]); the dextral, notably sole, as *boúglossos*, but even these equivalences are far from certain. Later the largest sinistral flatfish, brill and especially turbot, are distinguished by the name *rómbos*.[88]

Aristotle's *malákia* include cuttlefish, *sepía*, octopus, *poulypous* (cf. *Odyssey* 5.432), and squid, *teuthís*. These vary considerably in size and thus in their position in the menu. Little specimens, often given diminutive names, *sepídia, poulypódeia, teuthídia*, were fried or grilled in quantity and

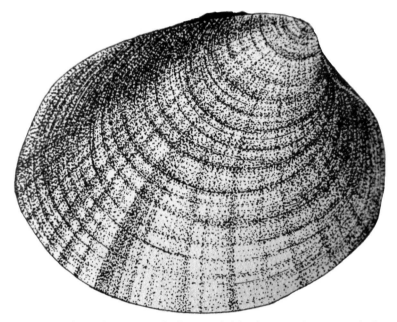

*Figure 13 Khéme leiá* or simply *leiá*. Probably the smooth venus, which is illustrated here from the drawing by Soun Vannithone in Davidson 1981

served as appetisers, side-dishes or at suppers and *sympósia*. Larger ones formed main relishes, treated with all the skill of a well-developed cuisine:[89]

> 'Three drachmas' worth of cuttlefish: I cut off the tentacles and the wings and stew them; the rest of the body I cut into many cubes, then, rubbing with ground salt and frying up while the diners have already begun to eat, I carry them in sizzling'.
> (Alexis 192 [Athenaeus 324c], cf. 84 [Athenaeus 326d])

A dozen kinds of shellfish occur as food in literary sources of the period. Among the best were certainly oysters, *óstrea*. Galen (*On the Properties of Foods* 3.32.2) is the first to remark that these can be eaten raw. *Kónkhe*, sometimes a general term for shellfish, may at other times denote a single kind, perhaps cockle. The remainder can be identified with varying levels of confidence: ormer, fan-mussel, horn-shell, limpet, mussel, scallop, smooth venus, warty venus, carpet-shell, top-shell, wedge-shell, triton and razor-shell can stand for the Greek names, respectively, *ótion*, *píne*, *keryx*, *lepás*, *mys*, *kteís*, *khéme leía*, *khéme trakheîa*, *peloriás*, *anarítes*, *tellíne*, *strómbos* and *solén*.[90] The last, from the phallic shape of the creature inside the shell, is amusingly described in one of Sophron's mimes (24 [Athenaeus 86e]) as 'a sweet-fleshed shellfish, object of widows' desires'.

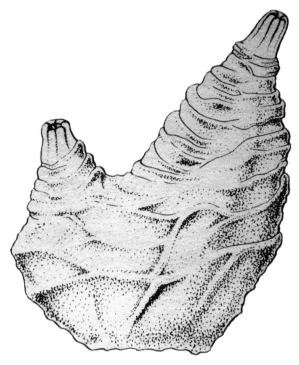

*Figure 14 Téthyon*: not an oyster – not even in the *Iliad* – but a sea-squirt, a delicacy still appreciated in Provence: an ancient recipe is supplied by Xenocrates (see below). *Source*: from the drawing by Peter Stebbing in Davidson 1981

Other sea creatures, too, appear as food in literary sources. Crabs, *kárkinos*, langoustes or lobsters, *ástakos*, langoustines, *kárabos*, cigales, *árktos*, and prawns, *karís*,[91] were common, especially the last; so was the much admired sea anemone, *akaléphe*, *kníde*, whose tentacles Archestratus (9 [Athenaeus 285b]) recommends frying with *aphyai*. Also sometimes found were sea-squirts, *téthyon*, venerable enough to be mentioned in the *Iliad* (16.747),[92] for which we can give a later recipe: 'It is cut and rinsed and seasoned with Cyrenaic silphium and rue and brine and vinegar, or with fresh mint in vinegar and sweet wine' (Xenocrates [Oribasius, *Medical Collections* 2.58.114]). Finally there was the sea urchin, *ekhînos*. An anecdote retailed by Athenaeus (91c-d) from Demetrius of Scepsis depends on the latter's unfamiliarity away from seaside towns:

A Spartan was invited to a banquet at which sea urchins were served at table, and took one. He did not know how this food is eaten and did not notice how his fellow diners handled it: he put the urchin in his mouth, shell and all, and cracked it with his teeth. He was getting on badly with his helping, having not come to terms with its surface resistance, and said,

'Pestiferous dish! I'm not going to weaken and let you go now – but I'll take no more of your kind!'

It is now known that sea urchins were part of the diet of seventeenth-century BC Akrotiri, along with tritons, limpets and other shellfish.

For some fish named as food by classical sources no likely identification has yet been suggested. These include *látos*; *glaúkiskos*; *anthías*, *aulopías*; *élops*; *brínkos*, *myllos*; *gnapheús*.[93]

## FISH SAUCE AND SALT FISH

The Greeks of the Black Sea coast appear to have been the first manufacturers of fish sauce, *gáros*, which, slowly but certainly, came to play a pre-eminent role in Greek and Roman cookery. One must look to a Roman Imperial source, Pliny, and to the Byzantine *Geoponica* (20.46)[94] for information on how it was made:

> The Bithynians make it thus. They take preferably small or large picarel, or, if none, anchovy or scad or mackerel, or also *álix*,[95] or a mixture of all these, and put them into a baker's bowl of the kind in which dough is kneaded. Then they knead in 6 Italian pints of salt to each peck of fish so that they are well mixed with the salt, and leaving it overnight put it in an earthenware jar which they leave uncovered in the sun for 2 or 3 months, occasionally stirring with a stick, then take [the fluid], cover and store.

As a salty fluid, a product of the fermentation of fish, Roman and Byzantine *garum* (*liquamen*) has a close modern analogue in the fish sauce of south-east Asia.[96] References in Greek sources, always less descriptive, begin in the mid-fifth century BC with Cratinus, Aeschylus and Sophocles. The comic playwright Plato is the first source to hint at the characteristic smell of the product with his phrase *en saprôi gároi*, 'in rotten fish sauce'.[97]

To those who make their living from the sea, such products are a profitable way of using whole small fish and parts of larger fish that would otherwise go to waste. Animals can be taken or driven to market alive, but it is troublesome to keep seafood alive once caught; yet fish quickly deteriorates once dead. Therefore, as Greeks spread across the Black Sea and the Mediterranean, there will have been a strong impulse to preserve, and so to make a less perishable commodity out of, the wealth of these seas. Whoever may have first tested it, *gáros* would soon have proved its economic potential.

There are alternatives too. Shellfish can be preserved in brine and vinegar. To judge by the space given to them in literature and by dieticians (e.g.

Diphilus of Siphnos quoted, with interruptions, by Athenaeus 90a–92a) shellfish must have been more than occasional food even for Greeks who did not live in fishing ports. The first literary evidence of pickled shellfish is from fifth-century BC Sicily,[98] outside the Aegean region, but later medical writers make it clear that they were available. Xenocrates' *On Seafood*, for example, refers in passing to pickled scallops and pickled venuses.[99]

Whatever may have been the nature and volume of the trade in earlier times, it is clear – not least from the number of technical terms in use – that salt fish had considerable importance in the fifth and fourth centuries. The salted tunny of Byzantium, called *horaîon*, *kybion* and other names depending on variety, age and preparation, was apparently widely popular. But fish was salted all over the Greek world by the mid-fourth century:

And a slice of Sicel tunny, cut before it is salted in the jars. But that Pontic relish, the *sapérdes*,[100] and all who praise it, I consign to eternal wailing: few men know what a poor and feeble food it is. Yet take a mackerel three days netted, before it goes into the brine, still fresh in the tub, half cured. And if you should come to the holy city of famous Byzantium, eat another slice of *horaîon* for me there: it is good and tender.

(Archestratus 38 [Athenaeus 116f])

Of similar date, perhaps, is a passage of verse that Euthydemus falsely attributed to the eighth-century poet Hesiod, a passage which shows that by its time sturgeon and sterlet from the Black Sea were being salted and exported to Greece, as was tunny from Byzantium, from southern Italy and from Cadiz, and eel from the River Strymon.[101]

Although salt, *háles*, was occasionally listed among kitchen supplies, it was probably wanted for curing and preserving rather than for the cooking of finished dishes. Much of the salt in ancient Greeks' diet surely came in the form of fish sauce and salt fish. Certainly it was so in Rome later, if we may judge from the recipes of Apicius: *liquamen* (fish sauce) occurs in almost every recipe, salt in only three out of over four hundred recipes for finished dishes and sauces.[102]

## FRUITS AND NUTS

Fruit can be cooked with meat, and can be eaten with bread; but in historical Greece it has not generally been used in these ways. The principal exceptions are the long-known olive and the more recently introduced tomato. Even wine, derived from fruit, was customarily drunk not with the main part of the meal but after it or at other times.

The *Odyssey*, for example, with all its set-piece descriptions of meals, never depicts the eating of a fruit. Yet to the poet of the *Odyssey*, pears, pomegranates, apples, figs, olives and of course vines made up a well-planned orchard, one that would produce fruit reliably through a long season:

> Outside the yard is a big orchard on both sides of the gates, of four acres, and a hedge runs along each side of it, and there tall leafy trees have grown, pears and pomegranates and shiny-fruited apples and sweet figs and leafy olives; and their fruit never fails or falls short, winter or summer, all the year, but forever the west wind, blowing, fertilises some and ripens others: pear upon pear grows old and apple upon apple, grapes upon grapes and fig upon fig.[103]
>
> (*Odyssey* 7.112–21)

Later sources fill in the gap for us: juicy fruits might be appetisers; sweet fruits, dried fruits and nuts were served on the 'second tables' to be chewed alongside wine, and likewise accompanied wine at *sympósia*. They were also, though literary sources tell us little of this, food for travellers, for workers in the field and for the poor.

The *Odyssey* tells us, then, of the planting of orchards, a practice for which there is no prehistoric archaeological evidence in Greece. Theophrastus' *Study of Plants*, however, gives sufficient indication that by its date (just before 300 BC) Greeks were giving much attention to the selection, tending and harvesting of fruit and vegetables, even if these skills had yet not reached the elaboration visible in the pages of Pliny's *Natural History* (about AD 60). Selection led to the development of varieties which had certain desired qualities: taste, suitability for storage, season of fruiting, suitability to specific climates and environments.

The early history of fruit trees has not been written. Where the initial steps were taken to domesticate each species and to propagate the domesticated forms is a question only now beginning to be answered. We can only say here that although most of the fruits used in Greece in classical times belong to species already known in the region from prehistoric archaeology, many of them had been drastically improved, somewhere, during the late prehistoric period. Although these improvements may, at least in some cases, have taken place in Greece itself, two details suggest that external influences should be looked for. One is the early flourishing of Near Eastern horticulture. The other is the strong bias, in Greek names for species and varieties, towards the acknowledgement of Anatolian sources. This seems to go together with a view among palaeobotanists that several species, wiped out in Europe during the last ice age, re-colonised Greece and the Balkans towards the end of the prehistoric period, having survived meanwhile in north-eastern Anatolia.

We shall begin with the less sweet fruits that typically belong to the appetisers rather than the desserts.

The apple, *mêlon*, will serve as an example. Its domestication may possibly have begun in Anatolia: the only early archaeological finds of cultivated apple pips are from Iraq, before 2000 BC, and later Israel, both of them south of the range of the wild apple. Real domestication came with grafting and vegetative propagation, as described by Theophrastus.[104] Greek sources emphasise the difference between wild apples, *hamamelís*,[105] and cultivated apples. Greek speakers generally included quinces with apples under the generic name *mêlon*: English translators have to say 'apple' and their readers have to bear in mind the difference in semantic range. There is indeed a superficial similarity between the fruits. The word was also used still more generally, to include other juicy round fruits such as pomegranates.[106] The gift of a *mêlon* was, at least in literature, a love token, and the *mêlon* served as a common metaphor for red-cheeked health.[107]

To the two varieties of quince that were at first recognised separate names were given, one of which suggests a Cretan origin, *kydónion mêlon*, 'Cydonian apple', and occurs in Greek poetry of the sixth century. The other well-known variety, *stroúthion*, had emerged by the fourth century. Akkadian records of the late second millennium list quinces among other fruits; for the present it seems possible that quinces were introduced from the Levant by the Minoans and spread northwards to Greece from Crete, but archaeologists have not yet been able to help with this species.[108]

The cultivated plum, *kokkymêlon*, descends from Prunus divaricata, native to south-eastern Europe and south-western Asia. Where domestication took place is unknown. The wild plum of Greece was the sloe, *brábilos*.[109] There are occasional references to plums from the earliest literature onwards: Hipponax (60 [*Epitome* 49e]) wrote of a wreath of plums. Something resembling the modern cultivated kinds is at once recognisable from a picturesque fragment of Alexis: 'Did you ever see a cooked calf's stomach, or a boiled stuffed spleen, or a basket of ripe plums? That's what his face looks like' (275 [*Epitome* 49f]).[110]

The sour cherry, *kérasos*, also probably came to the Greeks from Anatolia: literary sources and archaeobotany seem to be agreed.[111] To judge by Diphilus of Siphnos' comment on cherries, 'Finer are the redder ones and the Milesian, which are diuretic' [*Epitome* 51b], there were cultivated varieties on the eastern shore of the Aegean by the third century. But no Greek source says that these cherries were grown west of the Aegean,[112] and cherries do not occur in the literary menus.

The olive, *elaía*, was more important as a source of oil than as a table fruit, yet olives were a popular appetiser, wrinkled or underripe or fully ripe, *drypepés*, as in Aristophanes' metaphor: 'Old man, do you like the girls who are fully ripe or the almost-virgins, like firm olives, dripping with brine?' (fragment 148 [Athenaeus 133a]). And indeed olives were often served in brine, but also crushed and mixed with seasonings as a kind of 'cheese'.[113]

Watermelons and musk melons were both known in classical Greece: the seeds of both have been found at prehistoric Aegean sites. The watermelon, native to the deserts of north Africa and western Asia, was culti-vated in Egypt by 2000 BC. Of the musk melon, native to western Asia, a green-fruited variety, chate melon, which was not unlike cucumber, was also known in early Egypt. Both this and the better known sweet forms were grown in Mesopotamia by around 2000 BC. The sweet forms were apparently known in Akkadian texts as 'large' or 'ripe', reminiscent of the adjective *pepón*, 'ripe', by which certain kinds of melons were distinguished in Greek, where *síkyos pepón* is probably 'watermelon' and *melopépon* is probably 'sweet musk melon'. But the meanings of the Greek and Latin terms used by various authors at different times are difficult to sort out.[114]

Cucumbers, *síkyos*, native to the Himalayas, were a new fruit to early classical Greece. They have not shown up in Aegean archaeology, though cucumbers are known from Near Eastern archaeology and texts. There were several varieties of cucumber grown in Greek gardens by the fourth century BC. It is not now classed as a fruit by cooks, but its use as an appetiser in early Greece ranges it with fruits such as apples and olives.[115] With it may be listed bottle gourd, *sikya*, and colocynth, *kolokynthe*, the latter, a close relative of the watermelon, more of medical than gastronomic interest.[116]

We now deal with the sweeter fruits and the nuts that were served after a meal.

Anatolia was a prolific exporter of figs, *sykon*, as of so many other fruits: in ancient times Rhodes and Caria,[117] notably Caunus, were the best-known source, overshadowing the Smyrna region from which so many figs still come. But figs were widely grown, and, if served fresh, must necessarily not have travelled far: it was the dried fig, *iskhás*, that was the Anatolian export. Fig leaves, *thrîon*, pickled to reduce their bitterness, were required in a well-stocked larder: they served notably as wrapping for dishes resembling modern *dolmádhes*.[118] Figs were a well-known metaphor for the sexual organs.[119]

The spread of cultivated pears may have come through the grafting of cultivated clones on wild roots, and the beginning of the process may have taken place in Anatolia, as with apples. The cultivated pear, *ápios*, probably derived from Pyrus pyraster and P. caucasica, species not known in Greece in their wild form.[120] The pear was a metaphor for the fleeting ripeness of youthful beauty:

'Did you ever see pears served in water to men while they were drinking?'
'Lots. Lots of times. Obviously.'
'Doesn't each of the men always look for the ripest of the floating pears for himself and pick that?'
'Of course they do'.[121]

(Alexis 32 [Athenaeus 650c])

The native wild pear, *akhrás*, *ákherdos*, in classical times mainly of interest to the very poor, is dealt with separately in botanical and dietary texts, and the two names are distinguished by Galen (*On the Properties of Foods* 2.38.1) as denoting two different kinds.[122]

The introduction of the pomegranate, *róa*, and grape, *bótrys*, to the region have been discussed in chapter 2. Pomegranate seeds, *kókkon*, were used as an aromatic in ground form.[123] The main economic importance of the grape was of course in wine-making, see p. 87, but the fruit itself belonged among desserts, for which purpose fresh grapes were preserved in wine. Dessert grapes were, at least in later times, the produce of specially developed vine varieties.[124] Grapes were also, of course, dried, and as such served both for dessert and as flavourings in cuisine. A text of Roman Imperial date gives instructions:

> The ancients have written much on the making of raisins; I like to do it thus. Twist a bunch of ripe grapes and leave them to wither on the vine, then remove them and hang them in shade; then, when the bunch is dried, put them in a jar with sun-dried vine leaves under them. When the jar is full add more leaves on top, cover and place in a cold, smokeless room. Raisins made thus will last a long time and will be very good.
>
> (Florentinus [*Geoponica* 6.52])

Later, too, the tender shoots of the wild grape were pickled.[125]

The myrtle was well known in classical Greece both in wild and culti-vated form. Myrtle berries, *myrton*, were chewed fresh at dessert as they still are in Turkey.[126] Two other fruits have more rustic connotations. The preserving of sorbs, *óa*, is described by 'Aristophanes' in his tale of the origin of the sexes in Plato's *Symposium*: 'So saying he cut the people in half, like someone cutting up sorbs ready for pickling, or like someone slicing eggs with hairs' (Plato, *Symposium* 190d). Pickled sorbs were per-haps acceptable at dessert, though no text says so except a late and pastoral narrative by Dio Chrysostom.[127] Medlars, *méspila*, along with myrtle ber-ries, were brought to market at Athens in the fourth century. They are eaten when rotting; their first mention in the context of a meal comes, again, in Dio Chrysostom.[128] Galen (*On the Properties of Foods* 2.25) considered medlars and sorbs more useful as medicament than as food. The fruit of the strawberry tree or arbutus, *mimaíkylon*, occurs once in what definitely seems to be a list of desserts.[129] Five other minor fruits must be listed: the mulberry and blackberry shared the name *móron* because of their superficial similarity, though blackberry was also *batós*; the cornel, *kránon*, was edible but probably best known as having been food for Circe's pigs in the *Odyssey* (10.242); the winter cherry, *halikákabon*, was eaten at least later;[130] the hackberry is hard to pin down in classical texts at all, since *lotós* and *palíouros* were the names for other plants as well, but certainly *loutós* is one of its modern names, and certainly the use of hackberry wood can be recognised in classical references.[131] *Palíouros* was also the name for Christ's thorn with its edible berry.

To judge from surviving texts, the almond, *amygdalê*, was the most popular dessert nut in the classical period. Sweet almonds were widely grown: those of Naxos get special mention in the Athenian texts. Domestication of the species is thought to have taken place somewhere in the Levant, as early as the third millennium BC. Bitter almonds, fruit of the unimproved native tree or of the proportion of non-sweet seedlings originating from trees of the domesticated variety, were later said to be prophylactics against drunkenness, and almond oil would be a basis of perfumes.[132]

The walnut, according to pollen evidence, almost disappeared from southern Europe and western Turkey during the last ice age and spread there again only in the late second millennium BC, perhaps with human help. The prehistory of the sweet chestnut appears to have been very similar. The hazelnut and filbert, probably described together by Theophrastus (*Study of Plants* 3.15.1–2), were cultivated in the classical Aegean.[133] It is striking that the classical Greek names for these dessert nuts (which are easily stored and transported) mostly suggest Anatolian origin. *Káryon* meant 'nut' in general and walnut in particular, but the cultivated walnut was more specifically 'royal nut' or 'Persian nut', two adjectives of apparently identical meaning.[134] The hazelnut and filbert were later called 'little nut' and 'Pontic nut', named perhaps not after the Pontus or Black Sea, but after the Hellenistic kingdom of Pontus on its southeastern shore; earlier they had been 'Heracleotic nut' after Heraclea Pontica, a little to the west. Hazelnuts and filberts are still exported in great quantity from the Pontic regions of Turkey, as they were in the Middle Ages.[135] To the sweet chestnut was sometimes attributed an origin within Greece, 'Euboean nut', but more commonly it also was named after Anatolian sources, 'Castanean nut' and occasionally 'Sardian nut'. There was an older, non-geographical term for the chestnut, 'Zeus-acorn', but Hermippus (63 [*Epitome* 27e]), the first source for this word, describes Zeus-acorns as imported from Asia Minor like so many others – from Paphlagonia to be precise.[136] The names for all these nuts indicate that, even though the trees were grown in Greece, Anatolia remained a prolific source, exporting produce in some quantity, through the Greek coastal cities, in the first millennium BC, as it certainly has done ever since. Even for the almond, long known and used in prehistoric Greece, Anatolia (along with Thasos and Cyprus) was seen as an obvious source.[137]

Of minor importance, by comparison with these, were the lentisk nut, *skhînos*, and the terebinth nut, *términthos*; later, at least, not only the nuts but also the tender shoots of the two latter were pickled and eaten, like those of blackberry, dewberry and vine. Pine kernels, *kônos*, *stróbilos*, were also known as a food, especially as the chief ingredient of a sweetmeat made with spices and flour.[138] The lentisk tree had more importance as the source of mastic, *mastíkhe*, which one chewed to clean one's teeth and freshen one's breath. The best mastic came already from the island of Chios, as it does today.[139]

One fruit well known to the classical Aegean had to be imported to the region in bulk. The date, probably native to the Near East, was under cultivation there by 4000 BC and later became common in Egypt. Date palms had been planted in Crete in the bronze age; Odysseus' narrative (*Odyssey* 6.163) speaks of a date palm growing at Apollo's shrine on Delos, but these would have been ornamental trees, for dates will not ripen in Crete or Greece. Thus Herodotus (*Histories* 1.193.5) writes as if the fruit, but not its natural history, were familiar to his audience. Dried dates were typical dessert foods, like dried figs, though presumably more expensive.[140] *Fresh* dates were something new to Greeks who travelled in the Levant, like the mercenaries who went to fight for Cyrus the Younger in 401 BC:

> There was much grain, and date wine, and vinegar made from the same. As for the fruits of the date, any such as can be seen in Greece were what the servants had, while what the masters had were choice ones, surprisingly fine and big, and just like amber in colour. Some they dried and had for dessert. They were nice to eat with wine, but headachy.
>
> (Xenophon, *Anabasis* 2.3.15)

The date is good food and an excellent sweetener, easily stored and transported, yet the lack of finds of date stones in early Greece suggests that it was little known there before classical times.[141]

## VEGETABLES

Vegetables, like fish, are under-represented in archaeological finds. There must have been many more in the prehistoric diet than the prehistoric record tells us of, for early literature and science name a great many vegetables that were widely known. Many of them were grown in classical Greek gardens, including beet, blite, cabbage, cress, lettuce, orach, purslane, rocket, sorrel, basil, Roman hyssop, rue and salep, though this in itself does not prove, of course, that plants were used as food: gardeners also grew plants for decorative reasons, and for use in wreaths.[142] Several vegetables not yet found at Aegean sites but familiar in Greece by classical times happen to be archaeologically attested elsewhere in the Near East, including garlic, leek, lettuce, onion and thyme; but more numerous and just as important are the vegetables that were widely used in classical Greece (and in later Europe) and yet cannot be traced anywhere, in archaeology or in documents, earlier than Greek classical texts.[143]

It is possible to eat a great range of green plants gathered from the wild; this survey is of plants significant as food, and excludes numerous others that provided occasional nourishment but were not widely sought for or liked.

We begin with the vegetables that normally served as appetisers, side-dishes and pot-herbs, though despised as such by those who always went for fish and meat: that is the context in which dill, celery and cress are spoken of in a Eubulus fragment (35 [Athenaeus 347d]). These include asparagus, *aspháragos*, with its variant *órmenos* and a wild form *petraîon*;[144] beet, *teûtlon*, first used for its leaf (chard) which was the classic wrapping for baked eel, although a 'black' swollen-rooted kind was grown by about 320 BC;[145] blite, *blíton*; cabbage, *krámbe*, and a more open-leaved form, kale or rape, *ráphanos*;[146] capers, *kápparis*;[147] cardoon, *kinára*, ancestor of the modern artichoke, of which the bottom was edible but not yet the scales;[148] carrot, *staphylînos*, *daûkos*, *karotón*, in classical times known only for its seeds and foliage. Carrot seeds were found at iron age Kastanas (and the plant was known earlier in central Europe), but no classical Greek spoke of carrots with enthusiasm. Indeed, from the quotations gathered by Athenaeus on the subject, it seems clear that before Imperial times no one in Greece used the roots of carrot, as distinct from the seed and the leaves.[149] Celery, *sélinon*, had already been identified in Linear B texts, 'crinkled celery' in Theocritus' epithet;[150] chicory and endive, *kíkhora*, *séris*;[151] cress, *kárdamon*, well known to be popular in Persia but also used as a side-relish in Greece – the Greek name is of Assyrian origin;[152] dill, *ánethon*;[153] fennel, *márathon*, used in the marinating of olives and no doubt also as a vegetable;[154] grape hyacinth, *bolbós*, the much eaten and much despised 'bulb' of classical Greece, a reputed aphrodisiac, but palatable, it was said, only by virtue of sauces and seasonings: 'Look at the bulb, if you like: how much is spent on its good name! Cheese, honey, sesame, olive oil, onion, vinegar, silphium. All by itself it's a mean, sour thing' (Philemon 113 [*Epitome* 64e]);[155] leek, *práson*, a plant that apparently defined horticulture in archaic Greece to the extent of having provided the Homeric term for a garden bed, *prasía* (*Odyssey* 7.127, 24.247): the wild species *ampelóprason* was no doubt also used, as it was later;[156] lettuce, *thrídax*, known in Egypt from the third millennium BC;[157] mallow, *molókhe*, of which leaves, roots and flowers were all eaten;[158] mint, especially water mint, *mínthe*, *hedyosmon*, *sisymbrion*, seen as a pot-herb rather than a flavouring, one of which wild and cultivated varieties were distinguished: the first unambiguous reference to the use of mint in cooking, to accompany sea-urchins, is by Diphilus of Siphnos [Athenaeus 90a–92a] in the third century BC;[159] various mushrooms, *mykes*, *amanítes*, and truffles, *hydnon*, which were said by some to be produced by, or brought to light by, thunderbolts (Plutarch, *Symposium Questions* 4.2);[160] mustard greens, *anárrinon*;[161] nettle, *akaléphe*, young leaves gathered before the swallow

(a)  (b)

*Figure 15* Two greens: (a) *adráphaxys*, orach; and (b), nowadays much more commonly used, spinach (modern Greek *spanákia*) introduced to the region in medieval times. *Source*: from G. Hegi's *Illustrierte Flora von Mittel-Europa* (Vienna, 1912)

comes and boiled;[162] onion, *krómyon*, grown much earlier in Egypt and Mesopotamia, known to the Greeks in several varieties including *géteion* and *gethyllís* – perhaps 'spring onion' or 'chives' – some used as appetiser or side-dishes, some in cooking;[163] orach, *adráphaxys*, and Atriplex halimus, *hálimon*,[164] after which a district of Attica was named; purslane, *andrákhne*;[165] radish, *raphanís*;[166] rocket, *eúzomon*, which was food for Theophrastus' students according to Hippolochus [Athenaeus 130d];[167] samphire, *krêthmon*, which a later source says was eaten in vinegar (Dioscorides, *Materia Medica* 2.129);[168] sorrel and dock, *lápathos*, and from later evidence also curled dock, *oxylápathon*;[169] turnip and other closely related roots, *gongylís, bouniás, ráphys*;[170] water parsnip, *síon*.[171]

Certain vegetables, the sources suggest, were food only for the poor. Among these we may list asphodel, *asphódelos*; wild chervil, *skándix*; chervil, *ánthryskon*; a goosefoot, Chenopodium album (fat hen), not indeed identified in classical texts but known in prehistoric times (see Chapter 2) and now sometimes called *aghriospanákia*, 'wild spinach', in Greece; London-rocket, *erysimon*, a summer crop; hoary mustard, *lampsáne*;[172] nightshade, *strykhnon*; golden thistle, *skólymos* (Hesiod [*Works and Days* 582] remarks on the season at which golden thistle is in flower, a matter of importance because that is the right time to eat the root);[173] sow-thistle, *sónkos*, which Hecale once cooked for Theseus according to the Hellenistic poet Callimachus;[174] squill, *skílla*, an unprepossessing, woody bulb of which one garden variety was named after the ascetic Epimenides, but which also served later as a flavouring for vinegar.[175] Then there were alexanders, *smyrneîon*, cuckoo-pint, *áron*, star of Bethlehem, *ornithógala*, hound's tongue, *kynóglossos*, all of which were to be boiled together with fennel, wild asparagus, carrot and chicory, as a rustic vegetable dish, in Nicander's *Georgics* (fragment 71 [Athenaeus 371b]); cat's ear, *hypokhoirís*, groundsel, *erigéron*, hartwort, *kaukalís*, salsify, *tragopógon*, molokhia, *kórkhoros*, and knotweed or feverfew, *parthénion*, all six of which are listed as wild pot-herbs by Theophrastus (*Study of Plants* 7.7.1–2).[176]

Finally we come to the vegetables that served as flavourings, as herbs and spices, rather than as substantive dishes. Several foods already listed, and one or two still to be discussed, were also so used: almonds, sesame seeds, raisins, fennel, dill, capers, onion, leek, honey, must, vinegar, olive oil, salt, egg and cheese.[177] But we must now list wormwood, *apsínthion*;[178] anise, *ánison, ánnetos*;[179] basil, *ókimon*, eaten by slugs in fifth-century Greek gardens;[180] coriander leaf, *koríannon*, coriander seed, *koríanna*;[181] cumin, *kyminon*;[182] flax seed, *línon*, as an aromatic garnish on loaves;[183] garlic, *skórodon*, a cultivated plant of unknown ancestry already grown in the early second millennium BC in Egypt and Mesopotamia, a widely used flavouring and relish and in places a significant article of trade;[184] hyssop, *hyssopos*;[185] mustard, *nâpy*, likewise often listed among pot-herbs, not spices, in classical Greek written sources: the earliest explicit evidence of the use of mustard seed as a spice is in Nicander of Colophon's *Georgics* (fragment 70 [Athenaeus 133d]), 'mordant seeds of mustard' in a doggerel recipe for turnip;[186] oregano, *oríganon*;[187] pennyroyal, *blékhon*, hung up to store for use in dried form (pennyroyal was a flavouring in Demeter's *kykeón*, apparently [*Homeric Hymn to Demeter* 209] as it certainly was in the cheap vinegar drink of Byzantium, *phoûska*; otherwise its culinary use is not described by any Greek source earlier than Galen, who mentions it as a flavouring for lentil soup);[188] poppy, *mékon*, the seeds used as a garnish for loaves and as a flavouring for cooked dishes (the leaves were also eaten);[189] rue, *péganon*; Roman hyssop, *thymbra*;[190] safflower, *knêkos*, used, at least later, as a colouring for sauces and as a source of oil;[191] Greek sage, *elelísphakos* and *sphákos*;[192] salep, *orkhís*, *satyrídion*, the powdered tuber of Orchis mascula and other species, an aphrodisiac of fairly high repute, used then as it is now as an additive to soft drinks,[193] as Galen explains (*On the Properties of Simples* s.v.):

> *Orkhís*: the plant is also called 'dog's testicle'. Sweetish to the taste: the larger of the pair of tubers, taken in drinks, increases libido, the smaller represses and forestalls it. They are also eaten baked, like grape hyacinth bulbs;

and two species of thyme, *thymon*, typical of Athenian poverty, and *hérpyllos*.[194]

Sesame, *sésamon*, a lightly aromatic seed, was used as a garnish. Hipponax, in the sixth century BC, wrote of 'not biting bits of quail and hare, not drugging pancakes with sesame seeds, not drenching cakes in honeycomb' (Hipponax 26a [Athenaeus 645c]). The compound *sesamópastos*, 'sprinkled with sesame seeds', is used of a cake or sweet by Philoxenus. But in the same line Philoxenus uses the word *sesamótyron*, 'sesame cheese', which must have resembled tahini or halva and was used as a filling for cakes; Aristophanes seems to talk of sesame folded into a cake,[195] though the text is not free of *double entendre*. There is also the *krithaíe sesamóessa*, 'sesame-flavoured barley gruel (?)', of the *Homeric Epigrams* (15.7).

Of all the aromatics that had a place in the Greek diet by about 300 BC, only two did not grow in the Aegean region and needed to be imported. These were sumach and silphium.

Sumach, *roûs*, was probably one of the culinary delights listed in verse by Solon in the early sixth century, in an iambic poem (of which only disjointed fragments survive) on the life of luxury.[196] Sumach was certainly in use as a flavouring in Athenian kitchens by the fourth century. Although the tree grows all over the Mediterranean area it appears that the preparation of its ground fruit as condiment and medicine was only done in Syria.[197]

Silphium, *sílphion*, principally in the forms *opós*, '[dried] sap', and *kaulós*, 'stem', was one of the most valued exports of the kingdom founded by Greeks at Cyrene in north Africa. The plant, related to fennel and celery, was never naturalised elsewhere,[198] or even domesticated at Cyrene itself; silphium was brought there by the indigenous Libyans. It was said to have 'appeared seven years before they founded their city' about 630 BC; whatever the reliability of this tradition it is noteworthy as the only recorded dating of the introduction of a new food, anywhere in the Mediterranean

*Figure 16* A silphium plant, the traditional type of Cyrene, here paired with the horseman sometimes seen on the gold coins of the city. *Source*: Spink & Co

world, before late Hellenistic times, and this must say something of the perceived importance of silphium.[199] First mentioned in Greek literature in the early sixth century by Solon, silphium rapidly made itself indispensable. It was grated, along with cheese, vinegar and oil, on to birds for roasting, and similarly served with cheese and vinegar to flavour fish. It was an ingredient in marinades and sauces but never, I think, a separate dish: its role in luxury Greek cuisine was not unlike that of garlic in French or onion in English cookery. Its importance is evident both from the sheer number of technical terms connected with the trade, and from the way in which general words such as *kaulós* and *opós* were appropriated into its jargon. The austere *Study of Plants* of Theophrastus (6.3.1–7) finds room for an unusual level of detail on the plant, the edible parts of it, and the way it was prepared for export. The story of its disappearance and replacement by asafoetida is to be told in Chapter 6.[200]

## WINE AND OLIVE OIL

The importance of wine in the Greek diet has already been observed. Later (p. 93) something will be said of its gastronomic significance. The Greek term *oînos* is usually said to be a Mediterranean loan-word (and certainly it has relatives in Semitic languages), but a case can be made for its descent from proto-Indo-European, one's conclusion probably depending on one's view of Indo-European and Afro-Asiatic prehistory. The poetic *méthy* is certainly Indo-European: that word earlier meant 'sweet' or 'honey' or perhaps 'mead'.[201]

The vintage, the treading of the grapes to produce must, the tasting of the new wine, were landmarks of the farmer's calendar and of the religious year, illustrated on vases and reliefs – typically with satyrs, attendants of Dionysus, replacing the human workers. In some places it was customary to add sea water to the must before fermenting. This became the distinctive feature of Coan wine, and the most distinctive procedure in recipes for making 'Coan wine' outside Cos (Cato, *On Agriculture* 112–13). Numerous other aromatics were used as flavourings here and there. The subject is discussed at length by Pliny (*Natural History* 14.100–25) and many

*Figure 17 Magydaris*, the plant that so closely resembled silphium, flourishing on Rhodes

recipes are given by Dioscorides (*Materia Medica* 5.18–73). Wine was fermented in large, deep earthenware vats and transported and stored in smaller (but still big and heavy) amphoras, which came to develop distinctive shapes in different wine-producing areas. A producer city sometimes displayed its own amphoras on its coins. Expensive, high quality vintages, intended for long-term storage and for drinking at greater strength, came in smaller jars (Aristophanes, *Assemblywomen* 1119); a sensible arrangement, since if wine turns undrinkable it does so by the bottle, however large the bottle.

Fresh grape juice or must, *gleûkos*,[202] had its own uses, as did the boiled-down forms *síraion* and *hépsema*. Wine vinegar, *óxos*, was indispensable in cuisine, the first and most obvious kitchen necessity looked for by the cook in Alexis' *Pannychis* (179 [Athenaeus 170b]). In Roman and Byzantine times it would be mixed with water as a cheap wine substitute for the poor, *posca, phoûska*.[203]

The importance of olive oil was hardly smaller. Apart from its non-culinary uses as fuel and cosmetic, both equally essential to Greeks in their festivities, it was surely present in most cooked dishes, whether they were fried, marinated or basted in it or served with a sauce for which it was the vehicle. It was sometimes an ingredient in bread-making, and, in a plain snack, was sometimes the only relish that helped one's bread to go down,[204] for butter, which can serve a similar purpose for us, was scarcely used. Numerous vegetable oils were available in the ancient Mediterranean,[205] but of them all only olive oil was regularly used in food. The olive tree's economic importance was such that close attention was paid to its fruiting behaviour. It was inclined to fruit well only once in two years, 'for it is very weak and very delicate, and also suffers from the beating and breaking of its branches. Those who harvest otherwise, simply gathering windfalls or shaking the tree, say that it then produces more fruit annually' (Theophrastus, *Plant Physiology* 1.20.3).[206]

## STAPLE FOODS[207]

No single family of plants can be named as providing the staple food of classical Greece. Some of the poorest of country-dwellers may have relied regularly on acorns, *bálanos*. Several kinds were distinguished. Particularly palatable were *ákylos*, the acorn of the holm-oak and *fegós*, acorn of the Valonia oak.[208] They certainly served for human food on more occasions than that on which Circe fed *bálanoi* and *ákyloi* to Odysseus' men (*Odyssey* 10.242).

Some pulses and cereals, known in Greece, recognisable both in archaeological finds and in classical and later texts, had a place in the diet that is now difficult to define for lack of evidence. Among these less talked of pulses are bird vetch, *árakos*;[209] bitter vetch, *órobos*; grass pea, *láthyros*; Lathyrus cicera, *apháke*,[210] and Lathyrus ochrus, *ókhros*.[211] At least as despised as any of these, but more often mentioned in literature, was lupin, *thérmos*. The consumption of this bitter seed, 'not eaten raw by any animal' for indeed it is toxic until boiled, was a recognised symptom of destitution.[212]

Hence Zeno of Citium, very rough and bad-tempered to his acquaintances, became kind and gentle when he had taken plenty of wine.

Asked why he changed so, he replied that it was the same with him as with lupins. They too are extremely bitter before soaking, but when they have steeped they are sweet and very mild.

(*Epitome of Athenaeus* 55f)

Other pulses were far more significant in the diet, though it would be difficult in classical texts to find applied to them the praises regularly lavished on fine white bread. Pulses in general were dried, stored and used after soaking, though beans, peas and chickpeas were also liked fresh. Broad beans, *kyamos*, were one of Pythagoras' most famous interdictions, though nothing concerning Pythagoras' views can be considered certain. 'Abstain from beans, because, being windy, they have the greatest share of the spiritual; and because [you] will be more efficient if you are not governed by your stomachs': this statement is attributed to the philosopher by Diogenes Laertius (8.24). Another authority, however, said that 'Pythagoras recommended beans more than any other legumes, as being light on the stomach and digestible, and he himself ate them constantly'! (Aristoxenus [Aulus Gellius, *Attic Nights* 4.11]). Fresh beans were not only eaten as a dessert dish but also in meat stews.[213] Lentils, *phakós*, may have been the commonest of all pulses.[214] Peas, *písos*, were perhaps seen rather less often. Chickpeas, *erébinthos*, served both as a staple and as a dessert, for which purpose they were roasted or, if young and tender, eaten fresh.[215] Of calavance, *pháselos*, *dólikhos*, both the ripe seeds and whole immature pods could be eaten. Fresh tender calavance seeds served as dessert at Sparta.[216] Beans and peas could be made into a soup, *étnos*. This was also commonly done with lentils: lentil soup, *phakê*, was a filling everyday dish, typical workers' food, ideal for cynics but otherwise unlikely to be seen at rich men's feasts. 'When you cook lentil soup, don't add perfume' was proverbial – and was a line given to Jocasta in Strattis' comedy *Phoenician Women*.[217]

The less-known cereals of classical Greece are broomcorn millet, *kénkhros*, which Xenophon (*Anabasis* 2.4.13) at least assumes will be familiar to his readers; foxtail millet, *melíne*, *élymos*, sweeter but less robust than broomcorn millet, about which Herodotus (*Histories* 3.117.4) makes the same assumption;[218] and oats, *brómos*, of which a Byzantine dietician was to write: 'These are food for cattle, not people, except when extreme famine dictates that bread be baked from them. . . . Such bread has an altogether unpleasant flavour' (Simeon Seth, *On the Properties of Foods* 137).[219]

Finally we reach the two major cereals of Greece. Barley, *krithé*, was grown in most parts of the region. Two-row and six-row species were both known.[220] The most commonly grown wheat species was possibly still emmer, *zeiaí*,[221] *ólyra*. Einkorn, *típhe*, was also familiar; einkorn bread went especially well with Mysian cheese, said Galen later.[222] Club wheat, closely related to emmer, had been spreading across eastern and central

Europe in later prehistoric times. By now it was common in the Aegean region, and it may also have been imported to Greece from southern Russia:[223] it had the name of *pyrós*. Durum wheat, grown in the Levant but not yet in Greece itself, was imported from the Phoenician cities: this, although not improperly called *pyrós*, could be distinguished as *semídalis* and its flour could be given the same name, while the flour of *pyrós* was *áleuron* (cf. *Odyssey* 20.109).[224] *Álphiton* was the name for barley grains, especially when roasted and ground into meal;[225] *krímna* for a coarser meal or for cracked barley; and *khóndros* for the flour and cracked grain of emmer.[226] Darnel, the poisonous *aîra*, was all too well known: its presence in bread caused blindness.[227]

Surprisingly at first sight, in historical Greece the most ancient methods of using cereals coexisted with all the refined varieties of bread and sweet cakes. We will conclude by listing some of these fashions as they appear in written texts. None of these forms of cereal is named specifically in the Homeric epics.

A cake, typically served beside wine with the sweet fruits and nuts of the 'second tables', was *plakoûs*, of which there were many kinds, some being soaked in honey like many irresistible cakes of modern Greece. To accompany the hare or thrushes of an expensive supper was served cereal in its most delicate and elaborate forms, *ámes*, *amétiskos*, 'milk cake', and *ámylos*, 'frumenty', the latter also a suitable food for the toothless.[228] But at a main meal cereal took a simpler and more basic form, wheat loaves and barley mashes being the favourite according to literary sources. Both are already mentioned in Hesiod's *Works and Days* (442, 590).

Loaves were in practice more often made from emmer than from more advanced kinds of wheat. Barley was not so suitable for baking into bread. Both white bread and brown bread were familiar, as were the better digestive qualities of the latter. Much bread was unleavened, but raised bread was well known: baking powder, *nítron*, and wine yeast were both later used as raising agents.[229] A leavened wheat loaf was *ártos* and one with a savoury or sweet filling was *nastós*. Oven bread was *ipnítes*, crock-baked bread *klibanítes*. Bread baked under ashes was *spodítes*; drop-scones and pancakes were *eskharítes* and *teganítes*; mashes of barley and wheat meal were *mâza* and *kóllix*; porridges made of barley and emmer meal were *álphita* and *khóndros*.[230] Barley gruel was *ptisáne*, considered almost a panacea by some physicians (e.g. *Regimen in Acute Diseases, passim*); emmer gruel was *atháre*, *athéra*.[231] The armies of classical Greece, but not those of Imperial Rome, customarily ate *álphita* according to Galen; for Roman soldiers barley was a punishment.[232]

Several of these ancient methods are still found in use in Greece today. Their continued coexistence has been necessary, for those who have no millstones and no ovens must eat their staple in some other way than by making flour and baking bread. So it is that the contrast between oven-bread and the other forms of cereal has served, throughout this long period, to mark off rich from poor, urban from rustic, householder from traveller and soldier, luxury from moderation.

# 4

# IN THE FEASTS OF THE LYDIANS
The beginnings of Greek gastronomy[1]

Water and wine were plentiful enough, but they varied from place to place and only the wealthy could pick and choose the wine they drank. Broths, porridges, pulse soups and barley mashes and brown or 'dirty' wholemeal loaves, were the standard staple foods, familiar probably to all, while gourmets, over the centuries, preferred 'clean' white wheat bread, white puddings and light sweet cakes. To give a relish to their meals the poor and landless had the herbs and green plants that they gathered from the wild; the poor who fished or farmed had their own produce in its probably meagre variety; slaves and hangers-on of wealthy households had a chance, or at least a view, of more and better; the wealthy themselves had all the produce of their lands, all the fruits, vegetables, fish and meat of the market, all the time they wished to spend on choosing and haggling and every opportunity to experiment with menus, dishes, flavourings.

Archaeologists begin to distinguish the signs of unequal power, influence and wealth in Greece of the third and second millennia BC if not earlier. But only literature and iconography can begin to make visible the human context of these inequalities. From literature – beginning with the earliest literature of Greece, the *Iliad* and *Odyssey* – it is first seen that wines and foods could be selected and valued by those with the resources to do so. Wine came first.

### OLD WINE

Wine, with grain and olive oil, had been the stored wealth of the villages of Greece for centuries before it came to be catalogued in the Linear B tablets and before the *Odyssey* described the strong-room of Odysseus, 'where piled-up gold and bronze was lying and clothing in chests and plenty of good-smelling oil: and in it stood jars of old sweet-tasting wine, with the unmixed divine drink in them, packed in rows against the wall' (*Odyssey* 2.338–42). If long storage of great quantities of wine was a sign

*Figure 18* Heracles as dinner guest of Eurytius of Oechalia and his children. Didaeon shares his father's couch. At each table a dog awaits scraps. Corinthian *kratér* in the Louvre, no. E635 (see also the frontispiece and Figure 21)

of wealth and influence, as it is here, then the appreciation of old wine might develop rather naturally, as had already happened in Egypt, where newly-sealed jars of wine were stamped with the regnal year, and where a jar of thirty-three-year-old wine was entombed (among more recent vintages) with King Tutankhamun about 1325 BC.[2]

Certainly, by now old wine had begun to be appreciated in Greece, for in another passage of the *Odyssey* wine is 'unsealed and opened in its eleventh year' (*Odyssey* 3.391–2). Later Pindar would be amused by the contrast of 'old wine but the bloom of new songs' (*Olympian* 9.48) at dinner, and in fourth-century Athens the adjective *géron*, 'aged', properly applied only to people, was playfully used of wine.[3] The gourmet Archestratus (59 [*Epitome* 29b]) would judge Thasian wine to reach its best after 'aging for . . . many years'.

Attention to vintage went little further in Greece than an awareness that good wine improved with time. In Burgundy and Bordeaux and Alto Douro, and even in the Rhône valley and in northern Italy, the variable climate makes a big difference between one year's vintage and the next, a difference measured in flavour, in maturing time and in price. The vineyards of the eastern Mediterranean coasts produce a steadier harvest. As a matter of fact, in spite of the fame of the Opimian vintage of 121 BC – which was Pliny's benchmark for the beginning of Italian wine appreciation (*Natural History* 14.94) – it is not clear whether Horace's poetic appreciation of wine 'born, like me, in Manlius' consulship' (*Odes* 3.21.1) reflected any special quality in the Italian wines of 65 BC, or merely the general possibility that a really well-made wine could be allowed to mature for ten, twenty and even forty years. So it is, long afterwards, that the Emperor Diocletian's *Price Edict* permits 'old wine of best flavour' to fetch three times the price of 'table wine' – and higher still was the permitted price of certain wines of seven specified origins but not of specified age, which, we may suppose, a buyer could confidently lay down in his own storeroom.

For wine was not only easily stored but, in its big amphoras, easily transported. The *Iliad* (7.467–75) once depicts trade in wine, brought to Troy in ships from Lemnos from which the besiegers replenished their stock. This portability of wine might naturally lead, and in Greece had led even by the eighth century BC, to the appreciation of named kinds, the *prámneios oînos* of the *Iliad* and *Odyssey*, the *bíblinos oînos* of Hesiod.

The origin and nature of these two wines is unknown. As regards Pramnian, one cannot be sure that the poet of the *Iliad* himself attached a concrete meaning to the word. It is far from certain that fifth-century and later Greeks understood anything specific by either name. The dominant view – that Pramnian and Bibline derive from place-names in the Aegean – may well have been influenced by the fact that all the preferred wines in Greece in later classical and Hellenistic times had easily recognisable geographical appellations except Pramnian, Bibline and 'Psithian', a name that first occurs in fifth-century BC sources.

Bibline may indeed have been a geographical appellation, though if we accept this we have to choose to believe either in the Bibline stream on Naxos or the Bibline mountains of Thrace, mentioned in the suspiciously whimsical fragments of the Sicilian playwright Epicharmus. The wine from both Naxos and Thrace was adequate to sustain the legendary but vague reputation of Bibline.[4] But quite apart from geographical origin there are several distinctions that can be made among wines and that were already made in ancient times. Wines may be named after grape varieties recognised as common to more than one district: that is most likely the case with Psithian,[5] though no other variety is known to have achieved such status until Roman times (when, for example, 'Chian' grapes were grown in Italy).[6] Names may mark the inclusion of special ingredients, such as the brine that went into *anthosmías*, or some special treatment after vinification, like the Spartan and other wines that were boiled.

Names may also indicate vinification from specially treated grapes. It is clear that even by the time of the earliest Greek literature farmers were in the habit of setting aside a space for the partial drying of grapes to make especially sweet or strong wine, wine such as is now called *recioto* or *vin de paille*. Instructions – though for a relatively short drying period – for the work are given by Hesiod (*Works and Days* 609–14) as a farmer's September task:

> When Orion and Sirius reach the middle of the sky, and rosy-fingered Dawn observes Arcturus, then, Perses, bring your grape harvest home. You must show them to the sun ten days and ten nights; for five more, shade them; on the sixth, draw off into jars the gifts of joyous Dionysus.[7]

Although Hesiod does not use the word here, it is this process that may turn out to be implied in the term 'Pramnian'. It would explain the link made by post-classical sources between that term and the wine-producing districts of Crete, where, later, the juice that was tempted from fine sweet grapes as they dried made *prótropon* wines of notable sweetness or strength.[8]

## THE MEDITERRANEAN WINE TRADE

By the fifth century Greece had some part in the long-distance trade in wine that criss-crossed the eastern Mediterranean. Egypt, for example, produced red and white wine of its own; its meticulous records differentiated between the wines of 'the North', 'the South', 'the Southern Oasis' and several other appellations now less easy to identify. But in the fifth century BC, according to Herodotus, Egypt additionally imported wine 'from all of Greece and also from Phoenicia' (Herodotus, *Histories* 3.6) as it did in Roman times.[9] Perhaps it had done so long before, for in the northern Levant, even by the early second millennium, Egyptians knew that wine was far more plentiful than at home. This is clear from a fictional narrative of that period, in which a wandering Egyptian lands at Byblos in Phoenicia and travels inland: 'It was a good country.... Figs were in it, and grapes. It had more wine than water. Plentiful was its honey, abundant its olives' (*Story of Sinuhe* 82–4).[10]

Mesopotamian records frequently identify wine by its places of origin, and these included 'wine of Carchemish' on the Syrian bank of the Euphrates. Like that of Egypt, Mesopotamia's wine production was perhaps limited by its climate and failed to measure up to demand: according to Strabo (*Geography* 15.3.11) the 'Macedonians' were the first to succeed with vines in southern Mesopotamia. In both countries beer was more plentiful and cheaper, and was thus the drink of the populace, though it was perhaps rivalled in Mesopotamia by date wine.[11]

The Persians, in their turn, were said in later times to have had a preference for Syrian wine: 'The King of the Persians used to drink only

Chalybonian wine, which, says Poseidonius, is produced in[12] Damascus in Syria, where the Persians had planted vines' (*Epitome of Athenaeus* 28d). The *Letter of Darius* also claims that the king transplanted fruit trees from east of the Euphrates to the western parts of his empire. But the Persians did not create Chalybonian wine: 'wine of Helbon', surely the same name, was being exported from Tyre soon after 600 BC.[13]

Phoenicia and Syria, sources of wine for Egypt, Mesopotamia and Persia, were also in classical times supplying wine to Greeks. The literary evidence is not plentiful, but at least one fourth-century Sicilian connoisseur saw something to commend in the wine exported by Byblos:

> I approve the Byblian wine[14] from holy Phoenicia, though I do not equate it with [Lesbian]. If you taste it suddenly, having been previously unfamiliar with it, you will think it fragrant: more so than Lesbian; for it remains so for a remarkable length of time. But in the drinking it is worse by far, while the other will seem to you to have a nobility equal not to wine but to ambrosia. And if some foolish airy poseurs sneer that Phoenician wine is nicest of all, I take no notice of them.
>
> (Archestratus 59 [*Epitome* 29b])

'Phoenician wine', in this extract, was Athenaeus' cue for two further quotations, from the fourth-century playwright Ephippus, for whom, apparently, Phoenician wine helped to set up a feeling of good cheer: 'walnuts, pomegranates, dates, the rest of the nibbles, and small jars of Phoenician wine'. It is also mentioned on a Cretan inscription of around 400 BC and could evidently have come to the Aegean with the Ionian and Rhodian traders who took bronze and slaves to Tyre about 600 BC, as Ezekiel tells us (27.13).[15] Ezekiel's diatribe does not, however, link specific Tyrian exports to the Ionian or other merchants that are mentioned.

After the fourth century, Aegean sources say no more of Phoenician wine, popular though it was to be in Egypt and in Indian Ocean markets.[16] In Greece, perhaps, multiplying and improving local vintages drove it off the market. We must now consider the named *Greek* wines of the classical world, concentrating on those that were of special interest to gourmets.

## PREFERRED WINES OF THE CLASSICAL AEGEAN

Alcman, from seventh-century Sparta, had already named five or six vintages of Laconia in lyric verse, of which the *Epitome of Athenaeus* preserves ragged remains:

> Alcman somewhere calls 'unfired wine, flower-scented' the vintage of Five Hills, a place seven stadia from Sparta, and [?also mentions] that of a vineyard called Denthiades and that of Oenus and that of

97

*Figure 19* Drinking party in a vineyard. One guest plays the flute; another declaims; a third threatens the waiter, who pleads for mercy. Interior of an Athenian black-figure cup in the Ashmolean Museum, Oxford, 1974.344

Onogli and Stathmi: these [?are the vineyards] near Pitane – he says '*Oinountiàs* wine and *Dénthis* and *Karystios* and *Onoglis* and *Stathmítas*' – [?including in his list] that of Carystus which is near Arcadia. By unfired he means unboiled: they did use boiled wines also.[17]

(Alcman 92 [Epitome 31c])

Early Spartans were not averse to good food and wine. Was not King Cleomenes of Sparta supposed to have drunk neat wine and gone mad? Herodotus observed that there was a hereditary guild of cooks there.[18] A sixth- or fifth-century occasional poem, one in the collection ascribed to Theognis (879–84), praises the wine from a vineyard in a valley of Mount Taygetus.

This, like Alcman's vineyards, is never heard of again. Later Spartans wrote little. To outsiders Sparta seemed to glory in the discomforts of life. Thus it is hard to trace any continuation of a Spartan tradition of wine-making. In later classical times, references to wine from the Peloponnese betray little enthusiasm, though the Peloponnese would be a favourite source of wine for medieval Europe.

The only taste which is dwelt upon in either the *Iliad* or the *Odyssey* is that of the preternaturally strong wine that Odysseus says he was given by the priest Maron at Ismarus,

> drawing off the sweet unmixed wine in twelve amphoras, a divine drink; and none of the slaves or servants in his house had known it, but himself and his dear wife and one housekeeper only. And whenever he drank the honeyed red wine, filling a cup he poured it into twenty measures of water, and a marvellous sweet smell rose from the mixing bowl.
>
> (*Odyssey* 9.204–11)

Ismarus was the Thracian town sacked by Odysseus soon after leaving Troy.[19] At a time not far distant from the composition of the *Odyssey*, Archilochus does actually mention Ismarian wine in a brief fragment, but this is surely a cross-reference to the story of Odysseus: it is literary shorthand for 'north Aegean wine won by the spear'. It cannot be taken as a proof of Archilochus' familiarity with the same wine that Odysseus drank. If it were that, we could ascribe the appreciation of geographical appellations of wine not only to Archilochus and Alcman, but to the poet of the *Odyssey* himself:[20] however, such luxuries were for the lyric poets, not the singers of epic.[21]

But the general implication of the *Iliad* (7.467–75) and *Odyssey*, that wine came from the northern Aegean islands and the coast facing them, is wholly consistent with the fifth- and fourth-century evidence. There it was that the wine was produced which Greeks of classical times most appreciated. Apart from the appellations about to be mentioned, it is worth noting that grapes and vines figure on the fifth-century coins of Maronea and Abdera – the former a colony of Chios, the latter of neighbouring Clazomenae – and that Pindar wrote of Thrace 'of abundant grapes and of fine fruit' in a *Paean* celebrating Abdera (fragment 52b line 25).

From fragments of Athenian fifth- and fourth-century comedy, selected for this purpose by Athenaeus, we are allowed a survey of the Aegean wines that attracted contemporary Athenians. We generally do not know in what contexts these stage views were given, but the generalised list of good wines that can be derived from the comedy speeches is consistent enough. We are dealing with popular commonplaces. Speakers were characterised not so much by their choice of gourmet produce as by the way they expressed their choice. What is interesting, too, is that the selection varies slightly through time. The oldest useful list is in an extract from a play by Hermippus, an older contemporary of Aristophanes:

> 'Mendaean wine is what the gods piss in their soft beds. Sweet generous Magnesian, and Thasian over which the scent of apples plays, this I judge much the best of all the other wines after fine and

unhurtful Chian. There is a certain wine that they call *Saprías*, from the mouths of whose jars when they are opened there is a smell of violets, a smell of roses, a smell of larkspur, a sacred smell through all the high-roofed hall, at once ambrosia and nectar. This is the nectar; of this I shall give to my friends to drink at the happy feast: to my enemies, Peparethan.'

(Hermippus 77 [Epitome 29e])

We shall look briefly at what is known from fifth- and fourth-century sources of the individual wines listed here, beginning with Chian, often mentioned – and never criticised – in Athenian comedy. The historian Theopompus (115F276 [*Epitome* 26b]) implied that in his time Chian wine had already a long history: 'Theopompus says that black wine was first made among the Chians, who were the first to be taught to grow and tend vines by Oenopion, son of Dionysos and settler of their island.' Indeed it had already been exported to Smyrna in the eighth century BC according to archaeological evidence.[22] Chian wine would remain highly regarded in Roman times.

Thasian, too, was always praised by Athenian comedy speakers, both in the fifth century and the fourth.[23] We do not know the special features of Thasian at this period. To achieve a Thasian style of wine, according to the later recipe attributed to Florentinus [*Geoponica* 8.23], one must dry selected grapes in the sun; the addition of must and brine was required. The result will have been a *vin de liqueur*.[24]

Both Chian and Thasian figure in the Rabelaisian finale to Aristophanes' *Assemblywomen* (1119–39). Of 'little amphoras of Thasian' a slave-girl says, in terms supposed to be naive but not ironic, 'They stay in your head a long time.' The strength of Chian and Thasian wines is implied by the speaker of an Aristophanes fragment (334 [*Epitome* 29a]): 'I won't allow the drinking of Pramnian wine – or Chian or Thasian or Peparethan – or any other that makes their peckers stand up.' This example shows some of the dangers of using comedy fragments as evidence. Did 'Pramnian' really belong in the same list as the other three, or has the tone suddenly shifted from mock-epic to mock-gourmet? Was Peparethan (contrary to what Hermippus' character thought) just about as good as Chian or Thasian, or is Aristophanes' miserly and puritanical speaker running through an impatient list of wines from the heroically good to the ridiculously bad?[25]

The common adjective *saprós* means 'rotten'. Is the wine called *Saprías*, which seems to be associated with Chian in the Hermippus text, identical with the *Khîon sapr...*, literally 'rotten Chian', apparently listed in a play by Philyllius about the same time? 'I shall provide Lesbian, rotten Chian, Thasian, Bibline, Mendaean, so that no one will have a hangover', says a character in that play (23 [*Epitome* 31a]). When used of wine, this word *saprós* was somehow complimentary.[26] That is clear from a brief exchange in the mid-fourth-century play *Dancing-Girl* by Alexis (172 [Athenaeus 441d]), who seems here to be evoking Aristophanic satire at women's religious festivals:

'We women have all we need if we have all the wine we need.'
'Sure enough, by the two goddesses, there will be as much as we could want, and it will be very good too, toothless, rotten already, devilishly aged.'

Qualities that would render women undesirable make wine irresistible: Alexis' adjectival word-play reminds us of Pindar's contrast between old wine and new songs, mentioned earlier. But Hermippus' noun *Saprías* suggests that the quality of 'rottenness', whether good or bad, was not something that came to wine with age. The poet is naming a distinct variety of some kind. And it is even possible that this is the earliest literary evidence of the sweet wine that can be made from certain varieties of grapes when attacked by noble rot.[27]

Mendaean was 'fresh and white' according to a fifth-century comedy character (Cratinus 195 [*Epitome* 29d]). Fifth-century coins of Mende, a small town on the coast of Chalcidice, allude to Dionysus, Silenus and the vine. A group of amphoras found at Black Sea sites has been identified with Mendaean exports. A speech of Demosthenes names Mende and neighbouring Scione as sources of wine imported to Athens in the fourth century, and Eubulus seems to confirm that Mende was a byword for wine in mid-fourth-century Athens.[28]

Magnesian wine is less often heard of. It came, presumably, from the Magnesian peninsula of Thessaly. Hermippus' latest editors say 'We have found nothing from elsewhere on Magnesian', not noticing, perhaps, that two Magnesian towns, Meliboea and Rhizus, struck coins in the fourth century: both depicted vines. The enthusiastic Miles Lambert-Gócs,[29] whose celebration of modern Greek wines whets many an appetite, found 'something of berries with more of plums, and perhaps still more of stewed rhubarb' in the wines of Rapsáni, whose vineyards on the slopes of Olympus and Ossa probably overlap with those that once supplied Rhizus.

If we can judge by surviving passages of Athenian comedy, Lesbian wine came to favour later than the others. It is first mentioned, around 400 BC, in the fragment of Philyllius quoted above. 'I like the Pramnian wine of Lesbos', said a character in a play by Ephippus (28 [*Epitome* 28f]). Then, at about the same time as Archestratus' praise, also quoted,[30] comes an ironic reminder, in a fragment from a comedy by Alexis (278 [*Epitome* 28e]), that considerations other than those of pure taste may have affected the popularity of certain wines in a city such as Athens: ' "How nice of Bromius [Dionysus] to give duty-free status to Lesbians who bring wine here! If any of them is caught taking it to another city, even a spoonful of it, his property is forfeit to the god." '

As we consider the wine gastronomy of the Roman Empire and of the medieval Aegean, in Chapters 6 and 9, we shall see to what extent these famous names retained their reputation.

## WINE IN CONTEXT

In the early epics wine, bread and meat went well together, though wine could also naturally be taken without food. We seem to see a hint of a men's drinking party that was independent of a meal or followed on after it in Alcinous' house on Scherie (*Odyssey* 7.136–8), the classical *pótos* or *sympósion*, though those terms are not used in the *Odyssey*. In this particular scene, at the moment when the stranger arrives Alcinous' friends are not eating but drinking, and they continue to drink while, with customary Odyssean hospitality, a selection of food is brought for the visitor to eat.

We cannot see the wine-mixing ritual from the epic poets' point of view, for the 1:20 mixture of Maron's wine can hardly be called realistic. But

*Figure 20* A waiter dips wine from a *kratér*. Athenian red-figure cup of the mid-fifth century in the Louvre, no. G133

102

the mixing of wine with water was the universal rule in early Greece, as in some other Mediterranean countries.[31] A process that deserved such elaborate provision must be supposed to have as much importance, and as much ritual, attached to it in prehistoric as it certainly did in classical times. 'Never would anyone pour wine into the bowl first, but water and then wine on top', wrote Xenophanes (5 [*Epitome* 782a]), though we observe that he is describing a past practice, for which Athenaeus cites him in evidence. Theophrastus, too [quoted ibid.], was looking to the past:

> In the matter of wine-mixing, antiquity was opposed to modern Greek practice. They did not pour water on wine, but wine on water, so that they would have a more watery drink: quenching their thirst so, they would be less avid to continue. In any case, they threw most of it at the *kóttabos*.

Hesiod and Anacreon do however confirm the *Odyssey*'s detail: the pouring of wine on water, surprising as this was to later Greeks, was indeed once the custom.[32]

Discussion of these matters by later antiquarians and moralists fell too easily into the pattern of praising a simple and methodical ancestral lifestyle: the Theophrastus fragment, with its ironic tailpiece, shows up this tendency. The strength of the ancients' wine–water mixture aroused equally enthusiastic opinions among antiquarians. Here we need note only that the typical mixtures in the fragments of early lyric are 1:2 and 2:5. Hesiod spoke for 1:3, but he was writing of a farmer's lunch, not a *sympósion*.[33] At any rate, a single small cup of unmixed wine was all on which a symposiast might have to base his judgements of vineyards and vintages.

Certain foodstuffs were seen as a suitable dessert to be taken with the wine. This custom was of no interest to Hesiod and seems to be unknown to the poets of *Iliad* and *Odyssey*, if we except the *krómyon potôi ópson*, the 'onion, a relish to the wine' (*Iliad* 11.630), which differs so strongly from what most later drinkers would have chosen. Certainly it was thought by later Greek antiquarians that while refraining from drinking until the meal was over was, undifferentiatedly, 'ancient', the serving of desserts with wine, the so-called 'second tables', was not as old as Homer.[34]

By the beginning of the fifth century the separate dessert had certainly established itself, as Pindar makes clear: 'Dessert is sweet as dinner ends, even after limitless food' (Pindar fragment 124c [Athenaeus 641c]).[35] And Xenophanes now makes it clear that the drinking party had a ceremonial to match its social significance:

> And now the floor is clean, and the hands of all, and the cups; [one] distributes woven wreaths, another offers round sweet-smelling perfume in a jug. The mixing bowl stands full of cheer; there is wine ready,[36] mild in jars, that promises never to give way, flower-scented.

Among [us] incense gives a holy scent; there is water, cold and sweet and clean. Yellow loaves are set out, and a generous table loaded with cheese and rich honey. An altar in the middle is heaped with flowers, and song and festival fill the halls.

First the gods must be hymned by cheerful men in proper words and pure compositions. After libations, and prayers to be empowered to do right (for these come first) it is not wrong to drink as much as one can and still get home safe (all but the very old) without an assistant; and to honour the man who has drunk yet seems noble, who has the mind and the muscle for virtue; and not to draw up battles of Titans or Giants or Centaurs, fictions of earlier men, or vicious quarrels (there is no good in these); but always to have true respect for the gods.[37]

(Xenophanes 1 [Athenaeus 462c])

A mock-epic comedy fragment by Hermippus, soon to be quoted, speaks of Rhodian raisins and figs and of 'chestnuts and glossy almonds' from Paphlagonia: in this humorous context chestnuts and almonds, taking the place of the Homeric 'song and dance', are described in their turn as 'ornaments of the feast'. It is in the fifth century, too, that a character in a play by Eupolis (271 [*Epitome* 52d]) calls for 'Naxian almonds to chew and wine from Naxian vines to drink'.

## THE SEARCH FOR FOOD QUALITY

Turning, then, to food, in pre-classical Greece one can trace the beginnings of a gastronomic tradition in certain small but telling details. Athenaeus, or his source, observed (*Epitome* 25e) that it was a sign of the creation and appreciation of varied flavours if, on arrival at a Homeric household, guests were offered *eídata pólla*, 'many relishes', and *kreiôn pínakes pantoíon*, 'platters of all kinds of meats' (*Odyssey* 1.140–2): the difference is clear between the welcome offered by the rich and the shifts that the apologetic Eumaeus had to make: ' "Eat now, stranger, what servants have to eat: piglets, but the fat sows are eaten by the suitors" ' (14.80–1).

At household meals, too, the existence of such refinements allowed a poet to distinguish the wealthy way of life from that of the poor. The essential dining customs might not be very different: the host would still sacrifice before the meal and would still personally offer his guest a preferred portion. But culinary elaboration was not even hinted at. Again, a nobleman on campaign, though still provided with more than one kind of meat, might manage without the 'many relishes', a phrase that does not occur in the *Iliad*.

The fragment from Hermippus, referred to above, is the earliest clear literary evidence of a developed trade in gastronomic and other luxury goods within the Aegean region and of an observation, soon to be a commonplace, that some foodstuffs widely available were found at their best in specified localities:

'Tell me now, Muses whose dwellings are on Olympus, how many good things Dionysus has brought here to men in his black ship since he has plied the wine-dark sea: from Cyrene, [silphium] stem and oxhide; from the Hellespont, mackerel and all salt fish; from [Thessaly], wheatmeal and ox ribs; from Sitalces an itch for the Spartans; from Perdiccas many ships full of lies. The Syracusans send us pigs and cheese; and the Corcyreans, may Poseidon damn them in their slick ships, for they have shifty thoughts. . . . Africa provides much ivory for sale; Rhodes, raisins and dreamy figs. From Euboea, pears and fat apples; captives from Phrygia; mercenaries from Arcadia. Pagasae sends slaves and jailbirds; the Paphlagonians send the chestnuts and glossy almonds which are the ornaments of the feast. Then Phoenicia, bread wheat and the fruit of the date palm; Carthage, rugs and fancy pillows.'[38]

(Hermippus 63 [*Epitome* 27e])

This, like later similar lists, mingles information on local produce, and on the sources of Athenian food imports, with puns and political and racial satire; yet on the basis of this and other sources of the sixth and fifth centuries one may distinguish some true local contributions to the developing gastronomy of the Aegean coasts and the wider Greek world.

Though written a couple of centuries later, two historical fragments on the economic development of Samos under Polycrates in the second half of the sixth century – seen by the authors not as economic development but as an insatiable hunt for luxuries – may be thought to corroborate, from an entirely different viewpoint, the hypothesis of an increasing recognition of links between quality and geographical origin:

Clytus the Aristotelian in *On Miletus* says that Polycrates the Samian tyrant collected [produce] from everywhere for luxury's sake: dogs from Epirus, goats from Scyros, sheep from Miletus, pigs from Sicily. Alexis in *Samian Annals* III says that Samos was embellished from many cities by Polycrates, who collected Molossian and Laconian dogs, goats from Scyros and Naxos, sheep from Miletus and Attica. He also had craftsmen move there, offering very high wages.

(Athenaeus 540c–d)

Polycrates (or his farm manager) was not alone in these preferences. Hermippus' reference to the pigs that came from Syracuse has already been quoted, while Pindar knew the fame of the goats of Scyros:[39] 'from Taygetus the Laconian dog, a most eager beast for chasing the prey. Scyrian goats are most excellent for the giving of milk . . .' (Pindar fragment 106 [*Epitome* 28a]).

## INFLUENCES FROM THE PERIPHERY: LYDIA

Something can be traced of the cookery and gastronomy of Sumerians, Assyrians, Egyptians and Hittites.[40] Although the classical Aegean shared many foodstuffs with these earlier civilisations, and indeed borrowed many foodstuffs from them, culinary influences (narrowly defined) have not been traced. It is likely enough that they await finding, for there is no doubt of the preference, among affluent Greeks and Romans, for Levantine cooks and bakers. Meanwhile, gastronomic influences on classical Greece are certainly traceable from closer at hand.

The Lydians were credited with having taught the Greeks many of the arts of entertainment: Lydians, warlike enough in a Persian context, were in a curious contradiction characterised as flabby by Greeks,[41] for the simple reason that Lydians taught Greeks some of the usages of luxury. To wear perfumes was a Lydian habit: Greek cities and Greek men repeatedly criticised one another for adopting it, yet the scent of perfumes was part of the atmosphere of a Greek *sympósion*. *En deípnoisi Lydôn*, 'in the dinners of the Lydians', Greeks met the musical instruments and the music with which they were to entertain themselves at dinner. Greek, or at least Athenian, drinking rituals were also ascribed to Lydia, as by Critias; so were party games.[42] After his marvellous deadpan line, 'The Lydians share most of their customs with the Greeks, except that of prostituting their daughters', Herodotus (*Histories* 1.94) continues: 'They, first among people known to us, struck and used currency of gold and silver; and they were the first shopkeepers; and the Lydians say that the games[43] now instituted among themselves and the Greeks were their inventions.' Lydians may well have been the inventors of coinage (and their first coins were indeed of electrum, that is, of gold and silver mixed). They were not really the earliest shopkeepers, but they were in their time very active traders and shopkeepers. Certainly the first shopkeeper in Greek literature – a wine dealer – is in a fragment by the sixth-century poet Hipponax of Ephesus (79), who seems to have written in a mixed Greek–Lydian milieu. Settled retail trade was a necessity if gourmets were to learn to appreciate and demand a greater range of foodstuffs than could be looked for at market.

Two dishes appreciated in mainland Greece by the fifth century, the *kándaulos* and *karyke*, were said in much later times to have originated in Lydia. We shall return to the *kándaulos*, which certainly seems to have a Lydian name. As for *karyke*, a spicy sauce, it became so well known in fourth-century Greece that the word bred a family of derivatives: a character in Achaeus of Eretria's satyr play *Alcmaeon* called the men of Delphi *karykkopoioí*, 'sauce-makers'. In Menander's *Trophonius* 'dishes with spiced sauces', *tà kekarykeuména*, are seen from the viewpoint of Athens to be typical of the Aegean islanders, and the *kándaulos* and such *hypobinetiônta brómata*, 'lascivious foods', seem typical of the neighbouring Ionians.[44] Perhaps these sweet and spicy concoctions were among the specialities of the Chian cooks, a school of which nothing but its mere existence is now known.[45] They certainly came from the eastern half of the Aegean, perhaps from its eastern coast, and perhaps after all they did come from the inland kingdom which was the source of other details of Greek gastronomic culture.

Hipponax happens to be the first to name three delicacies soon to be widely spoken of in Greek literature: dried figs (124), tunny and *myttotós*, this last being a sauce with which tunny was eaten by one of Hipponax's enemies, whom he likens to a Lampsacene eunuch (26 [Athenaeus 304b]). Lampsacus was actually more likely than any other place mentioned in the surviving fragments of Hipponax to be well supplied with tunny, being on the Hellespont, their migration route between the Mediterranean and the Black Seas. We may accept from Hipponax, then, that sixth-century Lampsacenes, eunuchs or not, ate their tuna with *myttotós*, as approved by Ananius around the same date.

Ananius (as Athenaeus will observe in the following text) deserves a quotation of more than a line. Puzzling though the following passage is in one or two details, it is important as the first sketch of the relation between food and the seasons:

> Ananius writes as follows: 'In spring the meagre is best; the *anthías* in winter, but the best of all fine dishes is shrimp in fig-leaf. It is sweet to eat the nanny-goat's meat[46] in autumn, and the porker's, when [harvesters] turn and tread; then is the season for dogs and hares and foxes.[47] Mutton's [season] is when it is summer and the crickets chirp, and there is tunny from the sea, no bad food, but excelling all other fish when served in *myttotós*. The fatted ox, I think, is good to eat at midnight and in the day time.' I have given plenty of Ananius, noticing that the same kind of advice to pleasure-seekers is offered by him also.

(Ananius 5 [Athenaeus 282b])

What was *myttotós*? It became well known in fifth-century Athens as a sauce or relish containing garlic, leeks, cheese, honey, olive oil and, according to much later sources, eggs. From Theophrastus, at the end of the fourth century, we learn that a so-called Cyprian variety of garlic was especially suitable as an ingredient for *myttotós* since it had a foamy sap and did not need to be cooked.[48] In conjecturing that *myttotós* came to Athens from the Hellespont, one builds on the knowledge that salt fish, particularly salted tuna, certainly did come to Athens by that route.[49]

## SICILY

'The *kóttabos* is the most famous product of the land of Sicily', according to the jocular Critias, poet and philosopher (2 [*Epitome* 28b]).

The party game that we described in Chapter 1 was already known in the sixth-century Aegean, for it explains Alcaeus' line 'the *látages* fly from Tean cups' (322 [Athenaeus 481a]), *látages* being wine-drops in their special role as *kóttabos*-missiles. Slightly later, two scholars cited by Athenaeus (668de) seem to confirm that this much-loved party game did indeed come from Sicily: Dicaearchus, apparently commenting on this line of Alcaeus, and Callimachus, whose poetic conceit was to call *látages* 'Sicilian' (fragment 69). But it is doubtful whether Sicilian Greeks can have invented and transmitted *kóttabos* early enough for it to have become popular with Anacreon. Athenaeus himself does not insist on the Sicilian *origin* of the game: 'That *kóttabos* was liked by the Sicilian Greeks is clear from their having built special rooms for the game, as recorded by Dicaearchus in *On Alcaeus*. So, not unreasonably, Callimachus called the *látax* "Sicilian".' More likely Sicily was linked with *kóttabos*, the climax of symposiac festivity, as Sicily, in Greek minds, was linked with gluttony and symposiac festivity in general – for which the Italiots, the Greeks of southern Italy where wealthy Sybaris had stood, shared the credit. Aristophanes (fragment 225 [Athenaeus 527c, 484f]) spoke of 'Syracusan table and Sybaritic festivity'; Plato (*Letter* 7.326b) wrote censoriously to his Syracusan hosts of 'the life there called happy, filled with Syracusan and Italiot tables . . . a life of being filled up twice a day and never sleeping alone at night'.[50]

Certainly Sicily had more to offer to Greek cuisine than a party game. The Sicilian comedy playwright Epicharmus (58 [Athenaeus 282b]), early in the fifth century, had already alluded to Ananius' seasonal gastronomy quoted on p. 107. Other fragments of Epicharmus provide massive evidence of the variety of foodstuffs available in Sicilian cities in his time. Hermippus and Clytus, also quoted above (p. 105), show that by the sixth and fifth centuries the quality of the pork and cheese of Sicily was appreciated in Aegean Greece.

Sicilian cheese was quite a commonplace of Athenian comedy. It crops up often enough to show that its reputation is more than a literary reminiscence of the Cyclops episode of the *Odyssey*, which later readers universally pictured as taking place in Sicily. The Cyclops was certainly said to make goats' milk and ewes' milk cheese (9.218–23), as Athenian comedies and satyr plays often recalled.[51]

But Athenians were soon unambiguously crediting Sicily with an even more important contribution to gastronomy. It was from Sicily, so the comedies suggest, that skilled cooks had set out to conquer the gourmets of the Greek world. Their fame can be no better demonstrated than in the following brief fragment, clearly the first lines of a mythological comedy in which the speakers, probably Odysseus and one of his crew, must immediately let the audience know where they are, though they do not yet know for themselves:

> 'Do you sense what a sweet odour this country has, and how a rather fragrant smoke is rising? There must dwell in this chasm, it would seem, some purveyor of frankincense, or Sicilian cook.'
> 'Are you saying the two would smell the same?'
>
> (Cratinus the Younger 1 [Athenaeus 661e])

The gastronomic miracles wrought in Athens by Sicilian cooks became a cliché of fourth- and third-century comedy, in which the cook's grandiloquent pride in his art appears from the many quotations by Athenaeus to have been one of the most frequently recurrent set pieces. And Sicilian cooks not only practised, but also published.

## THE SICILIAN COOKBOOKS

The earliest author of a Greek cookery book seems to have been 'Mithaecus, who wrote the book on Sicilian cookery' to which Plato, in his *Gorgias* (518b), makes Socrates refer. The Socrates of the dialogue mischievously imagines that, just as Gorgias was claiming too much on behalf of current politicians, so he might have claimed 'very earnestly of Thearion the baker, Mithaecus who wrote the book on Sicilian cookery, and Sarambus the dealer, that they have been excellent at caring for us in a physical way, the first providing excellent bread, the second, cuisine and the third, wine'. Socrates goes on to argue that such provision tends to produce physical decadence, not health, and then reverts to his political discussion.

The cookery author is in interesting company here. Sarambus was a Plataean who dealt in wine at Athens, assuming that we are right to identify him with the Sarabus mentioned by the comedy author Poseidippus. Thearion was credited with inventing an oven for the mass production of bread, or, if he did not invent it, certainly with introducing it to Athens where it was widely taken up. He was alive when Aristophanes produced his *Aeolus the Cook* and was still remembered with honour by a speaker in an Antiphanes play in the mid-fourth century.[52] Thus Socrates is listing three non-Athenian contributors to the gastronomy of Athens. Even more strikingly, though it is difficult to show this in English translation, he coordinates his list with the three constituents of an ancient Greek meal: the cereal staple, the accompanying meats and other relishes with which cookery concerned itself, and the wine that followed these.

There are serious anachronisms in *Gorgias*, so it would be risky to argue that Mithaecus' book could have been known to Socrates and Gorgias by 427 BC, which is the earliest dramatic date that Plato could have intended for the dialogue.[53] It must, at any rate, have been in use by the first decade of the fourth century, when *Gorgias* was certainly written.

And the cookery book is not wholly lost, it seems. From Mithaecus, Athenaeus quotes just one recipe, for the fish called *tainía*, 'ribbon', a name known in Sicily in the early fifth century BC and apparently to be identified with the truly ribbon-like fish that the French call cépole:[54]

> Cépole: gut, discard the head, rinse and fillet; add cheese and oil.
>
> (Athenaeus 325f)

It is necessary to ask whether Mithaecus' book, *Opsartytikón* (*Cooking*),[55] as excerpted by Athenaeus, was the genuine work of the almost legendary fifth-century creator of the cookery book. The book from which Athenaeus quoted was in Doric dialect. This would be entirely natural for a Sicilian author and topic. Unfortunately it would be doubly natural for a later forger; the only biographical anecdote concerning Mithaecus is in an essay of Roman Imperial date in which he is said to have visited Doric Sparta and to have been expelled as a bad influence (Maximus of Tyre, *Dissertation 17*). The fourteen word quotation – a single sentence, the main verb being imperative – contains one otherwise unknown verb, *ekkoilíxas*, 'having gutted', one intransitive verb elsewhere always transitive, *apoplynas*, 'having rinsed', and one unique cognate accusative phrase, *tamòn temákhea*, 'having filleted' or 'sliced': 'Sicilian cookery' had, on this evidence, already developed a technical vocabulary and a laconic style. The vocabulary is an argument for authenticity (since only the most daring forgeries are linguistically adventurous); the style is again at least as suitable to a forged Mithaecus as to a genuine one. Athenaeus, though he is ready to comment on questions of authenticity, says nothing as to the genuineness of this work. It is not in itself surprising that he refers to it so seldom: he seldom quotes any cookery books, though they were certainly available to him, his preferred sources being literary and philological. The question of genuineness must be left open, for the name of Mithaecus as cookery author had been broadcast by Plato, and thus, if the real book had not survived the early period, there was every temptation for a falsifier to fill its place.

For all one knows, 'Mithaecus' may have consisted entirely of concise recipes. A certain Glaucus of Locri (in southern Italy) may have been more ambitious. He is the source for one of Athenaeus' two recipes for *hypósphagma*: 'But *hypósphagma*: fried blood and silphium and *hépsema*[56] (or honey) and vinegar and milk and cheese and chopped aromatic herbs' (Athenaeus 324a). *Hypósphagma* was a sauce to serve with meat: the other recipe, from Erasistratus [Athenaeus 324a], includes the meat. This recipe, like others, may have spread from Ionia or Lydia; at any rate the word probably did so, since it had already been used metaphorically by Hipponax (166 [Athenaeus 324a]) for cuttlefish ink, *sepíes hypósphagma*. The culinary extension of the term is easily explained since cuttlefish ink can be included in the sauce with which cuttlefish are eaten: Alan Davidson gives two modern Greek recipes.[57] But Glaucus also said something grandiose and generalised on the art of cookery, perhaps quoting the two lines of iambic verse on this topic that are retailed by Athenaeus (661e), lines which claimed it as an art unsuitable for slaves. It may be no coincidence, then, that Glaucus' recipe is a mere list of ingredients, part of a sentence which perhaps tabulated sauces in a work which might have been as much philosophical as practical, and was in the standard Attic–Ionic dialect of prose.[58] Yet it was known by the same title, *Opsartytikón*, as was Mithaecus', although, as we shall see, books with a title of this kind were far from uniform in content.

Something different again, perhaps, was the book by Hegesippus of Tarentum from which there survives (not necessarily verbatim) a list of the ingredients of *kándaulos*. This, variously spelt, was a new delicacy in Athens in the early fourth century, typically Ionian, something that not everyone could make – a rich savoury confection less fashionable a generation later. In the third century AD its origin was being traced to Lydia:

> The Lydians also spoke of a certain *kándaulos*, indeed not one but three of them, so versatile in luxury had they become; made, says Hegesippus of Tarentum, of fried/boiled meat and grated bread and Phrygian cheese and dill and rich broth.[59]

> (Athenaeus 516c–d)

In the third century the Alexandrian *Subject Index* listed a *plakountopoiikòn syngramma*, a 'text on cake-making', by Hegesippus. This reference, with the period of known popularity of the *kándaulos*, suggests a very tentative dating of Hegesippus to the fourth century BC. The 'text on cakemaking' may have been his only work: the *kándaulos* as described hardly sounds like a cake, yet it was classified as one (as a *plakoûs*, that is) by a Hellenistic scholar commenting on a fourth-century text.[60]

## THE STATE OF THE GASTRONOMIC ARTS

By the early part of the fourth century, then, much wine crossed the Aegean (though little of it now came to Greece from further afield). The geographical differences between wines were recognised and were the subject of praise and criticism. The arts of cooking meat and fish dishes, and of baking cakes, had reached the point of codification in writing. Recipes appear to have been transmitted across the Greek world even more widely than wine. We can make a start at judging the predominant flavours of classical Greek cuisine.[61] Medical authors were, as we shall see in Chapter 7, beginning to set out systematically their views on dietetics. Cities and regions of the Mediterranean world were becoming known for the quality

*Figure 21* Behind Heracles' couch, at Eurytius' feast, wine stands in a *kratér* and meat is prepared for dinner. Corinthian *kratér* in the Louvre, no. E635 (see also the frontispiece and Figure 18)

of their food and wine, and some were proud enough of it to allow food and wine to suggest the badges on their coinage.

And there is another point just as striking as any of these. Good food and wine had become subjects talked of in comic drama and written of in poetry. Literature of the fourth century, from Athens in particular, is for the first time plentiful and varied enough to show how these developments in gastronomy had become a part of the cultural mainstream.

And so from literature which for the first time treats food and drink as topics worth discussion in their own right, we can begin to speak more positively: for the meagre hints in seventh-, sixth- and fifth-century sources have led in this chapter to guesses and extrapolations rather than to established facts. It will become clear that gastronomic opinions – on the right way to cook a particular fish, or on the best place to buy it – were something more than whims of individual authors: they show a consistency which demonstrates that they were part of a widely accepted body of knowledge, present to the consciousness of popular audiences, open to controversy and to satire.

# 5

# SICILIAN TABLES
## The culture of fourth-century gastronomy

'But no, the bit of bluefish to simmer in brine, as before, I tell you.'
'And the bit of bass?'
'Bake whole.'
'The dogfish?'
'Boil in *hypótrimma*.'
'The piece of eel?'
'Salt, oregano, water.'
'The conger?'
'Same.'
'The skate?'
'Green.'
'There's a slice of tunny.'
'You bake it.'
'The kid?'
'Roast.'
'The other?'
'The reverse.'
'The spleen?'
'Stuffed.'
'The intestine?'
'He's caught me.'[1]

(Antiphanes 221 [Athenaeus 662b])

It was the peremptory style of the early cookbook, surely, which was mocked in this comedy exchange, perhaps an exchange between master and household slave:[2] we are to imagine a cookery book being consulted. In a culture such as that of fifth- and fourth-century Athens in which cooks were craftsmen, hired for the occasion of an entertainment and given temporary charge of the kitchen staff, there was every reason for a parsimonious host to save money and to please his own taste by arranging his dinner himself.[3] After all, the slaughtering and sacrifice of the meat, though unavoidable, did not have to be done in the presence of the host

113

or diners: the ritual work of the *mágeiros* could be got over in advance of the butchered meat's sale at market.

There was every reason, then, for cookery books to become popular: professional cooks might have transmitted their art by word of mouth,[4] but the host who took charge might well want an independent source of advice on his arrangements and suggestions for clear instructions to give to those in his kitchen. And indeed the public addressed by Athenian comedy was aware of the existence not only of bare cookery books but of more literary works on food and dining, all being classed together under the heading of *Opsartysía*, 'Cookery'.

## THE *DINNER* OF PHILOXENUS

In a second, and undoubted, comedy reference to cookery books it is possible to fill in a good deal of the background. The *Epitome of Athenaeus* quotes a fragment from the comic playwright Plato's *Phaon* (189 [*Epitome* 5b]):

> The comic author Plato has mentioned Philoxenus of Leucas' *Dinner*:
> 'Here in the wild I want to read through this book to myself.'
> 'Please do tell me what it is.'
> 'Some new *Cookery* by Philoxenus.'
> 'Show me it. What's it like?'
> 'All right, listen. "I shall begin with the grape-hyacinth, I shall end with the tunny . . .".'

The quotation (a further thirteen lines are given in the *Epitome*, and there was more in Plato) came from the playwright's imagination.[5] But there really was a Philoxenus who was the author of a wordy poem about food, and was well enough known to be mentioned with mock praise in Antiphanes' *Tritagonist*,[6] a comedy of the next generation. A passage from the real poem appears to be ridiculed in another play by Antiphanes, *The Parasite* (180 [Athenaeus 169e]):

> 'Get on with it.'
> 'A casserole, I mean – but you might want to call it a saucepan – '
> 'Do you think the name matters to me? Let people have fun and call it a casserole or a camisole,[7] as long as I know you mean a pot.'

Much of Philoxenus' *Dinner* survives in relatively long quotations by Athenaeus. I have published an annotated translation separately,[8] and will quote only the opening lines here. No persons or places are named in the surviving fragments, yet clearly they are parts of something in the form of a private poem: a description by one of the guests, addressed to an intimate friend, of a lavish banquet. Numerous diners shared many small tables in a single hall; they washed their hands before and after the main course; wreaths and perfumes were distributed:

> Philoxenus the dithyrambic poet in the so-called *Dinner* makes the wreath the beginning of the festivity, writing thus: 'A tender child came bringing water for the hands in a silver ewer, and poured it; then he brought a wreath plaited from the noble sprigs of a slim myrtle.'
>
> (Philoxenus a [Athenaeus 685d])

The number of different dishes was very large: fish predominated at the beginning, meat in the middle. Barley cakes as well as wheat bread accompanied the main course. Wine was served, without any accompanying food, after the main course and before the dessert,[9] which consisted (besides eggs, almonds and walnuts) of sweet confections in which safflower, honey and sesame had a prominent role. Afterwards the diners played *kóttabos*.

Some of the individual dishes named by Philoxenus are also mentioned in Athenian comedy and in the fragments of Epicharmus; the frenzied inventiveness of the language of the *Dinner* may account for the fact that most of the rest cannot be matched anywhere in Greek literature.

The description need not be read as factual. But it is worth considering where in the world such an entertainment might have been imagined by the poet as taking place. The whole organisation of it differs radically from anything described (after Alcman's time) from the Peloponnese and Crete, where communal dining became the general rule and tradition, by now, seems to have militated against gastronomic variety and innovation. On the other hand, the milieu is certainly Greek, and the course of the meal, and the behaviour surrounding it, resemble the dinner parties of Athens in many particulars.

But at Athenian dinner parties the guests were few. Among the Greeks before Alexander's time the only household famed for entertaining particularly large numbers to dinner appears to have been none other than that in which the dithyrambic poet Philoxenus of Cythera once used to dine: 'On the lavishness of Dionysius the Younger, tyrant of Sicily, Satyrus the Peripatetic says in his *Lives* that he used to fill thirty-couch rooms in his house with banqueters' (Athenaeus 541c). If a thirty-couch room might hold around sixty guests, the number is still not large by the standards of the rich and powerful in Hellenistic and Roman times. Indeed I suspect Athenaeus took the phrase from Satyrus in the singular and turned it into the plural to make it more impressive. But so far as one knows, no other fourth-century Greek had a house with a room large enough for thirty couches, and no one else was in the habit of filling such a room with dinner guests. The *Dinner*, therefore, tentatively ascribed by Athenaeus to Philoxenus of Cythera, may indeed describe an entertainment just such as the same Philoxenus might have enjoyed at the court of Dionysius the

Elder. It was in Syracuse, too, that diners were served with wine without any accompanying dessert.[10]

## READERS OF PHILOXENUS

The surviving passages of the *Dinner* are enough to show that the poem invited every criticism made or implied by the three contemporary authors who are known to have mentioned it. Its extravagantly lengthy compounds, sometimes consisting of lists of ingredients of stews and sweets, are particularly remarkable: as far as food is concerned, the only examples of this linguistic game that the author can have had before him are in the Athenian old comedy. Indeed much of the poem was a versified catalogue of dishes, and again the literary precedent was in Athenian drama,[11] this time paralleled to some extent in Sicilian literature by the lists of seafood in many fragments of Epicharmus.

We have to ask, in view of these precedents, how serious the author was in his purpose. One cannot be sure, and if the poem once had an introduction and conclusion, making all clear, Athenaeus did not preserve them. We should probably see it as a *jeu d'esprit*, a playful application of dithyrambic language to a less than elevated topic.

Contemporary intellectuals thought it a showy text, obscure in its vocabulary but obvious in its subject-matter, calculated to impress the half-educated, who might be observed 'speaking publicly... having read nothing except maybe the *Dinner* of Philoxenus, and not all of that' (Aristotle fragment 83 [*Epitome* 6d]). To such people it might appear a piece of serious but approachable literature, and it is against such people that Antiphanes' satire is directed:

> 'Far superior to all other poets: Philoxenus! First of all, he put new words of his own everywhere. And then, how well he watered down his lyrics with tones and colours. A god among men, he was, he really knew about literature.'[12]
>
> (Antiphanes 207 [Athenaeus 643d])

## THE *LIFE OF LUXURY*

This *Dinner* invited parody. Yet Plato's hexameters are not really a parody of it. Nor are they in the mock-epic tradition which is seen in different forms in satyr play, in some of the hexameter passages in old comedy and in comic poems like the *Battle of the Frogs and Mice* and the *Attic Dinner* of Matron of Pitana – a satirical piece, largely a cento from Homer, quoted at length by Athenaeus (134d–137c).[13]

Rather than that, they are a subversion of the Greek poetry of proverbs and lists and traditional wisdom. So is the hexameter fragment of Hermip-

*Figure 22* Red mullet have pride of place among the catch at a small harbour just south of Miletus on the Turkish shore of the Aegean – just as they did around 360 BC when Archestratus visited the place (ancient Teichioussa) and recommended its red mullet to the readers of his gastronomic poem. *Photo*: Professor R. B. Barlow

pus (63 [*Epitome* 27e]) quoted on p. 105. This genre, fruitful in gnomic statements lending themselves to brief quotation, goes back to Hesiod and the considerable body of poetry that was afterwards attributed to him, and was developed in the philosophical verse of the pre-Socratics. Tricks of style and vocabulary continually renew the links between such poems. *Arxomai*, 'I shall begin', says Plato's imaginary poet; Hesiod's word is *arkhómetha*, 'let us begin' (*Theogony* 36). And it is no easy task to draw a line between what is parody and what is not: the term belies the complexity of these poets' various purposes. Ananius' tone, in his fragment on the seasons quoted on p. 107 (5 [Athenaeus 282b]), is identifiably lighter than Hesiod's, but it is hard to pin him down more precisely. Hermippus is much closer than Ananius to parody, using puns and humorous juxtapositions to belie the seriousness of his introduction: the purpose here is laughter and the playwright's political agenda.

Somewhere between didactic poetry and its subversion lies the literary ancestry of Archestratus, whose home city was Syracuse or Gela (*Epitome of Athenaeus* 4e).[14] Much has been written on Archestratus recently, his historical context, the text of his work, its literary context; there is now an annotated translation, the first ever. Archestratus' only known work, his gastronomic poem, was probably called *Hedypatheía*, which means something like the *Life of Luxury*. It does not survive complete, but is known from many brief citations by Athenaeus, who once called him 'the Hesiod and Theognis of relish-eaters' (310a). Internal evidence dates the poem before Philip's destruction and enslavement of Olynthus in 348 BC: the advice (20 [Athenaeus 295c]) to 'go shopping for the head of a bluefish at Olynthus' would have been not only useless but extremely tasteless in a poem first circulated in the years after that traumatic event.[15]

While Philoxenus is mentioned several times in the surviving fragments of Greek comedy, Archestratus got in, at the most, twice – if it is true that Antiphanes' play *Archestrate* (*The female Archestratus* or *Archestratus' sister*) is really named after him. The one certain reference is in a typical middle comedy cook's speech in a play by Dionysius of Sinope (2.24 [Athenaeus 405b]).

His poem was, however, far from unknown. It (or at least its title) was known to readers of the early third century BC, notably to Clearchus of Soli and to Lynceus of Samos, who appealed to its authority in his *Shopping for Food* (Athenaeus 313f). Already to Clearchus, (81 [Athenaeus 285d]), Archestratus seemed so well known that gourmets could be described superciliously as *hoi perì Arkhéstraton*, 'the people with Archestratus', while Lynceus (Athenaeus 286a, 294e) expected a correspondent to understand his allusion to 'the author of the *Life of Luxury*'. It was even to be translated, or rather adapted, into early Latin in Ennius' *Hedyphagetica* from which eleven lines survive, suggesting that the poem was still in circulation in the late third century in Tarentum, near which Ennius was born.[16]

Repeatedly Archestratus criticised culinary elaboration and lavish entertainment. His views on the proper number of guests would have been quite at odds with those of the host of any dinner resembling Philoxenus': 'All to dine at one nicely-supplied table: there shall be three or four altogether or at most five, or it would be a tentful of plundering mercenaries' (61 [*Epitome* 4d]). It is at first sight strange that the *Life of Luxury* had no better a reputation than Philoxenus' *Dinner* among the philosophically inclined. Archestratus, quite unfairly so far as one can judge from the surviving fragments, came to be a byword for decadence – and decadence of all kinds.

Already, in his disapproval of the luxury he found in Sicily, Plato had linked Syracusan dinners with 'never sleeping alone at night' (*Letter 7*.326b, quoted on p. 108). Soon, writing in the late fourth or early third century, Clearchus of Soli (63 [Athenaeus 457c–e]) claimed to despise

> those people nowadays who set one another questions [at drinking parties] like which sexual posture is the most enjoyable, or which fish, or how cooked[?]; or which is in season now, or which is best to eat after Arcturus or after the Pleiades or after Sirius.... This is

typical of a man who is at home with the works of Philaenis and Archestratus, and has studied the so-called *Gastrológiai.*

This, by a pupil of Aristotle, no doubt was read by Chrysippus of Soli, who later in the third century coupled gastronomy with sexual experimentation in very similar dismissive terms [Athenaeus 335de]: 'books like Philaenis', and the *Gastronomy* of Archestratus, and stimulants to love and sexual intercourse, and then again slave girls practised in such movements and postures'; 'likewise not to study Philaenis, or the *Gastronomy* of Archestratus, with the expectation of improving one's life!'[17]

The coupling of gastronomy and sex in these strictures is natural enough. Dinner parties for men were all-round entertainments[18] designed to please every fleshly sense. With the taste of food and wine came the scents of perfumes and wreaths, the sounds of song and music and the sight of musicians and dancers; and the performers, and others of low status who were present, were in general not untouchable. Hence all these topics are appropriately dealt with by Athenaeus in the *Deipnosophists.* On such occasions, by their nature, no one was audience: all were performers. And men who disapproved of sensual indulgence (in shorthand, 'philosophers') might well wonder what part in the entertainment they themselves should properly be playing. Should they be the impassive observer, or the observer who succumbs to temptation, or the guest who leaves early?

> Once when one of these philosophers was drinking with us a flute-girl came in, and since there was room beside him the girl was going to sit there. He played cold and would not let her. But then later when we auctioned the flute-girl, as one does at drinking parties, he was very childish during the bidding, and shouted that the auctioneer had been too quick about closing the deal and giving her to someone else. Our cold philosopher finished the night with fisticuffs.
>
> (Persaeus 584F4 [Athenaeus 607d–e])

And since all these roles were so evidently open to ridicule,[19] should a philosopher really not be there at all?

## THE REAL ARCHESTRATUS

Archestratus' later reputation consists of a series of platitudes. A study of Archestratus himself will have little time for all this. We must survey his work as we have it, shorn of Athenaeus' context.

His language is direct, varied, forceful, often combative; his syntax and metre are notably rough. In confident mimicry of Herodotus he begins with the generous promise of 'an exposition of my research for all of Greece' (1 [*Epitome* 4e]).[20] The poem that followed was made up of a series of imperatives, directed, it seems, to two individuals, Moschus and

119

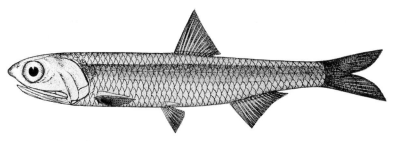

*Figure 23 Aphye*: the anchovy, *engraulis*. A panful of these tiny fish, fried for a
few seconds in sizzling oil, made a delicacy for which Salamis, Eleusis and
Phalerum were renowned. *Source*: from the drawing by Thosaporn Wongratana
in Davidson 1981

Cleandrus. They, or the reader, were told in which Greek towns they
might buy particular foodstuffs at their best, and in which towns they were
better avoided. For in spite of the imputations of his philosopher-critics,
Archestratus concentrated on food. He knew what fish to buy on the sea
front at Carthage (13 [Athenaeus 320a])[21] and in the market at Pella (30
[Athenaeus 328a]). He knew of the industrial bread ovens of Athens and
of the clay ovens of Persian-dominated Erythrae (4 [Athenaeus 111f]).
Those who followed his instructions would have made their purchases
under Phoenician (probably), Oscan, Macedonian, Persian and of course
Greek auspices.

One does not know what proportion of Archestratus' poem survives. It
is an interesting clue, however, that no place-names crop up so often in
the fragments as Ambracia and Byzantium (six times each). Ambracia was
a regular port of call for Sicilians and Italians sailing east; Byzantium was a
market for all the produce of the Black Sea, an unavoidable stopping place
on the route there, and a busy exporter of foodstuffs. These are just the
names that should recur if the poem is distilled from real travels and
experiences and if what survives is a fair sample of the whole.[22]

Among the many assertions of Archestratus concerning the origins of
good foods are several for which second opinions from classical authors
happen to be available. He approves the eels of Lake Copais, the bread
and cakes of the Athenian market, the small fry of the Bay of Phalerum,
the conger eels of Sicyon, the wines of Thasos and Lesbos. All these are
praised in other texts of the late fifth, fourth or early third centuries: they
could be called literary commonplaces. But we now see that they are the
tip of an iceberg, for they are expressed no differently from the scores of
other trenchant opinions in the surviving fragments of Archestratus. It is
as if, quite outside literature, there were already a consensus on the sources
of good foods in the region, and Archestratus, in spite of his verbal
fireworks, wrote in accordance with it. We have here not the unsupported

views of an individual, but a slice of the knowledge that passed among fishermen, fishmongers and fish buyers, among travellers, mariners and innkeepers.

The reader of Archestratus has to conclude that he was not an armchair gastronome. He travelled, and took a personal interest in his food and its preparation; whether as a merchant or a rhapsode or in some other capacity we have no idea, but he was hardly a mercenary soldier (61). His poem is classed as parody, yet the classification does not tell the whole story: it was a light didactic poem, lending itself to recitation to an audience in the right mood and to the memorising of precepts.[23]

Nearly all of Athenaeus' quotations from the *Life of Luxury* are very brief. The occasional slightly longer fragment, such as that on pearl barley and bread, gives a clearer picture of the work:

And first I shall recall the gifts of fair-haired Demeter, dear Moschus: take them to your heart. The best one can get, the finest of all, cleanly hulled from good ripe barley-ears, is from the sea-washed breast of famous Eresus in Lesbos, whiter than airborne snow. If the gods eat *álphita*, this is where Hermes goes shopping for them. They are passable at seven-gated Thebes and at Thasos and at some other cities too, but just like grape-pips as against Lesbian: know that for certain.

Take a Thessalian roll, a circling whirl of dough well kneaded by hand; they call it 'crumble' there, emmer-bread as others say. I also commend to you a child of durum-wheat, Tegea's bread baked under ashes. Fair is the loaf that famous Athens sells to mortals in her market-place; those from the clay ovens of vinous Erythrae, white and blooming with the gentle seasons, are a joy with dinner.

(4 [Athenaeus 111f])

## COOKS, GASTRONOMES AND COMEDY AUDIENCES

So much is said by cooks and of cookery in fourth-century Athenian comedies that for those who become enmeshed in the texts it is difficult to look beyond. Here we are not talking of complete works of literature, as we have pretended to do with the generous fragments of Philoxenus' *Dinner* and of Archestratus' *Life of Luxury*. We cannot: no complete comedies survive from the 'middle comedy' period, none in fact between Aristophanes' *Peace* and Menander's *Bad-Tempered Man*, a period in which great changes took place in the function and nature of Athenian comedy. Most of the readable fragments that survive do so because Athenaeus selected them for their food interest or for what they have to say of hosts, guests and cooks. There are not enough to allow the reconstruction of whole comedies. Yet the surprising thing is that there are so many fragments, from so many plays (and even so, Athenaeus did not quote them all – there is plenty about food and drink in Aristophanes and Menander that he could have selected and did not). Was food talked of in *every* Athenian comedy? What was the audience's view of this feast of food talk? What indeed was the dramatist's intention?

The enquiry can begin with the last of the three comedy references to cookery books. In Alexis' *Linus* (140 [Athenaeus 164b]) the youngster Heracles was encouraged to reveal his subconscious nature by choosing a book from Linus' library. He chose:

> '*Cookery*, the label says.'
> 'You're a wise man, clearly, with so many other books here, to take up the craft of Simus.'
> 'Who's Simus?'
> 'A very clever person. He's into tragedy now: among the performers, so his employers think, he's quite the best cook; among the cooks, as a performer....'[24]

Heracles' character in comedy and satyr play is all too well known: he was a byword for unregenerate, indiscriminate gluttony.[25] Can that be, at the same time, the character that an ancient audience would give to anyone who picked up a cookery book?

The cooks of middle and new comedy are characterised – to judge from their longer speeches and from the reactions to these – as imperious, ready to pontificate on all aspects of diet, tiresomely verbose, ridiculously grandiose in their claims for their craft.[26] Their interlocutors are evidently sometimes employers, sometimes slaves. Practically all of them eventually react to the barrage of professional boasting with an impatient and some-times violently rude interruption, though this follows an implausibly long and patient silence while the cook's monologue pursues its course. An extreme example of both the long patient silence and the eventual rudeness is in a fragment from Anaxandrides (42 [Athenaeus 131d]) which most readers must wish had been far shorter. Indeed, in these snatches of lost comedies, presumed employers can be distinguished from presumed slaves by the more brusque and authoritative way in which the former put an end to the gastronomic lecture.

On both sides of the dialogue these are stereotyped positions: the cook had to lecture, the hearer had to become impatient. Even Menander, rather less inclined to stereotypes than his competitors, allowed slave to express impatience with cook in the *Bad-Tempered Man* (546–51). But we have to suppose that the stereotypes did not conflict too strongly with the common assumptions of the audience. It is telling that one of the very few such exchanges in which no impatience is expressed, no outrageous claims are made, and the interlocutor takes more interest in the gastronomic details than the cook does, is the one written by the gourmet Lynceus (1

[Athenaeus 131f]): in this the knowledgeable interlocutor is to be a guest at the planned dinner. To judge from the careful way in which the characters are identified at the outset, this is the opening scene:

'Now, cook, your patron and my host is a Rhodian: I his guest am Perinthian. Neither of us likes Attic dinners. There is a sort of foreign unpleasantness about them. They serve you a big dish with five little dishes on it: one with garlic, one with two sea urchins, one with a sweet bird-pastry, one with ten shellfish, one with a bit of sturgeon. While I eat this, he's finished that; while he's still on that, I've finished this. I want some of this and some of that, my dear fellow, but I want what can't be had – So what have you got? Oysters?'
'Lots.'
'Then serve them on a dish by itself, a big one. Have you sea urchins?'
'That can be another dish. I bought it myself: eight obols' worth.'
'Then it is the only side-dish you need serve. So everyone will have the same, not one thing for me and another for him.'

The dilettante author (perhaps of only one play, of which no other fragment survives)[27] was in a minority: generally the audience was expected to be on the side of the interruptors, and to agree with them that recipes and dietary rules were to be made fun of.

Lynceus' interlocutor is unusual in his interest in the detailed arrangements for a meal. An enthusiasm for food could be shown by comedy characters other than cooks, but they are not characters with whom spectators would willingly identify: Lynceus' anonymous guest, and Alexis' young Heracles, are special cases of the generalised 'greedy uninvited guest' and 'hungry hanger-on or client'.[28] Aspects of these personalities can be identified in the oldest of comedies and mimes. ' "Not fire, not iron nor bronze prevents them getting to their dinner", like the flatterers of Callias satirised in the play!' (Plutarch, *Moralia* 778d): the play in this case being Eupolis' *Flatterers* (175) of 421 BC.

Sometimes they were fictional; sometimes they satirised real persons, such as a much-ridiculed late fourth-century figure, Chaerephon: 'I invite Ares and Victory to guide my path, I invite Chaerephon – he'll come even if I don't invite him' (Apollodorus of Carystus 31 [Athenaeus 243e]). Athenaeus gives plenty of examples of sniping at such figures. Ridiculed for subservience, for fawning praise, for unscrupulous pursuit of the necessities of life in the households and at the tables of the rich, the hangers-on in particular invited the spite and scorn of their companions and, surely, of the audience.[29]

They developed, almost insensibly, into the 'parasite' so widely known from Roman imitations and modern academic studies of Greek comedy. The stock character of the parasite was said by Carystius to have been created by the comedy author Alexis, and he was probably thinking of the play *Parásitos*, of about 350 BC, as argued by Arnott. Whether or not it can meaningfully be said that he created it, it is clear from very numerous excerpts made by Athenaeus that Alexis contributed greatly to the development of the stereotype.[30]

Ignoring such later elaborations and conflations, more and more owed to the stylisation of later new comedy and less and less to everyday life, it must be admitted that those who wrote enthusiastically about dinners (Philoxenus in the fourth century, Hippolochus in the third) fitted the early 'hungry hanger-on' stereotype pretty well. They praised their hosts, attempted to taste everything, ate to repletion or beyond. It is not after all so surprising that the greedy Chaerephon was not only gourmet but also author. Yes, the Alexandrian Library's *Subject Index* recorded, under 'Miscellanea', 'Authors of *Dinners*. Chaerephon, *To Cyrebion*, incipit: "Since you have often asked." 375 lines.'[31]

## THE GEOGRAPHY OF FOURTH-CENTURY GASTRONOMY

It is said that Xerxes, fleeing from Greece, left his impedimenta behind with Mardonius [whose camp the Greeks then captured]. When Pausanias [King of Sparta] saw Mardonius' tent decorated with gold and silver and embroidered drapes, he ordered the bakers and cooks to prepare dinner as if for Mardonius. They did as they were told. Then Pausanias, looking at the finely-draped gold and silver couches and gold and silver tables and the grandiose layout of the dinner, and amazed by the good things before him, ordered his own servants, for a joke, to prepare a Spartan dinner. There was a big gap between the two. Pausanias, laughing, sent for the Greek generals. When they arrived, he said, pointing to the one dinner and then to the other: 'Greeks, I have called you in to show you the foolishness of the Mede who, living in such luxury as *that*, came to rob us of such poverty as *this*.'

(Herodotus, *Histories* 9.82.1–3)

In the poverty that was Greece, within two hundred years of Xerxes' invasion, a gastronomic culture of startling complexity had developed. One of its chief features was a tradition of localised food and wine quality. It is not surprising that, as Greece became aware of its foods, local specialisation, local distinctions and excellences should have come to the forefront of the collective gastronomic consciousness. Indeed, there was a tradition of local rivalry that went beyond gastronomy: mention of Archestratus' work reminded Athenaeus [278e] of the Delphic oracle, 'Thessalian horses, Spartan women, the men who drink the water of fair Arethusa. . . .'[32] Geographically, Greece is a collection of micro-climates, in each of which a different selection of plants, animals and fish could be expected to flourish.

Politically, too, the country was remarkably fragmented. The fact that gastronomy emerged here, and at this time, helps to explain the route that has eventually been followed to such modern developments as *appellations contrôlées*.

To us, because of the source materials at our disposal, and to the classical Athenians for more obvious reasons, Athens was the centre of Greece. To citizens of other states this was not necessarily so at all, and, though we can reconstruct all too little of them, each will have had its own preferences both among its own products and among foods and wines that it imported from elsewhere. Fortunately, the Athenian bias, though strong, is not overwhelming. Aristotle and Theophrastus, in their studies of animals and plants, were alive to local variation, and some of their information came from food producers of various kinds: farmers, fishermen, bird-catchers, huntsmen, *rizotómoi* ('root-cutters', herbalists). And we have the fragments of Archestratus, surveyed on pp. 116–21, a Sicilian with an apparently insatiable interest in the food on Aegean markets.

We will conclude this chapter with a brief geography of Aegean gastronomy, based on fourth-century sources, but looking forward on occasion to Hellenistic and Roman times.[33]

Greeks of the Peloponnese certainly had their own favourite foods and wines. They wrote little that survives, however. The evidence that comes to us from outside the peninsula is weak. We know that Arcadia was famous for a doubtful gastronomic distinction, its staple diet of acorns.[34] Otherwise there is little more than the following list, which classes itself among the comic menus and may be a satirical feast for some temporary political alliance: 'A cook from Elis, a jug from Argos, Phliasian wine, bedspreads from Corinth, fish of Sicyon, flute girls of Aegium, Sicilian cheese, perfume from Athens, Boeotian eels' (Antiphanes 233 [*Epitome* 27d]). There certainly were vines at Phlius in later classical times, as there are now, for these are the vineyards of Nemea. The conger eels of Sicyon earned praise from others too.[35] But – to take Archestratus' work as an example – out of sixty-eight place-names, between Sicily and the northern Black Sea, that occur in the known fragments, only two are in the Peloponnese. Gastronomically speaking, to judge from surviving literature, the Peloponnese had no honoured place in the classical world. Not only the Arcadians, but even the cosmopolitan Corinthians had no gastronomic reputation. Although it was the mother city of Syracuse, Corinth is never mentioned in the fragments of Archestratus. The food market at Corinth in the fourth century was said by Athenians, perhaps inconsistently, to be a place where natives looked for expensive foreign wine in preference to their own, yet where lavish spending attracted investigation and punishment. Of the remainder of the Peloponnese little can be learnt. Tegea had its bread baked under ashes, Elis its truffles, Arcadia its oregano, Cleonae and Corinth their radishes.[36]

*Figure 24* Fruit as a punning coin type. Hellenistic bronze coin of Side in Pamphylia: obverse, head of Athena; reverse, pomegranate (*síde*). *Source*: Spink & Co

Significantly, when we come to Sparta, there is a certain contradiction in the evidence. Sparta attracted all the worst anecdotes for bad food and uncomfortable hospitality. The 'black broth' was legendary. 'Naturally Spartans are the bravest men in the world. Anyone in his senses would rather die ten thousand times than take his share of such a sorry diet', a Sybarite was supposed to have said (Athenaeus 138d). Their curious dining customs never failed to astonish other Greeks: 'Is it true, as it is said, that all comers are well feasted at their *kopís*, and that in their public-houses sausages hang from nails for the old men to snap at with their teeth?' (Cratinus 175 [Athenaeus 138e]).[37] Yet Sparta had its hereditary cooks,[38] and there is evidence, not directly gastronomic and not tainted by common-places, that there was good produce for them to work with – evidence from the works on gardening. From these we know that varieties of lettuce, of cucumber, of apples and of figs were all named after Laconia[39] – and we cannot adduce as many as four such examples from any other Greek city. It is in the abstract not surprising that a district we believe to have provided good farmland, and to have been managed as such for the benefit of a small number of landowners, should be the apparent source of several fine varieties of crops (it is necessary to say 'apparent source' because names can be deceptive and we know nothing of the real history of the varieties). Besides this, the wine of Sparta had had something to be said for it in archaic times; yet in the fourth century all that can be found is a mention, no doubt ironic, of Spartan vinegar.[40]

North from Corinth we find praised the apples (or perhaps rather pomegranates) of Side and the figs of Megara. The northern Saronic gulf, from Megara by Eleusis and Piraeus to Phalerum, sheltered by Aegina, had several fish specialities, most notably the small fry of which Chrysippus of Soli [Athenaeus 285d] observed that the best anchovy fry were caught at Athens but were not prized by the Athenians themselves. Aristotle (*Study of Animals* 569b10–14) specifies the best sources for anchovy fry as Salamis, Marathon and near the Themistokleion. Athens was also famous for its oven-baked bread and cakes, often soaked in Attic honey, and this honey no doubt retained the aroma of the thyme of Mount Hymettus. Good figs came from Aegilia in Attica.[41]

126

Boeotia's pride, if Athenian sources are to be trusted, was the eels of Lake Copais.[42] There were Boeotian varieties of radish and cucumber and Boeotian barley was not to be despised. Tanagra, like nearby Chalcis in Boeotia, was the origin of a breed of domestic fowl. Anthedon, on the Boeotian coast, had 'good wine and good food', especially hake. Wheat porridge and beef characterised the rich farmland of Thessaly. The gourds of the promontory of Magnesia were praised, as was its wine. There was more wine nearby: for just off this coast lay Sciathos and Peparethos.[43] Calydon, in north-west Greece, and Ambracia to Calydon's north, had fish specialities; among what are known to us as the Ionian islands, the wine of Leucas was beginning to be sought after.[44]

The Aegean islands were noted for fish and also for horticultural specialities. Euboea, the largest, was evidently the source of pears, apples and chestnuts on the Athenian market ('Euboean nuts' was indeed one common name for sweet chestnuts). There was a Chalcidic fig variety, grown in Italy in republican times. Chalcis, Eretria and Carystus, three cities of Euboea, were each praised by Archestratus for their fish, as were Delos and Tenos. Scyros produced the finest goat's milk, so Pindar had said. Naxian almonds, Naxian wine and Parian and Cimolian figs appear to have had a reputation.[45] The principal cultivated variety of quince was named after Cydonia, on the north coast of Crete, or so it was universally thought, and there was a Cretan onion too.[46] Cretan cheese and wine, and the fine cheese of Cythnos, will be mentioned in Chapters 6 and 9. Crete would become the most important producer of medicinal herbs in the Roman Empire.[47]

We move to the north coast of the Aegean. Archestratus knew of fish specialities at three towns on the Thermaic gulf: the squid of Dium, the maigre of Pella and the bluefish of Olynthus. Mende, in southern Chalcidice, produced wine that was widely noticed and praised; there was wine from Scione and Torone too, and Torone offered a species of shark that Archestratus liked. Near here were two freshwater sources of fish. The bass or mullet of Lake Bolbe were subject to an 'annual sacrifice, annual catch' by the people of the Olynthus district, who thus supplied themselves with salt fish for the year. The eels of the River Strymon were salted.[48]

We have already discussed the fame of Thasian wine. The big island of Thasos was also noted for its red mullet, rascasse and octopus, for its barley, its nuts and for a variety of radish known as Leiothasian or Thracian.[49] A variety of onion was named after Samothrace; Tenedos was a source of oregano. Along the Thracian coast, north and east of Thasos, a sequence of Greek cities boasted fine wine and fine fish: Abdera with its grey mullet and cuttlefish, Maronea with cuttlefish, Acanthus, Aenus with their mussels and *hyes*.[50]

It was seafood that came to the rest of Greece from the Hellespont, 'mackerel and all salt fish' (Hermippus 63 [*Epitome* 27e]). The oysters of

Abydos and the lobsters of the Hellespont were good; so were the truffles. Byzantium was 'a port of call, its people spending their time at the market and the harbour; they were lecherous and habituated to drinking in taverns' (Theopompus 115F62 [Athenaeus 526d]). It derived considerable profit from its unassailable trading position and was well known for a range of seafood: tunny, bonito, swordfish, parrot wrasse. Chalcedon, just across the Bosporus, could boast of sea-squirts and horn-shells. Byzantium was possibly even more renowned than it deserved: it was reputedly the source of foods that came to the Aegean from the further reaches of the Black Sea.[51]

Finally we deal with the eastern shores of the Aegean and the large islands off this coast. We shall see something of the later reputation of the wines and cheeses of north-western Anatolia in Chapter 6. Lesbos was famous not for its wine alone but also for the saupe of Mytilene, the scallops of Mytilene and Methymna, the truffles of Mytilene and the fine barley of Eresus, 'whiter than airborne snow. If the gods eat pearl barley, this is where Hermes goes shopping for it' (Archestratus 4 [Athenaeus 111f]), an assertion neatly matched by the coins of Eresus that carry a head of Hermes and an ear of barley.[52] Good cucumbers came from Smyrna – and, later, excellent sea-squirts. Inland from here was Lydia and its capital Sardis, a place of some gastronomic importance. Sardis was the source of a variety of onion – the whitest – and an exporter of dried figs, which in ancient times came threaded on strings. Sardis was also a source of thyme and one of the entrepôts for sweet chestnuts, sometimes called 'Sardian nuts'. Finally, Lydia was said to be the origin of those tasty sauces, *karyke* and *kándaulos*, 'lascivious comestibles' in Menander's phrase (see p. 107); and was presumably a place for good bread, since Archestratus recommended his reader to acquire a Lydian baker.[53]

Chios was another major wine producer, was apparently the origin of a school or tradition of cooks and was later a source of fine snails. Chios would also gain a reputation, which it still holds, as source of the best mastic, and a variety of figs was traced to the island. Across the straits from Chios were the mainland cities of Teos and Erythrae, both praised for red mullet, and Erythrae in addition for the loaves from her clay ovens. Archestratus has plenty to say of the seafood of Ephesus; its mussels are recommended by the dietetic writer Diphilus of Siphnos.[54]

The tunny of Samos, a crustacean (*chambre*) of Parium and four fish to be found at Miletus are also recommended. Miletus was apparently known for its cress and its chickpeas. Around the promontory from Miletus, the harbour of Teichioussa, near the well-known shrine of Didyma, offered red mullet; prawns were to be found, among other produce, at the fish-market of Iasus. Archestratus also recommended octopus from Caria. Astypalaea was later proud of its snails. Icaros, and later Cos and Cnidos, were known for their wine; a kind of onion came from Cnidos; Cos and

*Figure 25* The *agorá* at Ephesus. *Photo*: Professor R. B. Barlow

Calydna would produce fine honey. And it is not irrelevant to gastronomy to note that marjoram and quince perfumes were once made on Cos and a saffron perfume on Rhodes.[55] Rhodes was an important island for seafood and an exporter of raisins and dried figs. In the early Hellenistic period Rhodian wine was becoming better known; it was one of the two that Aristotle talked of on his deathbed, according to later legend.[56] The dried fruit of Rhodes probably came partly from the Carian coast opposite, an important source of dried figs (*Caricae*) in Roman times.

The local gastronomy of fifth- and fourth-century Greece was highly developed: yet it was parochial. From outside the region little was looked for except the staple wheat (from the Black Sea coast, from North Africa and from Phoenicia) and some valued flavourings. In Chapters 7 and 8 we shall see how this older Greek gastronomy became a part of that of the Hellenistic and Roman Mediterranean.

# Part III

# FOOD AND GASTRONOMY OF THE POST-CLASSICAL AEGEAN

# 6

# LEMONS OF THE HESPERIDES
## New foods of Hellenistic and Roman times

From the Mediterranean world of the first two centuries AD several detailed contemporary surveys of foodstuffs survive. One is Galen's *On the Properties of Foods*. A second is the *Materia Medica* of Dioscorides of Anazarba, which discusses the pharmacological properties of many natural and artificial substances, including foods. The third is Pliny's *Natural History*, which among its author's many other concerns does include a lengthy survey of the plants that provided food for the Romans of the Empire. A fourth, less systematic than these, is Athenaeus' *Deipnosophists*, whose principal concern is the food of earlier Greece. From these and from many other sources the present chapter sets out a history of the introduction of new foods and flavours to the Greek menu over the six centuries from 300 BC to AD 300.

In spite of the foregoing list, no work has survived to which the topic addressed here is central; though Pliny was interested in innovations and inventions, and Athenaeus did discuss the novelty of some foodstuffs in the *Deipnosophists*. Even the promising *Periplus of the Erythraean Sea*, an Indian Ocean Pilot of the first century AD, is far more relevant to the imports of Egypt and Rome than to those of Greece. Asides and incidental details make up most of the evidence: but there are enough of these to identify the significant new foodstuffs and to make it clear how they fitted into, and altered, the pattern.

## THE GROWTH OF THE FOOD TRADE

As a preliminary something needs to be said about the routes by which foods passed from producer to user, routes by which new foodstuffs would have to find their way. Greece is an unusual place: its main trade routes are maritime and its typical markets have therefore been not the periodic markets of much of the rest of the world – periodic markets for which there is good evidence from Roman Italy – but irregular, opportunistic harbour markets.[1]

Ever since the obsidian of Melos began to find its way to distant users,

*Figure 26* Fruit and vegetables in the modern covered market at Bodrum (Halicarnassus). Recently developed varieties, such as cauliflower, and exotics such as bananas, mingle with species that have been known in the Aegean for millennia. *Photo*: Professor R. B. Barlow

and certainly all through later prehistoric times, there was some transport of valuable products within the Aegean area. From the second millennium BC ruined storerooms and shipwrecked cargoes have been found which demonstrate that, among foodstuffs, at least wine and olive oil were so transported. Already at that time, and more fully in the first millennium BC, the Aegean was part of a wider, pan-Mediterranean network of trading links. Here it must be made clear that, according to the evidence available, merchants tended not to specialise, and the title of this section may mislead: 'There was no food trade, but trade in food was a large proportion of total trade.'[2]

Admittedly no mention of food or drink in the Homeric epics implies that it customarily travelled further than from country to neighbouring town, with the single exception of the shipload of supplies brought by a trader for the army at Troy, from which 'the long-haired Achaeans got wine, some in exchange for bronze, some for fiery iron, some for hides, some for whole cows, some for slaves' (*Iliad* 7.472–5). And that one incident[3] can hardly serve on its own as a sign of the regularity of trade in food and wine: how often in the prehistoric Aegean were armies to be found that were deprived of supplies from home and large enough to buy a cargo of wine? But it suggests that one of the main channels of trade in historical Greece, from the mid-first millennium BC to the present day, already existed: the harbour market, wholesale and retail, on the beach or quayside, activated not by a timetable (since sea travel is subject to unpredictable delays) but by the arrival of the fishing boats or of a trading ship. The very irregularity of such markets, requiring that something be available

134

to exchange for goods suddenly arrived in large quantities, will have contributed to the development of coinage, precisely in this region, a hundred years or more after the *Iliad* was composed.

In the smaller island and coastal towns, harbour markets may have been almost the only route by which foodstuffs passed in and out to reach buyers beyond the place where they were produced. But inland towns and towns with a hinterland attracted produce to their central market-places daily; and the markets of large towns, once they outgrew self-sufficiency, exerted a powerful economic influence on their neighbours to turn to specialised cash crops. Specialisation is enjoined, in any case, as we have seen (pp. 124–9), by the varied terrain and limited productivity of most parts of Greece.

In general, inhabitants of the Aegean islands and shores were no doubt responsible for nearly all the maritime trade in these semi-enclosed waters, though certainly the trade involved Phoenicians in archaic times, for they had taken to 'long voyages' (Herodotus, *Histories* 1.1), and Italians later. Greeks' interest tended to wane at the northern and eastern shores of the Aegean: at any rate Greeks *wrote* practically nothing about the land trade routes of western Anatolia and the Balkans. Obscure though they seem, these routes were all-important, acting as feeders to the markets of the mostly Greek coastal towns and so to the seaborne trade of the Aegean. The goods that passed along them, to or from the Aegean coasts, apparently moved under other auspices, or at least beyond the purview of Greek authors.[4]

Whatever the eventual predominance of local seamen, the harbour markets could as well be activated by a non-Greek as by a Greek vessel; the first legendary abduction in Herodotus' *Histories* occurs on the arrival of a Phoenician ship at Argos:

> On the fifth or sixth day after they had arrived, when they had traded almost everything, the king's daughter and a lot of other women came down to the sea (her name, the Greeks agree on this, was Io daughter of Inachus), and while they were standing by the stern of the ship bargaining for whatever it was they fancied from the wares, the Phoenicians spurred one another to make a rush for them. Most of the women ran away, but some, including Io, were seized.
>
> (Herodotus, *Histories* 1.1.3–4)

Longer voyages, no doubt, and greater investment, led to more carefully selected landfalls and more leisurely markets, especially before the general use of coinage. Herodotus' 'five or six days' seem more realistic than the 'year' that preceded a similar elopement with Phoenicians in a story in the *Odyssey* (15.455)!

By the fifth century BC there was already a ship-bound cheese trade, though we know nothing of its volume. A character in a comedy by Alexis speaks of 'fresh Cythnian cheeses', which were made from sheep's milk; we have seen something of the fame of Sicilian cheese at Athens, where it was already available for dogs to steal from larders at the time of Aristophanes' *Wasps*. Cheese from the Thracian Chersonese was also available at Athens in the fourth century. Semonides had written in iambic verse of the Tromilic goats' milk cheese of Achaea.[5] From various later sources we know of Cretan cheese and of Phrygian, Mysian and Bithynian cheeses, the last a cow's milk cheese.[6] Local honeys, too, began to earn fame: not only that of Hymettus in Attica, but also the honey of Calydna and Cos. The Latin storyteller Apuleius depicts an agent travelling Thessaly, Aetolia and Boeotia to buy cheese and honey.[7]

While local transport of wines, olive oil and other fine produce began to grow, the quantity and variety of imported foodstuffs that reached the Aegean from a distance were, as we have seen, at first very limited. In prehistoric times we know only of sesame; in the archaic period sesame, silphium, sumach, dates and Phoenician wine. Then, by the fifth century, as bulk transport of foods becomes safer and cheaper, wheat from Russia, Libya, Egypt and Phoenicia, salt fish and fish sauce from Russia and Spain, and hazelnuts and walnuts from Anatolia join the growing catalogue. But it is perhaps artificial to exclude consideration of the perfumes that made their own contribution to sacrifice and festivity: most of these came from Asia or Africa (Theophrastus, *Study of Plants* 9.7, *On Odours, passim*). It was the perfume trade, established even in Mycenaean times, that in Hellenistic and Roman times became the vehicle for the import of an increasing number of exotic aromatics now required not only as cosmetics and in religious ceremonies, but also in food.

Restrictions on free trade are known sometimes to have affected food and wine. The Thasians regulated (or attempted to regulate) the buying-up of their own wines and the import of others to the part of the Thracian coast that was under their control:

> Must nor wine, the fruit on the vine shall not be bought before the new moon of Plynteria: an offending buyer shall pay stater for stater. . . . No Thasian vessel shall land foreign wine between Athos and Pacheia, or it shall pay the same penalty as for serving water for wine, and the pilot shall pay the same. . . . [8]
>
> (*IG* XII suppl. 347)

The government of Cyrene attempted, but certainly sometimes failed, to keep a monopoly of the silphium trade: Strabo (*Geography* 17.3.20) mentions 'Charax, which served the Carthaginians as an entrepôt: they brought wine and got in exchange silphium stem and resin, secretly diverted there from the Cyrenaeans'. And we have seen (pp. 101–2) that one of the reasons for the popularity of Lesbian wine at Athens was its tax-free status.[9]

## EASTERN SPICES

The number of spices and aromatics in demand in the Roman Empire was considerable. J. I. Miller, in *The spice trade of the Roman Empire*, counted 'some sixty condiments mentioned by Apicius, [of which] about ten grew [only] outside and fifty within the Empire'.[10] Coriander, poppy-seed and silphium, long significant in Greece, were among the latter. This was only a proportion of the 'spice trade', for many of the products traditionally grouped as spices were not used predominantly for food. The evidence allows us to state impressions rather than to make assertions: the impression, then, is that imported spices were used in Greece and the Aegean to make perfumes and perfumed oils, to make medicines, to make aromatic wines, and, later and less ubiquitously, to flavour food. Three source references may be cited to reinforce this general impression before we move on to individual spices. First comes Theophrastus' reflection (*On Odours* 10): 'One might wonder why exotic and other fragrances improve the taste of wines when, so far from having that effect on foods – whether cooked or uncooked – they invariably ruin them.'[11] The second landmark will be quoted in Chapter 7 (p. 163): it is the late Hellenistic recipe for *myma* by Epaenetus [Athenaeus 662d] which calls for no fewer than thirteen flavourings, though all of them from the Mediterranean shores. The third landmark is the Latin recipe book *Apicius*, dating from the late Empire when we may suppose some homogeneity in dining fashions among the wealthy of the whole Mediterranean world. We do not know how many dined from the recipes of *Apicius* (though we know from its language that it is a book for use, not for display), but those who did so experienced complex mixtures of herbs and spices,[12] including several from beyond the Imperial frontier; many among them would have been considered by Theophrastus to ruin the flavour of food.

Black pepper, *péperi*, was certainly known in Greece for centuries in ritual use and as an ingredient in medicines before we can find any definite evidence that anyone in Greece had tried the practice of adding it to food. As one of Plutarch's speakers said, many older people in his time had not yet developed the taste for it (*Symposium Questions* 8.9).[13] Pepper came to the Roman Empire from the port of Muziris, near Cochin, on the Indian Ocean trading ships: 'They arrive with gold and depart with pepper', wrote a Tamil poet concerning the western traders at this port in Roman times (Tâyan-Kannanâr, *Agam* 149.7–11), and confirmation comes in the note on this coast in the *Periplus of the Erythraean Sea* (56).

The word *péperi* is of Indian origin – cf. Sanskrit *pippali* – but in Indian languages the word denotes long pepper, Piper longum. This spice, rather unfamiliar now, was regularly imported to the classical Mediterranean, where the price of *makropéperi* was double that of black pepper. Adulteration was a problem. The first clear mention of long pepper had come four hundred years before, in an appendix to Theophrastus' *Study of Plants* (9.20.1):

> Pepper is a fruit, and is of two kinds: one round like bitter vetch, with a shell and flesh like bay berries, reddish; the long kind with poppy-like seeds, and this is much stronger than the other. Both are heating; thus, like frankincense, they are antidotes to hemlock.

Later authors distinguish three kinds of pepper, but theirs is a less logical classification than Theophrastus': the third kind, white pepper, is simply black pepper with the shell removed.[14]

We first hear of ginger, *zingíberi*, in a Greek-speaking context when the Roman medical writer Celsus lists ginger as one of the ingredients in King Mithridates' famous poison antidote.[15] This would date the knowledge of ginger – at least among royal pharmacists in Pontus – to the early first century BC. In the following century the Greek pharmacist Dioscorides of Anazarba (*Materia Medica* 2.160), who says something of the ginger trade, hints that the Imperial provinces may not have been rich enough to share the expensive luxuries that were shipped to Rome. Dioscorides also correctly distinguished ginger from pepper:

> Ginger is a separate plant,[16] grown mostly in [Eritrea] and Arabia, where they make much use of it fresh, as we use leeks, boiling it for soup and including it in stews. It is a small tuber, like cyperus, whitish, peppery in flavour and aromatic. Choose roots that are not worm-eaten. Some [producers] pickle it (otherwise it deteriorates) and export it in jars to Italy: it is very nice to eat;[17] it is eaten pickle and all.

As for the geographical origin of ginger, Greek pharmacological authors had traditionally described it as Indian: this was misleading, though it is possible that some supplies of ginger came to the Mediterranean by way of south India. Pliny and Dioscorides of Anazarba, just quoted, were aware that some ginger was grown around the southern Red Sea.[18] None was aware that its original habitat was far to the east of India, the 'Spice Islands' of modern Indonesia.[19]

Pliny, the first classical author to mention cloves, says they were imported 'for their aroma'. Whatever this may or may not mean for the kitchen, by the end of the Roman Empire Greek medical authors knew of several uses for cloves, *karyóphyllon*.

> It belies its name, being rather of the nature of a flower of some tree, woody, black, almost as thick as a finger; reputed aromatic, sour, bitterish, hot and dry in the third degree; excellent in relishes and in other prescriptions.
>
> (Paul of Aegina, *Practice of Medicine* 7.3)

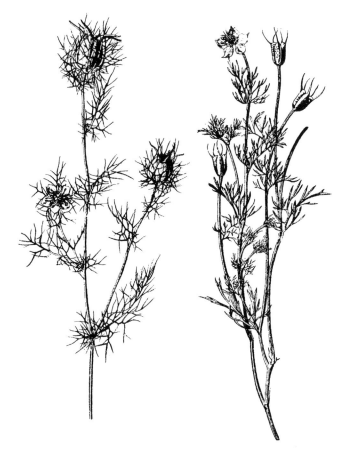

*Figure 27 Melánthion* and *kyminon aithiopikón*: the local substitute, love-in-a-mist, and the Indian spice plant, nigella. *Source*: from G. Hegi's *Illustrierte Flora von Mittel-Europa* (Vienna, 1912)

It is not called for in the recipes of *Apicius* yet was one of the flavourings needed in the kitchen according to the *Outline Apicius* of Vinidarius.[20]

Ajowan, *ámmi* or 'royal cumin', was a culinary ingredient according to Pliny and of medicinal use according to Galen. But it cannot have been really familiar to Pliny or to Dioscorides, because they both say that some thought ajowan identical to nigella while others distinguished the two.[21] Nigella, *kyminon aithiopikón*, was already known to Greeks at the latest in the third century BC: it is one of the older Levantine spices, having been identified from Tutankhamen's tomb, about 1325 BC, and in Akkadian texts.[22] Its European relative, love-in-a-mist, *melánthion*, was available as a substitute, at least in medicinal uses.[23]

Ajowan and nigella are both among the spices that are regularly used in Indian cuisine.

Cinnamon and cassia, *kinnámomon*, *kásia*, *malábathron* and other names, were a group of eastern exotics well known in classical times, and tall stories were told of their origin. But to find evidence of their use in food we must wait longer even than for pepper. Pliny goes into great detail on these spices. Cinnamon was most commonly ingested, in Greek dining, as one of the ingredients of absinthe wine.[24] It was not required in *Apicius* or in the *Outline Apicius* of Vinidarius.

Other aromatics of limited use in sauces and flavoured wines were two species of valerian, *nárdos keltiké*, *nárdos agría*, and Syrian nard, Cymbopogon iwarancusa, *nárdos syriaké*.[25]

While these newer spices were finding a place in the diet, however tenuous, what of the silphium of Cyrenaica? As attractive to Romans as it had long been to Greeks, yet never successfully propagated artificially, silphium was in due course over-exploited. Romans liked to eat the whole root and stem, sliced and preserved in vinegar: Theophrastus (*Study of Plants* 6.3.5) describes the method but appears not to have tasted the delicacy. It was perhaps this Roman demand, more destructive than the tapping of sap, that hastened the plant's extinction. Strabo (*Geography* 17.3.22) suggests an additional reason: 'It came close to dying out when the natives, in the course of some dispute, erupted and destroyed the roots of the plant. They are nomads.' For whatever combination of causes, silphium appears to have died out in the first century AD: 'For many years now it has not been found there . . . the single stem found within living memory was sent to the Emperor Nero' (Pliny, *Natural History* 19.39). Those who believe everything in the all too literary writings of Synesius of Cyrene (*Letters* 106, cf. 134) may, however, accept that a silphium plant still grew in his brother's garden in Cyrenaica around 400 AD.

But a silphium substitute had meanwhile come to notice in Iran, where it had been used as a spice by the soldiers of Alexander's expedition.[26] Earlier authors treated the Libyan and Middle Eastern plants as if they were identical. Thus Dioscorides could say (*Materia Medica* 3.80.1–2) that silphium 'grows in parts of Syria, Armenia and Media and in Libya', adding, however:

> The Cyrenaic, even if one just tastes it, at once arouses a humour throughout the body and has a very healthy aroma, so that it is not noticed on the breath, or only a little; but the Median and Syrian is weaker in power and has a nastier smell.

This silphium substitute was, beyond any doubt, asafoetida, brought to Greece and Rome as it was later brought to China and is now brought to India. In the Indian food trade its name is *hing*. It was 'rather windy' (Galen, *On the Properties of Simples* 8.18.16 [12.123]) and not so powerful, but Romans took to it with enthusiasm. There is a great number of recipes calling for *silfi* and *lasar* in the recipe book *Apicius*; *silpium* [*sic*] and *lasar* are still listed among kitchen requisites in Vinidarius' *Short Apicius*. Yet, though it continued to be in use in early Byzantine times as a medicament, there is no firm evidence that the Greeks of Greece substituted asafoetida for the lost silphium in their own cuisine. It comes, incidentally, from further east than Syria: Dioscorides' assertion to the contrary is explained by its having been a commodity in the trade of the Seleucid kingdom of Syria.[27]

The embattled frontier between Rome and Sassanid Persia will have become an obstacle to the trade in asafoetida, and will at all events have raised its price. To early medieval Europe asafoetida was probably unknown: it is not in Anthimus' late fifth-century *Letter on Diet*. Later still, however, with increased knowledge of Arabic medicine, it was reintroduced to the European pharmacopoeia. Arabic and Indian physicians valued it highly, and the learned Garcia da Orta, in his *Colóquios* (Goa, 1563), correctly identifying Indian *hing* with medieval *assa foetida* and ancient *laserpitium*, has several anecdotes of its medicinal and culinary virtues: 'Asafoetida has the most awful smell in the world, but in the Brahmins' vegetarian dishes it did not smell bad to me', he remarked. Galen may have thought it 'rather windy', but Garcia knew that it had effected a miracle cure:

A Portuguese in Vijayanagar had a very valuable horse which was terribly flatulent, and for that reason the King would not buy it. The Portuguese cured it by giving it *hingu* mixed with flour. The King paid a good price for it when it was healthy, and asked how it had been cured. 'With *hingu*', said the Portuguese. 'Then I am not surprised', said the King: 'what you gave it was the food of the gods; it is what poets call nectar.' The Portuguese said (but he said it in Portuguese and very quietly) that the King might better have called it the food of devils.

Alongside imported spices it is appropriate to deal with another food import from beyond the Roman frontiers: rice. This appears to have been domesticated in very early times in the crescent that links north-east India, inland south-east Asia and south China. Rice, *óryza*, first became known to Greeks after Alexander's expedition, and it was never grown within the Roman Empire. A long-distance import from India was bound to remain expensive; it is not surprising, then, that rice was rather little used in the Hellenistic and Roman world. Chrysippus of Tyana, writing in a Roman milieu, knew of a rice-cake (*oryzítes plakoûs*), though Athenaeus [647e] transmits no recipe for it. Perhaps more often rice was prized for medicinal reasons (as spices were too). Rice pudding for invalids is recommended by Galen as it is by the Byzantine dietician Simeon Seth.[28]

The wider availability of exotic spices, and an apparently increased readiness to use them as food flavourings, may have impelled Greek cooks to try the effects of some local aromatics that had not previously been used in food. The native cuisine of Italy, naturally sometimes a fashion-setter in the Roman world, also exerted an influence. At any rate, to the aromatics dealt with in Chapter 3 we must now add some apparent culinary novelties of local origin: saffron, juniper, lovage and caraway, the last two probably introduced to Greece from the west.

Saffron, *krókos*, may well have been first domesticated in Greece from the wild Crocus cartwrightianus. Pictures on Cretan pottery and frescoes suggest the saffron crocus, and a recently discovered fresco from Akrotiri shows women picking saffron. It was certainly grown in Greece, though in classical times the most aromatic saffron came from Cyrene according to Theophrastus. It was scarcely used in Roman cookery, finding its way into *Apicius* only as an ingredient in *apsinthium Romanum*, 'Roman absinthe wine', and in medicinal salts (1.2, 1.13). Similarly, the only Greek evidence from Imperial times for saffron in the diet is as an ingredient in spiced wine.[29]

Two species of juniper berries, *arkeuthís* and *kédrion*, served as medicines in classical Greece and had perhaps been exported from prehistoric Greece to Egypt for that or culinary purposes: they are found in Egyptian tombs from the fourth millennium onwards although the plant does not grow there. It is far later that a first reference is found in Greek authors to their use in food. They had at least a nefarious place in the classical diet as adulterants of pepper.[30]

Lovage was known to Dioscorides (*Materia Medica* 3.51) as a plant native to Liguria, whence its Greek name *ligystikón*: 'sour and aromatic to the taste ... digestive ... the local people use it instead of pepper, as an ingredient in sauces'. It was widely grown and used in food by others too; a herbal wine was made with it.[31]

Caraway, *karó*, like lovage, was used for flavouring meat; unlike most other herbs and spices, its culinary use was its principal one. Pliny thought, from its name, that it was native to Caria in south-western Anatolia but the fact that Greek authors of pre-Roman date never mention it is against this.[32]

## EXOTIC FRUITS

The conquests of Alexander brought great and lasting changes of perspective to Greece, which was less central now to the trade network that linked its colonies across the Mediterranean and the Black Sea. Instead, the Aegean lands began to be seen as a historical and cultural focus for the new Greek kingdoms of the East.

Meanwhile, on a Mediterranean scale, horticulture received its greatest impetus. Botanical investigations were carried out on Alexander's expedition: some of the results can be seen in the works of Theophrastus, Aristotle's successor. The Greek cultures that spread through the Near East in the wake of Alexander demanded Greek tastes, including the kinds of vegetables and fruits that were known in Greece. The result was experimentation and transplantation of stock in both directions, and this produced both novel varieties and improved methods of growing. Cultivated species now spread not only from east to west but along many paths. It was at this time, probably, that cultivation of the opium poppy spread eastwards as far as Egypt and the Near East. Hellenistic dynasts, such as the Ptolemies of Egypt, were enlightened in their encouragement of these developments. The Carthaginians and Romans also took a semi-official interest in the progress of horticulture and agriculture.[33]

Chapter 3 surveyed fruits and nuts that had become known in Greece before Alexander's time: quite a proportion of them came from northern and western Anatolia. But now new species from further afield, some of them originating in China, all of them long naturalised in the Levant, travel westwards to Italy and Greece. Literary evidence is fitful and sometimes ambiguous, but the species discussed in this section appear to have come to Greece during Hellenistic and Roman times, and all certainly have been grown there ever since.

We begin with citrus fruit. Here there is some dispute among modern authors as to what species were known in the ancient Mediterranean, a dispute that has not yet been resolved by archaeobotany. Much of the early evidence for Greek knowledge of citrus fruit is gathered by Athenaeus. The first clear sign of what must have been the citron, not yet grown in the Mediterranean basin but soon to reach it, is in the *Study of Plants* of Theophrastus (4.4.2 [Athenaeus 83d]):

> Among other produce, the land of Media and Persia has the so-called 'Persian' or 'Median apple'. This tree has a leaf similar to, and nearly the same size as that of the strawberry tree and walnut; thorns like the pear or pyracantha, smooth and very sharp and strong. The apple is not eaten, but it and the leaves of the tree are powerfully scented. If it is put with clothes it keeps moths off; is useful too if one has drunk poison – because taken in wine it turns the stomach and brings the poison up – and to sweeten the mouth – because the inside of the fruit, cooked in broth etc. and squeezed into the mouth and sucked, makes the breath sweet. . . .

The citron, then, a pithy fruit not especially attractive as food, was perhaps on its way westwards in the last centuries BC from a native habitat usually considered to be southern China or Indo-China. In Roman Imperial times it had certainly reached the western half of the Empire.[34] It is not surprising, since he is the first Greek author by some distance to mention the fruit, that in Theophrastus' time its nomenclature had not settled down. Uniquely among Greek authors, he sometimes applies the term 'Persian apple' to the citron. Perhaps he had heard the name, but not the description, of the peach, which was generally called 'Persian apple' by later Greeks, and mistakenly identified the two. The usual early term for citron, used by him and others, was 'Median apple': this name equally suggests a central Asian origin.[35] But by early Imperial times the fruit had a new Greek name, perhaps borrowed from Latin as Athenaeus (84d) suggests. Writing in the second century AD, Galen brings together the synonyms ('no longer called by anyone *mêlon medikón*, but rather *kítrion*': *On the Properties of Simples* 7.12.19 [12.77]) and describes the fruit carefully: 'There are three parts of it, the acid in the middle, the flesh of the fruit around this, and the skin on the outside. The latter is an aromatic, attractive not only for its scent but also for its taste' (*On the Properties of Foods* 2.37.2).

The citron, though now as in Galen's time its rind is used for flavouring, is otherwise of little value as food. It is, however, good-looking. Once it had become familiar in Greece as an imported exotic fruit, it asked to be identified with the 'apples of the Hesperides'. A passage in the *African Collections* of Juba, cited by Athenaeus [83b] makes precisely this point. Incidentally, it is the earliest certain reference to the citron in Greek literature after Theophrastus, and the earliest use of the name *kítrion*.[36]

More important would be the arrival of the lemon, a fruit that bears a strong resemblance to the citron but is smaller, more regular in shape, and much more juicy. It may be that we can date its appearance rather closely thanks to the observation by Athenaeus' speaker [84a], 'down to our grandfathers' time nobody ate it', an assertion which can be linked to that in Plutarch's *Symposium Questions* (8.9): 'We know that many elderly people have not learnt to enjoy the taste of watermelon, *kítrion* or pepper.' This edible *kítrion* (for the Greeks then, like the Germans now, did not distinguish the two species by name) was surely the lemon. The very earliest evidence for its presence in the Mediterranean comes from Pompeii: a lemon tree (and it does seem to be really that, and not a citron tree) is painted on a bedroom wall at the so-called 'house of the fruit orchard'. Some additional iconographical evidence from Italy in the late first and second centuries AD is available. But while the citron was widely familiar in the first to third centuries AD, the lemon, if we are right to recognise it here, remained for some time relatively little known. The lemon, like the citron, must have reached the Mediterranean from southern China by way of the Near East.[37]

The first Greek author who certainly mentions peaches is Diphilus of Siphnos. Athenaeus [82e] also attributes a remark on them to Theophrastus' *Study of Plants*, though his quotation is not to be found in the text of that work: if not misattributed, it may have come from some supplementary

Theophrastean notes on plants, now lost.[38] The peach appears to have been known in Greece, therefore, by the third century BC; indeed it seems possible that a pair of fourth-century comedy fragments quoted by Athenaeus [84a–c], thought by him to have to do with citrons, were really about peaches. They were at first called 'Persian apple'; 'they are now always called *persiké*, leaving out the "apple" '. Indeed, although a kind of peach was cultivated in China from a very ancient period, the familiar modern type, 'the golden peaches of Samarkand', came to China too from central Asia in historical times. In the Roman Empire peaches were only eaten fresh: 'some fruits will not take drying', said Galen, 'as mulberries, watermelons, muskmelons, peaches and such like' (*On Good and Bad Juices* 5 [6.785]). By the first century AD peaches were being planted in Italy; the Pompeiian still life that includes a half-eaten peach is well known.[39]

'Armenian apple', *mêlon armeniakón*, was the early name of the closely related apricot, which was known to both Romans and Greeks by the first century AD. Athenaeus, as it happens, does not mention this fruit. Apricots, like peaches, are well known in China and were domesticated there or in central Asia. They had been grown in Mesopotamia for many centuries before their introduction westwards. The original Greek name suggests that, like so many earlier fruits, they spread to Greece not from the Levant but from Transcaucasia. But by Galen's time, 'the old name of this fruit is not used. Everyone calls the fruit and the tree *prekókkion*' (*On the Properties of Simples* 7.12.18 [12.76]). This new name is through Arabic the ancestor of modern western European names for the apricot – a hint that its cultivation in the western half of the Mediterranean may not have continued through early medieval times.[40]

The jujube grows wild in central Asia and was presumably brought into cultivation there. The briefer history of its cultivation in Europe, under the name *ziziphus*, is given in Pliny's remark that Sextus Papinius brought the tree to Rome from Syria in Augustus' time.[41] The Romans thought higher of this fruit than did contemporary Greeks: but it may have remained unfamiliar in the Aegean. A Byzantine author, Simeon Seth (*On the Properties of Foods* 40), suggests this with his statement that 'the best *zínzipha* are the big ones from Edessa in Syria'. Perhaps, when Galen talks of *zízyphos* he means not this Zizyphus jujuba that Romans found in Syria but its close relatives, Z. spina-Christi and Z. lotus: for, from the perspective of his native Pergamum, he lists it among wild fruits like the cornel, arbutus and terebinth, and Christ's thorn was native to inland Anatolia. It was gathered in Egypt from pre-dynastic times and was known by report to very early Greeks if it was indeed the food of Odysseus' *lotós*-eaters.[42] It is certainly sometimes called *lotós* – also the name of several quite different plants in classical Greek – and sometimes *palíouros*, which was more properly the name of the hackberry.

More important in Greek everyday life than these berries has been the pistachio, *pistákion*. Closely related trees, terebinth and lentisk, are native to the eastern Mediterranean. The classical Persians were known to themselves and to others as 'terebinth-eaters'. But the true pistachio, native to central Asia, is first heard of in Greek literature when reported to Theophrastus as a tree, as yet unnamed, grown in north India, its branches and leaves resembling the terebinth but with a nut like an almond. It is also the edible 'terebinth' mentioned by Strabo. Writing in Augustus' time, Strabo had never travelled in central Asia and, like Theophrastus, relied on reports from Alexander's expedition: in this case specifically on Aristobulus.[43]

The poet Nicander, a century after Theophrastus and Aristobulus, refers to the pistachio in phraseology which is as close to Theophrastus' as any reader of Nicander could reasonably expect, and is the first source to name it: 'all the pistachios that grow like almonds on their branches beside the Indian flood of the resounding Choaspes' (*Theriaca* 890–1).[44] But the scientist Poseidonius, not much later than Nicander and a more serious informant, gave a detailed description and knew that the pistachio was grown in Arabia and Syria as well as further east. According to Pliny the pistachio tree was first brought to Italy by Vitellius, father of the emperor, who served in the Levant between AD 35 and 39. The pistachio is propagated by grafting. As it spread in Mediterranean lands it may well have been grafted most often on to already thriving terebinth trees, as it still is in Turkey.[45] This would explain why, although no other ancient authors make the identification, the Quintilii [Athenaeus 649e], authors of a farming manual, treated terebinth and pistachio as varieties of a single 'species'.

Carobs, *keratonía*, grew on the east coast of the Aegean, and on Rhodes, already by Theophrastus' time. Galen remarked on their constipating effect. They had long been common in the Near East: carobs were already food for the poor of Babylon around 1000 BC.[46]

With carob goes fenugreek,[47] strange though that may seem to modern cooks, who know carob as a chocolate substitute and fenugreek as an aromatic herb. This was another pulse that spread westwards in late classical times. Fenugreek had been domesticated by the fourth millennium in the Near East and in Egypt. It is mentioned in Greek literature of the fourth century BC onwards, though until Imperial times there is no clear indication from Greek sources that it was used for food. It had served earlier as a perfume, according to Pliny. It is Galen who assures us explicitly that the three Greek words *télis*, *boúkeras* and *aigókeras* are synonyms, all meaning 'fenugreek'.[48]

One further exotic addition to the Greek diet must be dealt with, though its importance was small. In Chapter 3 we noticed the introduction of the domestic fowl to Greece, apparently in the seventh century BC. Another Indian bird of more exotic appearance, the peafowl, *tahôs*, was already known to the Minoans to judge from iconography, but the peafowl has always remained far rarer and costlier, for it is not a prolific layer of eggs (Aristotle fragment 351 [Athenaeus 397b]). It was perhaps reintroduced to Greece in the fifth century BC, but as an ornamental denizen of gardens and a source of feathers, not as a food. The earliest mention of peafowl in literature is by Aristophanes; at the date of his *Birds* there were peacocks in Athens, exhibited as a rarity and seen by visitors from distant cities. By the fourth century BC there was a menagerie of peafowl at the Temple of Hera on Samos, so notable that peacocks appeared on Samian oins and a later antiquarian suggested Samos was the native island of the bird. An increasing fashion for keeping these birds is implied – with exaggeration – in a play by Antiphanes (203 [Athenaeus 654e]): 'Well, if someone imported a pair of peafowl it was a rare thing, but now they are commoner than quail.' Peahens' eggs were recommended as good food by cooks and dieticians who did not have to worry about the cost.[49]

## DEVELOPMENTS IN WINE

Wine remained a matter of pressing interest. Being more portable, and more durable in transport, than most foods, wine was the one Greek product that became a significant import to Italy at the time of the Roman conquest of Greece – along with such objects of trade as cooks and tutors. But of the appellations that had been well known to Aegean gourmets earlier, only Chian won a place on the Roman shopping list: it was joined by newcomers, Coan and Cnidian. These Greek vintages retained their prestige in Rome for a surprisingly long time. It would seem that fashion must have triumphed over taste, considering the violent treatment to which Greek wines were subjected to stabilise them for a long voyage: 'TO STABILISE WINE FOR EXPORT BY SEA. Strain through linen to remove solids, boil down to half, pour Attic honey into the bottom of the amphora before adding the wine: it then lasts a long time' (Diophanes [*Geoponica* 7.17]). But we should not forget that still-fashionable wines such as sherry, port and Madeira derive their style partly from the treatment they received during their sea journeys and in preparation for it. ('East Indian Madeira' was once sought after: its distinguishing feature was that it had travelled by sailing ship to Indonesia and back.)

Pliny, proud though he was of Italian produce, was not bold enough to compare Greek with Italian wines directly. His *Natural History* (14.59–72) contains a survey of Italian, Spanish and Gallic wines; the following passage (14.73–6) deals separately with *vina transmarina*, 'overseas wines', those of Greece, Anatolia, Egypt and the Levant. It is only in the fifth century AD that an appellation of Italy – a *recioto* of Verona, or something very like it – is at last stated by an Italian writer to be unequivocally better than any Greek wine (Cassiodorus, *Variae* 12.4). Yet clear signs of the decay of Greek wines on the market had come earlier. Diocletian's *Price Edict* (2.1–7) puts a price only on the major Italian vintages and on one Egyptian, ignoring all other appellations: a general designation of 'vin de pays' remains to class the wines of the rest of the Empire.[50]

In Greece itself, while Coan and Cnidian competed with the local wines of each district, there was perhaps not enough prosperity to sustain much of a long-distance trade. The Euboean peasants of Dio Chrysostom's oration (7.46, 76) are pictured making their own, and buying from the nearest town what extra was needed for a wedding feast. Lucius, a fictional visitor to Thessaly, is treated to good old wine, but wine not of any origin worth naming (*Lucius or the Ass* 2–3). A fictional letter by Alciphron (4.13), recounting a picnic somewhere near Athens – and claiming a fourth-century BC setting – remarks: 'The wine wasn't local, it was Italian, the kind you said you bought in small jars at Eleusis, very smooth.' This is the earliest hint in literature that Italian wines could be bought in Greece. Meanwhile, a tendency in local produce towards imitation and nostalgia becomes visible. Coan, one of the wines in whose manufacture brine was added to the must, was widely imitated: Cato (*On Agriculture* 112–13) had given a recipe in the second century BC. As has happened at other times and in other places, producers who could claim a link with some famous early name were not above appropriating it to make their produce saleable. A Roman general was persuaded that the wine he drank near Ismarus was as strong as Maron's had been in Odysseus' tale (Pliny, *Natural History* 14.54) and Pliny's report of the incident is unsceptical. Dioscorides and others give widely differing opinions of the places where Pramnian wine could be found.[51] Grape varieties were transplanted in both directions: Chian to Italy, so that 'Chian' at Roman banquets could be *maris expers*, 'innocent of the sea' (Horace, *Satires* 2.8.15), in at least two senses; Aminean, originally Sicilian or Italian, was transplanted to Bithynia.[52]

We may finally survey the major Hellenistic and Imperial wines of Greece and the Aegean through lists of them in sources of successively later date.

A certain Apollodorus, whose advice to a Ptolemy on the choice of wine is cited in Pliny's *Natural History* (14.76), recommended Oretic, Oeneate, Leucadian, Ambraciot and – best of all – Peparethan, though the last, he added, was ready to drink only after six years. Except for Peparethan and Leucadian, this list has nothing to do with any earlier or later ones, and even those two do not appear to have been widely praised.

Pliny's own survey (14.73–6) has already been mentioned. He begins by noting the historic fame of Thasian, Chian and then Lesbian. Among Chian wines, Ariusian had the highest reputation. In his own time Clazomenean, 'now with less sea water added', was most popular; Tmolite was a sweet wine to mix with others that were dry. Also highly regarded was the *protropum* of Cnidos: 'this is the name that some give to the must that runs out of its own accord before the grapes are pressed' (ibid. 14.85). Ephesian and Catacecaumenite are also mentioned from western Anatolia, the latter coming from the volcanic district near Sardis. Lesbian had a natural tang of the sea: Lesbian, Myconian and Sicyonian are the wines that Pliny selects from the Greek mainland and Aegean islands. In a discussion of wines from semi-dried grapes (ibid. 14.80–5) he seems to class Cretan highest:

> Some make this from any sweet, early-ripening, white grapes, drying [bunches] in the sun till little over half their weight remains, then beat and gently express the must.... The more painstaking dry in this same way, pick the individual grapes and soak them, without the stalks, in fine wine till they swell, then press them: this type is considered better than any other.

In the following century Galen is the principal source: 'As it is most noxious to children, so it is most useful to the old', he says of wine (Galen, *Health* 6.5 [6.334]). He, too, deals with Italian and Anatolian wines separately, seldom comparing them:

> Sometimes the best wine to prescribe, of those available in those parts, will be Ariusian or Lesbian. Lesbian, as is clear from its name, is made in Lesbos; Ariusian is grown in certain districts of Chios. There are three cities of Lesbos. The least aromatic and sweet comes from Mitylene, more aromatic and sweeter from Eresus, then Methymna. Get the unmixed, so called because there is no sea water mixed in.... But they have not usually included sea water in their best wines (and I am talking of the best wines) on Lesbos or in Chian Ariusium.
>
> (*On the Therapeutic Method* 12.4 [10.830–4])

'Always try to get the best', Galen insists, and he goes on to list a number of other fine wines of the eastern Aegean and western Anatolia: Mysian, Perperine 'black', Nicomedian, Aegeate 'black', Aphrodisiaean, dry and sweet Tmolite and the wine of Thera (Santorini), one of the very sweetest. Aphrodisiaean and Tmolite were amber-coloured, *kirrós*, like Lesbian. He scarcely mentions the wines of peninsular Greece.[53]

In spite of these conflicting preferences for specified vintages, preferences that now seem chaotic because of the length of time that separates each surviving source from the next, we can pick out a few details of long-term interest. Lesbos and Chios had produced wine that was praised through many centuries of history. Cnidian and Coan had a renown that was possibly briefer but may well have reached a wider market. The sweet wines of Crete and Thera, first picked out for us by Pliny and Galen, were to be noted again in medieval and early modern times. Galen's Nicomedian marks the beginning of the good repute of Bithynian wines.

And meanwhile there was much experiment with spiced and aromatic wines. Aelian, indeed, considered myrrh wine already an ancient indulgence, citing the comic poet Philippides in evidence. Little is said of them as yet in literature, yet flavoured wines too have some historical significance, for we must recognise in them the forerunners of modern mixtures such as vermouth. It is already of absinthe-flavoured wine, vermouth's direct ancestor, that we hear most: the Roman recipe of *Apicius*[54] can be compared with those given by Dioscorides (*Materia Medica* 5.39):

> *Apsinthítes* is made by a complicated method. Some add to 48 pints of must one pound of Pontic wormwood and boil down to two-thirds: then adding 90 pints of must and half a pound of wormwood and mixing carefully they bottle and (after straining) store. . . . Others chop 3 (or 4) oz. wormwood and 2 oz. each Syrian nard, cinnamon, cassia, sweet reed, ginger-grass, date spadix into one amphora of must, seal and set aside for two months, then strain, bottle and store.

The two recipes for myrtle wine given by Dioscorides can again be compared with the careful instructions for myrtle wine, myrtle-flavoured mead and myrtle juice in the Roman farming manual of Columella.[55]

Dioscorides gives the first surviving instructions for flavouring wine with a bouquet of pine resin, to produce the ancestor of modern retsina (*Materia Medica* 5.34), a taste that Plutarch considered typical of Euboea.[56] More will be said of the flavoured wines and drinks of Greece in Chapter 9.

Finally, a new perspective on the wine trade of the Roman Empire is given by a surviving instruction from the farming author, Florentinus, who appears to have written in general of conditions in Bithynia. This, then, we may say, is how farmer and buyer dealt in the Nicomedian wine that Galen happened to recommend:

> WHEN AND HOW TO TASTE WINE (Florentinus). Some taste wines when the wind is northerly, because wines are then unstirred and uncloudy. But wine experts prefer to taste when the wind is southerly, because that does stir up the wine and demonstrates its qualities. One should not taste on an empty stomach, which dulls the taste; nor after a drinking session, nor after heavy eating. One should not taste after eating bitter or very salty food or food that will affect the taste, but after eating as little as possible of some digestible food. Buyers, of course, should be encouraged to taste when the wind is in the north. Some, wishing to deceive buyers, keep an empty tasting-cup which they have soaked in the finest old aromatic wine; its qualities linger, and seem to belong to the wine that is served afterwards, and so those tasting are tricked. Other dealers, more dishonest still, put out

*Figure 28* Hecamede mixes *kykeón* for the white-bearded Nestor. Interior of an
Athenian red-figure cup in the Louvre, no. G152

cheese and nuts in their wineries, so that visitors are tempted to eat,
and the accuracy of their sense of taste is ruined. I set this down not
for us to imitate, but to avoid being deceived ourselves. The farmer
should taste [his] wine frequently, both the new and the old, or he
may not notice when it is about to turn.

(*Geoponica* 7.7)

# 7

# STRYMONIAN EELS
## Greek gastronomy in the Hellenistic world

In the early centuries influences on Greek gastronomy had come from the edges of the Greek world, from Lydia and Sicily. The conquests of Alexander and the establishment of the kingdoms of his successors, at the end of the fourth century BC, are the most obvious political corollaries of a group of cultural influences from quite different sources. The first of these that becomes evident derives from Macedonia itself. It is a sign of Macedonia's change in status with respect to Greece that what was recently seen as a barbarous kingdom, destined for gradual Hellenisation, turns into a source of new ideas of the fashionable and the civilised.

'You will get a big meagre in Pella (and it is fat in summer) and in Ambracia', said Archestratus (30 [Athenaeus 328b]) in the mid-fourth century. He was the first to comment on the eels of the River Strymon, though he does not say where he ate them: perhaps they were already pickled, and so would travel, as was the case in late Hellenistic times.[1] Archestratus knew of the squid that could be bought at Dium, the Macedonian religious centre a little to the south, and of the bass and grey mullet (*képhalos*) of Lake Bolbe. These fish of Bolbe were subject to an *apópyris*, 'annual sacrifice, annual catch', by the people of Olynthus, who thus supplied themselves with salt fish for the year. Salt *képhalos* was better than fresh, Galen thought.[2] Archestratus also wrote of Olynthus itself shortly before King Philip of Macedon destroyed it, again finding something to praise: 'Buy me the head of a bluefish at Olynthus and Megara, for it is noble and is caught in shallow water' (20 [Athenaeus 295c]).

The wines of Mende were certainly popular, as we have seen, but this little Greek town was hardly perceived by Greeks as belonging to Macedonia. Outside the pages of the adventurous Archestratus, Macedonia proper had no gastronomic reputation in the mid-fourth century. The royal capital was satisfied with the wines of neighbouring districts, of Mende, Mende's neighbour Torone and Thasos: on this point archaeological evidence agrees with the texts. Pella was not even a place where good slaves could be bought, it seemed.[3]

From mainland Greece, looking northwards, one's eye needed to reach only as far as Thessaly, noting the generous beef and porridge and the comfortable dining furniture, to be distressed by an un-Greek greediness and seeking after luxury:[4]

Some of them spend their time with dancing girls and flute girls, some pass their days in dicing and drinking and similar licentiousness, and they are more interested in ensuring that the tables served to them are full of all kinds of relishes than that their lives are respectably led.

(Theopompus 115F49 [Athenaeus 527a])

The Thessalians' love of extravagance and luxurious entertainment were said to have been the reason for their sympathy with the invading Persians, whom they longed to emulate.[5] A hundred and fifty years later, the same traits left their politicians open to Macedonian blandishments:

Knowing that the Thessalians were licentious and unrestrained in their life style, Philip got up parties for them and tried all kinds of amusements with them, dancing, kômoi, every licentious act. He was a vulgar man himself, getting drunk every day and enjoying the sort of pastimes that lead in that direction. . . . He won over most of the Thessalians that came in contact with him by parties rather than by bribes.

(Theopompus 115F162 [Athenaeus 260b])

Thessaly, then, was bad enough. Beyond Thessaly, and outside the Greek colonies, one saw nothing but danger and boorishness. Did not King Seuthes of Thrace, at a dinner to which Xenophon and his companions were invited, throw bread around the hall? – a custom which Xenophon and the rest politely copied, no doubt creating some confusion. Had not Persian ambassadors to the Macedonian court once been murdered at dinner, by young noblemen dressed as women, because they had demanded to be allowed to dine with the ladies of the Macedonian royal family?[6] Was a Greek woman captive from Olynthus whipped, at a dinner party of Macedonians and their Athenian diplomat guests, because she would not sing?[7] Not all these stories are true, but they are all stories that Greeks could be expected to believe.

For the outsider it requires an exertion of imaginative sympathy to understand how Thessalian and Macedonian behaviour could look so bad to Greeks of the south. Was their own behaviour not rather similar?

The immediate difficulty with the Thessalians was their excellent farmland and hence the ready availability of beef. We have seen how little, and in what contexts of Herculean gluttony, beef occurred in classical literary menus: we have seen Nicander Nucius' later characterisation of the English as 'meat-eaters, insatiable for flesh'. To southern Greeks, the regular eating of meat equated with greed and unrestrained animal impulses. Meanwhile, the difficulty with Macedonians and Thracians was the culture of generosity that maintained their rulers' status. Through gifts and entertainment these northern kings obliged men into their service. Athenians, to take them as example, had painfully thrown off a similar custom: hence the sniping in fifth-century comedy at Callias, the last Athenian who did not expect to be invited back to dinners just like his own. Eminent Athenians invited one another to dinner, or paid their shares: the obligations were as tight, but the entertainment was reciprocal. They despised as *parásitoi* those unable to play a proper part in the exchange. All those who accepted Philip's invitations were, in the eyes of Athenians, *parásitoi*.

But all this would soon look different. With the enduring hegemony, so successfully initiated by Philip and Alexander, that came to be wielded by Macedonian rulers over Greek cities, things Macedonian rapidly gained prestige.

The conspicuous consumption that now became fashionable at entertainments of the rich and powerful owed much to the Macedonian culture just outlined. It owed something too to the riches that the Macedonians had won in the east, and perhaps to the fashions that they themselves adopted as possessors of the Persian Empire. Athenaeus actually investigates mathematically whether the Persian monarchs had been spendthrift in the resources that went into the 'King's Dinner'. He concludes that they had not been: but then his yardstick is Alexander's customary expenditure at dinner with his friends. Athenaeus may have proved no more than that Alexander, trained in Macedonia, had learnt to be a Persian monarch. If Athenaeus had had at his command a comparison with expenditure at pre-Hellenistic Greek dinners, he might well have found both Persian and Macedonian courts spendthrift (Athenaeus 146c). The only Greek estimate Athenaeus adduces comes from a passage of comedy which estimates a dinner party at nearly a talent; and it reads like exaggeration, at that (Menander fragment 264 [Athenaeus 146d, 364d]).

A new example was certainly set in Athens by the entertainments of Antigonus, of Demetrius Poliorcetes and of Ptolemy, when these kings successively visited the city before and after 300 BC. All three were guests of honour at banquets. Athenian custom was observed in parody: Demetrius' hostess, for example, was the famous *hetairá* Lamia. She had received so much subvention from the city for her dinner that a comedian declared she deserved the name of 'city-capturer' even more than her royal serenader deserved it.[8]

We know something more of Macedonian festivity through the narrative of a banquet given in Macedonia about this time, the wedding feast of a certain Caranus. In this, again, Greek custom, including religious observances, can be seen selectively mixing with Macedonian and, probably, Persian. The resulting congeries may be compared with that in the almost contemporary description by Callixeinus of the grand procession of Ptolemy Philadelphus.[9] At Caranus' dinner there were numerous courses, all

*Figure 29* Drunkenness in the later stages of a *sympósion*. A flute-girl, naked but for a necklace, plays on. Athenian red-figure cup in the Lewis Collection, Corpus Christi College, Cambridge

separated by distributions of wreaths and perfumes. There were gifts of jewellery and gold cups, which must first be drunk dry, 'but one of the guests, poor fellow, could not drink up, and sat and cried at not getting his bowl until Caranus made him a present of an empty one'. There were performances by huge numbers of singers, dancers and acrobats, some of them naked. There was far too much meat, mostly of wild animals and birds, to be eaten by the guests. Some of the surplus was passed outwards to the slaves who waited around the edge of the banquet, and some was taken away by the diners for distribution. The narrator, Hippolochus [Athenaeus 128a–130e][10] gives no evidence of being a stylist or a gourmet, though he enjoyed the banquet.

## MACEDONIAN CUISINE

The increasing prestige of Macedonia is also visible in fashions for cuisine. Macedonians were more lavish than the majority of Greeks in their use of meat, obtained, traditionally, by hunting. They were also, it seems, more adventurous with meat in culinary terms. It was at this time, and under Macedonian influence, that Athenians learnt to include meat in the dessert course of their meals. In Menander's *False Heracles* (fragment 451

[Athenaeus 172a, 644c]), a play that also obliquely criticised the licentious behaviour of the Macedonian king Demetrius Poliorcetes at Athens,[11] the change is remarked on by a host or household slave:

> Cook, you seem very tiresome. This is the third time you have asked me how many tables we are going to set out. We are sacrificing one little pig. What does it matter to you whether we set eight tables or one? . . . No need to make a *kándylos* or to do your usual *karyke* with honey, bread-wheat flour and eggs. Everything's upside down now: the cook makes *énkhytoi*,[12] bakes cakes, boils porridge and serves it after the salt fish, along with a *thrîon* and grapes; while the pastry-chef, his new rival, roasts bits of meat and thrushes as dessert. So a man lying down to dinner gets dessert to eat, and then when he's had some more perfume and a fresh wreath [ready for dessert], he gets his dinner, thrushes and honey-cakes!

The epitome of the meaty supper or dessert was the dish known as *mattye*, one mentioned with pride by a comedy cook in a play by Nicostratus (7 [Athenaeus 664b]): 'Good, gentlemen, very good: but with my *mattye* I shall so affect you that I think not even this fellow will speak against me afterwards.' It recurs in several texts of the mid- to late fourth century, all in contexts that in one way or another suggest drunkenness and licence. The longest relevant fragment is an ironic passage, spoken possibly by a northern traveller disdainful of the poor meat and dilute wine of Athens, in a play by Sophilus (5 [Athenaeus 640d]):

> 'It's always nice to get together with Greeks. A good time is had. "Won't you kick in twelve ladlefuls?" somebody goes. "One's off for a *kômos* at the girl from Tanagra's: we'll lie down to supper there and have a donkey *mattye*!" '

There was a dispute, it would seem, whether the *mattye* originated in Thessaly, but a general opinion was that it was introduced to Athens by the Macedonians.[13] The first list of ingredients more generally attractive than that just quoted comes in a recipe from the first-century BC *Glossary of Cookery* of Artemidorus the Aristophanean. He knew of it as a dish of chicken with other strong flavours, to be served *parà póton*, 'during the drinking' [Athenaeus 663d–e]: for chicken was still in Artemidorus' time classed with hare and game birds, not with the sacrificial animals of a main course.[14]

For a while, in late fourth-century Athens, the *mattye* exemplified the life of hedonism: drunken revelry, serenading a *hetairá* and, assuming her compliance, a late supper, of which the central feature would be the spiced, salted, sauced roast meats that helped to make the wine go down.[15] Sophilus' perspective is matched by that of a character in Alexis' *Demetrius*, another play that linked the Macedonian monarch with the decline in

Athenian morals. A woman is addressed: 'You get this dish (it's compulsory), you prepare it, you have your party, you drink to your lovers, you suck cocks – you've had a *mattye*!' (Alexis 50).[16]

To take another example, the costly custom of roasting big animals whole, stuffed with smaller creatures and other delicacies, a custom so famous from descriptions of Roman banquets,[17] is traceable to Hellenistic Macedonia:

> Next was served a treasure rather than a dinner! a silver dish (with quite a broad gold rim) big enough to take a whole roast porker, and a very large one, which lay on its back displaying all the good things its carcass was full of. Baked together inside it were thrushes and wombs and an infinite number of beccafici, and yolks of egg poured over them.
>
> (Hippolochus [Athenaeus 129b])

Finally, there is no earlier evidence than third-century Macedonia for the use of a flat loaf of bread as a plate for meat, a function which bread continued to perform in the *pide* of Turkey, the *píta* of Greece and Bulgaria, the *pizza* of southern Italy and the 'trencher' of medieval Europe. Although meat and other 'relishes' were seen in earlier Greece as accompaniments to cereal, the cereal had taken other forms.[18]

It is odd, at first sight, that Macedonian produce itself did not gain in fashion. There seems no doubt that it did not. Strymonian eels and the wine of Chalcidice, both known by the fourth century, both from borderlands, remained the only fine foods for which Macedonia was known. No one praises the cattle or goats or game of any particular Macedonian district, and the mountain cheeses of Macedonia do not achieve notice in literature until early medieval times. The reason is clear. There had been no tradition of farm development. When Macedonians suddenly became rich and powerful, they began to demand the things whose possession and consumption was known to bring immediate respect, the products of Greece and the East. The result was not the development of Macedonia but rapid monetary inflation elsewhere.

## THE OBSERVANT TRAVELLERS

If for Clearchus of Soli, and for Stoics such as Chrysippus, Archestratus' *Life of Luxury* was an exemplar of decadence, comparable to a sex manual, for others in the tradition of Aristotle it might have had a different resonance. Theophrastus was the systematiser of botany, alert like his mentor Aristotle to geographical variation; Lynceus of Samos, a student of Theophrastus,[19] gave a sympathetic reading to Archestratus' poem, which he might have thought comparable in its light-hearted way to the results of some of his mentor's researches.

Lynceus was a miscellaneous writer who had lived in Samos, Rhodes and Athens and has something to say on food customs in all three. He is known only from quotations by Athenaeus, and the fragments of his works have never been brought together in print. His *Letters*, among which *Shopping for Food* (one fragment) might be counted, his comedy *Centaur* (one fragment) and his *Anecdotes* and *Reminiscences of Menander* are all relevant to social history. He conducted a gastronomic correspondence with Hippolochus and published letters to at least three other correspondents; a letter to Diagoras, comparing Athens and Rhodes from the gourmet's point of view, will be discussed below.[20] The literary letter – addressed to a single person but intended for publication – had a history of at least a century by Lynceus' time. It is a history that is now difficult to trace because so many letters attributed to fifth- and fourth-century notables are Hellenistic or Imperial forgeries. All those ascribed to Phalaris, Themistocles, Socrates and others have long been discredited. Some of those of Isocrates, Plato, Aristotle and Theophrastus are probably genuine, but which? The uncertainties are so great that it is hard to say how much originality was being shown by Lynceus and his friends in the early third century in exchanging and publishing light, amusing letters about such topics as gastronomy.

Both in the *Letter to Diagoras* and in *Shopping for Food* Lynceus cited 'the author of the *Life of Luxury*'. In the former he wanted corroboration for his own high valuation of the *alópex*, a kind of dogfish caught off Rhodes [Athenaeus 285f–294f]. In the latter he advises an unnamed correspondent how to haggle with fishmongers:

> To quell their steely gaze and unwavering prices it is not ineffective to stand over the fish and criticise it, recalling Archestratus who wrote the *Life of Luxury* or some other poet, and saying this line:
> *The inshore morme, a poor fish, never worthy;*
> and if it's spring,
> *Bonito? Buy in autumn!*
> and if it's summer,
> *Grey mullet's wonderful when winter comes!*
> There are many possibilities. You will frighten off most of the shoppers and bystanders, and the man will have to settle at the price you choose.[21]

[Athenaeus 313f]

Of the *Letter to Diagoras* enough fragments survive[22] to show some of Lynceus' stylistic quirks. He was, like his mentor Theophrastus, careful of rhythm and sparing of repetition. Throughout the letter he referred to Rhodes as 'she' and Athens as 'they' to avoid repeating the place-names. The *Letter to Diagoras* is crucial here because it is evidence of a new stage in Greek gastronomy: the eclecticism which allowed a host to compare the choice, preparation and serving of food and the table etiquette, across the Greek world, and to choose what suited him.

'When you lived in Samos, Diagoras, I know you were often at the drinking-parties at my house, at which a flask beside every man used to be poured out to give each a cupful at pleasure' [Athenaeus 499c]. We are to notice a contrast with Athenian *sympósia* of the traditional style, where part of the ritual was deciding the ruling strength of the wine-and-water mixture; a wine-waiter kept each participant's cup filled, and the host supervised the inebriation of the participants.[23] Lynceus' more urbane practice permitted his guests to regulate their alcohol intake by allowing them to fill their own cups. He had opinions, too, on the suitability of foods as appetiser and dessert: 'figs, by the way, I have sometimes served not after dinner, as they do there, when fullness has spoilt the palate, but before dinner when the appetite is virgin' [Athenaeus 75e]. It is quite in accordance with his known interests that in the only surviving fragment of his comedy *Centaur*, quoted on p. 123, Lynceus depicted a gourmet discussing with a hired cook the best way to serve hors d'œuvres.[24]

For the observation, comparison and conscious selection in social behaviour, here exemplified by Lynceus' views on food, a double ancestry may be traced. On the one hand Archestratus, ahead of his time, had claimed to disapprove of his own countrymen's drinking habits:

And as you imbibe, chew on some such dessert as this: tripe or boiled sow's womb marinated in cumin and sharp vinegar and silphium, and the tender tribe of birds, such as are in season. But have nothing to do with those Syracusans who simply drink, like frogs, without eating anything. You must not give in to them: eat the food I tell you to.

(62 [Athenaeus 101c])

On the other hand, the eclecticism of Lynceus seems altogether at home with the researches initiated by Aristotle that resulted in the *Constitutions* compiled under his direction and equally in his own *Study of Animals* and Theophrastus' *Study of Plants*: the latter, for example, continually refers to the ecology of specific regions, from Euboea and Magnesia to Ida and Tmolus.[25] In Lynceus, at any rate, we can identify a shift from the general fifth- and fourth-century ways of thinking, in which someone else's way of life was contrasted with one's own in order to idealise it, as Xenophon and Plato did with Sparta, or to mock it, as was usually the case in the comedies. The tone of the discussions between cook and patron in two such texts, by Diphilus of Sinope and Menander, though they are superficially on the same topic as that in Lynceus, is wholly different: the aim in those texts was to characterise non-Athenians by their laughable food preferences.[26]

If one can be eclectic about etiquette, one can be eclectic also about food preparation. It is so obvious to us that a menu may contain recipes consciously based on several regional (and foreign) cuisines that it may be hard to see such a development as innovative; yet in the Greek world of the third century BC it was indeed new. Earlier, certainly, recipes and other aspects of cuisine had in practice been imitated and so gradually spread from one town or region to another; wines and foods able to travel did travel widely in trade; migrant cooks had brought their skills with them. But when Archestratus advised his readers to prize the special loaves and cakes of one city or another, his advice must usually be to go there and buy them. It was in the Hellenistic period that one might first find, in a single household, at a single meal, 'cakes of every kind, Cretan and your own Samian, my dear Lynceus, and Attic, each set out in its individual container' (Hippolochus [Athenaeus 130c]).[27]

## COOKERY BOOKS AND DIETARY MANUALS

Such an innovation demanded an innovation in the contents of cookery books. Admittedly an 'Assyrian stew' and an 'Elamite stew' occur in the cuneiform collection of Akkadian recipes *YBC 4644*,[28] but no continuity can be traced between the culinary tradition of early second-millennium Mesopotamia and that of the Greek world, and the few fragments of fifth- and fourth-century Greek cookery books do not include any recipes with regional names. The third century marks a change.

Athenaeus cites two titles, *Bread-Making* and *On Cakes*, by an author Iatrocles. The one scrap of information ascribed to his *Bread-Making* reached Athenaeus through the first-century AD lexicographer Pamphilus, and – in spite of the title – is about a cake or sweetmeat, not bread. This suggests that Pamphilus and Athenaeus knew the same work under two different titles,[29] or perhaps rather that Iatrocles' name had become attached to a book which continued to evolve after his time: this happens with many cookery books, such as Mrs Beeton's, and with comparable manuals on other subjects. If this were the case here, Athenaeus might cite through Pamphilus a passage of 'Iatrocles' which he had not found in the edition to which he himself had access. Iatrocles is mentioned by no other source, and so is difficult to date. He may be later than the fourth century, because he apparently was not in Callimachus' list of authors on cake-making.[30]

Two of the names of cakes on which Iatrocles is cited as an authority appear to be known from earlier Sicilian authors, although in both cases the link is brought about by a conjectural emendation of the text of Athenaeus. An impression of the geographical breadth of Iatrocles' survey remains: the few fragments that are known describe cakes from Cos, perhaps Thessaly, probably Syracuse, certainly Athens (the *pyramís*). He could, on this evidence, have been a traveller and gastronome with interests more specialised than those of Archestratus. It seems more likely, however, that he was a technical author who reflected in his writing the eclecticism of Hellenistic culture.[31]

Perhaps from the second half of the third century comes a fragment from Baton's comedy *Benefactors*, which gives a further indication that cookery books had taken to distinguishing the origins of recipes, though this time attributing them not to places but to famous cooks: 'Right, Sibyne, we don't sleep at nights – we don't even lie down; with lighted lamp, with book in hand we work out what Sophon has bequeathed to us, or Simonactides of Chios, or Tyndaricus of Sicyon, or Zopyrinus' (4 [Athenaeus 662c–d]). There is no need to take the word of Athenaeus alone that cookery is the subject of discussion here. Sophon of Acarnania was indeed a famous cook,[32] and Pollux, in his second-century AD *Onomasticon* (6.70–1) repeats the list, without acknowledging Baton, though clearly drawing on him. Pollux assumes, with uncertain justification, that all these were authors of cookery books: they could, to judge from Baton's text, have been nothing more than the inventors of recipes.

The little that is known of the *Cookery* of Heracleides of Syracuse reflects two additional Hellenistic developments already discussed (p. 154). Athenaeus cites this author twice on the ingredients of cakes: the second of the citations is ascribed to a work of a different title, *On Offerings*, and describes a cake used in a ritual at Syracuse, reminding us again of the eclecticism of Hellenistic Greek culture in matters of religion. And Heracleides is cited in the *Epitome of Athenaeus* on quite a different question: 'Epaenetus and Heracleides of Syracuse in *Cookery* say that the best eggs are peahens', next best being those of shelducks. They put hens' eggs third.' Peafowl had been introduced to the Greek world in the fifth century, as we have seen, but they were expensive creatures, and the eating of peahens' eggs, which must always be far rarer than those of hens and quail, is a form of conspicuous consumption. If they are prized by gourmets, it is for their cost more than for their flavour.[33]

Those who live lavishly can afford expert advice on health, and are likely to need it. By the end of the fifth century, in the treatise known as *Regimen* or *On Diet* that forms part of the Hippocratic collection, foodstuffs had been catalogued for their real or imagined dietary effects; moreover, the seasons of the year and the various human physical types had been matched with appropriate 'regimens' of diet, exercise, hygiene and sexual activity.[34] In the Hellenistic period dietetic advice and dietetic writing flourished. In the early third century eminent Greek physicians were employed by the royal courts of the Hellenistic monarchies (as they had already been at the Persian court). One of these was Diocles of Carystus, author of *To Pleistarchus on Health*, from which Athenaeus quotes a number of passages. To Diocles are also attributed two surviving brief manuals of diet and regimen, one in the form of a letter to King Antigonus Gonatas, and a set of dietary rules for travellers (142 [Oribasius, *Medical Collections* 5.228]).[35] A second, perhaps, was Diphilus of Siphnos, author of *Diets for the Sick and the Healthy*, another lost work known mainly through quotations by Athenaeus: Diphilus 'lived under King Lysimachus' of Thrace.[36] A third, evidently, was the Apollodorus whose advice to a Ptolemy on the choice of wine is cited in Pliny's *Natural History.*[37]

Pliny even attributes the eminence of Lesbian wine to the influence of a fourth-celebrated physician, Erasistratus of Iulis on Ceos.[38] Erasistratus was a figure of considerable importance, his influence on medicine reaching much further than the study of diet. But he does appear to have had a more practical concern with diet even than his colleagues, for he wrote a work *On Cookery.* Athenaeus quotes it once [324a] for the ingredients of a sauce: '*Hypósphagma* for roast meat: the blood to be blended with honey, cheese, salt, cumin, silphium – these heated together.' Erasistratus' recipe differs from the earlier one by Glaucus of Locri (see p. 110) only in standardising: cumin is now called for specifically in place of the 'aromatic herbs' of the older writer. Owing to the extreme brevity of both recipes, it is not clear whether there is a difference in the cooking procedure. Erasistratus also gave attention to the quality of drinking-water: 'Compare, for example, the water of Amphiaraus with that of Eretria, one brackish, the other excellent: there is no difference between them as to weight' [*Epitome* 46c].

Other comparable writings of the third and second centuries were *On Comestibles* by Mnesitheus of Athens, several times quoted at length by Athenaeus and also cited by Galen; a work of uncertain title by Dieuches;[39] and *On Food* by Phylotimus, again known through quotations by Athenaeus. All three of these went into sufficient detail to provide, through surviving fragments, information on food preparation that almost amounts to recipes. So did Euthydemus of Athens, author of the most specialised titles so far in this subject area, *On Vegetables* and *On Salt Fish.*[40] The dietetic works of Xenocrates of Aphrodisias, not used by Athenaeus but often quoted by Galen and later medical compilers, appear to have been similar.

The early Hellenistic period appears to have been a golden age for dietary writing, as it was in general for the codification of Greek culture. But, so far as available fragments take us, it is a codification of existing Greek dietary opinion that is in view, not an extension of it to new species such as were certainly available, if wanted, to the kitchens of the Hellenistic monarchs. Athenaeus lists Nile fish from his own knowledge: he quotes no Ptolemaic physician for their digestive qualities. The survival of Hellenistic medical writings even into Imperial times was surprisingly patchy.[41]

## COOKS OF THE WIDER MEDITERRANEAN

One cannot follow the later history of gastronomy in Greece without an awareness of developments well beyond the Aegean region. Trade continued to increase in volume. Migration grew too, in its multiple forms:

colonisation, the spread of merchants and specialists, the slave trade, movement from country to city and from city to country in the search for livelihood. Those who travelled, those who migrated carried with them cultural influences of very varied kinds: the people, languages and civilisations of the Mediterranean were becoming more and more intermixed. Greek influence on the Levant took new and powerful forms when, after Alexander's conquests, Greek became the language of power in the Middle East. Rome, as its power spread, drank Greek culture and was influenced too by Carthage, whose sphere of influence Rome gradually engulfed. The western Mediterranean, long open to Greek and Phoenician influences, began to turn to Rome. During the first few centuries of the Christian era the Mediterranean was politically, culturally and economically more unified than it has ever been before or since.

Within the present subject area this openness is reflected in two quite different, though connected, ways. One is the movement of cooks, recipes and dining customs. Its corollary, observed in Chapter 8, is the sharing of terminology between languages.

Perhaps the latest of the Hellenistic cooks whose names are preserved, Epaenetus is cited ten times by Athenaeus and quoted verbatim twice: of the two quotations one is a discussion of fish names.[42] The names, incidentally, are mainly Sicilian. The remaining verbatim quotation is a recipe for *myma*. This dish marks, as far as we can know, a new departure in Greek cuisine, for the *myma*, a meat stew not mentioned in any surviving sources of earlier date than Epaenetus and his approximate contemporary Artemidorus the Aristophanean, calls for no fewer than thirteen flavourings:

> A *myma* of any sacrificial animal, or chicken, is to be made by chopping the lean meat finely, mincing liver and offal with blood, and flavouring with vinegar, melted cheese, silphium, cumin, thyme leaf, thyme seed, Roman hyssop, coriander leaf, coriander seed, *géteion*, peeled fried onion (or poppy seed), raisins (or honey) and the seeds of a sour pomegranate. You may also use it as a relish.[43]
>
> (Epaenetus [Athenaeus 662d])

With one exception, concerning eggs, the remaining citations of Epaenetus are all on matters of vocabulary, which of course may reflect the interests of Athenaeus or of intermediate sources rather than those of Epaenetus.[44] The fish-names cited from Epaenetus are remarkable not only for their rarity but also for their linguistic newness: they tend to be obvious derivatives or compounds of ordinary Greek words. The most attractive explanation for this phenomenon is that they are calques from foreign languages, which would be a sign that Greek familiarity with the food resources of the Mediterranean was now spreading beyond the older colonies and incorporating the knowledge and experience available in areas which had come under Greek influence more recently.

If this is an acceptable inference, Epaenetus provides evidence of the second Hellenistic revolution: the incorporation into a Greek-language gastronomy of food resources, and of combinations of ingredients, that had been foreign. The term 'Greek-language' is used intentionally; where Epaenetus wrote, and for whom, is unknown. But surviving fragments set him apart from Iatrocles and Heracleides, whose horizons appear to have been limited to the traditional Greek world, and link him with others whose cuisine was more cosmopolitan.

At any rate Parmenon of Rhodes' *Cookery Lessons* are cited by Athenaeus for a use of vocabulary that differed from that the early Hellenistic Phylotimus and Euthydemus, while Harpocration of Mendes, author of *On Cakes*, was Egyptian not only in his domicile but in at least some of his subject-matter, which included a recipe for an Alexandrian sweetmeat that came wrapped in thin papyrus. Chrysippus of Tyana, from whose *Bread-making* Athenaeus gives two rather long quotations, wrote notably bad Greek interlaced with Latin words.[45] He came from Cilicia in Asia Minor, and on Athenaeus' evidence his work included recipes linked to Asia Minor itself, to Crete, to Syria and to Egypt, but in much greater number to Rome and Italy, where it must be assumed that he wrote.

On the evidence of a statement in the frame narrative of Athenaeus' *Deipnosophists*, Paxamus may be likened to Chrysippus as a Greek technical author read in Rome and possibly working in Rome. ' "I am ashamed to name" *isíkia* to Ulpian, though I know how much he likes them. Still, my authority Paxamus mentions them, and I do not care about Attic usage', says Athenaeus' fictional cook (376d).[46] *Isicia*, the name of a type of sausage, was a colloquial Latin word, though this Greek citation may be as early as any of the surviving Latin ones. Paxamus was a man of wide interests, according to a Byzantine lexicon: 'Paxamus, author. *Cookery* in alphabetical order. *Boeotica* in 2 books. *The Twelvefold Art*: this is about sexual postures. *Dyeing*, 2 [books]. *Farming*, 2 [books]' (*Suda* s.v.). He wrote in time to be read by Columella, whose Latin work *On Farming* appeared at the middle of the first century AD. Columella placed Paxamus' writings on 'the feeding of mankind' in the tradition that began with the voluminous Carthaginian writer on farming, Mago, whose work was translated into Latin and Greek after the destruction of Carthage.[47] Columella is here talking of Paxamus' work on *Farming*, which, in the tradition of the Greek and Latin technical literature, will have included instructions on the making of wine and *garum*, tasks which were traditionally classed with farming rather than with cuisine. Columella dealt with them in his work *On Farming*: so, it seems, did Mago; so did Paxamus. His *Farming* is frequently acknowledged in the Byzantine collection on that subject, *Geoponica*, compiled under Constantine Porphyrogennetus in the tenth century. As for the book on *Cookery*, this was certainly in use for about two centuries (since it is cited as if current by Athenaeus' cook), but there are no other references to it. Paxamus is in a sense still remembered: a barley biscuit, first recorded in the second century and well known in Byzantine and modern Greece, is supposed to have taken its name *paxamâs*, *paximádion* from him.[48]

Having deduced what can be deduced of Chrysippus and Paxamus, one is not surprised to find other evidence that Greek cuisine had an early and strong influence on that of Rome. Cato, in the earliest surviving work of Latin prose, *On Agriculture*, included several recipes for bread and cakes. Two of these had names borrowed from Greek: *placenta* from Greek *plakoûs*, though Cato's *placenta* was a single type of cake, a baked cheese-cake, while the Greek term had a far more general meaning; *encytum* from Greek *énkhytos*, a fried cheese pastry.[49] Four more, wherever they were invented, had names of Greek form: *spira*, *scriblita*, *spaerita*,[50] *panis depstic-ius*. This last is to be compared with similar names of loaves, *artoptíkios*, *phournákios*, *klibaníkios*, given by Chrysippus of Tyana, all three of which recur in Latin. It would be more precise than 'of Greek form' to say that such words are 'of Latino-Greek form', for indeed they are a little odd in either language. Cato and Chrysippus of Tyana have at least two cakes in common, *spîra* and *skriblítes*.[51]

Parallel evidence of the growth of a Mediterranean culinary culture is to be found in writings beyond the narrowly technical farming and cookery manuals: in dietetic and pharmaceutical texts, for example.

In late Hellenistic times Hicesius of Smyrna had compiled a work *Perì hyles*, literally *On Materials*.[52] This lost work is several times cited by Athenaeus. One important fragment [689c] will be quoted here as it is a reminder that Greek festivity was properly regarded as an activity in which all the senses were engaged, for, unlike any modern dietician, Hicesius considers the perfumes of the *sympósion* as germane to his subject as the foods:

> Some perfumes are ointments, some are waters. Rose fragrance is suitable for a drinking party, as are myrtle and quince:[53] the latter is stomachic and appropriate to lethargics. Meadowsweet fragrance, a stomachic, also keeps the mind clear. Marjoram and mother-of-thyme fragrances are also suitable for a drinking party, and saffron when not mixed with much myrrh. Myrrh oil [*stakté*] is also suitable for a drinking party; spikenard as well. Fenugreek fragrance is sweet and gentle. Gilliflower is aromatic and very digestive.[54]

Now, in the first century AD, Dioscorides of Anazarba's *Materia Medica* (a work that survives complete) sets a new standard for comprehensiveness in the study of natural substances of all kinds, their man-made derivatives and their digestive and pharmacological properties. Relentlessly methodical, it draws on the flora, fauna, food products and indeed minerals of the whole central and eastern Mediterranean.

165

Medical dietetics, too, continued. We know of herbalist and dietary writings by Rufus of Ephesus, who probably worked in the late first century AD: his writings on diet survive, but in Arabic translation, and as yet unpublished.[55] Athenaeus of Attaleia was probably an older contemporary: there are excerpts from his work in the fourth-century *Medical Collections* of Oribasius. This Athenaeus – not to be confused with the gastronomic author – summarised the seasonal qualities of meat and fish in a fragment reminiscent of Ananius:

> Pigs are worst from spring until the autumn setting of the Pleiades, and are best from then till spring. Goats are worst in winter, and begin to improve in spring up to the setting of Arcturus. Sheep are worst in winter, but they fatten after the equinox up to the summer solstice; while cows fatten when the grass goes to seed as spring ends and through the whole summer. As for birds, those that appear in winter – the blackbird, thrush and wood pigeon – are best then, francolins in autumn, and blackcaps, greenfinch, and quails are fattest at that season. Hens are not very healthy in winter, especially when the wind is in the south: the turtle dove is finest in autumn. Of fish some are best when carrying eggs, shrimp, langoustine and the soft-bodied squid and cuttlefish, others when they ovate, such as the *képhalos* grey mullets: these are thin and poor as food when they fill with roe, still more so when they deposit their eggs. The tunny is fattest after Arcturus, worse in summer.[56]
>
> [Oribasius, *Medical Collections* 1.3]

In the second century AD Galen of Pergamum, doctor and prolific author working in Rome,[57] discusses in *On the Properties of Foods* the dietary value of the foodstuffs of Rome, Egypt, Greece, Asia Minor and elsewhere. The work opens with a review of earlier writings on the subject, notably *Regimen* (attributed to Hippocrates), the *Hygiene* of Diocles of Carystus and *On Foods* of Mnesitheus. Systematic but attractively anecdotal, *On the Properties of Foods* is the one of Galen's works that is most relevant to our subject, and nothing demonstrates better the central role that diet played in the thinking of ancient physicians than the almost obsessively careful observations and deductions made here on such subjects as the boiling of eggs (3.21.1) and the making of pancakes (1.3.1–2):

> Let us find time to speak of other cakes, the ones made with club wheat flour. *Tagenitai* as they are called in Attic, *teganitai* to us in Asia, are made simply with oil. The oil is put in a frying pan resting on a smokeless [very hot] fire, and when it has heated, the wheat flour, mixed with plenty of water, is poured on. Rapidly, as it fries in the oil, it sets and thickens like fresh cheese setting in the baskets. And at this point the cooks turn it, putting the visible side under,

next to the pan, and bringing the sufficiently fried side, which was underneath at first, up on to the top, and when the underneath is set they turn it again another two or maybe three times till they think it is all equally cooked. Obviously this food is pachychymic and astringent.... Some mix it with honey, and others again with sea-salt.

There are useful shorter studies and asides throughout Galen's writings, including careful assessments of Italian, Greek and Anatolian wines.

Some decades earlier than Galen, the *Satiricon* of Petronius, evoking a subculture of Graeco-Roman Italy, had demonstrated in its consciously colloquial language and its incomparable narrative of Trimalchio's dinner the full extent of the interpenetration of Greek and Roman cultures. The same coalescence may be seen in a slightly different context in the first surviving discussion of *social behaviour* around food, Plutarch's *Symposium Questions*. Like Athenaeus' *Deipnosophists*, the *Symposium Questions* take the form of dinner conversations, and they deal with many other subjects besides food. A contemporary of Galen, Plutarch lived at Chaeronea in Greece and reflects (though he would not have put it thus) the provincial culture of a minor subject province of the Roman Empire.

Athenaeus himself, in the early third century, perhaps wrote in Rome; certainly he set his fictional dialogue in Rome (and chose 'Galen' as one of his speakers), as if Rome were the natural home of a Greek intelligentsia and indeed of Greek cooks.

# 8

# THE IMPERIAL SYNTHESIS

Thus we return to the *Deipnosophists* of Athenaeus, the work that is not only the first and most important scholarly survey of the present subject, but also the single most important collection of literary and historical source material. Much of what is most relevant is quoted in the *Deipnosophists*, and very many of these quotations are from works that no longer exist. Athenaeus was a native of Naucratis in Egypt, familiar with the life and food of Alexandria and of Rome. As to the date at which he wrote, a *terminus post quem* is provided by the fact that he could write of the death of Ulpian – if we allow the identification of the real jurist Ulpian, who died about AD 223, with the pedant Ulpian of the *Deipnosophists*:

'And, as if in a play, I shall make that my parting word.'
It was as if he had predicted his own falling silent, for, not many days after that, he died, fortunately, allowing no space for illness, but causing much grief to us his companions.

(686c)

Admittedly it would be very odd to say that the real Ulpian died 'fortunately', since he was murdered.[1] The only true *terminus ante quem* is supplied by the fact that Athenaeus' work was used by the lexicographer Hesychius in the fifth century. But it is generally assumed, I think rightly, that Athenaeus lived and wrote at the beginning of this range. 'Athenaeus', the narrator of the *Deipnosophists*, speaks to 'Timocrates' as if he had lived under the Emperor Commodus ('the Emperor Commodus, in our own day . . .' [537f]), and it is reasonable to suppose that this applies to the author.

The *Deipnosophists* was not his only work, for, within it, the speaker Masurius says (211a) that Athenaeus had written something on the rulers of Syria. He seems to claim in his own voice (329d) to have compiled a commentary on the fifth-century BC comedy *The Fishes* by Archippus, a contemporary of Aristophanes. This play was surely forgotten by almost everybody else in Athenaeus' time. But it was highly relevant to Athenaeus' own interests, for with the play's chorus of fishes Archippus mined the

168

same vein of satire as Aristophanes' *Birds* and in doing so supplied any later philologist with a rich ichthyological vocabulary.

## THE *DEIPNOSOPHISTS*

The *Deipnosophists*, a work in fifteen long books, takes the form of a series of fictional dinner discussions set in Rome in the early third century AD. In obvious imitation of Plato's *Republic*, these discussions are reported, in a frame conversation, by 'Athenaeus' to 'Timocrates'. Timocrates speaks only at the outset of book 1 (*Epitome* 2a), but he is addressed by 'Athenaeus' at the beginning and end of most of the individual books.

The dramatic date of the first of the discussions is before the death of Galen in AD 199. The date of the last is just before the death of Ulpian about AD 223 (see above). Both these datings depend on whether the speaker in question is to be identified with the known and famous personality of that name.[2] The dramatic date of the frame conversation is a little while later still, when the discussions are supposed to have attained fame (*Epitome* 2a) and Ulpian was dead.

The dialogue and the speakers must of course be treated as fictional, even though they have points of contact with the real second-century world. It is clearly possible that Athenaeus had known the real people whom he includes in the dialogue, though he mixes them with others who are almost certain to be inventions. It is rather unlikely that these eminent people were united in a regular dining club, as the frame conversation suggests: we might expect to have known of it from some other source. It is hardly to be imagined that they really spent their time in the culinary and antiquarian byways into which the speakers of the *Deipnosophists* wander. These are the researches of Athenaeus himself.[3] He no doubt would have considered the precedent set by Plato's practice in his dialogues fully to justify both the bringing together of real contemporaries in a fictional meeting, and the attribution to them of discussions that went far beyond their own studies and enthusiasms in the direction of those of the author.

These semi-fictional speakers, then, are scholars and pedants who are ready with all sorts of quotations on a given topic. They include cynics, doctors, whose special interests naturally include medical and dietetic literature, the pedant Ulpian, who demands the classical authority for many a strange word and item of food, and others less clearly differentiated. A partial list of speakers is provided by the Epitomator.[4] They interrupt themselves and others; in asides they question the texts and attributions of their own quotations and throw similar doubt on the quotations of others. The linking subject is the food and drink and entertainment of the Greeks and some of their neighbours in the first millennium BC. The speakers, and the narrator 'Athenaeus', not infrequently say something of the food

*Figure 30* A flute-player oblivious to her audience's inebriation. Athenian red-figure cup of the mid-fifth century in the Louvre, no. G135

and social life of Rome and Alexandria in their own time. However, apart from these contemporary allusions, the sources of their information are almost exclusively written: partly literary (comedies, memoirs, epics), partly scientific, partly lexicographical.

There is a sequence of topics, a sequence that at times is almost lost in continual digressions. Book 1 dealt with the literature of food, food and drink in Homer and wine; books 2–3 hors d'œuvres, bread; book 4 the organisation of meals, music; book 5 lavish display and luxury; book 6 parasites, flattery; books 7–8 fish; book 9 meat, poultry; book 10 gluttony and more wine; book 11 cups; book 12 social behaviour; book 13 love, women; book 14 more music, desserts; book 15 wreaths and perfumes. To make a full index to the *Deipnosophists* is a lengthy task.

Several hundred authors are quoted in the *Deipnosophists*.[5] References are normally scrupulously accurate, giving author, title and book number. It is clear that Athenaeus took many of his briefer quotations from intermediaries (such as glossaries of obsolete and dialect words, commentaries on archaic poets) because his speakers say so explicitly and engage in criticism of these intermediate sources. But it is also hard to dispute that Athenaeus read and excerpted a great range of works himself. Possibly the most recent author cited in the *Deipnosophists* is mentioned at the end of a survey of names for loaves, a survey (115b) that is put in the mouth of Pontianus:

> '...Allow me not to list – since, sadly, memory fails me – all the cakes and sweets given by Aristomenes of Athens in *Religious Requisites* III. I myself, when young, knew this author as an old man, an actor in classical comedy and a freedman of that very cultured monarch Hadrian, who used to call him "Athenian Partridge".'
>
> 'Freedman!' said Ulpian. 'Now which early author used that word?'
>
> Someone said that *Apeleutheroi, Freedmen*, is the title of one of Phrynichus' plays, and that Menander uses 'freedwoman' in his play *The Smacked Girl*.
>
> He would have gone on, but Ulpian asked: 'And what about the difference between *apeleutheros* and *exeleutheros*?'
>
> But we agreed to leave that for the present, and were about to get to grips with the bread when Galen said:
>
> 'We shan't start dinner before we have told you what the medical fraternity have to say about bread....'

The quotation exemplifies the conversational exchanges of the *Deipnosophists*: the reader soon finds, however, that these do not bulk large in comparison with disquisitions, sometimes many pages in length, attributed to single speakers.

Attributed quotations make up a very high proportion of the whole text. So it comes as a surprise to find occasional evidence that further works are cited without attribution: Athenaeus certainly on occasion used the works of Plutarch and of Lucian unacknowledged. These two authors are more recent than any of those cited by name.

This fact gives the handle for those who wish to argue that a much higher proportion of the work than is evident is actually drawn from secondary sources now unknown to us, that were recent in Athenaeus' time. As regards the longer quotations, those from Hellenistic sources, and those relevant to fact rather than to lexicography, the hypothesis is unlikely in the extreme: for we know of no kind of compilation that would have united such quotations in handy form, pre-designed for the highly unusual reader that Athenaeus was. However, as regards the smaller but still considerable number of briefer citations that are of lexicographical and grammatical interest (for these are interests that Athenaeus shared with many Greek scholars of Hellenistic and Roman times) the possibility is not to be discounted. Scholars of all periods have been caught re-quoting quotations found in dictionaries and encyclopaedias, and the dictionaries and encyclopaedias are not acknowledged as often as they deserve. It may be argued, for example, that when an author or work is introduced in two or three different ways in different passages of the *Deipnosophists*, this is because a different intermediate source has been drawn on for the citation.[6]

## ATHENAEUS AS WRITER AND SCHOLAR

As a littérateur Athenaeus' accomplishments are generally agreed to have been limited.[7] The dialogue format certainly gave him the excuse to incorporate masses of fascinating material that any other structure would have excluded. It also allowed him to lay down quick, trenchant, even scurrilous opinions (as narrator or through the mouths of his characters) on a host of subjects, opinions which would have had to be toned down, or justified at length, if he had been writing plain history or literary criticism.[8] But although he had these good reasons for choosing to write his book as a dialogue, Athenaeus did not care to tackle the artistic problems of his chosen literary form. Real conversation is desultory, inconsequential, repetitive: so are Athenaeus' Deipnosophists.[9] The dialogue is not carried through carefully, or consistently, or purposefully enough to permit any normal reader to suspend his disbelief. It has even been argued, notably by Ullrich and Kaibel, that Athenaeus, having planned a dialogue, would have written it more conscientiously, and thus that the present state of the dialogue in the *Deipnosophists* is evidence of a seriously mutilated text: Kaibel adduced other arguments in support of this view,[10] which is still held by some scholars.

The half-hearted nature of the dialogue framework in the *Deipnosophists* is, in fact, for the best: no one reads the book for the sake of the dialogue, rather for the information embedded in it, and we must presume that that was Athenaeus' intention. Indeed, although Plato put immeasurably more skill and effort into the dialogue form in the *Laws*, the final result there was equally unconvincing and its effect on the real success of the work was equally marginal.

As a student of cultural history, Athenaeus' achievement deserves a high estimate. He had the advantages of wide reading, lack of prejudice and untiring enthusiasm.

One of his favourite categories of sources was certainly the Athenian comedy of the fifth to third centuries BC: of these plays, mostly lost now, we would know little if it were not for Athenaeus. He quotes them briefly, for incidental mentions of foodstuffs or other details of social history; extensively, for boastful speeches by cooks and for menus of dinner parties. Other classical and Hellenistic poetry is also quoted: Sicilian comedy and mime; hexameters of the fourth to second centuries BC; less frequently, archaic lyric, elegy and hexameter. Tragedy, no doubt less prolific in snippets relevant to food and drink, is little used. Coming to prose, there are numerous extensive extracts from dietetic writings of Hellenistic and early Imperial times, most of them otherwise lost, some also to be found excerpted in late medical compilations. There is also a wealth of extracts from popular and anecdotal history books of Hellenistic times, and much is drawn from philological works such as lexica, dialect glossaries and commentaries.

Athenaeus is notable for his detached treatment of historical and literary controversy. This is not to say that he does not take sides in quarrels over minutiae of classical Greek culture such as the spelling of words, the genuineness of lines of Homer, the moral character of Plato and of Archestratus. His speakers take sides very fiercely, and in non-dialogue passages 'Athenaeus' the narrator, addressing the almost silent Timocrates, takes sides too. To those who wish, it is open simply to suppose that these *parti pris* positions represent the author's views, held by him as firmly and uncomplicatedly as they are stated. But we are, after all, reading the work of an author who will assist us to reach our own opinions on these matters. If it is a question of a debate between scholars, both sides of the debate are quoted. If it is a question of interpretation, or of morality indeed, the dubious text is put before us for us to decide. And although many of the arguments in the *Deipnosophists* are tendentious, the texts appear to be sacrosanct – at least in the following sense. It was, admittedly, hard for ancient authors to quote accurately, especially any authors who drew on as wide a range of sources as Athenaeus, because of the difficulty of access to texts, the difficulty of finding precise passages in papyrus rolls, and the consequent tendency in all concerned to rely on memory. Athenaeus has been praised for accuracy and has also been criticised for inaccuracy. But he has never been caught adjusting quoted texts to suit an argument.

In one further way the dialogue form suited Athenaeus rather well. Although it might have been relevant to his subject, Athenaeus was evidently not interested in technical writing on subjects such as farming, wine-making, cookery and the organisation of banquets. And, conveniently, his semi-fictional, eminent, scholarly speakers would not have been avid readers of such books either. Thus, of all the categories of earlier writing that had a bearing on the subject, technical books are cited least.

Among Athenaeus' weaknesses was that he was easily confused by changes in the meaning of words. He quoted texts from the eighth century BC to the second century AD, roughly a thousand-year period. During much of this time the written Greek language changed little: texts in the Attic dialect (or a slightly modified Attic) of the fifth and fourth centuries BC had gained the status of classics and literary models. It was easy for readers and even scholars at the end of the period, in studying earlier literature, to work on the assumption that nothing at all had changed. It was not true, as Galen knew:

This is not written for people who choose to speak Attic (probably they will not want to read it, despising health as they despise common sense) but for doctors in particular, who do not care much for Atticisms, and for any others who live like logical beings. . . . For these, I know, the more clearly I write the more useful it will be, so I shall use the words they know, whether they would have made sense to the ancient Greeks or not.

(*On the Properties of Foods* 2.11.1)

And in fact there had been a multitude of small changes, a multitude of new words and changed meanings; very often they accompanied new patterns of behaviour. This is true of many words denoting food, drink and etiquette at meals, and Athenaeus did not always realise it. Therefore he did not always understand his sources. Here too, however, since he tends to give verbatim quotations and full references, we are often in a good position to see what may have gone wrong.

## THE FATE OF THE *DEIPNOSOPHISTS*

Athenaeus' great work survived the medieval period in one manuscript, copied by John the Calligrapher in Constantinople in the tenth century and brought to Italy by John Aurispa in the fifteenth.[11] It is a large and carefully written volume now in the Biblioteca Nazionale Marciana in Venice and is known from its former class-mark as Marcianus 447. From this unique copy the whole of books 1–2, the beginning of book 3, part of the final book 15 and a few other pages, adding up perhaps to about a fifth of the whole work, disappeared many centuries ago.[12] For these sections, therefore, the *Epitome of Athenaeus* provides an indispensable substitute.[13]

The *Epitome* is an abridgement made in late Byzantine times. It survives complete in several manuscripts, two of which are of independent value.[14] Comparison of the *Epitome* with the *Deipnosophists* in books 3 to 15 shows that the *Epitome* naturally omits most of the conversational exchanges of the full work, retaining a fairly large selection of the quotations. Where the full work cites author, title and book number of nearly every source used, title and book number are lacking in the *Epitome*, and the quotations themselves are often trimmed of words or sentences not immediately relevant.[15] Even so, the *Epitome* quite often provides a more convincing version of some disputed passage than the Marcianus does[16] and so it is important to know whether this may originate from a lost, possibly good, manuscript and not merely from a late Byzantine scholar's conjecture. It is now in fact generally agreed that the *Epitome* was made from a better text than the Marcianus, or, to put the matter more precisely, the Epitomator had a stronger manuscript tradition to depend on than is represented by the Marcianus alone.[17]

In all current editions of the *Deipnosophists*, extracts from the *Epitome*, interpolated from other sources such as the *Suda* where relevant, are printed in the gaps left by the missing sections of the complete text. These gaps are at 1a–73e; 781b–784d, inserted at 466d; an unnumbered passage inserted at 502b; and 701a–702c.[18]

Besides the Epitomator, a few other later authors used the *Deipnosophists*: they sometimes preserve readings that differ from those of the direct manuscript tradition, and sometimes these readings are preferable. Hesychius' fifth-century *Lexicon*, in one of its many citations of Athenaeus, seems to betray an awareness of a version divided into thirty books.[19] The Byzantine lexica *Suda* and *Etymologicum Magnum* certainly quote Athenaeus from a better text than the Marcianus.[20] Psellus knew the fuller text of books 1–2, now missing from the Marcianus, and cites them in his *Lexicon*. Eustathius of Thessalonica frequently makes unacknowledged quotations from Athenaeus in his commentaries on the *Iliad* and *Odyssey*.[21] Not all the useful readings to be found in these sources have yet been included in editions of the *Deipnosophists*. It was argued by Kaibel that the Latin writer Macrobius, author of *Saturnalia*, a literary and historical miscellany with some superficial resemblances to the *Deipnosophists*, had drawn directly on the latter, but this is unlikely.[22]

It is clear from rubrics in the manuscript that there was once an alternative division of the text, and that each of the present fifteen books represents two books of the alternative division.[23] But Athenaeus built the present book divisions very elaborately into his text, while the openings of the intercalary book divisions are not heralded in the text in any way. They are probably an unofficial expedient of an editor or copyist who found Athenaeus' books inconveniently long.[24] Few antiquarians have been as persistent in pursuit of their subjects as Athenaeus, who extended his patchy dialogue to fifteen long books and quoted over seven hundred authors, many of their works being highly obscure in his time, many of them wholly unknown now except from his quotations. Dare one believe that there was a later, more obsessive, antiquarian who was able to find enough additional matter to double Athenaeus'?

The *editio princeps* of the *Deipnosophists* was the Aldine, published in Venice in 1514. This was based on a transcription of the Marcianus manuscript and incorporated many sensible corrections by Marco Musuro. The standard text divisions, through which passages of the *Deipnosophists* are nearly always identified, are the page numbers of Casaubon's 1597 edition, which was printed with a parallel Latin translation and followed by a commentary in 1600. The standard edition of books 3–10 is still Kaibel's; Gulick's text of books 11–15, based on a new collation, replaces Kaibel's.[25] Gulick's English translation, though not infallible, is generally sound and has of course been very frequently used by social historians who cannot read Greek. The most extensive commentary, incorporating much of Casaubon's work, is that by Schweighäuser.[26] Gulick took relatively generous space for notes in his later volumes. But these works do not add up to a satisfactory modern commentary on the *Deipnosophists*: in particular, editions of and commentaries on nearly all the poets, historians and philosophers quoted by Athenaeus have appeared during the last two centuries, and a great deal of scholarly work relevant to the *Deipnosophists*, and to Greek social history, has built up in the form of studies, translations and annotated texts of these authors.

## USING THE *DEIPNOSOPHISTS*

The *Deipnosophists*, like any historical source, must be used circumspectly.

The convenience of the dialogue form to Athenaeus' approach to his subject has been outlined above. The great advantage of it to any historian using the book is that it allowed the bringing together of verbatim quotations from many genres, bearing on the topic in different ways, contributing to a more rounded picture of many aspects of Greek social life. There is a risk attached. It is easy to forget that quotations, attributions and interpretations – most emphatically the latter – are given on the authority of the speakers (and sometimes the narrator), not of the author. The expression 'Athenaeus says that . . .', sometimes found in social histories, would often have been better avoided. Athenaeus vouches for few facts. His speakers make some incidental assertions from their own knowledge, for example, on the availability and prices of foods at Rome and Alexandria. They make statements which are by their nature open to challenge, for example, on the earliest authority for particular words or on the origin of particular customs and beliefs. The fact that *some* such statements are actually challenged by speakers reminds us that *all* might be open to challenge. An example:

> On the subject of citrons the Deipnosophists fell into a long controversy as to whether there is any reference to this *kítrion* in classical authors. It was Myrtilus who started us students on the wild goat chase by claiming that Hegesander of Delphi mentioned it in his *Notes*, but that he could not recall the text just now.
>
> Plutarch disagreed with him. 'It happens', he said, 'that another of our friends, citing some research notes by a reliable person, told me just as firmly as you that Hegesander has this word in his *Notes*; whereupon I read them all through for this sole purpose, and I maintain that he has not used the word at all. So it is time you looked for another authority, friend Myrtilus.'
>
> Aemilianus said that Juba, King of the Moors, a very learned man,

refers to the citron in his *African Collections*, claiming that Africans call it 'western apple' and that it was from Africa that Heracles brought to Greece what were called from their colour 'golden apples': 'and the story that the "apples of the Hesperides" were brought forth by Earth at the so called Wedding of Zeus and Hera is in *Egyptian Studies* LX by Asclepiades'.

Democritus glanced across and said: 'If Juba has put down any of that, then goodbye to his *African* books along with the *Voyages of Hanno*. I say that the word *kítrion* is not found in classical authors; but the thing is there in Theophrastus of Eresus, so described in his *Study of Plants* that I have to take it he is writing of citrus fruit. In *Study of Plants* IV this is what the scientist says: "Among other produce, the land of Media and Persia has the so-called 'Persian' or 'Median apple'. This tree has a leaf similar to, and nearly the same size as that of the strawberry tree and walnut..."'

(Athenaeus 83a–d)

A long and accurate quotation ensues, followed in turn by extracts from fourth-century comedy. And indeed Athenaeus' speakers do practically always quote, or cite, an earlier written authority for their statements.

Many scholars think of the *Deipnosophists* solely as a mine of quotations of some author or authors in whom they are interested. The approach of social historians is typically quite different. They are pursuing a topic, and are likely to be interested in all the texts in which a topic or key word is mentioned, whether or not Athenaeus had originally brought them together with the same topic in mind. This approach entails risk of misunderstanding. Before any of Athenaeus' quotations can be used, it is necessary to ask some questions. Where and when did the quoted author write? Is the text authentically his? Was he writing fact or fiction? Did he mean what he said literally, ironically or in some special context? Is he being quoted accurately? The speakers will sometimes comment on these questions: whether they do or not, the reader must always have them in mind.

The question of authenticity is an important one. Forgery was a challenging literary exercise, testing one's facility with metre and dialect and one's familiarity with the recorded life and known works of an author or historical personage. In the text above, Democritus throws doubt on the authenticity of the *Navigation of Hanno*. That text survives – and the doubt remains unresolved.

Many quotations are of passages of dramatic dialogue. There is very often room for disagreement as to who said what within these extracts, and the answer may affect one's view of what may be fact, what may be irony, what may be a lie; the manuscript gives no reliable help here. In the case of prose, meanwhile, there may be no way of knowing whether what seems to be a verbatim extract really is so: what little punctuation is found in the manuscript is not reliable. In particular it can be hard to know where a quotation stops. Athenaeus liked to interweave quotations.[27] Sometimes a speaker will take one authority and repeatedly revert to it, interspersing short quotations from other authors; stylistic incongruities may be the reader's only clue that this is taking place. The practice can be seen in effect in the following quotation (109b). Here, in a single sprawling sentence, a list taken from the scientist Tryphon provides the link for a chain of quotations from plays and other sources. To clarify Athenaeus' practice his syntax has been imitated as closely as possible in this translation, while the list taken from Tryphon is italicised:

'There is a classification of bread in the *Plants* of Tryphon of Alexandria, if I can bring it to mind', said Pontianus, getting in first: *'leavened, unleavened; flour bread, meal bread; wholemeal*, more laxative, he says, than *white; emmer bread, einkorn bread, millet bread* (meal bread is always made from the lesser wheats, he says, it cannot be made from barley); then those named after the method of baking: *oven-bread*, mentioned by Timocles in *Honest Robbers* ("I discovered a warm tray lying there, so I ate some of the warm oven-bread"); *drop-scones*, mentioned by Antidotus in *Chorus Leader* ("took hot scones – why not? – folded them over and dunked them in must") and by Crobylus in *The Suicide* ("and taking a tray of white scones") while Lynceus of Samos, in his *Letter to Diagoras*, comparing the foodstuffs made in Athens with those at Rhodes, says: "Even the loaves of the market-place are exalted among them. They bring them in at the beginning of dinner and in the course of it till none is left, and when the diners have finished and are full they serve up what are called 'dipped scones', a very pleasant affair so compounded of sweets and softness and so symphoniously soaked in must that a true miracle occurs – hunger recurs in the eater through the joy of eating, just in the way that sobriety frequently recurs in the drunkard"; *atabyrites*, as Sopater in *Woman of Cnidos* ("There was an atabyrite loaf, a jaw-ful!"); *brockets*, mentioned by Semus in *Deliad* VIII, who writes that they are made for processions ("They are large loaves; the feast is called Great Loaves, and they say as they carry them in, 'A goat, a brocket full of suet!' "); *pitta bread*, mentioned by Aristophanes in *Age* (he depicts a baker-woman who has her loaves stolen by men who have thrown off their old age, and says, " 'What's happened here?' 'Hot ones, child!' 'Are you mad?' 'Pittas, child!' 'What do you mean, pittas?' 'And very white, child!' "); *ember-bread*, mentioned by Nicostratus in *High Priest* and by the magic gourmet Archestratus, whom I shall quote in due course; *toast*, as in Eubulus' *Ganymede* (" 'Hot toast!' 'What's toast?' 'Sexy bread!' ") and Alcaeus' *Ganymede*; and then *crumpets*, which are thin and light, and *muffins* even more so (Aristophanes mentions the former in *Assemblywomen*, saying, "Crumpets are baking", while Diocles of Carystus refers to muffins in *Health* I, stating, "Muffins are lighter that crumpets")'.

This extract will serve here as a last example of the wealth – and the complexity – of the evidence provided by Athenaeus' *Deipnosophists*.

## THE CULINARY SYNTHESIS

Relatively little of Athenaeus' vast work concerns Rome and its Empire in AD 200. There are a few remarks on what foods were available, and at what price, in Rome and Alexandria. There are discussions of foods and words that are supposed to be familiar to the Deipnosophists, and of others that are supposed to be unfamiliar to them. Very occasionally we are told of foods that were served at the fictional dinners of the dialogue: but these appear to be literary mirror-images of the foods under discussion. So, for example, the pig served whole, stuffed with smaller animals, at a dinner of the fictional *Deipnosophists*, is a clear imitation of a dish described by Hippolochus at an apparently historical dinner of the third century BC, though indeed such concoctions were known in Rome too.[28]

There are other sources for the food and cookery of the Roman Empire in the third and fourth centuries: a subject that forms, in the present context, a link between the food of earlier and of later Greece. Dishes, usually luxury dishes, are named in the *Historia Augusta*, the semi-historical collection of Imperial biographies written about AD 300.[29] Foods of relatively wide and general importance are listed in Diocletian's *Price Edict*, a short-lived attempt to fix maximum prices of commodities sold in the shops and markets of the Empire. But the single most informative source on cookery and cuisine is certainly the Latin collection of recipes, apparently of the fourth century, known by the name of *Apicius*,[30] a legendary (but real) gourmet of early Imperial times: it has been traditional since Renaissance times to say that the work is 'by' him or 'attributed to' him.

A collection of recipes may be intended for armchair perusal rather than for use in connection with cooking. This has been argued for *Apicius*: the rather uniform richness of a large proportion of the recipes suggests to some that they were intended to whet the literary rather than the physical appetite.[31] But this is to ignore the evidence of the language in which the book is written, for *Apicius* is one of the major sources for Vulgar Latin, the spoken language of the Roman Empire which is the ancestor of the modern Romance languages. This is to say that it was not written for people of culture, or to be read for pleasure. It is written in a technical jargon, and one that was used by people of little formal education. As such it gives an unrivalled picture of the linguistic interaction that was at work in one particular trade during the later Roman Empire – and thus, indirectly, of cultural interaction.

It is no surprise, then, that *Apicius* contains many recipes for dishes with Greek names and many other culinary terms borrowed from Greek. The same is true of the later, briefer, *Outline Apicius* of Vinidarius, a compilation with no clear textual link to the earlier *Apicius*. But *Apicius* is far from marking the beginning of any tradition. Dishes for which recipes are given in *Apicius* and the *Outline Apicius* crop up earlier: in the first century in passages of Petronius' *Satiricon*; in the second century in the *Daily Conversation* attributed to Pollux. The author of that interesting phrasebook is a 'hypercorrector', attempting, by eliminating the diminutives that proliferated among the new words of later Latin and Greek, to restore an illusory standard. Thus for *ofellae*, 'meat pieces' (*Apicius* 7.4; Vinidarius 3–6), *Daily Conversation* has *offae*; for *rapulatus*, 'coated in turnip paste and deep-fried' (Vinidarius 7), *Daily Conversation* has *rapatus*.

Roman cookery at its most elaborate surpasses, in complexity and in sheer number of ingredients, anything that we have yet seen of the cuisine of Greece. The spikenard, kuth, cardamom, camomile, sage, cyperus and gentian that Vinidarius (Preface) apparently expected a fifth-century Roman cook to have at hand were not called for in any earlier Greek recipe. Roman menus added to the native produce of western Europe all the animal and vegetable foods that had come to them from the East – and native produce included such un-Greek delicacies as rabbit and dormouse.

## THE NAMES OF FOODS IN LATER GREEK AND LATIN

The tendency of which *Apicius* provides the fullest evidence – that of the mixture of Greek and Latin in the later Roman language of cookery – was nothing ephemeral. In Greek it explains many Latin borrowings in the medieval and modern language: as to Latin, meanwhile, it presages numerous Greek elements in the vocabulary of the modern Romance languages. Greek and other outlandish terms in *Apicius*, unique or rare in surviving Latin texts, recur regularly in the etymological dictionaries of Spanish, Portuguese, Catalan, French and Italian. This is the time to look more closely at the linguistic evidence. In part this comes from medieval and modern Greek and the medieval and modern Romance languages; occasionally, too, from other languages of the Mediterranean basin. It also comes from Greek and Latin texts of late antiquity, especially non-literary texts: most borrowings did not belong to the learned but to the colloquial languages.

First, it is rather to be expected that newly devised or newly familiar foods and recipes should take their names with them from language to language. Thus the sausages called *isicia* naturally had the same name in Latin and Greek: it was considered a Latin word.[32] Thus a third-century

Greek literary author like Athenaeus might well make some difficulties over using what was still perceived to be a foreign word: one widely enough used to survive (through its compound *salsicia*) in modern French *saucisse* as well as in later Greek. The compound, probably deriving from a phrase *salsa isicia* – but unrecorded as such – was certainly used in both Latin and Greek, for in Greek we have the useful phrase *seirà salsikíon* 'a string of sausages' (*Miracles of Saints Cosmas and Damian* 2). And certainly with the popular smoked sausage *loukánikon*, named after a region of Italy, it is clear that not only the word but some details of the recipe have been borrowed from language to language. The method was brought to Rome, we are told, by soldiers of the late Republic who had served in southern Italy; *Apicius* gives the first surviving recipe. The word is first recorded in Greek in fourth-century papyri and in the joke-book *Philogelos*. *Lucanica* are familiar today from end to end of the Mediterranean and far beyond: in southern Italy, Greece and Cyprus; in Bulgaria; in Portugal and Brazil as *linguiça*; in Spain as *longaniza*; in the Arabic-speaking Levant and among Levantine Jews.[33] Modern *lucanica*, under these various names, are usually spicy, usually smoked, usually formed of a single long casing which is not twisted into segments. Quince paste or marmalade was most often called *kydonâton*, a Greek stem with Latin suffix;[34] this or a similar Latinised form lies behind Provençal *codonhat* and French *cotignac*. It is a Latin source that gives us our first recipe for something like an omelette, *ova spongia*. This term reappears in Byzantine Greek: Damascenus Studites made an object-lesson out of the way that *sphoungâton* was made, and the word also occurs in the twelfth-century *Prodromic Poems*.[35]

Second, there are the new names for foodstuffs that were already known. Very often these are to be explained as names for newly developed varieties. In Hellenistic and Roman times gardeners and farmers put great effort into plant breeding, a subject on which Pliny and the Latin agricultural writers have much to say. New varieties sometimes became so widely popular that the name that came with them (and this in its origin was sometimes a newly invented name for the variety, sometimes a foreign name for the whole species) eventually replaced, in Greek, the older species name. An analogous process may be invoked to explain how, in Hellenistic or even earlier times, some Greek plant names had become established in Latin: *asparagus* beside Latin *corruda*, 'asparagus', *malum* and later *melum*, 'apple'. In Imperial times the movement tended to be in the other direction: the earlier Greek names for apricot, peach, plum, citron, endive and lettuce have all been supplanted in modern Greek by terms first recorded in the first or second centuries AD, some of them definitely variety names in origin, some of them clearly Latin, most of them surviving in the Romance languages as well. An early variety of apricot was called *praecox*, 'precocious', in Latin. This gave rise to the new Greek word for 'apricot', *brekókion* (Chapter 6).[36] A kind of peach was given the not very distinctive epithet *duracinus*, 'hard-kernel':

hence later Greek *dorákinon* and, after transposition, modern Greek *rodáki-non*.[37] Rome liked the Damascus variety of plum, *damascenum*: this is still a variety name in most of Europe – English *damson* – but in Greek, as in Portuguese, it has become the name for all plums.[38] Though the usage is not attested in Latin, modern Greek *maroúli*, 'lettuce', seems clearly to come from a Latin variety name *amarula*, 'bitterish'.[39] For less evident reasons Latin *citrus*, in a Greek form *kítrion*, replaced the older Greek term *mêlon medikón* for 'citron'. The Greeks themselves appear, from the multiplicity of names for 'chicory' and 'endive', to have developed several varieties of these species: the usual name in most modern European languages for the endive comes from another term first recorded under the early Empire, *intibus*, though in this case its linguistic origins are unknown. Whatever precisely was the nature of earlier *petrosélinon*, usually translated 'parsley', an improved kind called *petrosélinon makedonikón*, 'Macedonian parsley', is first recorded in the second century: it is this that has given its name to parsley in modern Greek, *maidonós*.[40] Finally the new name for carrots, both in modern Greek and in many western languages, seems to have been a variety name that originated not in Latin but in Greek: *karotós*, 'headed'. Carrots as we know them, with their red, swollen, nutritionally rich roots, are not so much as heard of in classical or Hellenistic texts. For the first time in the first century AD, as an appendix to the description of the plant, one finds: 'the root as thick as a finger, pointed, aromatic, edible boiled', and it is at this time also that the new term is found.[41]

Interaction between Greek and Roman cultures sometimes resulted not in borrowings but in linguistic calques: it was not the phonetic form but the semantic form of a word or phrase that was adopted. A gastronomic example is Greek *sykotón*, Latin *ficatum*: the Greek word initially meant 'force-fed goose liver, foie gras'. Which language was the originator? The answer is that the Latin seems to be a calque on the Greek, and not vice versa, because it was Greek geese that were actually force-fed *with figs*, and 'stuffed with figs' is the literal meaning of both Greek and Latin terms. However, their usual meaning is simply 'liver': indeed the Latin word is actually recorded only with this sense. It occurs first in *Apicius*. 'Liver' is the meaning of the modern descendant words, modern Greek *sikóti*, Spanish *higado*, French *foie* and Romanian *ficat*.[42]

An obvious outcome of all this interchange, which is just as evident in legal and administrative terminology, is that the Greeks of Byzantium, in writing of their own food and its surroundings, used a high proportion of terms borrowed from Latin – though some authors were more assiduous than others at hunting out classical Greek words from early texts and glossaries. A butcher, no longer doubling as a cook, would now be a Latinised *makelários* unless one remembered to devise a pseudo-classical term for him, *kreôn prátes* 'vendor of flesh'.[43] A wineshop would now be a *tabérnion* rather than a *kapeleîon*.

But to treat the phenomenon as one of borrowing from a foreign language is to oversimplify. Cultures were actually mingling and a technical term from one of the two languages might seem the only good way to denote a newly developed institution or concept. More significantly, in the case of many of the new technical terms of Latin and Greek that are first recorded during the Roman Empire it is not easy to say which language they started in. This was evident already with the breads and cakes of Chrysippus and Cato (Chapter 7). It is evident again with the new fruit and vegetable names above, and with the names of exotic imports that first reached the Mediterranean in the early centuries AD, for example, cloves (Chapter 6, p. 138). *Karyóphyllon* looks Greek, but 'nut-leaf' makes little sense, and Latin *gariofilum* does not look like a good attempt at Latinised Greek. The word is probably neither Latin nor Greek in origin, but borrowed from some eastern language and then reshaped in Greek by folk-etymology.[44] Finally, the doubt over word origins occurs with the names of new food terms such as *copadia*, 'small slices of meat served with a dip'.[45]

As the vast scale of borrowing from Greek to Latin and from Latin to Greek during this period gradually becomes apparent – we have dealt only with some examples from a single semantic field – we begin to grasp that a kind of coalescence was under way; a coalescence more advanced in some milieux than in others; a coalescence that began but was never completed, as the division first made by Diocletian between eastern and western provinces hardened, long after Diocletian's time, into a cultural and linguistic frontier.

*Figure 31* Preparing a meal on the beach: Alonnisos, about 1930 (unknown photographer)

# Part IV

# THE BYZANTINE AND LATER AEGEAN

# 9

# BISCUITS FROM BYZANTIUM[1]

## ROMAN AND BYZANTINE LITERATURE AND THE FOOD OF GREECE

In the centuries of Roman domination there is all too little evidence for the gastronomy of Greece. Athenaeus shows no knowledge of contemporary Greece: his antiquarian compilation reconstructs the food behaviour of a lost, ancient Greece. In this he was firmly in the scholarly tradition of the Hellenistic diaspora, for in all the capital cities where Greeks had clustered, Antioch, Pergamum and most of all Alexandria, there had been lavish patronage for research on the classics of their literature. In Greece itself, by contrast, not very long before this, Plutarch (in *Symposium Questions*) had sketched the dining customs of Greece as a Roman province, more different from those of earlier Greece than he himself realised.[2] Plutarch in any case says little of what was eaten at his semi-autobiographical *sympósia*; but his work is a sign that strong influence from Rome should already be expected in culinary and social matters.

From Byzantine sources, written when the Greek-speaking world was contracting once more and no longer stretched so far beyond the Aegean region, it is once again possible to find copious information on the food and the social history of the region – and thus to investigate how deep had been the long-term influence of Hellenistic and Roman cuisine on that of Greece itself.

Byzantine literature poses its own problems for those looking for evidence of this kind. Traditional education continued to privilege the now long-distant classical past, its language, its literature, even its non-Christian mythology. Thus there is a deep, often creative, contradiction in the writings of the Byzantine Empire between the reality of every day and the paths of schooled thought and approved expression. It is through engagement with this contradiction that a new history of Byzantine social life will be written.

Dietetics was a concern of doctors, and, we must suppose, of those who consulted doctors, throughout the Byzantine period. Oribasius (*c.*

325–400), a contemporary of the Emperor Julian (and a main character in Gore Vidal's novel *Julian*), marks an end and a beginning with his vast collectanea, addressed to the Emperor and compiled at his suggestion not only from Galen's works but also from numerous lesser authorities.[3] The first five books of these are devoted to the dietary properties of foodstuffs. They are important as a guide to the inherited dietary wisdom of the period and also as preserving many passages from lost works. Compilations by Aetius of Amida, who worked *c.* AD 550,[4] and by Paul of Aegina, *c.* 640, are comparable. An outline of medicine by Theophanes Nonnus, *c.* 950, dedicated to Constantine Porphyrogennetus, is accompanied in many manuscripts by a short anonymous work *On Foods*.[5] There are several other brief and approachable dietary manuals. A Latin *Letter* by the exiled Byzantine physician Anthimus to his new patron Theodoric, *c.* 475, can be counted first in this genre – first, that is, in succession to Hellenistic and Roman works of the same kind.[6] A dietary survey by Simeon Seth, *c.* 1075, is arranged by food origins: it reflects its period in the inclusion of eastern foods, eastern varieties and Arabic dietary opinions unknown to earlier Greek authors.[7] Of about the same date is Michael Psellus' poem *On Medicine*. And there is a family of brief manuals setting out the regimen appropriate to each month of the year in diet, exercise, baths and sex – the latter forbidden in July. Some of these handbooks, in prose, are attributed to 'Hierophilus the Sophist'; one, abridged and versified, is by Theodore Prodromus (*c.* 1150); others, prose and verse, are unattributed.[8] Pharmacological works, and pharmacological sections of the general medical textbooks, are also informative on food sources; botanical investigations survive as comment, annotation and illustration of Dioscorides' *Materia Medica* and in lexica of botanical terms.[9]

Not unlike the medical collections, textbooks of agriculture in late Hellenistic and Imperial times had also developed in the form of collectanea. But the agricultural textbooks are largely lost. The Byzantine compilation of *c.* 950, dedicated to Constantine Porphyrogennetus and known as the *Geoponica of Cassianus Bassus*,[10] attributes its information – with questionable reliability – to numerous ancient authorities, including Paxamus. It is not quite the sole survivor of its genre, but an earlier Greek *Geoponicon*, perhaps to be assigned to Anatolius of Berytus, *c.* 365, is now known only in Syriac and Armenian translations. Finally, Byzantine knowledge, both agricultural and dietetic, is applied to a new generation of plant and animal varieties in the *Geoponikón* of the monk Agapius of Crete, first published in Venice in 1647 – a modest and useful work that was still being reprinted for farmers' use in nineteenth-century Greece.[11]

And to set beside all this is the non-specialist literature, from law manuals to saints' lives and secular satire, that happens to offer insights on food and its social context.[12]

## THE FOOD AND DRINK OF BYZANTIUM

The Byzantine rule, that educated writing must wear the disguise of classical Attic, has been unfortunate for the reputation of Byzantine culture. It asks to be judged by classical standards – and by those standards is judged stiff, unoriginal and artificial. Those who have read the Imperial portraits by Psellus (*Chronographia*) and the bitter lament that is the *History* of Nicetas Choniates, know that Byzantium was far more than a poor imitation of classical Greece and Rome. Its life and culture, like those of most other societies, certainly did arise from a synthesis of what had gone before; a synthesis that continued to develop and did not cease to innovate.

So it is with food and gastronomy. Constantinople naturally inherited the culinary knowledge of the Roman Empire, but novelties are to be found.[13] Alongside the meat foods known in earlier times, the Byzantines experimented with dried meat, one of the forerunners of the *pastirma* of modern Turkey. The attention that they paid to inland Anatolia and Syria is reflected in the high reputation as game of the gazelles of the Near East, '*dorkádes* commonly called *gazélia*': these, practically overlooked by earlier authors, were recommended above all other game by Simeon Seth. The emperors had their hunting parks, and in particular their herd of wild asses – though one wonders whether the cynical Bishop Liutprand was right and the wild asses of tenth-century AD Constantinople, prized by gourmets, were semi-feral herds of the domesticated species after all. Closer to home, sparrows, *pyrgítes*, were among small birds that were caught to eat. Of domestic animals one seems to detect a preference, stronger than in earlier texts, for the suckling young; but this did not preclude a liking for offal of all kinds, including the udder of a suckling sow.[14]

Constantinople, classical Byzantium, modern Istanbul, has always been famous for its seafood. The medieval dietary manuals specify a great many kinds, singling out this or that quality in each. There are some names unfamiliar to readers of classical texts.[15] And again there was room for gastronomic novelty. The Byzantines appreciated salt roe, botargo, whose name is Greek in origin: *oiotárikhon* is literally 'egg pickle'. Botargo is first mentioned by Simeon Seth (*On the Properties of Foods* 125), who said that it 'should be avoided totally'! In the twelfth century Constantinople tasted caviar, *kabiári*, the new fish delicacy of the Black Sea, and, still later, imported kippered herrings, *réngai*, from distant Britain.[16]

Herbalists, gardeners and food collectors could still draw on all the native plant species whose properties were set out in the *Materia Medica* of Dioscorides. Dieticians could recommend to invalids vegetarian meals, eaten with vinegar or other dressing.[17] Newly introduced species included the aubergine, *melitzána*, and, later, the orange, *nerántzion*.[18] New flavours and combinations continued to be tried. Where classical cooks had wrapped food in pickled fig leaves, *thrîa*, it seems to have been in late Roman or

189

early Byzantine times that stuffed vine leaves were used in similar recipes, thus becoming the parents of modern *dolmádhes*. Vine leaves were in any case stripped from the vine in the course of the summer to assist the ripening of the fruit.[19] The unprepossessing bulb of squill, *skílla*, poisonous according to modern sources of information, was used in flavoured wines and vinegars: a recipe is already given by Dioscorides and it is not surprising that this is excerpted in the compilation of Oribasius, for, though known to the Romans, squill vinegar appears to have come into its own in Byzantine recipes.[20] Rosemary, *dendrolíbanon*, again well known in the earlier Roman Empire, was for a long time not used as a food flavouring, though it was popular for wreaths: it is however recommended for roast lamb, quite in the modern fashion, by Agapius.[21] Saffron, whose only known place in the earlier Greek diet was as an ingredient in spiced wine, was certainly used in Byzantine cookery.[22]

The bakers of Constantinople were in the most favoured of trades, with a range of privileges specified in a document of *c.* 895 (*Book of the Eparch* 18): 'bakers are never liable to be called for any public service, neither themselves nor their animals, to prevent any interruption of the baking of bread'. Bread, colloquially *psomí*, came in many of the varieties already known from classical texts: white and brown were distinguished as *katharós*, 'clean', and *ryparós*, 'dirty', among other terms. *Silignítes*, made from bread wheat, becomes far more common in sources of the Byzantine period than it had ever been before; barley bread was also baked. Sweets and cakes continued to be devised.[23]

The cheese available in Greece begins in Byzantine texts to resemble more closely the range that we know from the modern Aegean. *Mízithra* is recognisable. So is *féta* under its medieval name *prósphatos*: '*prósphatos*, containing plenty of salt, is soft, pleasant to taste and nourishing' (*Poem on Medicine* 1.209). They were produced respectively by the Vlachs of Thessaly and by the Cretans. The cheese of Paphlagonia, a region of north-west Anatolia, was also well known in Constantinople.[24] The marketing of *féta* in Crete is described in some detail by an Italian pilgrim, Pietro Casola, who visited Candia at the end of the fifteenth century:

> They make a great many cheeses; it is a pity they are so salty. I saw great warehouses full of them, some in which the brine, or *salmoria* as we would say, was two feet deep, and the large cheeses were floating in it. Those in charge told me that the cheeses could not be preserved in any other way, being so rich. They do not know how to make butter. They sell a great quantity to the ships that call there: it was astonishing to see the number of cheeses taken on board our own galley.[25]

The use of imported spices in European cuisine was still growing to its medieval peak. Byzantine Greeks used nutmeg to sprinkle on pease

*Figure 32* Honeycombs on sale in the spice market in Istanbul

pudding for fast days.[26] They also imported cane sugar, *sákhar*. This was first brought to Greek attention long before, in a report by Eratosthenes of 'large reeds, sweet both by nature and by the sun's heat' (Strabo, *Geography* 15.1.20), but once more the first evidence of its use in European food comes in middle Byzantine times.[27] The trade routes that led to Byzantium passed through Trebizond, through Alexandria and through Mesopotamia: 'the best cinnamon comes from Mosul', we are told (Simeon Seth, *On the Properties of Foods* 55), and must understand that in the eleventh century the best cinnamon available in Mediterranean markets had come from India by way of that city. One fact stands out. Where earlier dieticians, from the Hippocratic *Regimen* to Oribasius, had said very little of the effect of spices in food, the Byzantine dietary manuals insist on the point over and over again, urging different strengths and combinations of aromatics depending on the eater's physical condition, on the season of the year and even on the time of day. And, more than any earlier such texts known to us, they give the impression of being written for non-specialists. Spices and seasonings were, more than ever before, an integral part of the diet, used both during the cooking process and at table to adjust the flavour and the dietary qualities of each dish.[28] For example, fresh figs, if eaten in July when sweet foods were inappropriate, must be taken with salt.

It is among sweets and sweet drinks that we can perhaps best recognise the distinctive flavour of Byzantine cookery. There are dishes that we would recognise as puddings: *groûta*, a sort of frumenty, sweetened with honey and studded with carob seeds or raisins; rice pudding served with honey. Quince marmalade has already entered the repertoire; other jams or conserves now make their appearance, including pear and citron or lemon, sugar, as it becomes commoner, being a realistic substitute at last for honey. High-quality biscuit, *biscoctum delicatum*, was bought in Constantinople by William of Rubruck. Rose sugar, a popular medieval confection,[29] may well have originated here.

Flavoured soft drinks were by no means unknown under the Roman Empire. There is an impressive list of them, with recipes and nutritional information, by a dietician Philagrius: his work survives because it was excerpted by Oribasius. But it is in Byzantine times that sources such as Hierophilus' *Dietary Calendar* indicate the frequent use of such concoctions.[30]

Flavoured wines were even more popular, if we can judge by the available sources. They also had a long history: but it is in the later years of the Roman Empire, and after, that they seem to have gained in importance. Three are listed in Diocletian's *Price Edict*. The price of the complex, multi-spiced *conditum* was fixed at 24 denarii per Italian pint, three times that of *oînos ágrios*, *oînos khydeos* – 'vin de pays, vin de table'; absinthe wine and rose wine were to fetch almost as much.[31] But there were far more varieties than these three. In our texts of Oribasius' *Medical Collections* (5.33) there is a lengthy list, which, to judge by some of its vocabulary, was partly or wholly added to the text after Oribasius' time. Among these wines, the ones flavoured with mastic and aniseed may be set beside the rose and absinthe wines of the *Price Edict* as already of fairly wide use. They are distant ancestors of the mastiha, vermouth, absinthe – now outlawed – and pastis of the modern Mediterranean.[32] Let us borrow a classicist locution and call the compiler of these recipes 'pseudo-Oribasius'. This anonymous Byzantine physician or druggist gives us evidence that a remarkable range of new aromatics, unknown to earlier inhabitants of the region except as perfumes or in medicines, belonged to the liquid diet of Byzantium: spikenard, *nardóstakhys*; gentian, *gentiané*; yellow flag, *ákoron*;[33] stone parsley, *sínon*; spignel, *mêon*; Valeriana Dioscoridis, *karpésion*; kuth, *kóstos*; tejpat, *phyllon*; benzoin, *styrax*; ginger grass, *skhoínanthos*; chamomile, *khamaímelon*; violet, *íon*. Several of these, with pepper, cinnamon and cloves, could be ingredients in Byzantine *conditum* (ibid. 5.33.8–9), of which a daily glass, strong in spikenard, was recommended in March in Hierophilus' *Dietary Calendar*: *anisâton* was appropriate for April.

William of Rubruck, a thirteenth-century traveller, looking for worthwhile presents to take from Constantinople to Khazaria, had chosen 'on the advice of merchants, fruit, muscat wine and fine biscuits to . . . make my passage easier, since they regard no one with favour who arrives empty-handed' (*Report* 9). The fruit was no doubt dried, candied or preserved in must or honey. Of wine – colloquially *krasí*[34] – he would have found a considerable variety. Constantinople was already the *Wînburg*, the city of wine, to Anglo-Saxon tradition in the seventh century (*Widsith* 76–8). We know something of the trade from the *Book of the Eparch* (19). We know too that the dieticians, following Galen's example, ruled on the kinds of wine that suited each season.

There were two grape varieties that provided the favourite sweet wines of the medieval Aegean. One, yielding the *vinum muscatos* to which William referred, is still widely grown in many Mediterranean countries. Its name is borrowed by most modern languages from the medieval Greek, in which *moskhâtos* meant 'musk-flavoured'.[35] The vineyards of Samos and Lemnos today produce muscat wine very much of the style that William might have selected. The other variety was the *monembasiós*, French *malvoisie*, English *malmsey*, the typical sweet grape of Crete. Its product, in later Byzantine times, was beginning to be exported to western and northern Europe through Monemvasia, hence its name.[36] This grape is now less widespread in Greece, but was in due course found to be ideally suited to the volcanic slopes of Madeira.

We may now list wine-producing districts favoured by Byzantine authors – bearing in mind the difficulty that literary men liked to drop classical names, such as Pramnian and Maronean, into their texts. The highly literate Michael Psellus, in a poem of apparently contemporary reference (*To a Shopkeeper*), went so far as to borrow Italian wines out of the list at *Epitome of Athenaeus* 26c–d! From the much longer unselective list that could be gathered the namings more likely to be honest are those with less of a classical resonance. Chian and Lesbian, however, were still appreciated by travellers even in the Ottoman Empire, so there is no good reason to doubt that Byzantine authors who said that they liked these two meant what they said. In one of the *Prodromic Poems*, Cretan, Samian and Ganitic – from Mount Ganos in Thrace – are listed as good, beside Varniote, from the Black Sea port of Varna, which was not so good. Elsewhere Euboean and Rhodian are set beside beside Chian; Monemvasiote appears for the first time, with Triglian from Bithynia; Nicaean also appears from Bithynia and the wine of Cuzinas from the Thracesian theme. In the fourteenth century the Florentine merchant Francesco Pegolotti (*Pratica della Mercatura*) listed Triglian and Monemvasiote with Cretan and Theban wines.[37]

There are signs in the middle Byzantine period that the attractions of neat wine were beginning to assert themselves. Even dieticians, somewhat cautious authorities, permitted their Byzantine readers a dose of neat wine on a winter morning, and were inclined to recommend rather stronger than half-and-half mixtures.[38] By the sixteenth century, Pierre Belon

*Figure 33* Pierre Belon, sensitive observer of early Ottoman Greece and of Venetian Crete. *Source*: from the second edition of his *Observations* 1555

(*Observations* 1.4), on a visit to Venetian-governed Crete, found a difference between ancient sources and observed custom:

> [The Greeks] all consider it bad to put water in their wine. Their present practice is to drink equally and by turns, especially the Cretans... with frequent little sips of their strong malmsey.... It must be understood that the Greeks' tables are usually very low, and their custom is to drink as they sit, by turns, never getting out of sequence. If anyone asked for wine out of turn he would be considered rude. The quickest at pouring has the wine-jug and pours for all the company. The custom is to drink from a small glass without a stem, and to drink all that is poured out, not leaving a drop.... They always have the water urn at hand and drink water as well, in big mouthfuls, to restore themselves. Women never take part in their banquets, and are not present when they drink and eat in company.

As we have seen, Aegean wines were exported westwards in some quantity in the Middle Ages. Cretan malmsey, like earlier Greek wines intended for long distance export, was specially treated. Belon's description of this practice (*Observations* 1.19) shows that the *solera* method of blending sherry, and the 'cooking' undergone by French fortified wines such as Banyuls and Maury, may both be traceable to medieval Greece:

> The wine we call malmsey is only made in Crete, and we are able to assert that what travels furthest, to Germany, France and England, has first been cooked, for the ships that come to Crete to carry it abroad insist on loading that of Rethymo. This is well known to keep its quality for a long time, and the more it travels the better it is. In the town of Rethymo there are big cauldrons all along the harbour side, which they use for boiling their wines each vintage. We do not say that all malmseys are boiled. Those of the town and district of Candia, which are only exported as far as Italy and are not expected to turn sour, are not boiled. But, refreshing their wines annually, they correct the old with the new and reinforce the new with the old. . . . Crete also produces very good muscat. . . . There is muscat and malmsey of two kinds, one sweet, one not sweet . . . but the latter is not exported, because it is not cooked as the sweet is, and does not keep so long.

To judge by the very limited evidence available from earlier times, which we have noted in Chapters 4 and 6, these methods of wine production 'for export' have a much longer ancestry still. The Spartan wine that was 'boiled', the classical wines prepared 'for transport by sea', and even the Phoenician and Lesbian wines 'in small jars', are all part of the same story.

## BYZANTINE FOOD IN ITS CONTEXT

> In Galatia there is a village called Syceon. . . . The post road ran through this village, and on the road stood an inn kept by a very beautiful girl, Mary, and her mother and sister. . . .
>
> There lived at the house a God-fearing man called Stephanus who used to make skilfully prepared dishes. The women by this time had become quite respectable, for they had abandoned their profession as prostitutes and followed the path of sobriety and godliness. They now relied upon the quality of the cooking when they entertained the many governors and officers who came to the inn, and they congratulated Stephanus who had made the food so tasty.
>
> (*Life of St Theodore of Syceon* 3, 6)

This early Byzantine text is a landmark in gastronomic history – the first such record anywhere in the world. In the ancient world travellers went to inns because they had nowhere else to go: if wise, they brought their food with them and kept a close eye on its preparation. Those were the travellers that Archestratus had had in mind. To find an inn that was sought out for the sake of its food is, in this context, little short of miraculous. Whatever the truth of this, there are no more such records. In Greece and Turkey, until the increase in European-style travelling in the late nineteenth century, the usual 'inn', *xenodokheîon, han*, seemed to foreign travellers more in the nature of a hostel, and a very down-at-heel one. They had often been founded as charities, housing the sick and the homeless equally with unprovided travellers: 'no one is refused who comes there, Jew, Christian, Idolater or Turk', said Belon (*Observations* 1.59) in the sixteenth century. These hostels provided free food – but not good food. The American Nicholas Biddle, shortly after 1800, summarised the situation that had held, for those with introductions, for two thousand years and more: 'there being no taverns in Greece you are always lodged in the houses of individuals'. The same observation was made by an Iranian traveller, Mirzâ Mohammad Hosayn Farâhâni, who visited Istanbul in 1885: 'all of the travellers who have an acquaintance go to the home or lodging of the acquaintances'.[39]

For those who had to use them, the food provided at inns no doubt resembled the porridges of classical times and those that belonged to the basic food of the Ottoman Empire, to be described in due course (p. 201). For such people, too, there were wine shops that served the wine of the poor, *phoûska*, Latin *posca*. Sellers of *posca* were already to be found in the first century AD. It was a vinegar and water mixture, with little of the flavour and less of the potency of wine, sometimes flavoured with penny-royal,[40] just as ancient *kykeón* had been. Taverns that dealt in true wine were subject to a curfew in the tenth century (*Book of the Eparch* 19) to prevent 'violence and rioting' under the influence of drink.

The food of the poor was certainly limited, and no doubt usually veg-etarian: a list of the contents of a poor family's larder (*Prodromic Poems* 2.38–45) includes numerous vegetables and locally grown fruits, but also a considerable list of flavourings, vinegar, honey, pepper, cinnamon, cumin, caraway, salt and others. Cheese, olives and onions also helped to take the place of meat. Another poem in the same collection (4.49–70) describes a cobbler's daily routine: his meals are meaty enough, though relying partly on offal, and he can afford Vlach cheese. *Timarion* (17), a satirical poem also of the twelfth century, offers a salt pork and cabbage stew as a typical poor man's meal, eaten with the hands as in contemporary western Europe.

The basic food of the Byzantine army[41] was cereal, in several convenient forms. Of great importance was the barley biscuit that was possibly named after the late Hellenistic cook Paxamus (Chapter 7, p. 165). It was probably the food that the future Emperor Justin II, uncle of Justinian, carried in his knapsack, the food that kept him alive on his long walk from Illyria to Constantinople; it was certainly food for soldiers and for frugal priests as well. Knowledge of it spread onwards from Byzantium more widely, perhaps, than the fame of many luxuries. The Greek *paximádion* – still known in the countryside today under that name – is Arabic *bashmat*, *baqsimat*, Turkish *beksemad*, Serbo-Croat *peksimet*, Romanian *pesmet* and Venetian *pasimata*.[42] A second typical food was the crock-baked bread, close to pita bread in style, *klibanítes*, suitable for army use because the *klíbanos* in which it was baked was portable. Also well known was millet porridge, *píston*.[43]

But for those who had the money and the opportunity to buy and prepare good food, Constantinople offered dazzling variety, high quality and tempting quantity in food and wine. As the centre of what was at first little less than a world empire, the city attracted trade from a wide hinterland. The *Book of the Eparch* tells us something of how this trade was regulated, although, by contrast with Evliya Çelebi's description of the annual procession of the trades of Istanbul before the Sultan, the *Book of the Eparch* gives little idea of the range that must already have been available in the shops and markets of Byzantine Constantinople. Lively letters of many a Byzantine notable list the fine foods and wines that were given and received as gifts.[44]

Byzantium was a Christian Empire. Its Christianity led to certain changes in food habits as compared with the earlier Roman Empire and before, and for those in monasteries food and drink were regulated as they had been for few in earlier times. There were the weekly fast days. In the satirical third *Prodromic Poem*, abbatial abstinence from meat and fish, enjoined every Wednesday and Friday, allows the impressive ingenuity of Byzantine cooks to be expended on making shellfish and vegetable foods as attractive as the flesh on which the abbots were able to gorge themselves on the other five days of the week. But for most in monasteries, there is no doubt, fasts were really severe, and occupied not only two days of each week but also certain longer periods: Lent, the fast of the Apostles, the fast of St Philip. Monks ate only once on each fast day, and on these days their food was eaten without oil or seasoning. The rule in brief was *xerophagía*, 'dry eating', and *hydroposía*, 'water drinking', though the water might be flavoured with pepper, cumin and anise.[45]

Judaeo-Christian culture brought also some specific prohibitions, not necessarily easy to impose and maintain against the resistance of custom and tradition. The eating of foods made from animal blood – in origin a Jewish taboo – was forbidden by the 58th *Novel* of Leo VI; yet some such foods were still being made and eaten, as close to the capital as Adrianople, in the twelfth century according to Theodore Balsamon's *Commentary on the Canons of the Council of Trullo*. The 'foods made from blood' to which Balsamon refers must have been some sort of black pudding.[46]

Food had its symbolism in Byzantine times as in earlier Greece. Vryonis gives examples of the association of fruit with love and marriage:

> The emperors of the eighth and ninth centuries chose their brides in a beauty contest by presenting an apple to the future imperial consort; golden apples or pomegranates were part of the ceremonial connected with the empress's procession to and from the bath after the wedding. As early as the fourth century and into the medieval epoch the groom was showered with apples when he came to take the bride from her parents' house.[47]

## A CHARACTER OF BYZANTINE GASTRONOMY

We have seen classical Greek food through Greek eyes – and perhaps occasionally via Greek opinions of external views. Greek cuisine of the Roman Empire is privileged in another way. We do know something of Romans' reaction to it. But, by employing Greek or eastern cooks, by importing and paying high prices for Greek and eastern delicacies, by assiduously transplanting Greek and eastern plant varieties, by adopting Greek names for foods and for finished dishes, Romans appear to have displayed in this area, perhaps uncritically, their general ambition to emulate Greek culture and eastern luxury. The occasional impatient counterblast by a moralist or an old-fashioned politician was never a sufficient corrective.

With Byzantium it is different: here, for the first time, we can read and compare both native and foreign views of the culture and the cuisine. Byzantine cookery pleased natives, or so it seems from the lingering, mouth-watering descriptions in Byzantine satirical poetry such as *Timarion* and the third *Prodromic Poem*.

In spite of their exaggerated local pride Byzantines abroad tended to be impressed by the food they found.[48] Foreign ambassadors to Constantinople were not uniformly complimentary. Strong, indeed supercilious, views on many aspects of Byzantine life and culture were expressed by Bishop Liutprand of Cremona, ambassador from Germany to Constantinople in 949–50 and again in 968: Liutprand's lively if querulous Latin *Embassy to Constantinople* and *Antapodosis* are rich sources for the food that the bishop ate and disliked in the course of his mission.

Greek wine, he reported, was 'owing to its mixing with pitch, resin and gypsum, undrinkable by us' (*Embassy* 1). We have seen a little of the long history of retsina: Liutprand was not the last traveller to have disliked it. In the fifteenth century Pietro Casola was equally disgusted by the resinous flavour of the wine of Modon. Even the Byzantine author Michael Choniates, Archbishop of Athens in the twelfth century, disliked the local retsina; Nicephorus Basilaca, around the same date, disapproved of the resinous

wine of Philippopolis in Thrace.[49] Liutprand may have been right in recog-
nising also the aroma of pitch – though the two are not always distinguished by disdainful palates. Pitch, used in the preparation of amphoras
for wine-making and storage, was also sometimes added for its aroma or
flavour.[50] In the western Mediterranean, however, barrels had long ago
taken the place of amphoras. Liutprand will no doubt have been taken
aback to sense resin or pitch instead of oak. Gypsum, among other minerals, is quite commonly used in the fining of wine, as it was in Roman
times, but its overuse could indeed impair the flavour.[51]

Liutprand reports on the first formal dinner he attended at the Palace
(*Embassy* 11):

> I sat fifteenth from [the emperor] and without a tablecloth. Not only
> did no one of my suite sit with me: they did not even set eyes upon
> the house where I was entertained. This dinner ... was quite nasty
> and unspeakable, drunkenly awash with oil and seasoned with
> another very unpleasant liquid made from fish. ...

Graeco-Roman tradition, made manifest in the smell of fish sauce and
squill vinegar, had clung tenaciously to Byzantine cuisine: and a generous
use of olive oil is one of the most frequently criticised features of modern
Greek cookery. Liutprand's fish liquor is surely *gáros*, though indeed he
will in due course refer to that substance by name. In a passage that may
be ironic in its praise Liutprand remarks on a dish sent to him at his
lodgings: 'The sacred emperor lessened my woes with a big gift, sending
me one of his most delicate dishes, a fat kid of which he had himself
partaken – proudly stuffed with garlic, onion, leeks, awash in *garum*'
(*Embassy* 20). This fermented fish sauce, by now just about dead in the
western Mediterranean, was still much used in Byzantium.[52]

Liutprand's dry wit allows us only a hint of the range of Byzantine
cuisine. He remarks elsewhere on the marine delicacies available at Constantinople. But an enthusiasm for fish cookery in the Greek tradition had,
it seems, been joined by a newer willingness to put effort into meat and
vegetable dishes such as the stuffed kid: this kind of meat cookery, so
*Apicius* indicates, had been Roman rather than Greek. We would suspect
nothing from Liutprand of the roast pork basted with honey wine, of the
baked *kítharos* spiced with caraway, of the wild duck with its sauce of
wine, *gáros*, mustard and cumin-salt; we would know nothing of the
calavance cooked in honey vinegar.[53]

## FOOD OF THE OTTOMAN AEGEAN

The last centuries of Byzantium were a nightmare of war and civil strife.
None of the inhabitants of the once-favoured central lands of the once-
great Empire could consider themselves safe from capture, expropriation

or death. Therefore the years that followed the Ottoman capture of Constantinople in 1453 appear, through the eyes of contemporary travellers,
as something of a new golden age. The French naturalist Pierre Belon
(*Observations*), for example, considered the Greeks who lived under the
Venetian domination of Crete, last survivor of the medieval political frag-
mentation of the Aegean, no better off than those who were Ottoman
subjects. Belon's visit to the Levant had a scientific purpose – the discovery,
or rediscovery, of plants and drugs known from classical sources – but his
lively mind found much of interest in the social behaviour of his Greek
and Turkish hosts.

It is appropriate to begin with one or two of Belon's rediscoveries. It is
to his work that we owe the latest clear description of the making of *gáros*,
fermented fish sauce, in the region:

> There was a liquor called *garum* which was once as widely used at
> Rome as vinegar is now. We found it as popular in Turkey as it ever
> was. There is not a fishmonger's shop in Constantinople that has not
> some for sale.... The *garum*-makers of Constantinople are mostly
> in Pera. They prepare fresh fish daily, sell it fried, and make use of
> the entrails and roe, steeping them in brine to turn them into *garum*.
> It matters a good deal which fish is used. Only the *trachurus*, which
> the Venetians call *suro* [scad], and mackerel, will do.... There is a
> another product made of sturgeons' eggs, universally called *caviar*,
> which is so common at Greek and Turkish meals throughout the
> Levant that there is no one who does not eat it except the Jews, who
> avoid it because the sturgeon has no scales.[54]

(1.75)

*Gáros* had been worthwhile enough in medieval eyes, as a contributor to
cuisine, to find imitators: the *murri* of the medieval Levant is an analogous
fermented sauce, though made from grain, not fish. But in Greece this was
the last gasp of *gáros*: at any rate I have as yet found no mention of it by
later travellers. Fish was said not to be in favour at the Palace.[55]

Belon also (*Observations* 1.66) found yoghurt in common use, identifying it with classical *oxygala*. His description can be compared with Galen's,
cited in Chapter 2 (p. 66):

> All the carmen and muleteers of the caravan had a kind of sour milk,
> called *oxygala*, which they carry in cloth bags hanging at their beasts'
> flanks. Although quite liquid, it stays in the bag without seeping
> through. The Greeks and Turks customarily take cloves of garlic and
> beat them in a wooden mortar and mix them with this yoghourt. It
> makes a lordly dish.[56]

Though foreshadowed in earlier Aegean sources, yoghurt appears to
have become a much more significant part of the diet in Ottoman times.

The same may be said of dried meat, *pastirma*, which according to Michel Baudier was already a prized delicacy in his time.[57]

Belon (*Observations* 1.59) gives a description of that useful substance *trakhanás*, a porridge, well known in the modern Aegean, made from cracked emmer (or other grains) that has been mixed with sour milk and dried in balls. He describes it as a *potage* which he found regularly served at hostelries in the region. He is not quite right in identifying it with ancient *mâza*, barley mash, which appears to have been eaten in a more solid form. *Trakhanás* was in fact the *tragós* or *traganós* of earlier texts: its making is described in the *Geoponica*.[58]

Ottoman cuisine had not stood still. Some kinds of cultivated vegetables and fruits that are familiar now would have been unknown in the region at earlier periods. The currant (literally 'Corinthian') vine cannot be traced in early texts. Its produce was noticed by Nicholas Biddle[59] at Zante and Patras. He says of 'the currants of Corinth', 'when preserved they are exquisite'. The artichoke, a cultivated variety of the cardoon, was developed only in fifteenth-century Italy, according to historians of horticulture, and soon spread to Greece.[60] Other varieties of fruits, introduced now or slightly earlier, owe their existence to Levantine plant breeding – such as 'the so-called Saracen melon' of Simeon Seth. And lemons, if not actually new to Greece at this period, are now clearly distinguished from citrons for the first time as *lemónia*.[61]

The entirely new foodstuffs that were introduced in Ottoman times came from India, Indo-China and of course the New World. Among aromatics we can name tarragon, highly important in Arabic cookery, and chilli, already known to Agapius as *spétsiai*, 'spices'. The legumes of genus Phaseolus, notably haricot beans in all their variety, now appear. In view of their unfamiliarity Agapius gives rather full advice on their preparation. He recommends cooking them with vinegar, oil, mustard and pepper. Potatoes, tomatoes and spinach, *patátes*, *domátes*, *spanákia*, were now for the first time introduced to the Greek diet.[62]

In spite of these various novelties, travellers to the Aegean lands tend to notice the foodstuffs that have been there for a long time – grapes, figs, pomegranates and of course cheese and wine. Rather than the range and choice of foodstuffs they are struck by aspects of cuisine: not always those aspects that we might have expected. Belon (*Observations* 1.59) noted a singularity in cooking technique which will not surprise readers of *Apicius*:

> Their method of cooking differs much from ours. When the meat is cooked they take it out of the pot and then put in whatever it is that they will use to thicken the sauce, stirring it, if they have a large quantity, with a long wooden stick.

Turkish custom had fully adopted the love of sweets and sweet drinks that we noticed as a characteristic of the Byzantine palate. The sherbets of

*Figure 34 Orkhís, satyrídion*: the bulbs of Orchis mascula are the favoured constituent of *salep. Source*: from G. Hegi's *Illustrierte Flora von Mittel-Europa* (Vienna, 1912)

Istanbul soon became famous – refreshing drinks made of lemon juice, sugar, water, sometimes perfumed with ambergris, Greek *ámbar*,[63] and in summer chilled with mountain ice. Evliya Çelebi knew not only of ambergris, but also of rhubarb, roses, lotuses, grapes and tamarinds as flavourings for sherbets.[64] Refreshments of seventeenth-century Istanbul also included the *salep*, enriched with ground orchid root, whose early history in the Aegean diet we traced in Chapter 2:

> There are 200 salep-sellers; they have no shops. The salep is commonly called 'fox's testicle', and grows on high mountains such as the Olympus of Bursa. . . . It grows like an onion, and when dried is ground to a powder, cooked with sugar like a jelly, and sold in cans heated by fire. They cry, 'Take salep, seasoned with rosewater: rest for the soul, health for the body!' It is a fortifying and invigorating beverage, and sharpens the eyesight.
>
> (Evliya Çelebi 155)

Spoon sweets are often described as offered to visitors by both Turks and

Greeks. Biddle noted: 'On entering a house you first are presented with a pipe, then coffee, and sometimes a spoon full of citron and a bowl of water.' Bitter orange and lemon jam have indeed been among the most popular of spoon sweets.[65]

At first little difference was seen between the lifestyle of Turks and Greeks: the Turks ate simply, it appears from sixteenth-century travellers' reports, so that any difference in wealth was less noticeable. Belon (*Observations* 1.27) gives the following sensitive description:

> The governor of Lemnos, the *vaivode*, invited us to dine with him and treated us as friends, giving us the opportunity to observe what the Turks normally do for guests whom they invite to eat with them at home. If they wished to treat an ambassador or the like with greater ceremony, clearly they could arrange to provide fancier dishes than was done for us on this occasion: but we shall describe what they normally do. The first dish was of raw cucumbers without vinegar or oil, and that is how they eat it, with no other seasoning but salt. After that we had raw onions and raw *mouronne*,[66] and beside this there was a soup of *trachanas*, and honey and bread. Also, since there were Christian Greeks among the company, we drank wine, brought by some monks of the neighbourhood. This is how the Turks dine – and there is no fuss over napkins and white table-cloth. They make no difficulty about mixing with Christians.

In the later Ottoman period, those entertained by Greeks found their hosts' resources slight. Dodwell had possibly hoped for better. At any rate he sounds disappointed:

> [The Bishop of Salona] lives with all the simplicity of the primitive Christians; there was nothing to eat, except rice and bad cheese; the wine was execrable, and so impregnated with rosin, that it almost took the skin from our lips! ... We dined at a round table of copper ... supported on one leg or column, like the *monopodia* of the ancients (Livy 39.6). We sat on cushions placed on the floor. ... The Bishop insisted upon my Greek servant sitting at table with us; and on my observing that it was contrary to our customs, he answered, that he could not bear such ridiculous distinctions in his house.[67]

At the other extreme from the poverty of most Greeks was the fabled wealth of the Saray of Ottoman Istanbul. Michel Baudier wrote of 'an admirable organisation, as contrasted with the chaos of most royal palaces'. A hundred sheep, a hundred lambs or kids, forty cows, forty geese, two hundred brace of chickens and a hundred brace of pigeons were its daily requirement, he added. Twice a year shiploads of pulses, spices and sugar came from Alexandria destined for the Saray. Dates and plums came to it from Egypt, apples from Wallachia and Transylvania, olive oil from Coron and Modon in the Peloponnese, butter from Moldavia. Apples and olive oil for the Sultan's own use, however, were specially imported from Crete, and the Venetians of Istanbul imported Milan cheeses for the most favoured. Wheat came here from Bursa (Prusa) in Bithynia.

> Special mills at Constantinople grind it, the great ovens of the *Serail* bake it into bread, and this impressive organisation distributes it as is laid down, twenty loaves a day to the Sultanas, ten to the Pashas, eight to the Mufti, and to lesser personages in smaller quantity, down to one per head.[68]

Wine, forbidden to Muslims, was not in use in the Palace; Evliya Çelebi carefully and repeatedly denies having tasted the numerous wines listed in his survey of the Empire. Foreign travellers gradually swell the reputation of Samian muscat wine:

> The muscat grapes are the finest and best fruits of the island. When they are ripe, the vineyards are full of people, everyone eating as much as he wants from wherever he chooses. The wine would be good if they knew how to make and keep it; but the Greeks are dirty, and also they cannot be persuaded not to put water into it. I have, however, drunk very good muscat of Samos, carefully made for our Smyrna merchants, though it had less of the taste of the grape than does muscat de Frontignan.[69]

Tournefort's discussion of Cretan wine includes a very early mention of the raki or brandy of the island:

> The wines of Candia are excellent, red, white and *clairet*. The vines of this climate do have sufficient *verdeur* [acid] to correct their sweetness. Far from being insipid, this sweetness is accompanied by a delicious perfume which makes those who have enjoyed the wines of Candia dislike all others. . . . Excellent spirit could be made from it: but in fact the brandy, *raki*, which is drunk on Crete and all over the Levant is detestable. To make this liquor one adds water to grape marc: after fifteen to twenty days' steeping it is pressed with heavy stones. The first half of the resulting *piquette* is distilled, the remainder discarded. They would do better to discard the lot: their brandy has no strength and a merely burnt flavour. It is brownish in colour, and soon spoils.[70]

Flourishing to the extent that peace prevailed rather than war, profitable when government and landlords did not appropriate too high a proportion of rural income in taxes and rents, the trade and distribution system of the Ottoman Aegean may be viewed as a development from the Byzantine. We begin to hear more of annual fairs, weekly markets and daily markets,[71] whose antiquity is sometimes quite unclear. We hear, for example, of the annual fair at Istanbul of the salt beef merchants, 'infidels of Moldavia and Wallachia', lasting forty days from the feast of St Demetrius (Evliya Çelebi 148). Already in Byzantine times we knew of the annual fair at Thessalonica, outside the city gates, beginning six days before the same saint's day. 'The most important held in Macedonia', it attracted not only Bulgarians and Vlachs but also Catalans, Italians and French (*Timarion* 4–5).[72]

Istanbul, centre of a wide empire, was naturally a hub of trade in food as in many other commodities. The single most informative source of information on its trades and professions in the early Ottoman centuries is the extensive and discursive description of the annual procession of the guilds of Istanbul before Sultan Murad IV, compiled by Evliya Çelebi (104–250): 'All trade and craft is suspended at Istanbul, on account of this procession, for three days, during which the riot and confusion fills the town to a degree which is not to be expressed in words.' There were a thousand and one guilds, said Evliya, though by his translator's count he reached only number seven hundred and thirty-five,

> the tavern-keepers: there are in the four jurisdictions of Constantinople one thousand such places of misrule, kept by Greeks, Armenians and Jews. . . . Besides the open wine-, brandy- and beer-houses there are many secret spots known to amateurs by their particular names, of which, however, I am ignorant.

In his time, incidentally, coffee was 'an innovation which curtails sleep and the generating power in man. Coffee-houses are houses of confusion', or so the butchers' guild had claimed in a celebrated debate on precedence (137). On the way to the tavern-keepers Evliya had listed apothecaries, herb-collectors, rose-water merchants and perfumers; greengrocers; thirteen guilds of bakers; bakers of *paksimat*, classed apart from the others among millers; dealers in Egyptian goods, rice, lentils, sugar and imported sweets, musk-sherbets and coffee; many kinds of cooks, butchers, milkmen, cheese merchants, makers of sweet and hot drinks (including *salep*), confectioners; many guilds of fishermen (but no makers of *gáros* that I can find); grocers, butter merchants, oil merchants; fruit merchants, with a separate guild of watermelon sellers; poultrymen; and finally the dealers in alcoholic beverages: *buza*, 'barley wine', millet beer with its many flavourings, rice wine, mead, arrack and cooked wine or must.

## FOOD AND WINE OF THE MODERN AEGEAN

Greek wines have not yet recovered the good name they had in the Roman and medieval West. Yet in modern times a far greater variety of Greek wines is available on the international market. We know that in ancient times Greek wines were 'cooked' for long distance transport; we know in what small quantities they were served at Roman banquets; we know

*Figure 35* The coffee shop, *kafeneío*, a traditional masculine preserve which thus serves one or two of the functions of the ancient *sympósion*. *Photo*: Rena Salaman

that the Greek wines exported to sixteenth-century northern Europe were 'cooked', and sometimes blended like sherry: even those that made the relatively short journey to Italy had to be sweet muscats. Whatever the alcoholic strength of them, then, we can feel sure that the Greek wines encountered by non-Greek authors in earlier centuries had something of the taste and heaviness of the modern fortified wines and *vins doux naturels* of the Mediterranean. Greece still exports such wines: the Mavrodaphne of Patras, made by a sherry-like process introduced – or rather reintroduced – to Greece a century ago by Baron Clauss; the muscat of Samos and of Lemnos. But the drier and less elaborated wines of other Greek vineyards, which declined in the last Ottoman centuries, have in many cases revived, and modern bottling and modern transport allows them to travel over long distances for the first time.

As yet a relatively low proportion of Greek wine is bottled for distribution and retail sale, and a low proportion again of this is available abroad. The legislation introducing *appellations contrôlées* to Greece, which commenced in 1969, now specifies more than twenty areas of production, with their grape varieties and vinification methods, that qualify for *appellation*. They spread across Greece, from Naoussa of Macedonia and Côtes de Meliton of Chalcidice to Sitia of Crete; from Cephallenia to Lemnos and Samos and Rhodes. Greece is unusual among wine-producing countries in terrain and in climate. Parts of it are still untouched by the phylloxera that forced the rest of Europe, a century ago, to replant every vineyard with vines grafted on Vitis labrusca stocks. Local grape varieties remain pre-eminent not only in wines that qualify for *appellation*, but in most others as well. Few of these local varieties have been found to do well elsewhere (muscat, malmsey and liatico being the principal exceptions). Flavours, and even colours, of well-made Greek wines can be quite start-lingly distinctive – and those who wish can occupy a most enjoyable study trip attempting to match ancient flavours with modern.[73] Some good wine is made on the eastern shores of the Aegean. The Islamic prohibition of alcohol is a restraint on trade, though it may have encouraged the survival of an ancient taste for concentrated must or grape syrup, the modern Turkish *pekmez*.

The Greek enthusiasm for retsina was not shared by medieval travellers to Greece from abroad: many modern travellers agree. Even where pine resin is not used, fresh pine wood is allowed to add its flavour to must in parts of modern Greece, as it was in medieval Attica. Retsina is now made chiefly in central and southern Greece and some of the Aegean islands; in Attica even a fizzy retsina can be found.[74] The old spiced wines survive, in altered form, in the oúzo and mastíkha, the spirits flavoured with aniseed and mastic that are still popular in the Aegean. It is to travellers of Ottoman times, incidentally, that we owe the earliest full description of the mastic harvest and of the use of mastic in food as well as its more ancient use for cleaning the teeth and freshening the breath. Tournefort visited Chios and observed the process, a royal monopoly and source of revenue:

> They begin the tapping of the lentisks on the first of August, making several diagonal cuts into the bark with a long knife but not touching the young branches. On the day after cutting, one observes the nourishing sap flowing out in drops, which gradually coagulate into tears of mastic. They harden on the ground, often forming quite large concretions: this is why the bases of the trees have to be kept so clean. The bulkiest harvest is in mid August, if the weather is dry and fine. . . . The Sultanas consume most of the mastic that goes to the Palace. They chew it, all through the morning, on an empty stomach, both to pass the time and to sweeten their breath. Tears of mastic are also put in stews, and in bread before it is baked.[75]

The story of modern Greek food is a story both of survivals and of innovations. The taste and price of fish was (so comedy assures us) ever present to the consciousness of ancient Athenians: fine fish cuisine is the principal aim of many of the best restaurants of Istanbul and of modern Greece, where typically fish is selected with care by the prospective diner

*Figure 36* The Easter lamb: Alonnisos, about 1980. *Photo*: Rena Salaman

and is then cooked – and priced by weight. For fish, as for other foods, there are long traditions of local excellence; undoubtedly these are not always independent of the reading of classical texts. We may think ancient literature had something to do with Nicholas Biddle's report from Attica of 'the best honey that any of us ever tasted'.[76] Yet Attic honey can be very good indeed.

The ancient preference for eating mutton in spring – a matter of flavour – may not be unconnected with the Christian Greek tradition of lamb at Easter. We have seen that the Byzantine Empire was already part of a new cultural synthesis, one in which Christian beliefs took their place, though certainly not supplanting earlier ones. Vryonis brings together information on animal sacrifice among Christians – Greek and Armenian – and Muslims in medieval and modern Anatolia. Christians sacrificed to saints, on particular occasions or for specific purposes. This practice is surely to be linked, as Vryonis argues, with the official Byzantine slaughtering and roasting of animals on the occasion of major religious festivals. Clearly both kinds of sacrifice can be seen as deriving from ancient sacrificial practice, both public and private. The apportioning of certain parts of the sacrificial animal to priests, as has been customary among Anatolian Muslims, is likewise strongly reminiscent of classical customs. Non-meat sacrifices resembling earlier pagan rituals were sometimes observed. Edward

Dodwell, while in Greece, saw Turkish women performing a religious ritual, which he desecrated after the celebrants had departed. They had placed in a cave a cup of honey and white almonds, a cake on a small napkin and a bowl of burning aromatics.[77] And in any case it is clear that, just as in the fourth-century BC Athens of Menander's *Bad-Tempered Man*, religious observances, sometimes of city-wide significance but sometimes meaningless outside an individual family, are still the primary occasion for good food and festivity, often linked with births, betrothals and weddings.

In the modern Greek and Turkish menu[78] there are items that would have been unfamiliar before the Ottoman centuries: the tomatoes that have only recently won their place in Mediterranean cuisine, the spinach that has usurped the place of earlier greens, the chillies that now add their heat to cooked dishes; and then sweet oranges and bananas, and coffee and tea and spirits. Others can first be traced in Byzantine texts: aubergines, bitter oranges and perhaps lemons, sugar and sugary sweets and jams and sweet soft drinks. Others go back to the Romans and the centuries that followed Alexander's expedition: citrons, peaches and apricots, and the use *in food* of aromatics like pepper and cinnamon and cloves. But most of the menu has certainly been there since the classical centuries, the fifth and fourth centuries BC, and little of it was new to the Aegean even then. With grapes and wine, raisins and figs and honey, wheat bread and barley cakes,[79] onions and garlic, kid and lamb, fish and shellfish and octopus and squid, the Greek kitchen had established much of its range of ingredients three thousand years ago and more, and given the simple methods that have characterised the best Greek cookery, both in Archestratus' time and today, Europe's oldest cuisine has never lost its original and unique flavour.

*Figure 37* A sixteenth-century sherbet-vendor

Si le lecteur trouve de l'ennui au récit de cette matière de cuisine, qu'il considère que, sans ce chapitre, les autres qui composent l'Histoire ne seraient point.

(Michel Baudier, *Histoire générale du Serrail*, p. 67)

# NOTES

## 1 THE WAY THESE PEOPLE SACRIFICE

1 Literary evidence on classical Greek dining and entertainment is balanced by iconography, by inscriptions and by archaeological finds. For the iconography see e.g. Lissarrague 1987 and Schmitt-Pantel 1990, who sensibly gives attention to contexts – to the scenes that were combined with banquet and *sympósia* scenes on Athenian vases.

The most popular field in recent scholarship has certainly been that of 'the *sympósion*', and no apology is necessary, therefore, if *sympósia* occupy a restricted space in the present work. Schmitt-Pantel's work (especially 1985 and 1990) and two recent conference volumes (Murray 1990; Slater 1991) will help to repair the imbalance. Sacrifice and libation have been a major subject of study for French structural anthropologists (e.g. Detienne and Vernant 1979; Vernant *et al.* 1981; Lissarrague 1985).

2 It is because of the archetypes of Menander, more than of any other single author, that romantic comedies of later repertoires, for over two thousand years, have so often been set in a fantasy Athens at a fairy-tale time, or at any rate in a world where any number of coincidences might happen. Out of Menander's plays, themselves building on the traditions of fifth- and earlier fourth-century tragedy and comedy, came the hero's best friend and the clever servant, as well as the 'recognition scene', the story of the foundling whose satisfactory parentage is to be revealed at the right time.

This is an unpromising set of relationships: does not such material, imbued with the fantasies of wish-fulfilment, make an unsteady basis for deductions on social history? But Menander's work, now that some of it can again be read in connected form, must be read afresh, independently of its derivatives. Its recognition scenes are found to be less ubiquitous than theirs, its servants less farcical and its heroes' friends less stylised. Its atmosphere is found to be less comic, a source of complaint to those modern readers who were expecting something at least twice as funny as Terence, the *dimidiatus Menander*, 'half-sized Menander', of the Roman stage.

Menander's plots generally develop through the reaction of strongly differentiated characters to love and to preoccupations of family, wealth and honour. Later playwrights of this tradition, whose settings (Athens or elsewhere) were tied to no reality known to their audiences, could adapt society and circumstance more freely to fit the demands of plot. But Menander's usual setting was his audience's own home city, and the time was their own time. This is not to say that every incident, every twist of plot, every extreme of characterisation can be taken as realistic; it is rather to say that audiences are likely to have been dissatisfied when the characters' responses to events fell outside the range of what might be expected from social norms and from their own previously-established personalities. Athenian plays such as the *Bad-Tempered Man*, being in origin scripts for performance, tie the author very closely to the demands of his contemporary audience.

3 Cf. Demosthenes, *Against Meidias* 79.

4 She is named and addressed once at the most – if she is Parthenis. But Parthenis and Plangon may both be maids. If so the daughter's name is unknown. Line 953 shows that at least two slave girls were supposed to be at the festivities later. One is led to presume that the daughter is there only because all the family appears to be there, and because Gorgias might have expected a glimpse of her before accepting Sostratus' invitation to marry her.

5 We are reminded of Ottoman Istanbul. The traveller was advised never to 'look too closely at the veiled women. . . . No allusion must be made to the ladies of the family, who are regarded as under a veil' (Baedeker 1911 pp. xxv–xxvi).

6 Schaps 1977. Polite English society shares this rule, with its *Mrs Smith* and *Miss Smith*!

7 The argument pursued here is, as will be seen, relevant to the question of women's attendance at Athenian drama. It does not answer the question: it explains why it is so difficult to answer. If women were present, they were not present in their own right and not part of the conversation.

8 Menander, *Bad-Tempered Man* 448; Athenaeus 146e. The emendation of 'couches' to 'caskets', so much more suited to the modern stereotype of an ancient sacrifice, was first made by Grotius and adopted by most editors (e.g. Kaibel 1887–90 vol. 1 p. 332 – Kaibel does not even mention the manuscript reading; and Gulick 1927–41 vol. 2 p. 168).

It is not clear to the modern reader, and perhaps it was not clear to the ancient audience, whether the family meal of the *Bad-Tempered Man* is taking place under a roof: all that is clear is that it is behind the central door of the universal three-door 'scene' of classical Athenian drama. In this case, like the door on the right that led to Cnemon's farmyard, the central door might be supposed to give on to an open space, the sacred precinct, rather than a building. Gomme and Sandbach (1973) suppose that the meal is taking place in the cave that was the central feature of the shrine: perhaps, indeed, we are to imagine that: but there is an unbridgeable difference between the landscape of the real place in Attica named by Menander and the landscape that an audience saw and pictured when watching the play.

9 The *Bad-Tempered Man* was first translated into English under the upbeat title *The Feast of Pan*. This was misleading because of its implication that the impulse for sacrifice and festivity came from something of the nature of a religious calendar. It is clear, however, from lines 260–3 that this is not so: cf. Menander fragment 264 [Athenaeus 364d].

10 Aristophanes, *Assemblywomen* 348–9; Menander fragment 385, which is from the play *Synaristôsai*, *Women Lunching Together*, a scene from which may well be illustrated in a well-known mosaic from Pompeii.

11 Here I draw on material earlier brought together in Dalby 1993a; see notes there.

12 Gomme and Sandbach 1973 pp. 330, 264.

13 Commentators see an inconsistency here with Sicon's claim (646–7) of superiority to a *trapezopoiós*, 'table-setter'. See e.g. Gomme and Sandbach 1973

p. 282. The argument smacks of modern restrictive practices. After all, the *mágeiros* may delegate table-setting to a *trapezopoiós* if there is one, and look down on the *trapezopoiós* as member of a non-sacred trade, and yet still regard table-setting as work he himself can properly perform, especially if, as in this case, no lavish expenditure is envisaged and no *trapezopoiós* has been hired.

14 'Dionysus', i.e. wine, as a marginal note in the papyrus explains.

15 Machon, whose subject was the gossip of late fourth-century Athens, wrote at least sixty years later in distant Alexandria.

16 *Odyssey* 19.59–64. Campbell 1964 p. 151, quoted on p. 15.

17 Pherecrates 73 [Athenaeus 159e]; Aristophanes, *Lysistrata* 856; Matron [Athenaeus 137c]; Alexis 172 [Athenaeus 441d], etc. Dalby 1993a.

18 Menander, *Bad-Tempered Man* 943, where, whatever the text to be restored, Getas must have done some of the work; Apollodorus, *Against Neaera* 34. The exceptions were meals at which *hetairaí* were the hosts, see pp. 20, 154–7.

19 There were specialised cooks in the Greek world as early as the late sixth century BC, when Cyniscus, who called himself an *ártamos*, dedicated to Hera an axe-blade found at Santa Agata dell' Esaro in Calabria (*IG* 14.643; Rankin 1907; Orth 1921a; Berthiaume 1982). In Athens the work of the *mágeiros* was well known by the later fifth century. Cf. Sokolowski 1969 no. 10 A lines 25–8, 55–8; Euripides, *Cyclops* 397; Sophocles fragment 1122 [*Epitome* 68a]; Aristophanes, *Peace* 1017–18. Athenaeus 660a–e; Berthiaume 1982 pp. 9–12.

20 Alexis 177 [Athenaeus 386a], 259 [Athenaeus 164f]; quotations at Athenaeus 170d.

21 On this character see Rankin 1907; Dohm 1964; Gomme and Sandbach 1973 pp. 431–2.

22 See Berthiaume 1982 for this part of the work of the *mágeiros*. For the ritual see Burkert 1966, and for its vocabulary Casabona 1966.

23 Cf. Dohm 1964 pp. 228–30.

24 *Odyssey* 14.407–38; Dio Chrysostom, *Euboean Oration*.

25 Theophrastus, *Characters* 22.4.

26 Chester Starr, in 'An evening with the flute-girls' (Starr 1978), discusses this trade, attempting (like Athenaeus 658e–662d on cooks, but with less success) to show that its exponents were free and independent.

27 The best discussion of Xenophon's *Symposium* is by Körte 1927; on the *gelotopoiós* see now Fehr 1990. Fehr perceptively observes that such uninvited guests 'played themselves', rather as Odysseus played the beggar. But, deceived by the results of this role-playing, Fehr himself estimates the social status of Philippus and the parasites lower than it probably was.

28 Bruit 1995; Ziehen 1949.

29 Athenaeus 613c–614d, 234c–262a. Wüst and Hug 1949 is the fullest modern study of the *parásitos*; see also Nesselrath 1985. Like *hetairaí* and flute-girls, these male performers had their analogy in early modern Japan, where the *hokan* or joker was in past centuries a frequent guest at dinners; cf. Dalby 1983 p. 56.

Leo 1912 p. 106 and Arnott 1968 observe the interesting formula, 'the young men all called him . . .', in comedy but do not comment on the parallel in the *Odyssey*.

30 Aeschines, *Against Timarchus* 75; Ephippus 20 [Athenaeus 572c].

31 Cf., for example, Demosthenes, *Olynthiac II* 19 on the flatterers and jokers that were said to surround Philip: see Herman 1981. It is in this context of parasites and flatterers, hangers-on of the rich and powerful, that a commentator glossed Homeric *therápontes* ('attendants') with *kólakes* 'toadies'.

32 'Not comparable to the other artisans' quarters, but actually the place that cooks were hired from': Pollux, *Onomasticon* 9.48, citing Antiphanes 203.

33 Murray 1982; Schmitt-Pantel 1987.

34 See the study and collection of references on entertainment at the *prytaneîon* by Miller 1978. See also Schmitt-Pantel 1980, 1985; Osborne 1981; Henry 1981, 1983.

The view has been taken that 'the main occasions for meat consumption at Athens were furnished by religious festivals at which meat was distributed from animals sacrificed at public expense' (Sallares 1991 p. 311).

35 Demosthenes, *Against Conon* 4; Aristophanes, *Assemblywomen* 306–8; Aristophanes, *Acharnians* 164–6. On the provision of soldiers' food see Pritchett 1971–; Dalby 1992.

36 Xenophon, *Management* 7.30; Aristophanes, *Frogs* 549–62, *Wasps* 612–18.

37 *Regimen* 2.60.3.

38 Lysias, *Against Alcibiades for Desertion* 14.25, *For Simon* 3.6.

39 For example, Plato, *Symposium*; Xenophon, *Symposium*; Apollodorus, *Against Neaera* 34. Murray 1990.

40 This is to draw the distinction between public and private where the evidence implicitly draws it, and where Pauline Schmitt-Pantel draws it in a recent debate: Schmitt-Pantel 1990 pp. 24–5.

41 Demosthenes, *Against Euergus and Mnesibulus* 53–5.

42 Menander, *Bad-Tempered Man* 427–518; Lysias, *Against Simon* 6.

43 These can be called *hestiatória* or *hestiatéria*. The words are uncommon in literature: the first reference is in Herodotus, *Histories* 4.35. See Frickenhaus 1917; Roux 1973; Miller 1978; Börker 1983; Bergquist 1990 and her bibliography.

44 For example, Athenaeus 138f on Sparta: see Bruit 1990; Cooper and Morris 1990 p. 76. Aelian, *Miscellany* 4.9; Aristophanes, *Thesmophoriazusae* 624, see scholia on this passage.

45 Cooper and Morris 1990 especially p. 78.

46 For example, Plato, *Republic* 372b; Theocritus, *Idyll* 13.34. Dunbabin 1991.

47 Cf. Aeschylus, *Agamemnon* 1594; Euripides, *Cyclops* 544–89. Fraenkel 1950 vol. 3 pp. 754–5 oversimplifies the contrast between Aeschylus and Euripides on this point, failing to observe that the Euripidean examples are both from satyr plays.

48 Aristophanes, *Wasps* 1208–20; on this passage, and the social context of reclining in general, see Cooper and Morris 1990 pp. 77–80.

49 For example, Timotheus 1 [Athenaeus 243c]. Bergquist 1990; McCartney 1934.

50 Cf. Bergquist 1990.

51 Athenaeus 245a–c citing Lynceus, Timocles 34, Menander fragment 238 and Philochorus 328F65; Athenaeus 532d–e citing Theopompus 115F249 and Duris of Samos 76F35.

52 Chares 125F4 [Athenaeus 538c]. Borza 1983; Bergquist 1990 and her references. See also the discussion on the size of parties in Plutarch, *Symposium Questions* 5.5.

53 Campbell 1964 p. 151; du Cange 1688 col. 269.

54 Lysias, *Against Simon* 7; Menander fragment 452.

55 Aristophanes, *Knights* 42–60, 1164–1220, *Assemblywomen* 468–70, 595.

56 Dentzer 1969, 1970, 1971a and b, 1982; Fehr 1971.

57 Artemidorus, *Dream Interpretation* p. 271; see Dentzer 1982 p. 535; Folsom 1976 plate 52.

58 At this point Athenaeus evidently skips some lines.

59  For example, Boardman 1975 figures 27, 38.1.

60  Antiphanes 57 [Athenaeus 666f] is a scene in which a novice is taught to play the game. Some have thought that the target was 'originally' human, adducing Aeschylus 179 [Athenaeus 667c] and Euripides 562 [Athenaeus 666c]. See Hayley 1894.

61  For example, Sophilus 5 [Athenaeus 640d].

62  See for many examples Machon [Athenaeus 577d–583d]; Lynceus and other sources [Athenaeus 583f–585f]. At a *hetaírá*'s house the waiters might well be her female slaves [ibid. 584d]: 'Men drinking at Gnathaena's knocked over the bulb-and-lentil soup. The girl cleaning it up scooped the lentils up to her chest. "She's planning boob-and-lentil soup", said Gnathaena.'

63  See e.g. Figueira 1984 (with a relevant comment in Foxhall and Forbes 1982).

64  Nafissi 1991.

65  For a longer description of the dining customs of Lyttus on Crete see Dosiadas [Athenaeus 143a–d].

66  For example, Polemon [Athenaeus 138e–139c]; Polycrates [Athenaeus 139d–f], and accompanying citations from other historians to 141f.

67  Apollodorus of Athens 244F151 [Athenaeus 172f], cf. *Homeric Hymn 3*.51–60; Criton 3 [Athenaeus 173b]: by his time a *parásitos* was a commonplace of traditional comedy, a greedy sponger; Hypereides, *Delian Oration* fragments. Deonna 1948.

68  Antiphanes 233 [*Epitome* 27d]; cf. Epicrates 6 [Athenaeus 655f].

69  This is the boast underlying Anaxandrides 40 [Athenaeus 299f], in which a speaker lists the foods that an Egyptian won't eat but a Greek will.

70  Some 'barbarians' disagreed: see Xenophon, *Anabasis* 5.4.

71  Terpsion [Athenaeus 337b via Clearchus of Soli]; Clearchus of Soli 102 [Athenaeus 317b]. Later, Belon, *Observations* 1.65; Clusius, Belon's Latin translator, adds an amusing reminiscence (p. 153) of how he had shocked Balkan observers, during a campaign in 1579, by eating a tortoise and failing to die.

72  *Epitome of Athenaeus* 65f; Diogenes Laertius 8.19.

73  An identical passage is Eubulus 148 [*Epitome* 65c]. On the naming day festival see e.g. *Suda* s.v. *Amphidrómia*.

74  Burkert 1983; Berthiaume 1982; Isenberg 1975.

75  For example, Philochorus [*Epitome* 38c]; Theocritus, *Idyll 14*.18, *Idyll 2*.152. Gow 1952 vol. 2 p. 60.

76  Davidson 1995. For appetisers e.g. Athenaeus 131f, 133a. For desserts, citations at Athenaeus 640a–643e.

77  A late word (see the discussion in *Epitome of Athenaeus* 58b–c) whose etymological meaning 'pre-drinks' implies, I think, that wine was drunk before the meal alongside these appetisers, which must be likened to modern *meze*.

78  Davidson 1993; cf. Athenaeus 277a.

79  Koukoulès 1947–55 vol. 5 pp. 31–4. 'Opson, Attic. *Prosphágema*, Hellenic': so Moeris asserts in *Attic Glossary* s.v. *ópson*. See also the quotations given by du Cange 1688 cols 1654–5 s.v. *prosphági* and the extract on p. 15 above.

80  Gallo 1989; Braun 1995.

81  Hesiod, *Works and Days* 232–3, 442, 582.

82  Plutarch fragment 26 [Scholia on Hesiod, *Works and Days* 41]; *Epitome of Athenaeus* 58f.

83  Theophrastus, *Study of Plants* 7.7.2; Lucian, *On Salaried Posts in Great Houses* 26; Galen, *On the Properties of Foods* 2.65. Byzantine references: Koukoulès 1947–55 vol. 5 pp. 89–90. For more on the Hesiod passage and subsequent

references see West 1978 pp. 152–3. West documents the modern use of mallow with salt and pepper or lemon juice or in salads, while Sallares 1991 p. 459 n. 322 shows that mallow was useful in Greece during the First World War. Several species of mallow grow wild in Britain, though few eat them.

84 Theophrastus, *Study of Plants* 7.12.1, 7.13.1–4; Pliny, *Natural History* 21.108; Galen, *On the Properties of Foods* 2.63; Aulus Gellius, *Attic Nights* 18.2.13; Plutarch, *Banquet of the Seven Sages* 157f.

85 Theophrastus, *Study of Plants* 8.7.3.

86 Galen, *On the Properties of Foods* 1.25.2. We must take it that he bought his lupins ready cooked. On calavance, *ôkhros* and the salty fish sauce *gáros* see Chapter 3.

87 Ibid. 1.23. Sallares (1991 pp. 360–1; see also p. 492 note 203) seems unwise to conclude that the lupin was 'not much used in classical times'. See also Hondelmann 1984, and, for further quotations from Greek sources, *Epitome of Athenaeus* 55c–56a.

88 Timocles 25 [Athenaeus 567e]; Demosthenes, *Against Androtion* 22.15; Andocides [*Suda* s.v. *skándix*].

89 Alexis 167 [*Epitome* 55a]; Poliochus 2 [*Epitome* 60b]; Antiphanes 225 [*Epitome* 60c].

90 See also Aristophanes, *Wealth* 544 (dry vegetable leaves instead of bread).

91 According to the scholia this detail comes from Philoxenus' *Cyclops or Galatea*.

92 The scholia add: 'Some say he is parodying Hesiod', presumably Hesiod, *Works and Days* 41, though the resemblance is not close.

93 And even the aged poor, in philanthropic Byzantium, might be given all these. The allowance in *gerokomeîa* (old people's homes) in the twelfth-century *Typikon of Pantokrator* included bread, wine, dried pulses, cheese, and oil.

94 Chrysippus of Soli [Athenaeus 137f].

95 Antiphanes 179 [Athenaeus 74e] and the further citations of Athenaeus 112a–e.

96 On huntsmen's food see Xenophon, *Constitution of Sparta* 6.4–5.

97 The anecdote, relating to a 'not very ancient' dinner, comes from the third-century BC philosopher Chrysippus of Soli [Athenaeus 137f].

98 Thucydides, *Histories* 2.38.2 (from the funeral speech put in the mouth of Pericles).

99 'To the fish' and 'to the relishes'. These are not the kind of place-names that can be cited in a nominative form. For ancient sources see Wycherley 1957.

100 Callimedon, for example (in exile by 318 BC), was said to spend heavily on food: Alexis 57 [Athenaeus 104d], 149 [Athenaeus 340c]. For another such spendthrift see Alexis 47 [Athenaeus 338d].

101 Eubulus 117 [*Epitome* 8b].

102 They were relished by Sicilians, says Clearchus of Soli (59 [Athenaeus 518c]), but perhaps he says so only as a result of a reading of Archestratus, whose work he certainly knew and disliked.

103 For example, Theocritus, *Idyll* 16.27–8; Gow 1952 vol. 2 p. 311.

104 Theocritus, *Idyll* 14.18; Gow 1952 vol. 2 p. 252.

105 Plutarch's tale that Lycurgus made Spartan sacrifices cheap, so that the less well-off would not be shown up, sounds more like the Greek dream of the good old days than anything relevant to Sparta itself (Plutarch, *Sayings of Kings and Generals* 172b).

106 Cf. Machon quoted by Athenaeus 579e.

107 The passage is said by Athenaeus (364b) to be a parody of the *Greater*

*Catalogue* attributed to Hesiod. The final lines appear in elegiac dress as *Theognis* 467–9.

## 2 THE GARDENS OF ALCINOUS

1 Vickery's survey of the food of prehistoric Greece, published in 1936, is on a larger scale than this chapter. It is still useful, particularly for its references to early excavation results, often overlooked in modern studies.

Jane Renfrew's handbook *Palaeoethnobotany*, which appeared in 1973, is important not least because Renfrew always asks that indispensable, practical question, implied in her title: how were these plants actually used? Renfrew's book is usefully supplemented by her 1979 paper. Zohary and Hopf are the authors of what is now the standard manual, in its second, 1993 edition, of the development and spread of cultivated plants of the Old World – though they omit many herbs and spices. Zohary and Hopf are relatively weak in their use of early written evidence: to judge from their references they tend to approach this material through unreliable secondary sources. The general survey of plant origins by Candolle (1882) is still sometimes cited, as is Hehn's work, last revised by Schrader *et al.* (1911): the latter is still found useful by some classicists for its collection of source references. Vavilov's work on the centres of diversification of cultivated plants is best known from the 1950 compendium in English (though it is also reflected in Zhukovskii 1933 and in the work of other researchers of the doomed school of Vavilov). Stearn's 1965 paper is a useful evaluation of Vavilov's work.

All the books mentioned so far, except Vickery's and Hehn's, are about plant foods only. To set alongside Renfrew there is Sándor Bökönyi's study of the archaeology of domesticated animals in south-eastern Europe, published in 1974.

Surveys of the food of other Levantine countries are often useful, for example, Darby *et al.* 1977 on Egypt, supplemented by Hepper 1990 on the finds in Tutankhamen's tomb. Darby's hefty pair of volumes (Darby *et al.* 1977) appears well-informed on Egyptian texts and archaeology, but uses Greek and Latin texts (or rather, English translations of them) uncritically.

In this chapter references have been kept to a minimum. In tracing the history of any item of food the works just mentioned should always be consulted: their bibliographies will be found indispensable. In investigating finds at specific sites the works referred to in endnote 6 will be helpful starting-points.

2 For more on Greek transhumant pastoralism see: palaeolithic: Bailey 1983; Bailey *et al.* 1986 p. 77; neolithic: Jacobsen 1984; classical: Georgoudi 1974; Osborne 1987 pp. 47–52; Skydsgaard 1988; cf. Theocritus, *Idyll* 7.111–15; medieval: Bryer 1979; modern: Hammond 1976; Wace and Thompson 1914; Campbell 1964. For the general Mediterranean picture see also Lewthwaite 1981; Whittaker 1988; Braudel 1966–7 vol. 1 pp. 76–93.

3 Some of the early finds have been noted in this chapter, though modern authors tend to ignore them. But the identifications of plant and animal remains at these early excavations were frustratingly vague. We are told of beans at the Palace of Knossos 'of a sort identified by the workmen as of a kind now imported from Egypt and known as *kikià misiriotiká*'. We hear of 'wheat or some other grain' found in the Kamares Cave near Phaistos (references in Vickery 1936 pp. 15, 19).

4 Renfrew and Wagstaff (1982), reporting a vain search for such signs, conclude

that visits to Melos were so fleeting as to leave no evidence. They could have given more weight to the probability that later natural processes, notably erosion and the changes of sea level, have effaced or concealed what evidence there may have been. On obsidian, Torrence 1986.

5 The date is highly controversial. For the view adopted here see Bernal 1987– vol. 2 pp. 274–319.

6 Selected references on these sites: Frankhthi: van Andel and Runnels 1987; Jacobsen and Farrand 1987; Hansen 1992. Asprokhaliko, Kastritsa and Klithi: Higgs et al. 1967; Bailey 1983; Bailey et al. 1986. Argissa Magoula: Hopf 1962; Boessneck 1962. Sea level questions: van Andel and Lianos 1983; van Andel and Runnels 1987. Sidari: Sordinas 1969. Lerna: Hopf 1964. Prodromos: Halstead and Jones 1980. Sitagri: Renfrew et al. 1987– . Nea Nikomedia: Rodden 1962, 1965; van Zeist and Bottema 1971. Sufli, Marmariani, Dimini and Sesklo: Tsountas 1908; Kroll 1979. Knossos: Jarman and Jarman 1968. Hacilar: Helbaek 1961. Chevdar and Kazanluk: Dennell 1978. Aghia Triada: Follieri 1986. Tiryns: Kroll 1982. Therasia and Akrotiri: Fouqué 1879; Doumas 1978–80, 1983. Kastanas: Kroll 1984.

7 Van Andel and Runnels 1987 pp. 50–1; cf. Byrd 1989; Soffer 1989.

8 Vickery (1936) is, I think, wrong to suppose that rabbits were caught. They were first noted in Spain, in due course bred in Italy, but still unfamiliar in classical Greece (Polybius, *Histories* 12.3.10 [Athenaeus 400f]; Varro, *On Farming* 3.12.6; Bodson 1978).

9 Doumas 1983 p. 118 and plate 85.

10 Bailey et al. 1986 p. 18.

11 On modern uses see Stol 1979 pp. 2–5. The species concerned are Pistacia lentiscus, P. terebinthus and P. atlantica. Some, including Renfrew (1973 p. 157) and Doumas (1983) (see also De Laet 1994 pp. 492, 507), have confusingly described these prehistoric finds as 'pistachio': see Sancisi-Weerdenburg 1995. Greeks' first knowledge of the pistachio, P. vera, can be traced in Hellenistic texts (Chapter 6): it is a larger nut, native to central Asia, which has always been distinguished by name from the others.

   Botanists differ on the range of the three Mediterranean species (e.g. Zohary and Hopf 1993 p. 197; F. Yaltirik in Davis 1965–85 vol. 2 pp. 544–8). The prehistoric finds at Greek sites are most often assigned to P. atlantica.

12 It is the Pyrus amygdaliformis of many botanists.

13 Renfrew 1979. There is a whole spectrum of possibilities between cultivation of fully domesticated plants and opportunistic gathering from the wild, an area of controversy in prehistoric archaeology: several papers in Harris and Hillman 1989 are relevant to the subject. Those of L. Costantini (on Grotta dell' Uzzo, Sicily) and of Hillman, S. M. Colledge and Harris (on Tell Abu Hureyra, Syria) are complemented by several on modern societies which offer parallels.

14 Osborne 1987 pp. 29–52; cf. Garnsey 1988 pp. 10–14; S. Cane on Australian aboriginal food gathering, and other papers in Harris and Hillman 1989.

15 Gamble 1986 pp. 54–9.

16 Dembinska 1988 p. 14.

17 Van Andel and Runnels 1988: see their references.

18 Gamble 1986 pp. 331–8.

19 The same is true of the domesticated dogs of neolithic south-eastern Europe. Those of Argissa Magoula, for example, were similar to those of the Near East and unlike the dogs of central and northern Europe. Dogs, though

sometimes eaten, were probably not bred for food. See Bökönyi 1974 p. 318; Bökönyi in De Laet 1994 pp. 389–97.

20  See van Zeist 1988.

21  Bryer 1979 p. 380. The question of where cattle and pigs were domesticated remains controversial. Bökönyi's latest view (in De Laet 1994 pp. 391–3) is that Near Eastern domesticated specimens of these two species were the ancestors of the neolithic European animals, though the archaeological record does not yet support him.

22  Payne 1972; Halstead and Jones 1980.

23  Sherratt 1981, 1983.

24  See Athenaeus 375b and *Epitome* 9d for further evidence of rules governing kill-off patterns in classical animal husbandry.

25  Vickery 1936 p. 72; Renfrew and Wagstaff 1982 pp. 161–71.

26  The later prehistoric evidence is collected by Buchholz *et al.* (1973). Octopus, cuttlefish and squid are absent from the archaeological record, but pictures from Crete suggest that by the second millennium people knew all about them (Vickery 1936 pp. 77–8; Thompson 1947 p. 208): doubtless they served for food. On fish in Minoan iconography, cf. Gill 1985; Marinatos 1985.

27  Renfrew 1979. On acorns see Mason 1995.

Danewort (or dwarf elder), Sambucus ebulus, classical (*khamai*)*aktê*, modern *vouziá* is a close relative of the elderberry, classical *aktê*, modern *zaboúkos*, *froxiliá*, and is native to southern Europe. In Greece it was later collected for medicinal purposes and as a dye, not a food. It was plentiful at bronze age Kastanas in Macedonia, where blackberries were also used (Dioscorides, *Materia Medica* 4.173; Kroll 1984).

28  Renfrew 1979.

29  Vickery 1936 pp. 66, 80–5; Buchholz *et al.* 1973.

30  For example, Halstead and Jones 1980.

31  Grant 1995.

32  Kroll 1979.

33  Triticum turgidum subsp. compactum is also often known as T. aestivo-compactum. Some early finds have been identified in the past as bread wheat, T. aestivum, which is now thought to be a hybrid from the southern Caspian region that did not reach the Mediterranean in prehistoric times.

34  Gunda 1983; Zhukovskii 1933.

35  Hansen 1988 pp. 39–44.

36  West (1978 pp. 214–15) rightly observes on this passage that *drûs*, 'oak', and *bálanos*, 'acorn', were less precise terms than their nearest English equivalents, covering also the sweet chestnut tree and its nut (which could be more specifically called *Díos bálanos*, literally 'Zeus's acorn', see Chapter 3, p. 81 and n. 136). It is relevant that the Italian dialect word *válano*, derived from Greek *bálanos*, means 'roast chestnut' (Meyer-Lübke 1911 p. 60).

37  On the nature of human exploitation of bees before true domestication compare Gunda 1968.

38  Crane 1983.

39  Kroll 1991. Although Hansen (1988 pp. 47–8) doubts that even the latest pips are large enough to be from 'cultivated' varieties, she does not offer an alternative explanation of the gradual increase.

40  For grapes in Sumerian and Akkadian records see Postgate 1987. On wines in the Linear B tablets see Perpillou 1981; Stanley 1982.

41  Vavilov 1950 p. 35.

42  Janushevich and Nikolaenko 1979.

43 See Ventris and Chadwick 1973 no. 234; B. Bohen in Murray 1983 p. 199; and, on the pottery of the neolithic period and its social implications, Cullen 1984.

44 Boardman 1976; Runnels and Hansen 1987; Hansen 1988 pp. 44–7; Sallares 1991 pp. 304–9. There is a strong current tendency to emphasise the lateness of olive cultivation in the Aegean region, opposing the views of, for example, Colin Renfrew (1972).

45 Shelmerdine 1985; Melena 1983; cf. Georgiou 1973.

46 Zhukovskii 1933 pp. 863–4, cf. Kalças 1974 pp. 5, 71. Vavilov, however (1950 p. 33), considered aniseed native to south-eastern Anatolia. See also Renfrew 1973; this plant is not dealt with by Zohary and Hopf 1993.

47 Keimer 1924 pp. 37, 99.

48 Zohary and Hopf 1993 p. 189: they cite no source.

49 Gulick (1927–41) generally translates *kyminon* 'caraway'. I don't know why. Caraway is native to central Europe and does not appear to have been familiar in early Greece. It became known to Greeks of the Roman Empire under a different name, *karó* (p. 142).

50 For this gloss Athenaeus possibly relies, as he does elsewhere, on the commentary on Alcman by the Hellenistic scholar Sosibius.

51 Probably a seed is intended, in view of the context and the quantities (so Chadwick and Baumbach 1963). Sesame seeds have not been identified with certainty at Greek archaeological sites, or indeed at Near Eastern ones, and there is widespread doubt whether Akkadian *shamashshammu*, clearly in the ancestry of the Greek word, actually did denote sesame (for references see Zohary and Hopf 1993 pp. 126–7; see also Sallares 1991 pp. 363–4, p. 493 n. 207; Bedigian and Harlan 1986) – although classical Greek *sésamon* certainly did (for example, Theophrastus, *Study of Plants* 8.1).

52 The hypothesis of African origin is based on the fact that most of the wild species of the genus are native to Africa, but it is rendered less likely by the statement of the first century AD *Periplus of the Erythraean Sea* (14) that in those times sesame oil was exported from Iran or India to east Africa.

53 On Mycenaean herbal remedies see Janko 1981. On aromatics generally, Georgiou 1973; Wylock 1972.

Coriander and *ku-pa-ro* – the latter probably Cyperus longus, 'English galingale', ancient *kypairos*, modern *aghriokíperi* – were certainly used at Pylos in the manufacture of aromatic oils (Pylos *Un08* and *Un09*). Rather large quantities of coriander and cyperus together with much smaller quantities of an unidentified substance *po-ni-ki-jo*, perhaps purple dye, were inventoried at Knossos (*Ga415, Ga418, Ga517, Ga675, Og424*; see Melena 1976 pp. 185–7 and his references). Both coriander and cyperus grow in Greece (Theophrastus, *Study of Plants* 4.10.1, 7.1.2) but cyperus has not often been used in cookery; for two exceptions, extremely heady and expensive sauces for roast meat, see the Roman cookery book *Apicius* (7.5.2, 7.5.4). It is unlikely, all things considered, that the Pylos and Knossos tablets are here listing stores for culinary use. Admittedly Melena 1976 pp. 183–4) identifies *ku-pa-ro* with chufa, Cyperus esculentus: he is most probably wrong, however, since its tubers, though they are edible after cooking, were not used in later Greece (Theophrastus, *Study of Plants* 4.8.1–12). They have been important in both ancient and modern Egypt but have nowhere else been considered so valuable as to be worth the trouble of inventorying.

Terebinth resin, which can be used for flavouring wine (Dioscorides, *Materia Medica* 5.30) but was more probably wanted for the perfume industry, was probably the *ki-ta-no* available in large quantities at Knossos (e.g. *Ga1530*, *Ga1532*; see Melena 1976 pp. 180–3).

Some of these aromatics were used for wreaths in classical Greece: a wreath of coriander, Pollux, *Onomasticon* 6.107 citing Anacreon; a wreath of cyperus, Alcman 60 [Athenaeus 681a]; a wreath of mint, Hipponax 60 [*Epitome* 49e]; a wreath of celery, Pindar, *Olympian* 13.33. And *Odyssey* 5.72 suggests appreciation of the scent, rather than the taste, of celery.

54 Postgate 1987.
55 Stol 1987.
56 There is as yet all too little that can be said of the actual diet of individuals, and how it might have varied with economic circumstances. Studies such as those of Bisel and Angel 1985 make a beginning.
57 For some continuities of technical vocabulary in viticulture see Perpillou 1981. On olive cultivation, against the view taken here, Sallares 1991 pp. 304–9.

# 3 DIVINE INVENTIONS

1 Athenaeus' *Deipnosophists*, the only work of scholarship that covers the whole field of classical Greek food, dining and entertainment, is likely to be the constant companion of those who read this and the next two chapters.

It is more than a century since any extensive survey was attempted of the food of classical Greece: curiously, two had appeared in the same year, both as part of encylopaedic works (Fournier 1882; Hermann and Blümner 1992 pp. 17–31 and 214–35). Since then, work in this field has resulted chiefly in monographs on particular foodstuffs and their names (references to many such will be found in this chapter). Bommer and Bommer-Lotzin's work (1961) depends on secondary sources. Miha-Lambaki's thesis (1984) is really an index to food names in Aristophanes' comedies. There are chapters on ancient Greece in the world histories of food, wine and cookery, but, if they use ancient sources at all, they rely heavily on excerpts from Gulick's translation of Athenaeus, generally attributing to Athenaeus remarks made by his sources and often treating comic dialogues as if they were statements of fact.

To make this chapter easier to read I use modern English names, not scientific Latin names , for the animals and plants that provided Greeks with their food. These names – indeed, any names that one might choose to use – mask problems of identification, the most important of which will be found outlined in the following endnotes.

A classical Greek term is given for each species, in the nominative singular, as a rule, whatever the syntax of the surrounding sentence, so as to assist cross-referencing between this chapter and the Greek index. Scientific names and modern Greek and Turkish terms can be found in the Greek index.

2 Most references in the chapter are to writings from this period (down to about 250 BC) and from the region. Later authors, and authors from elsewhere in the Greek world, have also been cited if the information they offer is in some way complementary. Reference is often made to the appropriate section of Athenaeus in cases where he quotes a useful selection of sources from the right time and place.

3 Sardis: K. L. Gleason in Hostetter 1994; Hanfmann 1983; Greenewalt 1976. Other Aegean sites: Renfrew 1971; Renfrew 1988; Karali-Yannakopoulos 1989. Pompeii: Casella 1950; Mayer 1980; Jashemski 1979–93; Meyer 1989. Stobi: Davis 1981. There is a useful historical outline of Bulgarian foodstuffs by Johnson (1981). On Roman foodstuffs see André 1981.

4 Aristophanes, *Birds* 959; Polemon [Athenaeus 138f]; Ananius 5 [Athenaeus 282b]; Aristotle, *Study of Animals* 579a9. Richter 1972.

5 As suggested by the remarks in *Regimen in Acute Diseases* 88. An all-too-similar story is told of two sophists of Elis, Anchimolus and Moschus, who drank nothing but water and ate nothing but figs. They, too, were healthy, but their sweat smelt so bad that everyone avoided them at the baths (Hegesander [*Epitome* 44c]). The tale appears to be an ancient 'urban myth'.

6 Machon [Athenaeus 579e, 580d]; Molpis [Athenaeus 141e].

7 Bodson 1977; Orth 1921b.

8 Philoxenus b [Athenaeus 146f]. Suckling lamb: Crates Comicus 1 [Athenaeus 396d]. Lamb and kid together: Molpis [Athenaeus 141e]; *Regimen* 3.82.2.

9 A *kríbanos* as usually understood (a dome-shaped baking crock) was not a place for boiling or stewing. Aeschylus is not always precise with technical terms, but may be picturing the utensil used as a cooking pot on top of a fire rather than a crock under it.

10 *Epitome* 7c. Dohm 1964 p. 158, and, in general, Orth 1921a.

11 For example, Ananius 5 [Athenaeus 282b]; *Odyssey* 14.80–1; perhaps, with all its *double entendre*, Aristophanes, *Acharnians* 786–8; Pherecrates 49 [Athenaeus 396c].

12 *Odyssey* 3.441. The term used here, and occasionally elsewhere, is *oulaí*: more explicitly *oulaí krithôn*, 'groats of barley', Herodotus, *Histories* 1.160. The word is explained as 'grains of barley mixed with salt, thrown on at sacrifices' (Scholia on Aristophanes, *Knights* 1167).

13 Hippolochus [Athenaeus 128c]. Gulick (e.g. 1927–41 vol. 1 p. 413) tries the translation 'beef' for Greek *kréas*, 'meat'. While 'meat' is indeed used as a euphemism for 'beef' in certain modern languages, especially in south and south-east Asia, there is no reason to suppose the same euphemism to have been necessary in classical Greece.

14 Greenewalt 1976; cf. Gow 1952 vol. 2 pp. 36, 38; Pope 1972.

15 Another source seems to contradict Galen: 'The Greeks do not eat dog or horse or ass' (Porphyry, *On Abstinence from Animal Foods* 1.14; cf. 2.25). The two could be reconciled by supposing that Galen's asinine men are not Greeks: but if he is speaking of non-Greek dietary practices he usually says so explicitly. If Pollux (*Onomasticon* 9.48) is right that there was a recognised market area for ass meat at Athens, *Memnóneia*, this suggests the domesticated animal, for wild asses can hardly have been so plentiful.

16 For offal, citations at Athenaeus 94c–101b. Sow's womb, Athenaeus 96e and especially Archestratus 62 [Athenaeus 101c]. Miscarried womb, citations at Athenaeus 101a.

17 Citations at Athenaeus 399d–401b; Nicostratus 4 [*Epitome* 65d]; Antiphanes 295 [*Epitome* 65e]. 'With swaying hips' may well not be the original meaning of the Homeric epithet *eilípous*, but this is surely how Eupolis expected it to be understood.

18 Alcaeus Comicus 17 [Athenaeus 399f]. *Mímarkys*: Aristophanes, *Acharnians* 1112 and scholia; Hesychius, *Lexicon* s.v. *mímarkys* citing Pherecrates 255.

19 Citations at Athenaeus 401b–402b; Xenophon, *Hunting* 10.

20 *Odyssey* 9.154–65; Hesiod, *Shield of Heracles* 407.

21 Sophilus 5 [Athenaeus 640d]. This passage reeks of irony; but cf. Galen, *On the Properties of Foods* 3.1.9, quoted on p. 60, and Liutprand of Cremona, to be cited in Chapter 9, p. 189.

22 Ananius 5 [Athenaeus 282b]; Theocritus, *Idyll* 1.48–9; cf. Galen, *On the Properties of Foods* 3.1.11.

23 Aristotle, *Study of Animals* 579a4–9; Xenophon, *Hunting* 9; *Odyssey* 17.295.

24 Aristotle, *Study of Animals* 579b6.

25 Aristotle, *Study of Animals* 556b7; Aristophanes fragment 53 [Athenaeus 133b]; Davies and Kathirithamby 1986 pp. 127–9. The context of the Aristophanes passage is unknown. Is the speaker perhaps not human? Or in a desert, where no other foods are available? But grasshoppers also occur in an interminable list of what are certainly human foods, Anaxandrides 42 [Athenaeus 131e]. On whether locusts, *akrís*, were eaten at Athens see Aristophanes, *Acharnians* 1116–17; Davies and Kathirithamby 1986 pp. 141–2; Beavis 1988 p. 76.

26 Poliochus 2 [*Epitome* 60b]; Theocritus, *Idyll 14*.17; citations at *Epitome* 64a. Thompson 1947 pp. 129–31.

27 But hedgehog meat is assessed in *Regimen* (2.46.4) in a context which makes it plain that hedgehog, and not the homonymous sea urchin, is the subject.

28 Pollard 1977 especially pp. 104–9. The source materials are gathered in Thompson's indispensable *Glossary of Greek birds* (1936).

29 Aristophanes, *Birds* 531–8, 1579–90; cf. Archestratus 57 [Athenaeus 399d]. Pollard 1977 p. 107 attributes this treatment to their being regarded as 'inferior eating'.

30 Aristophanes, *Birds* 13–18, 529–32, 1079–85; citations at *Epitome* 64f-65d; Eubulus 120 [*Epitome* 65e]. Kislev 1992. For the blackcap, admittedly, a non-Athenian source, Hippolochus [Athenaeus 129b]. All identifications are approximate. *Sykalís* is traditionally translated 'fig-pecker' rather than 'blackcap'.

In the Eubulus fragment their juxtaposition with hares seems to guarantee that these birds were meant to eat rather than to keep as songbirds. I leave out of account the last line of the fragment, which, as preserved in the *Epitome of Athenaeus*, requires the purchase for food of parrots and kestrels. For brief comment see Hunter 1983 p. 222.

31 Athenaeus of Attaleia [Oribasius, *Medical Collections* 1.3].

32 See also Galen, *On the Properties of Simples* 11.1.37 [12.360], citing Aristophanes and Theocritus.

33 Citations at Athenaeus 395c.

34 Polemon [Athenaeus 388c], a rather late source. Greek *porphyríon* is either moorhen, Gallinula chloropus, or purple gallinule, Porphyrio porphyrio. The latter identification, though often accepted, is the more doubtful as the species is not now found in Greece. Thompson 1936 pp. 252–3.

35 Eupolis 226 and other citations at Athenaeus 392a–393c; Aristotle, *Study of Animals* 613b5.

36 *Odyssey* 15.160–74; Pollard 1977 p. 87. From a later period, Diocletian's Price Edict (4.21–2) distinguishes the prices of wild and farmyard geese.

37 These texts, with Nicander, *Alexipharmaca* 228, tilt the balance against the view of Wilkins and Hill (1994 p. 92). Commenting on Archestratus' instruction to 'feed up the young goose' (58 [Athenaeus 384b]), they argue that this 'does not necessarily signify forced feeding'. Later, in any case, the force-feeding of geese with cereal (*siteutoí*), which has been the usual method, is discussed by Athenaeus (384a–c): instructions for a Roman readership are given by Cato (*On Agriculture* 89).

The earliest source in any language that explicitly mentions foie gras as a delicacy is a Roman poet (Horace, *Satires* 2.8.88). 'They are much sought after in Rome', says a speaker in Athenaeus 384c. But Eubulus 101 (quoted ibid.) is a strong hint that fourth-century BC Athenians already saw something of special interest in goose livers.

38 Aristophanes, *Clouds* 109. In the second century BC they were said to be plentiful in the estuary of that river (Agatharchides of Cnidos 86F15 [Athenaeus 387c]). Athenaeus elsewhere argues from a passage of the *Commentaries* of Ptolemy Physcon (234F2a [Athenaeus 654c]) that pheasants were rare in the second century BC: the monarch had apparently never tasted them. But rarity in Egypt did not mean rarity in Greece.

39 Alexis 58 [Athenaeus 395b]; cf. Nicander fragment 73 [Athenaeus 395c], Aristotle, *Study of Animals* 562b3–563a4. Identification of Greek names for pigeons and doves is uncertain. If the trend of the sources quoted by Athenaeus 394c–395c is to be relied on, that *peleiás* and *peristerá* are not distinct as other species are distinct, but that one is wild and the other domestic, then *peleiás* is Columba livia, ancestor of the domestic pigeon. The other species are fitted to Greek names tentatively rather than confidently.

40 Eubulus 148 [*Epitome* 65c], similar to Ephippus 3 [Athenaeus 370c]; Molpis [Athenaeus 141e].

41 Aelian, *Nature of Animals* 4.58. In general, Tepper 1986.

42 Aristophanes, *Acharnians* 786, 875: identifications tentative.

43 For example Aristophanes, *Assemblywomen* 1169.

44 Or 'Greek partridge'. Alectoris graeca is distinct from the partridge, Perdix perdix, of northern Europe. Its eggs were later recognised as good food for invalids. Dioscorides, *Materia Medica* 2.96; Athenaeus 388e; Aristotle, *Study of Animals* 613b5. Thompson 1936 pp. 234–8.

45 Tournefort 1717 vol. 1 p. 412; Thompson 1936 pp. 60–1.

46 Galen, *On the Properties of Foods* 3.19.2; Simeon Seth, *On the Properties of Foods* 30. Witteveen 1986–7; Langkavel 1868 p. vi. The fourth-century source for crane as food, Anaxandrides (42 [Athenaeus 131f]), adds swan and pelican (*kyknos, pelekán*). In this text, a fearsomely long fantasy menu for a wedding in Thrace, most of the items did actually serve as food in contemporary Greece, but there is no further evidence on these two.

47 Cf. Murray 1980 p. 192; Pollard 1977 p. 88. Vickers 1990 p. 114 discusses the date of Athenian vase-paintings depicting domestic cocks. Cock-fighting, later legend said, was introduced to Athens by Themistocles after the defeat of Xerxes – in 480 BC – see Aelian, *Miscellany* 2.28. In general see also Mason 1984.

It has been argued that hens were known in Minoan Crete, but the evidence is weak (Vickery 1936 p. 68; West and Zhou 1988; Sallares 1991 p. 233). See also Darby *et al.* 1977 pp. 297–309 on Cretan antiquities found in Egypt and on the incomplete evidence for the introduction of the hen to Egypt itself: the first knowledge of it there may have come as early as the fifteenth century BC, but the relevant text is fragmentary.

48 Aristophanes, *Birds* 705–7; citations at Athenaeus 373a; Aristotle, *Study of Animals* 613b5. Gow 1952 vol. 2 p. 234. Chicken was certainly eaten in classical Greece (see also *Regimen* 2.47.2; Chrysippus of Soli [Athenaeus 373a], Diocles of Carystus 141 (Oribasius, *Medical Collections* 3.168–9)), but, like hare and small birds, it does not occur in the grand literary menus. It was a supper luxury, not a sacrificial and dinner dish. It seems to have taken a long time for chickens to become accepted as sacrificial animals: Alciphron (*Letters* 4.13) here, as often elsewhere, introduces an anachronism to his romantic picture of the fourth century BC.

49 Aristophanes, *Wasps* 878; Aristophanes fragment 581 [Athenaeus 372b]; Eubulus 74 [Athenaeus 640b]; Varro, *On Farming* 3.16.26; Pliny, *Natural History*

11.34, 21.57. Schuster 1931; Solomon 1995 n. 25. Pliny knew the importance of thyme for the flavour of Attic honey.

50 Cf. Dickson 1978. It is not surprising that mead is little known around the Mediterranean. It can be a pleasantly aromatic wine, but not pleasant enough to compensate for the costliness of honey as compared with grapes. Greek *méthy*, though etymologically linked with the English word, should not, of course, be translated 'mead'.

51 For example, Herodotus, *Histories* 1.216, 3.23. The statement of Herzog-Hauser (1932) that 'milk formed, after wine and mead, the principal beverage of the Homeric age' is two parts fantasy.

52 The same term, *boútyron*, is used (appropriately enough) for 'ghee' in the *Periplus of the Erythraean Sea* 14.

53 For example, Menander fragment 451 [Athenaeus 172a, 644c]. This is the *méli kaì gála sympakton* of Philoxenus b.36 [Athenaeus 147e]; cf. Gow 1952 vol. 2 p. 212 on the *paktâs* of Theocritus (*Idyll 11*.20).

54 Athenaeus 516e, 646e; Scholia on Theocritus, *Idyll 9*.19, where several mutually contradictory recipes will be found. Gow 1952 vol. 2 p. 188.

55 Empedocles 33 [Plutarch, *Moralia* 95a]; *Geoponica* 18.19.2; Galen, *On the Properties of Simples* 6.4.9 [11.865], 10.1.7 [12.265]; Lysias, *Against Pancleon* 23.6; Aristophanes, *Frogs* 1369, *Knights* 480; Diocletian's *Price Edict* 5.11, 6.96. Richter 1968 pp. 62–4; Kroll 1919.

56 Athenaeus 542f; Cicero, *Letters to Friends* 9.16; Aristophanes, *Acharnians* 1125; Theodoridas [*Anthologia Palatina* 6.155].

57 Purcell 1995; Dölger 1922–43; Engemann 1968; Höppener 1931; Gallant 1985; Davidson 1993; Sparkes 1995.

58 Vickery 1936 pp. 76–9; Buchholz *et al.* 1973; Casteel 1976.

59 Many names given by the early fifth-century playwright Epicharmus in the surviving fragments 41–70 of his *Heba's Wedding* have been passed over in silence here. Some coincide with names found elsewhere, but others are rare or unique and cannot be identified with certainty. Epicharmus was very much a Sicilian writer: naturally he listed species and names that were familiar locally. In any case the fish in this play were guests at the legendary wedding, not food on any table.

60 If the numerals have been correctly interpreted. The unit, X, is a *khalkoûs*, a bronze coin, supposed here to be worth one-twelfth of *I*, a small silver *óbolos*. The price for belly of tuna, the most expensive legible price, is given as *IIXX*. Prices are supposed to be by weight, the local *mnâ* probably rather more than a pound. See Schaps 1987 and references given there.

61 The user of this indispensable work should be aware of two minor faults. Thompson was a careless reader of Athenaeus (admittedly a confusing author), sometimes misattributing quoted texts because he did not observe where one quotation was supposed to give way to another. On p. 296, for example, at *ótion*, a dietetic rule by Diphilus (second century BC) is attributed by Thompson to the poet Archippus (fifth century BC). Thompson was an enthusiast for Egypt, an enthusiasm which he on occasion assumed in others. On p. 146, at *látos*, he took it that Archestratus was writing of the Egyptian fish so named when there is no evidence that Archestratus had travelled anywhere southeast of Rhodes. I have found Alan Davidson's *Mediterranean seafood* (1981) a useful guide to modern food species and modern names, sometimes suggesting corrections to Thompson's identifications.

Beside literary sources there is also iconographic evidence (Delorme and Roux 1987), particularly that of south Italian 'fish-plates', probably used for serving fish at dinner, but so called because they illustrate fish (McPhee and Trendall 1990, 1987, where unfortunately no attempt is made to identify the fish; Kunisch 1989; Lacroix 1937). These, however, are not strictly relevant to Greece.

62 In Plato's comedy *Phaon* (189 [*Epitome* 5b]), a character claims to be reciting lines from a versified cookery book. Some have thought these to be extracts from a genuine work. A telling argument against this idea is that they recommend the serving of whole shark, *karkharías*, making nonsense of the distinction between what can practically and appropriately be brought to the dining room whole and what cannot. Thompson 1947 p. 107 argues the other way, taking it from the cookery book's recommendation that *karkharías* was a small fish. Against this, Archestratus 23 [Athenaeus 310c], quoted below, instructs his reader to buy steaks of it, as we would expect for one of the sharks.

One feature of the exaggeration in Matron's Homeric parody [Athenaeus 134d] is that it describes the serving of several very large fish whole, including eel, catfish, moray eel, dolphin-fish and dogfish.

63 Vickery 1936 pp. 76–7.

64 Aristotle, *Study of Animals* 607b2; Archestratus *passim*; Lynceus [Athenaeus 313f].

65 For this list see Ephippus 12 [Athenaeus 322d]; Antiphanes 130 [Athenaeus 295f].

66 Swordfish, citations at Athenaeus 314e. Dolphin-fish, Coryphaena hippurus, is the most probable identification for ancient *híppouros* and *koryphaina* (citations at Athenaeus 304c; see Thompson 1947 pp. 94, 293).

67 The correct reading is likely to be *góngrou*, '[the head] of a conger', since that is what was always prized. The manuscript reading talks of the purchase of a whole conger.

68 Carp: Dorion [Athenaeus 309a]. Pike: citations at Athenaeus 323a. Catfish and sheatfish: e.g. Diodorus Comicus 2 [Athenaeus 239e]; Diphilus of Sinope 17 [Athenaeus 132c]. For identification see Thompson 1947 pp. 43–8, 233–7. The *kápros* (e.g. Philemon 82 [Athenaeus 288f]), so Thompson (1947 pp. 101–2) suggests, may be another name for the *glanís* of the River Achelous. I would like to feel certain that the *kápros* of one particular fragment, Archestratus 15 [Athenaeus 305e], is indeed a fish – 'boar-fish' as Wilkins and Hill 1994 translate it – and not a wild boar, the original and commonest meaning of the word.

69 Archestratus 34 [Athenaeus 301f]; Strabo, *Geography* 5.2.6, 5.2.8; cf. Theocritus, *Idyll* 3.26; Polybius, *Histories* 34.8.1 [Athenaeus 302c]; Philoxenus b.21 [Athenaeus 147c]; citations at Athenaeus 301e, 315c, 319a.

70 For example, Lynceus [Athenaeus 132a], though Thompson (1947 p. 17) takes this and other texts as early references to caviar. Two classical texts that probably allude to sturgeon, though they do not name it, are the Hesiodic verses quoted by Euthydemus of Athens [Athenaeus 116a] and a fragment of Archestratus (39 [Athenaeus 284e]).

71 Citations at Athenaeus 306d.

72 For example, Archestratus 47 [Athenaeus 286d]; cf. Davidson 1981 p. 168. This is modern Greek *vatrakhópsaro*, 'frog-fish', called by some translators 'fishing frog' after the Latin *rana piscatrix*.

73 Anaxandrides 31 and other citations at Athenaeus 295b–297c. Literally 'grey', and traditionally called 'greyfish' by translators. Pomatomus saltator is 'a fish of the high seas which approaches the coasts in summer ... a good fish ... well known in Turkey' (Davidson 1981 p. 100).

74 Conger: Archedicus 3 and other citations at Athenaeus 288c–294c; Archestratus 18–19 [Athenaeus 293f]. Eel: Aristophanes, *Acharnians* 889–94; Strattis 45 [Athenaeus 327e]; Archestratus 8 and other citations at Athenaeus 297c–300c; Hicesius [Athenaeus 298b]. Moray: Archestratus 16 and other citations at Athenaeus 312b.

   Greek *myraina* should not be translated 'lamprey' (as it is by Gulick (1927–41)) though Latin *muraena* does sometimes mean 'lamprey': see Thompson 1947 pp. 162–5 for examples.

75 Citations at Athenaeus 294c, 306d, 310a.

76 Sotades 1.2 [Athenaeus 293a]; Archestratus 21 and Lynceus [Athenaeus 285e]; Aristotle fragment 310 [Athenaeus 294d]; Archippus 23 [Athenaeus 227a].

   Angel shark is Squatina squatina, also called 'angel fish' or 'monkfish', but the latter term is ambiguous, also denoting the anglerfish (see p. 68), Lophius piscatorius (*Multilingual dictionary* 1978, cf. Wilkins and Hill 1994 p. 85).

77 This is the normal North American usage (differing from British). The stingrays and electric rays are seldom now considered good food (Davidson 1981 pp. 33–4). Greek *nárke* also meant 'numbness', such as is caused by the sting of the fish. Eupolis 174 and other citations at Athenaeus 286b; citations at Athenaeus 314a.

78 Archestratus 46 [Athenaeus 319d]; Archestratus 31 and other citations at Athenaeus 305f. On the basis of the name it is tempting to identify the latter fish with the guitar-fish, Rhinobatus rhinobatus. For the problems see Thompson 1947 pp. 114–15.

79 Citations at Athenaeus 310e, 319b, 315a; Archestratus 45 [Athenaeus 311a]; Cratinus 154 [Athenaeus 315b]; Eubulus 109 [Athenaeus 311d]; Antiphanes 130 [Athenaeus 295f]. To be precise this 'comber' will have been Serranus scriba, modern Greek *pérka* (Davidson 1981 p. 73), usually called 'perch' or 'sea perch' by translators.

80 Ananius 5 [Athenaeus 282b]; Archestratus 30 [Athenaeus 328a].

81 Hermippus 63 [*Epitome* 27e].

82 Davidson 1981 pp. 74–89. *Synagrís* denoted either the same species as *synódous* (probably Dentex dentex, denté) or another closely related one (Athenaeus 322b; Thompson 1947 pp. 253–4). *Hépatos* (e.g. Archestratus 27 [Athenaeus 301c]) was like *phágros* and *erythrînos*, according to Speusippus [Athenaeus 327c], and therefore a bream; but it was *petraîos*, a wrasse or something like it, according to Diocles of Carystus 135 [Athenaeus 301c]. If *hys* (Archestratus 22 [Athenaeus 326e]) is the same as the later *hyaina* (Numenius [Athenaeus 326f]), then it may be identifiable with the sheepshead bream, Puntazzo puntazzo: but the descriptions make it hardly big enough to match this species.

83 Epicharmus 63 [Athenaeus 321d]; Davidson 1981 p. 88. Gilthead: citations at Athenaeus 328a. Sar: Archestratus 36 [Athenaeus 321c]. Pagre: Archestratus 26 [Athenaeus 327d]. Morme: Lynceus [Athenaeus 313f].

84 Aristotle, *Study of Animals* 488b7; Archestratus 13 [Athenaeus 320b]. *Skaren*, perhaps the same species, is valued low in the *Acraephia Price List*, where several other names belonging to this group also occur. Davidson 1981 p. 109.

85 Two species were distinguished, the larger (red) and smaller (dark), corresponding to Scorpaena scrofa and S. porcus. The latter was better (Archestratus 29 [Athenaeus 320f]; cf. Numenius and Hicesius [Athenaeus 320d]).

86 The latter is *gelabrias* in the *Acraephia Price List*. See Archestratus (14), who seems to consider them identical, and other citations at Athenaeus 315e.

87 Nausicrates 1 and other citations at Athenaeus 325c; Antiphanes 204 and other citations at Athenaeus 309b; citations at Athenaeus 313a; Aristotle, *Study of*

*Animals* 569b25; Antiphanes 123 [Athenaeus 287e]; citations at Athenaeus 284f, 328c; *Acraephia Price List*.

88 Athenaeus 330b.

89 Citations at Athenaeus 323c, 316a, 326c.

90 For example, Archestratus 56 and other citations at Athenaeus 85c–94b. Oysters, Andrews 1948b; for most of the latter list, Thompson 1947. Explicit references naming the *khéme leía* as food begin in the third century with Diocles of Carystus 133 [Athenaeus 86b] and Hicesius [Athenaeus 87b]. This is probably the shellfish intended by Archestratus' single word *leíai* (56 [Athenaeus 87b]. *Peloriás* was probably carpet-shell, Venerupis decussata, French *palourde*: not unlike the clams, but larger (Athenaeus 92f). *Tellíne*: wedge-shell, Donax trunculus, is Italian *tellina*. *Strómbos* is often a general term for a spiral shell; but see Thompson 1947 pp. 252–3 and Gow 1952 vol. 2 p. 190 for occasions on which a large specimen, such as a triton, is probably meant.

91 Archestratus 24 [Athenaeus 105a]; Eupolis 174 [Athenaeus 286b]; citations at Athenaeus 104c; Archestratus 56 [Athenaeus 92d], 25 and other citations at Athenaeus 105d. I believe that *astakós* denotes larger creatures such as Homarus gammarus (lobster) and Palinurus vulgaris (spiny lobster); *kárabos* denotes the smaller ones such as Nephrops norvegicus (langoustine or crayfish or Dublin Bay prawn). *Karís* is the name for prawns of the families Palaemonidae, Penaeidae, especially for the larger ones.

92 Translators of the *Iliad* traditionally write 'oyster', their excuse being the imprecision of the Scholia (A) on *Iliad* 16.747, which explain the term as 'one of the marine shellfish'. On the basis of Aristotle's description (*Study of Animals* 531a8–30) the creature is satisfactorily identified as Microcosmus sulcatus, sea-squirt, French *violet, figue de mer* (Minchin 1987 n. 13; Thompson 1947 pp. 261–2; Davidson 1981 p. 216).

93 *Látos*, Archestratus 51 [Athenaeus 311e]. *Glaúkiskos* e.g. Lynceus [Athenaeus 285f]. *Aulopías, anthías*, e.g. Ananius 5 [Athenaeus 282b]; *Acraephia Price List*; Archestratus 33 [Athenaeus 326b]. *Elops*, citations at Athenaeus 282d–e, 294e–f, 300d–e. *Myllos, brínkos*, Ephippus 12 [Athenaeus 322d]. *Gnapheús*, Athenaeus 297c citing Dorion and Epaenetus. In general, Thompson 1947 s.vv. Some other names could be added from the *Acraephia Price List*.

94 Pliny, *Natural History* 31.93. The Bithynian recipe given here, one of the four in *Geoponica*, is probably from Florentinus, like most of the other special Bithynian information in the collection, though in this case it is unattributed.

95 Latin *hallec*, a salted fish paste.

96 Thai *nam pla*, Vietnamese *nuoc mam*, now widely available: the similarity was pointed out to classicists by Grimal and Monod (1952). The comparison with anchovy sauce, made by Daremberg and Saglio (1877–1919 s.v. 'Garum') and repeated even by some recent English-language authors, is misguided; anchovy sauce is not the product of rotting or fermentation, and could hardly be said to be 'of the same colour as old *mulsum* [honeyed wine]' (Pliny, *Natural History* 31.95), while good *nam pla* can indeed be likened to Malaga in colour – if not in flavour.

The closest analogue may be the home-made *padek* of Laos and northern Thailand. While *nam pla* is entirely liquid, *padek* has 'chunks of the fermented fish still in it' (Davidson in Phia Sing 1981 p. 23), as *gáros* must sometimes have done, since fish bones are found in excavated amphoras that once contained it. Another comparable product is soy sauce, likewise the product of fermentation.

97 Cratinus 312 [*Epitome* 67b]; Aeschylus fragment 211, Sophocles fragment 606, Plato Comicus 215 [all at *Epitome* 67c]. Further references and full discussion: Curtis 1991; Ponsich and Tarradell 1965; Zahn 1912.

98 The meaning of Epicharmus 42.6 [Athenaeus 85d] is too uncertain to be conclusive, however.

99 Xenocrates [Oribasius, *Medical Collections* 2.58.67–71, 2.58.125].

100 For the highly contradictory explanations of this word see Thompson 1947 p. 226.

101 The pseudo-Hesiodic verses of Euthydemus of Athens [Athenaeus 116a]; cf. Sopater 12 [Athenaeus 119a]). On the tunny fishery see Dumont 1976–7; Anfimov 1983. On *tárikhos* see further Foucher 1970; Sanquer and Galliou 1972; Besnier 1909 s.v. 'Salsamentum'.

102 Solomon 1995. On salt, Nenquin 1961; Besnier 1909.

103 Cf. *Odyssey* 11.589–90, 24.336–44.

104 Citations at Athenaeus 80e. Zohary and Hopf 1993 pp. 162–6; Olck 1894.

105 But there is much variation in spelling and in the interpretation of this term. Athenaeus 650c; Galen, *Hippocratic Glossary* s.v. *epimelís*; Dioscorides, *Materia Medica* 1.118. Gow 1952 vol. 2 p. 109; Gulick 1927–41 vol. 6 p. 513 note c.

106 So, probably, Euphorion 11, and also Nicander fragment 50 [both at Athenaeus 82a]: on the latter see Gow and Scholfield 1953 p. 207. On quinces, Trumpf 1960.

107 Gow 1952 vol. 2 pp. 107, 161; Brazda 1977; cf. Vryonis 1971 p. 493.

108 Stesichorus 187 [Athenaeus 81d]. *Farming* attributed to Androtion and others [Athenaeus 82c]; Theophrastus, *Study of Plants* 2.2.5. Akkadian sources: Postgate 1987. Quince is late Akkadian *supurgillu*, cf. Arabic *safarjal*.

For botanical reasons Vavilov (1950 p. 34) considered that quinces were first domesticated in the Levant. Quinces have up to now been overlooked by the archaeobotanists. In Zohary and Hopf's second edition (1993 pp. 172–3) they are listed, but evidently as an afterthought: 'Literary sources seem to indicate that also the quince reached the Mediterranean only in classical times.' No references are given.

The problem comes from the absence, so far, of archaeological information and the use of Greek *mêlon* to cover both 'apple' and 'quince'. The terminological difficulty caused by the lack of a single distinct term for 'quince' led to confusion even in ancient times (e.g. citations at Athenaeus 81a–f), and in one work at least to the grouping of quinces under the name 'winter apples' since they blossom early (Phylotimus 11 [Athenaeus 81c]), while true apples, Malus pumila, could be called 'spring apples' (Androtion [Athenaeus 82c]. For a discussion of this term, considering and rejecting the hypothesis that it referred to apricots, see Powell 1987.

The meaning of Alcman's word *kodymalon* (Alcman 100 [Athenaeus 81f]: context unknown) was disputed by Hellenistic philologists: some thought he meant 'quince', and if so this would be the earliest mention of the fruit in Greek texts. Some think that Alcman used the word *kydónion*, too (e.g. Davies 1991– p. 107 [Alcman 99]), but this is to misunderstand Athenaeus (81d) who merely refers forward, in a way that he often does, to his coming citation of *kodymalon*.

109 For example Theocritus, *Idyll* 12.3. Gow 1952 vol. 2 pp. 166–7.

110 'The earliest records of plum planting and grafting come from Roman times' (Zohary and Hopf 1993 pp. 169–71).

111 Prunus cerasus was probably a cross between P. avium, the sweet cherry or gean, and the 'ground cherry', P. fruticosa. The former is native to temperate

Europe, northern Turkey and the Caucasus region; the latter to central and eastern Europe and north-eastern Turkey. A cross between them is most likely to have arisen in north-eastern Turkey (Zohary and Hopf 1993 pp. 171–2), the ancient Pontus, exactly where ancient sources say that the *kérasos* came from.

Roman history claims a precise date for the cherry's spread westwards: 'There were no cherries in Italy before L. Lucullus' defeat of Mithridates, A.U.C. 680 [74 BC]. He brought them here from Pontus; within 120 years they have crossed the ocean to Britain' (Pliny, *Natural History* 15.102). 'You forget that the Roman general Lucullus, victor over Mithridates and Tigranes, first brought this tree to Italy from *Kerasoûs*, a city of Pontus. It was he who called the fruit *kérasos* after the city, so our [Roman] historians report' (*Epitome of Athenaeus* 50f).

The last claim, by Athenaeus' fictional speaker Larensius, is immediately given the lie by an interlocutor. The word was not invented by Lucullus: it had been in use in Greek for centuries. In fact it is more likely that Cerasus was named after the fruit, just as neighbouring *Trapezoûs*, with its table-like acropolis, was named after Greek *trápeza* 'table'. Cerasus is unlikely to have been founded earlier than the first occurrences of the word in Greek literature.

Pliny's statement, 'There were no cherries in Italy . . .' helps to make it clear that *cerasus*, to Roman authors, meant principally the fruit of Prunus cerasus rather than that of P. avium, the wild sweet cherry that is native to much of Europe, which the Romans called *cornus* and, later, *cerasus silvatica* (André 1981 p. 78): from this late usage it comes about that reflexes of *cerasus* are the modern names for P. avium in most of Europe, whereas P. cerasus has quite different names, for example, French *griotte*, German *Weichsel*. These *kérasoi* were an Anatolian speciality, present on the eastern Aegean coast by the sixth century, present in great numbers in north-eastern Turkey, but transplanted to mainland Greece and Italy far later.

112 They are first mentioned by Xenophanes (39 [Pollux, *Onomasticon* 6.46]), who was from Colophon, not very far from Miletus. Theophrastus, himself from the island of Lesbos off the Anatolian coast, had informants from many regions, and does not say where his information on cherries came from (*Study of Plants* 3.13.1–3); his description here, incidentally, applies more to Prunus avium than to P. cerasus. *Lakáre*, a term used twice by Theophrastus (ibid. 3.3.1, 3.6.1: spelling uncertain), may be the specific name, otherwise unrecorded in Greek texts, of P. avium.

113 Citations at *Epitome* 56b; Besnier 1904. Compare the recipe for *epítyron*, olive relish, given by Cato, *On Agriculture* 119.

114 Citations at *Epitome* 58f, Athenaeus 372b. Zohary and Hopf 1993 pp. 181–3; Akkadian sources, Stol 1987; in general, Andrews 1956; Sallares 1991 p. 483 n. 117. See the fairly full descriptions by Galen, *On the Properties of Foods* 2.4–5; Pliny, *Natural History* 19.67–8. Pliny thought the *melopepo* a newly developed variety of cucumber. Andrews, not yet aware of archaeological finds, demonstrated from texts (against doubts of Candolle 1883 and others) that the watermelon was known in classical Greece.

115 Theophrastus, *Study of Plants* 7.4.1; citations at *Epitome* 73d, Athenaeus 74a. Zohary and Hopf 1993; Charles 1987; Stol 1987.

116 Bottle gourd, Theophrastus, *Study of Plants* 7.3.5. For both, citations at *Epitome* 58f and Athenaeus 372b. One or both of these terms is sometimes translated 'marrow', 'pumpkin' or 'squash', but the plants to which those names belong, Cucurbita spp., are native to the Americas and were not known in the classical world (Sallares 1991 p. 483 n. 117).

117 For Rhodian figs see e.g. Lynceus quoted by Athenaeus 652d and 75e. In addition Rhodes may well have supplied Carian figs to Athens. Latin was to adopt the word *carica*, etymologically 'Carian', for 'dried fig'.

118 Citations at Athenaeus 74d, 652b. Olck 1909. *Thrion*, Alexis 179 [Athenaeus 170b]; Dalby 1989.

119 Henderson 1991 pp. 117–19, 134–5; Buchheit 1960.

120 Citations at Athenaeus 650b. Zohary and Hopf 1993 pp. 166–7.

121 Cf. Gow 1952 vol. 2 p. 161.

122 For example, Alexis 167 [*Epitome* 54f]. Gow 1952 vol. 2 p. 429.

123 Nicander, *Alexipharmaca* 489–93; citations at Athenaeus 651e; Solon 40; Epaenetus [Athenaeus 662e]. Engemann 1983.

124 Citations at Athenaeus 653b; Eubulus 48 [Athenaeus 653e]; Justinian, *Digest* 50.16.205.

125 Galen, *On the Properties of Simples* 6.1.32 [11.826].

126 Plato, *Republic* 372c; Apollophanes 5 [Athenaeus 75c]. Kalças 1974. Incidentally, English translators generally render *myrton* 'myrtle berry', Myrtus communis, while French translators sometimes plump for *myrtille*, Vaccinium myrtillus, English 'bilberry'. Although not closely related, the two actually do have a certain resemblance, even in flavour, but assuming that Vaccinium myrtillus (or a close relative) is correctly identified with the *vaccinium* of Pliny, which he does not link with myrtle, Greek *myrton* is best taken as denoting Myrtus communis. The English seem to be right here.

127 Dio Chrysostom, *Euboica* 75. Both 'cultivated' and 'wild' sorbs were known to Theophrastus, *Study of Plants* 3.2.1. His wild kind may be the rowan, Sorbus aucuparia, which is known as 'wild sorb' in some modern languages (e.g. Romanian *scorus-de-munte*).

128 Eubulus 74 [Athenaeus 640b–c]; Dio Chrysostom *Euboica* 75. Baird and Thieret 1989.

129 Pherecrates 158 [Athenaeus 653e]. This fruit is generally said to be edible but no more (e.g. Pliny, *Natural History* 15.99), and the other citations of Athenaeus on the subject (*Epitome* 50e) might be taken as ironic rather than as confirming the tree-strawberry's place at dessert. Its Latin name *unedo* was said to mean 'I eat only one'. I have not tasted it.

130 Phaenias of Eresus 42 and other citations at *Epitome* 51b; *Regimen* 2.55.3; Galen, *On the Properties of Foods* 2.38.5.

131 Theocritus, *Idyll* 24.45. Lindsell 1937.

132 For almond and other nuts see citations at *Epitome* 52b–54d; against drunkenness, Plutarch, *Symposium Questions* 1.6.4, but the experiment is not recommended; in perfumes, Pliny, *Natural History* 13.8,19. Zohary and Hopf 1993 pp. 173–7.

133 Walnut: Zohary and Hopf 1993 pp. 177–8 citing work by Bottema. Chestnut: ibid. pp. 178–9 citing work of van Zeist. Hazelnut and filbert were certainly both present in the classical and later Aegean. For their names see notes 134–6. Zohary and Hopf (1993 p. 179) say of the hazel: 'apparently this shrub was already planted by the Romans (White 1970)', as if that were the earliest evidence. Note the references to cultivation in Theophrastus (*Study of Plants* 3.15.1–2).

134 Liddell and Scott 1925–40, and Gulick 1927–41 vol. 1 p. 227, translate *káryon*, when used narrowly, 'walnut', in accordance with Galen's statement (*On the Properties of Foods* 2.28.1) that 'some name *basilikà kárya*, royal nuts, what everyone these days calls simply *kárya*. So *Epitome of Athenaeus* 52a–b, citing Epicharmus 150 and Sophocles fragment 759. See also, later, *Diocletian's Price*

*Edict* 6.50–3, which distinguishes *nuces abellanae*, 'hazelnuts', from *nuces*, 'walnuts' (cf. Italian *noce*, French *noix*, etc., 'walnut'); the edict is fragmentary in Greek at this point, but the Greek equivalents were probably *leptokárya*, 'hazelnuts', and *kárya*, 'walnuts'. For a less likely identification of *káryon* with 'hazelnut' see Hort 1916–26 vol. 2 p. 455.

'Royal nut': Theophrastus, *Plant Physiology* 4.2.1. 'Persian nut': Theophrastus, *Study of Plants* 3.6.2, 3.14.4; Diocles of Carystus 126 [*Epitome* 53d]. It is Dioscorides, *Materia Medica* 1.125.1, who states that the two terms are synonymous, cf. Pliny, *Natural History* 15.87.

135 Bryer 1979 pp. 384–5. *Leptokáryon* 'little nut', *káryon Pontikón*, 'Pontic nut': Galen, *On the Properties of Foods* 2.28.1 and Dioscorides, *Materia Medica* 1.125.3 (the earliest source for *leptokáryon*) both give the two terms as synonyms. There are much earlier uses of *káryon Pontikón* in third-century BC papyri, P.Cair.Zen.59012.48, 59013.24, 59702.22. 'Heracleotic nut': Theophrastus, *Study of Plants* 3.15.1–2, etc.; Mnesitheus [*Epitome* 54b]. Hort (1916–26 vol. 2 p. 455) identifies *Herakleotiká* specifically as 'filberts', but it is noticeable that no author distinguishes them from *Pontiká* (or even uses both terms). Hort's *Herakleotiká* = filberts becomes necessary only because of his unlikely *kárya* = hazelnuts. Diocles of Carystus 126 [*Epitome* 53d] identifies *Herakleotiká* with Zeus-acorns 'chestnuts', but that seems to be an aberration.

136 This passage is missed by Liddell and Scott (1925–40 s.v. *diosbálanos*) and misunderstood as referring to an edible acorn by Gulick (1927–41 vol. 1 p. 121).

Theophrastus, *Study of Plants* 4.5.4, etc. ('Euboean nut'), 4.8.11 (*Kastanaiká*, 'Castaneans', in an aside on a different plant). Mnesitheus quoted in the *Epitome of Athenaeus* 54b is the first source to state that these two terms are synonymous. For the various word-forms and the doubts over their origin cf. Liddell and Scott 1925–40 s.v. *kástana*, and for another view on identification see Gleason in Hostetter 1994 p. 83. 'Sardian nut': Diphilus of Siphnos [*Epitome* 54c]; Phylotimus 8 [*Epitome* 53f]; Dioscorides, *Materia Medica* 1.106. The *Epitome of Athenaeus* (53b–54d) gives several other names for this species or close relatives of it, twice referring to Nicander's *Farming* (fragments 76 and 77). Whether one believes that chestnuts had sometimes also been called 'Pontic nuts' depends on one's faith in the text of the sentence of the *Epitome* (53b) that cites Nicander fragment 77. I would consider it no more than a reference back to fragment 76, a reference that has become garbled in the process of abridgement. On this sentence, incidentally, Desrousseaux (1956 p. 131 note 1) concludes: 'D'ordinaire "noix du Pont" désigne la châtaigne. Ici, ce serait l'aveline.' The truth is precisely the opposite.

137 Hermippus (63 [*Epitome* 27e]); Diphilus of Siphnos [*Epitome* 54b].

138 Theophrastus, *Study of Plants* 9.1.2; Theophrastus, *Study of Plants* 4.4.7; Galen, *On the Properties of Foods* 2.58.2; cf. 2.38.5; citations at Epitome 57b; Aeschines, *Letter* 5.2; cf. Athenaeus 126a. Gow and Page 1968 vol. 2 p. 253.

139 *Comica Adespota* 338 Kock; Dioscorides, *Materia Medica* 1.70; Galen, *On the Properties of Simples* 7.1.2 [12.68]. Salaman 1993; Howes 1950.

140 Herodotus' was the first mention of the fruit (as opposed to the tree) in Greek literature, if we accept Athenaeus' doubt (652a) that the passage he cites from the even earlier Hellanicus (4F56) is genuine. Theophrastus, *Study of Plants* 3.3.5; citations at Athenaeus 651b. Zohary and Hopf 1993 pp. 157–62; Charles 1987; Darby *et al.* 1977 p. 724; Reder 1967; Vickery 1936 p. 60. Greeks named the date palm *phoîniks*, evidently after the Phoenicians from whom they got its fruit (cf. Hermippus 63 [*Epitome* 27e]: the text is doubtful), though since

there was a Greek community trading in northern Syria in the sixth and fifth centuries Greeks might have had a hand in the trade. The fruit was the *bálanos*, 'acorn', of the tree, or later *dáktylos*.

141 Melena (1976 p. 186) withdraws his earlier suggestion that the *po-ni-ki-jo* of the Linear B tablets was the date.

142 Garden plants, e.g. Theophrastus, *Plant Physiology* 2.5.3, *Study of Plants* 7.1.2; Strattis 66 [*Epitome* 69a]. Carroll-Spillecke 1990; Vatin 1974; Thompson 1963; Capelle 1954; Olck 1912. Use in wreaths, e.g. Nicander fragment 74 [Athenaeus 683a].

143 Epicharmus (159–61 [*Epitome* 70f–71a]) provides the first clear mention in Greek literature of poppy leaves, fennel, lettuce, radish, cabbage, chicory or endive and cardoon. As a Sicilian writer he cannot be confidently assumed to have been writing of foods known in the contemporary Aegean, though no doubt most of them were.

144 Asparagus, Theophrastus, *Study of Plants* 6.4.2; citations at *Epitome* 62d; Nicander fragment 71 [Athenaeus 371b]. *Ormenos* is identified as wild asparagus, Asparagus acutifolius, by A. C. Andrews (in Jones 1980 p. 528), as Joseph sage, Salvia viridis, by Hort (1916–26 p. 467, using the name Salvia horminum).

145 Pherecrates 113 [Athenaeus 268f]; Theophrastus, *Study of Plants* 7.4.4; Diphilus of Siphnos and other citations at Athenaeus 370f; Galen, *On the Properties of Simples* 8.19.2 [12.138]. Zohary and Hopf (1993 p. 187) underestimate the age of the cultivation of chard and beet: 'Greek, Roman and Jewish literary sources provide clear evidence that already in the first century BC the crop was represented by several leafy forms (chards). Cultivars with swollen roots appeared later.'

146 Citations at Athenaeus 369e. Saint-Denis 1980.

147 Nicostratus 1 [Athenaeus 133c]; Antiphanes 63 [Athenaeus 161e].

148 Theophrastus, *Study of Plants* 6.4.10–11; citations at *Epitome* 70a. Theophrastus described 'another kind [of *káktos*, which is] edible but cannot be stored'; Athenaeus, surely correctly, identified this with the *kynára* or *kinára*, which had been named in fifth-century sources but without reference to its edibility (*Epitome of Athenaeus* 70a–71c). The *káktos* itself, according to Theophrastus (*Study of Plants* 6.4.10–11) grew only in Sicily, though it grows in Greece now and Theocritus (*Idyll* 10.4, cf. Lindsell 1936–7) plants it on Cos.

149 Diphilus of Siphnos and other citations at Athenaeus 371b. Theophrastus, *Study of Plants* 9.15.5, 9.15.8, 9.20.2. *Daûkos* refers to more than one species, including candy carrot, Athamanta cretensis: cf. Hort 1916–26 vol. 2 p. 444. Some have translated *staphylînos* 'parsnip', but parsnip is not native to Greece, and even now is known there little if at all. Cf. Dioscorides, *Materia Medica* 5.32; Andrews 1949b, 1958b; Steier 1932.

150 Theocritus, *Idyll* 7.68; Aristophanes, *Clouds* 982, a comic speech stuffed with pederastic innuendo. Andrews 1949a; Lindsell 1936–7.

151 Theophrastus, *Study of Plants* 1.10.7.

152 Xenophon, *Education of Cyrus* 1.2.8, cf. Nicander, *Theriaca* 876–7; Eubulus 35 [Athenaeus 347d]. Sancisi-Weerdenburg 1995; Stol 1985.

153 For example, Eubulus 35 [Athenaeus 347d]. Lindsell 1936–7.

154 Hermippus 75 [*Epitome* 56c]; Epicharmus 159 [*Epitome* 70f]; Galen, *On the Properties of Foods* 2.56.

155 Other citations at Epitome 63d–64f. For the identification see Hort 1916–26 vol. 2 pp. 443–4; and for the 'bulb' as a food in classical Rome, André 1981 pp. 20–1. The identity of the bulb was already a matter of confusion in Roman times ('some wrongly think daffodil is meant by *bolbós*': Galen, *Hippocratic*

*Glossary* s.v. *bolbós*), but not, presumably, in Greece itself, where the grape-hyacinth bulb has always been eaten. Some modern translators riskily choose 'iris bulb', which under the pharmacists' name of 'orris root' is the source of a powerful purge. By contrast, it is some slight confirmation of the usually accepted identification with grape-hyacinth, Muscari comosum, that this bulb is now used in the chemotherapy of cancer, for a Byzantine scholion on Dioscorides, *Materia Medica* 2.170, states that 'edible bulb, boiled with barley meal and pigs' fat, causes *oidémata* and *phymata* [tumours] quickly to rot and break up' (Riddle 1984 p. 100).

156 Surely the garden leek, Allium porrum (Hort 1916–26 vol. 2 p. 471), though it has been argued that the leek grown in Egypt in the second millennium BC was Allium kurrat, still known in the Near East (Darby *et al.* 1977 p. 673). There are also references in Sumerian and Akkadian texts (Stol 1987; cf. Zohary and Hopf 1993 p. 183). Wild leek, Galen, *On the Properties of Foods* 2.44.3.

157 Citations at *Epitome* 68f. Zohary and Hopf 1993 p. 186.

158 Hesiod, *Works and Days* 41 and other citations at *Epitome* 58d; Plutarch, *Moralia* 158e.

159 Theophrastus, *Study of Plants* 7.7.1; Strabo, *Geography* 8.3.14 [344c]. Andrews 1958a; Steier 1932. Bergamot mint and peppermint are modern varieties or hybrids, unknown in ancient times.

160 Mushrooms, Nicander fragments 72 [Athenaeus 372f] and 78–9 with other citations at *Epitome* 60b–61f. There is relatively little information from Greek sources: see Houghton 1885; and, from Roman sources, Maggiulli 1977; also useful is a list of edible mushrooms gathered in modern Bulgaria (Johnson 1981). Truffles, Theophrastus fragment 167 and other citations at *Epitome* 62a.

161 If this 'caused tears when eaten' (Aristotle, *Problems* 925a34) and was similar to radish, turnip and *ráphys* (Speusippus [Athenaeus 369b]), it was probably mustard greens, Brassica arvensis.

162 Aristophanes, *Knights* 422; Theophrastus, *Study of Plants* 7.7.2. On the time-table, *Apicius* gives similar instructions (3.17): 'when the sun is in Aries'. The nettle was still important in Byzantine times (Koukoulès 1947–55 vol. 5 pp. 89–90).

163 Aristophanes, *Knights* 677; citations at Athenaeus 371e; Aristotle, *Problems* 925a28 discusses why it makes the eyes water. Zohary and Hopf 1993 p. 185; Darby *et al.* 1977 p. 661; Charles 1987; Waetzoldt 1987; Stol 1987.

164 Theophrastus, *Study of Plants* 7.4.1; Antiphanes 158 [Athenaeus 160f]. Andrews 1948a.

165 Theophrastus, *Study of Plants* 7.4.1.

166 Citations at *Epitome* 56d.

167 Theophrastus, *Plant Physiology* 2.5.3.

168 Cf. Nicander, *Theriaca* 909–14.

169 Theophrastus, *Study of Plants* 7.4.1, 7.6.1; cf. *Geoponica* 2.5.4.

170 Aristophanes fragment 581 [Athenaeus 372b]; Nicander fragment 70 and other citations at Athenaeus 369a. André 1981 esp. pp. 15–16; Andrews 1958b. On food gathered from the wild in Roman Italy see Frayn 1979 pp. 57–72.

171 Cf. Theocritus, *Idyll* 5.125. The identification is uncertain.

172 Dioscorides, *Materia Medica* 2.116; Andrews 1942.

173 *Asphódelos*, Hesiod, *Works and Days* 41. *Skándix*: Aristophanes, *Acharnians* 478. *Anthryskon*: Pherecrates 14 [Athenaeus 316e]; Theophrastus, *Study of Plants* 7.7.1. Goosefoot: Reynolds 1995; Kalças 1974 p. 19; Renfrew 1973. *Erysimon*: Theophrastus, *Study of Plants* 8.1.4, 8.7.3. *Strykhnon*: Theophrastus,

*Study of Plants* 7.7.2, 7.15.4; Galen, *On the Properties of Foods* 2.49. *Skolymos*: West 1978 p. 304; cf. Theophrastus, *Study of Plants* 6.4.7.

174 Callimachus fragment 250 [Pliny, *Natural History* 22.88]; Nicander fragment 71 [Athenaeus 271b].

175 Theophrastus, *Study of Plants* 7.12.1. See also Chapter 9, pp. 190 and 199.

176 *Kaukalís*, a difficult area: there are too many Greek names for the available species. For other identifications of *kaukalís* see Gow and Scholfield 1953 pp. 188, 231. But of *séseli, órdeilon, tórdylon, kaukalís*, only the last is described by ancient sources as a food plant. Tordylium apulum, small hartwort, is still considered edible in parts of Greece according to Facciola (1990 p. 19). *Kórkhoros* is variously identified: as molokhia (Jew's mallow), Corchorus olitorius, by the Linnaean botanists and by A. C. Andrews (in Jones 1980 p. 502); as Anagallis caerulea, blue pimpernel, by Hort 1916–26 vol. 2 p. 458. *Parthénion*, too, is variously identified: with a knotweed, Polygonum maritimum (and also with some less edible plants), by A. C. Andrews (in Jones 1980 p. 530; cf. also Gow and Scholfield 1953 p. 234); as bachelor's buttons (better known to many as feverfew), Pyrethrum parthenium, by the Linnaean taxonomists and by Hort 1916–26 vol. 2 p. 469.

  Theophrastus' list contained at least two more names, garbled in the manuscripts. One was reconstructed by Schweighäuser as *apápe*, dandelion: Theophrastus, however, elsewhere described *apápe* as inedible (*Study of Plants* 7.11.4), though fresh dandelion leaves are eaten in modern Greece. The other, as Salmasius saw, might have been *khóndrylla*, gum succory, Chondrilla juncea, since that appears in a section of Pliny's *Natural History* (21.89) which is a confused version of Theophrastus' list.

177 Alexis 132, 179 [Athenaeus 170a–b]; Archestratus 36 [Athenaeus 321c]. The reader will note two mistranslations in Gulick's version of this last passage (1927–41 vol. 2 p. 273): for 'anise' read 'dill'; for 'kale' read 'silphium stem'.

  There are Englishmen still living who learnt at their mothers' knees that herbs and spices are used in foreign cuisines to mask the taste of rotting meat. For a reasoned refutation see Riley 1993.

178 Diphilus of Sinope 17 [Athenaeus 132e].

179 Theophrastus, *Study of Plants* 9.7.3 lists *ánnetos* as one of the aromatics and not native to Europe. Hort 1916–26 wrongly translates this word 'dill', but Theophrastus knew that that was grown in Greece and he called it *ánethon*. With an inconsistency characteristic of Theophrastus (or rather of his varied sources of information and gradual collecting of information), at 1.12.1 *ánnesos* is the term used for 'aniseed'. It should be noted that 'aniseed' is a variant reading slightly earlier in Alexis 132 as quoted by Pollux, *Onomasticon* 6.65 mss. F, S (but the spelling is *ánoitton*): Athenaeus 170a, who quotes the same fragment, read *skórodon*, 'garlic', instead of *ánoitton*.

180 Strattis 66 [*Epitome* 69a]. But it is not quite certain that humans ate it: in the modern Near East basil is widely known and grown but almost unknown in food (Chase 1993a).

181 For example, Alcaeus Comicus 17 [Athenaeus 399f]; Antiphanes 71 [Athenaeus 169e]; cf. Galen, *On the Properties of Foods* 2.50.2, 2.51.5.

182 For example, Anaxippus 1 [Athenaeus 403f], a text that suggests a fashion against strong flavourings in the third century BC (but see Gowers 1993 on this passage). Lindsell 1936–7.

183 Alcman 19 [Athenaeus 111a].

184 Aristophanes, *Acharnians* 164–5, *Wasps* 679, etc. Zohary and Hopf 1993 pp. 183–5; Waetzoldt 1987; Stol 1987; Crawford 1973b.

185 Archestratus 22 [Athenaeus 326f]. In spite of problems over the occurrence of this term (it is not used by Theophrastus: Galen, by contrast, does not use *amárakon* or *sámpsykhon*, and always lists *hyssopos* next to *oríganon*) Andrews 1961c argues that in classical sources it normally denotes hyssop (Hyssopus officinalis), not marjoram or oregano (cf. Thiselton-Dyer 1913–14 p. 199).

186 For that combination of flavours see also Diphilus of Siphnos [Athenaeus 369e]; it is probably implied by Alexis 132 [Athenaeus 170a]. In general, citations at Athenaeus 366a and see Galen, *On the Properties of Foods* 2.68.2.

187 Andrews 1961c. The word is often inexactly translated 'marjoram'. True marjoram, Origanum majorana, *amárakon*, *sámpsykhon*, was a well-known aromatic (e.g. Pherecrates 138 [Athenaeus 685a]) apparently used only medicinally and in wreaths.

188 Aristophon 16 [*Epitome* 63a]; Galen, *On the Properties of Foods* 1.18.6. Steier 1932 s.v. *Minze*; Andrews 1958a.

189 Alcman 19 [Athenaeus 111a]; cf. Philostratus, *Gymnasticon* 44; Pliny, *Natural History* 19.168; Euphron 10 [*Epitome* 7d]; Theophrastus, *Study of Plants* 9.12.4; Epicharmus 159–61 [*Epitome* 70f–71a]. Kritikos and Papadaki 1967; Andrews 1952, who is right to stress the plant's usefulness as a food; Steier 1932.

   Thucydides, *Histories* 4.26.8 corroborates Alcman on the use of poppy seeds as food at Sparta.

190 Satureja thymbra, often translated 'savory', a name that really belongs to two other species of the genus Satureja.

191 Philoxenus e.11, e.19 [Athenaeus 643b–c]; *Regimen* 2.54.8; Dioscorides, *Materia Medica* 4.188.1; Pliny, *Natural History* 21.90.

192 Cf. Cratinus 363 [Phrynichus, *Ecloga* 81].

193 Theophrastus, *Study of Plants* 9.18.3; cf. Petronius, *Satiricon* 8.4, 20.7. The relevant passage of Theophrastus is entirely excised in Hort's edition (1916–26 vol. 2 p. 310, see n. 2) and must be sought in Wimmer's (1866 pp. 160–1). There are interesting notes in Grieve 1931 pp. 602–5; see also Kalças 1974 p. 47; and now Chase 1993a. I am grateful to Holly Chase for the impulse to investigate this undeservedly obscure foodstuff.

   The plant was grown in gardens, where it attracted slugs, according to Strattis (71 [*Epitome* 69a]). This poet's reference to *satyrídia makrókerka* has been a bit of a puzzle to editors. They have suggested 'baby satyrs' and 'long-tailed animalcula', (for references see Kassel and Austin 1983– vol. 7 p. 656), but neither of these is known to be subject to attack by slugs. Strattis meant, of course, 'long-tailed orchids' – and the adjective does not really describe the orchids, but is a broad hint at their aphrodisiac power.

   In later authors the term used is *satyrion* (Dioscorides, *Materia Medica* 3.128), and in Latin *satureum* (for example, Ovid, *Art of Love* 2.415; Martial 3.75.4 (*improba satureia*, 'naughty salep')). The *Oxford Latin dictionary* and most others gloss this word '[garden] savory, and the aphrodisiac made from it' (thus *sarriette lascive* of the Budé translator of Martial). But no aphrodisiac is made from garden savory, and, even if it were, Ovid could hardly have described it as 'poison'.

   On Salep in Ottoman times, see p. 202.

194 Antiphanes 166 [Athenaeus 108e]; Hippolochus [Athenaeus 130d]; Theophrastus, *Study of Plants* 6.7.2 [Athenaeus 681f]. For a find of a sprig of a related species, Thymbra spicata, in Tutankhamun's tomb, see Hepper 1990 pp. 64–5. It must have come to Egypt from some more northerly country.

195 So scholion ad loc. citing Menander fragment 910. Alcman 19 [Athenaeus 111a]; Philoxenus e.18 [Athenaeus 643c], cf. *Battle of the Frogs and Mice* 36;

Aristophanes, *Peace* 869. Sesame oil was unfamiliar in early historical Greece. Herodotus (*Histories* 1.193.4) writes: '[In Babylonia] they use no olive oil, but make [oil] from sesame seed.' The phrasing suggests that Greeks in his time did not make or use such oil. Later, sesame oil is mentioned, in a brief entry suggesting it was little used, by Dioscorides, *Materia Medica* 1.34. See also Bedigian and Harlan 1986.

196 Solon 41 (Photius, *Lexicon*: '*roûn*: the seasoning. Solon') to be linked, probably, with fragments 38–40.

197 Antiphanes 140 [*Epitome* 68a]; Alexis 132 [Athenaeus 170a]; Galen, *Substitutes* [19.741], *On the Properties of Simples* 11.1.31 [12.353], *On Compounding of Drugs, Arranged by Parts of the Body* 6.4 [12.922]. One variety was used in tanning (Pliny, *Natural History* 13.55): hence Scribonius Largus (*Pharmacopoeia* 111, 113) specifies 'the Syrian sumach that cooks use'.

198 Armchair gardeners have tried to plant silphium on the European coasts of the Mediterranean. The mistranslation by Gulick (1927–41 vol. 1 p. 123) of Eubulus 18 [*Epitome* 28c]) misled Long (1986) on this point. Gulick wrote 'silphium-stalks from Carthage, silphium and thyme from Hymettus', but he ought to have written 'silphium stalk and sap from Carthage, thyme from Hymettus'. Again, Ahrens, in emending the unknown *otóstyllon* to *opóphyllon* 'silphium fruit' in a list of wild foods in Epicharmus (161 [*Epitome* 71a]), boldly transplanted silphium to Sicily. There were, however, really attempts to plant silphium in Ionia and the Peloponnese according to the Hippocratic treatise *On Diseases* 4.34; they failed.

199 The arrival of the fodder crop lucerne, known to Greeks as (*póa*) *mediké*, 'Median grass', was dated by Pliny (*Natural History* 18.144) precisely to Darius' invasion of Greece. Pliny's authority is unknown: the first surviving reference to the plant is by Aristophanes, *Knights* 606. Media may indeed have been the origin of cultivated lucerne. It was taken eastwards from there to China in the second century BC (Laufer 1919 pp. 208–19).

200 Antiphanes 88 [Athenaeus 100f]; Herodotus, *Histories* 4.169; Theophrastus, *Study of Plants* 6.3.1–7, 9.1.7; Solon 39; Hermippus 63 [*Epitome* 27e]; Aristophanes, *Birds* 531–8, 1579–90; Archestratus 45 [Athenaeus 311a]; Lynceus [Athenaeus 100f]. For an exhaustive survey, covering all identifications possible and impossible, see Amigues 1993. See also Arndt 1993; Dalby 1993b; Chamoux 1953 pp. 246–63, 1985; Vikentiev 1954; Andrews 1941; Werlhof 1875.

201 Cf. Mallory 1989 p. 275 n. 20. On wine in Greece in general, Chapot 1916; Billiard 1913.

202 For example, Aristophanes, *Wasps* 878. See Stanley 1982 on the meaning of this term, sometimes confined to the prized free-flow must that was obtained from fully ripe or over-ripe grapes before treading, and, he claims, sometimes denoting the fermented product of this must (but his appeal to the Thasian inscription *IG* XII suppl. 347 (cf. p. 136) on this point betrays misunderstanding of Greek legal phraseology).

203 Amouretti 1990; Kislinger 1984.

204 Citations at *Epitome* 66f; *Regimen* 2.65. Hadjisavvas 1992; Amouretti 1986; Besnier 1904.

205 Cf. Pliny, *Natural History* 15.7.

206 See further Galen, *On the Properties of Simples* 6.5.4 [11.868–72].

207 Apart from works cited below note Währen 1974; Jasny 1944, 1950; Heichelheim 1935; Jardé 1925.

208 Hesiod, *Works and Days* 232–3; Plato, *Republic* 372c; Alexis 167 [*Epitome*

54f]; Theophrastus, *Study of Plants* 3.8. Gow 1952 vol. 2 pp. 188–9; Mason 1995.

*Fegós* is often translated 'beech nut' (Latin *fagus*). But beech is classical Greek *oxye* (e.g. Theophrastus, *Study of Plants* 3.10.1), modern *oxiá*. The identifications given in the text are the most probable ones on the basis of ancient descriptions and of edibility. Valonia oak is Quercus macrolepis (Q. aegilops). In translating *ákylos*, for holm-oak some would substitute kermes-oak, Q. coccifera, whose acorn has a bitter flavour.

209 An uncertain identification, but *árakos* must denote one or more of the Lathyrus or Vicia species. Hort (1916–26 vol. 2 p. 441) suggests Vicia Sibthorpii.

210 A tentative identification, but supported by modern Greek *afáka*, which does denote dwarf chickling, Lathyrus cicera.

211 Aristophanes fragment 428 [Galen, *On the Properties of Foods* 1.27]; Phaenias of Eresus 43 [*Epitome* 54f].

212 Theophrastus, *Study of Plants* 8.7.3. Alexis 167 [*Epitome* 55a]; citations at *Epitome* 55c. Zohary and Hopf 1993 p. 117.

213 Phaenias of Eresus 43 [*Epitome* 54f]; Polemon [Athenaeus 139a]. On the prohibition, see also Aristotle fragment 195 [Diogenes Laertius 8.34]. Delatte 1930.

214 For example, Solon 38 [Athenaeus 645f].

215 Xenophanes (22) and other citations at *Epitome* 54e.

216 Citations at *Epitome* 56a; Theophrastus, *Study of Plants* 8.3.2; Polemon [Athenaeus 139a].

*Pháselos* arouses surprising difficulties of identification. Many authors translate it and its Latin derivatives 'kidney bean, haricot bean' (e.g. Gulick 1927–41: for defences of this view see Bernad Aramayo 1977; Bolens 1987), yet botanists insist that that species is of New World origin. It was domesticated in Peru around 8000 BC. André (1981 p. 196) and others would identify *pháselos* with the species known in English as calavance, cowpea or black-eyed pea, a species still familiar in the Mediterranean. There has been at least equal confusion in the botanical nomenclature of this species. André's Vigna sinensis, identified with V. unguiculata by others, is the same species as the Dolichos melanophthalmus of A. C. Andrews (in Jones 1980 p. 530).

217 Aristophanes, *Lysistrata* 1061, *Knights* 1171; Theocritus, *Idyll* 10.54; Aristophanes, *Wealth* 1004; Strattis 47 and other citations at Athenaeus 156a–160b. On pulses generally see also Galen, *On the Properties of Foods* 1.18–22.

218 Theophrastus, *Study of Plants* 8.7.3.

219 Sallares 1991 pp. 362, 492 n. 205, 495–6 n. 227.

220 Theophrastus, *Study of Plants* 8.4.2; cf. Columella, *On Agriculture* 2.9.14–16.

221 Often translated 'spelt' in old-fashioned scholarship. The identification with einkorn, in Liddell and Scott 1925–40 p. 753, is unexpected. In particular it does not suit Herodotus (*Histories* 2.36), who is writing of Egypt, where einkorn was not grown.

222 Mnesitheus 28 [Athenaeus 115f]; Galen, *On the Properties of Foods* 1.13.19.

223 It is perhaps more likely that what was imported from Russia to Greece was bread wheat (Zohary and Hopf 1993 p. 53; Sallares 1991 pp. 323–32), not yet distinguished by a Greek name of its own.

224 *Semídalis*: Hermippus 63 [*Epitome* 27e]; Antiphanes 36 [Athenaeus 127b]; *Regimen* 2.42.2. The word is borrowed from a Semitic language (cf. Akkadian *samidu*). Sallares 1991 pp. 316–61 examines with great care and close argument the complex botanical, agricultural and lexicographical problems of classical wheat.

Archaeobotanical evidence has now begun to come together with plant genetics (see e.g. Zohary and Hopf 1993). *Pyrós*, it is now clear, cannot be bread wheat (Triticum aestivum: so Liddell and Scott 1925–40) since *pyrós* was well known in Greece from the time of the earliest literature, while bread wheat, archaeobotany suggests, will have been almost or entirely unknown there at that time. *Semídalis* is also unlikely to be bread wheat, since *semídalis* came to Greece from Phoenicia, which, archaeobotany suggests, was not close to the main areas where bread wheat was then grown. Bread wheat, its flour and its bread are probably Greek *silígnion*, *sílignis*, a term that may be read conjecturally in Theophrastus, *Study of Plants* 8.4.3: cf. Galen, *On the Properties of Foods* 1.2.5.

225 Note that Galen, *Hippocratic Glossary* s.v. *álphita*, distinguishes *álphita* from *áleuron* not by species but by grade: *áleuron* is fine flour, *álphita* coarser, and *krímna* coarser still. But this is not necessarily truly applicable to the common Greek of Galen's time or earlier: the purpose of the exposition is to justify the term 'wheaten *álphita*' in a Hippocratic text. On the meaning of *álphita* see also Braun 1995.

226 *Khóndros* was similar to, if not identical with, Latin *alica* (Sallares 1991 p. 320). Much archaeological information is available on milling and baking in classical times (Moritz 1958; Runnels and Murray 1983).

227 Paxamus (a Hellenistic source) in *Geoponica* 2.43.

228 Archestratus 62 [Athenaeus 101c]; citations at Athenaeus 643e–649e; Alexis 168 or Antidotus [Athenaeus 642d]; Teleclides 1 [Athenaeus 268a]. Orth 1922. 'Milk-cake' is the usual translation for *ámes*, but there is no evidence how this delicacy was made.

*Amylos*, cf. Philoxenus e.9 [Athenaeus 643b]; Theocritus, *Idyll* 9.21. Gow 1952 vol. 2 p. 189. The neuter form *ámylon* usually meant 'starch' (Dalby 1987 n. 23).

229 Galen, *On the Properties of Foods* 1.10; Tryphon 117 [Athenaeus 109b]; Didymus in *Geoponica* 2.33. Braun 1995; Battaglia 1989; Amouretti 1986; Benndorf 1893.

230 Nicostratus 13 [Athenaeus 111c], cf. Athenaeus 646e; Theocritus, *Idyll* 4.34. For all these terms, citations at Athenaeus 108f–116a: see the translation of this passage in Dalby 1990. On the nature of *mâza* see Amouretti 1985.

231 Thompson 1995; Darmstädter 1933.

232 Galen, *On the Properties of Foods* 1.11.2; Vegetius 1.13.

# 4 IN THE FEASTS OF THE LYDIANS

1 Research on Greek cookery writers begins from the following data.

There are some fragments and testimonia. Bilabel (1920) collected the known verbatim fragments of prose *Opsartytiká*, 'cookery books' – alongside an interesting fragmentary papyrus cookbook, which, because of its Egyptian provenance, will not be dealt with here. In another work, Bilabel (1921) cited all literary references to Greek cookery books.

There is a list of cookery authors in Pollux, *Onomasticon* 6.70, but this, as we shall see in Chapter 7 (p. 161), is deceptive. It is based, unacknowledged, on a couple of lines of the late comic author Baton, whose speaker was listing famous cooks and inventors of recipes, not *necessarily* authors of cookery books.

There is a much longer list at Athenaeus 516c. It is introduced as a list of authors who gave recipes for *karyke*, but is concluded in more general terms:

'Glaucus of Locri, Mithaecus, Dionysius, the two Syracusans called Heracleides, Agis, Epaenetus, Dionysius [again], Hegesippus, Erasistratus, Euthydemus, Criton, and in addition Stephanus, Archytas, Acestius, Acesias, Diocles,
Philistion: all these, I know, have written *Opsartytiká*.' This appears to be a
miscellaneous list including some of the prose authors from whose works
Athenaeus had drawn actual recipes. Some are medical or scientific writers,
notably Erasistratus, Diocles and Philistion.

    Finally there is a list derived from Callimachus' subject index to the library
of Alexandria. Callimachus fragment 435 [Athenaeus 643e] is a list of authors
on cake-making: 'Aegimius, Hegesippus, Metrobius, and then Phaestus.' Hegesippus, who occurs in both lists, is discussed in this chapter (p. 111). The
other three are otherwise unknown to us as they probably were to Athenaeus.
It is possible that Aegimius is the early doctor and dietician mentioned more
than once by Galen (e.g. *Health* 2.12 [6.159]).

2 Lesko 1977.

3 Eubulus 121 [*Epitome* 28f]; Epinicus 1 [Athenaeus 432b]; Menander, *Bad-
Tempered Man* 946; Alexis 172 [Athenaeus 441d].

4 A character in a play by Eupolis (271 [*Epitome* 52d]) wants 'wine from Naxian
vines'. Naxian wine had been compared to nectar by Archilochus according
to the *Epitome of Athenaeus* (30f). For Thracian wines see p. 99. On Bibline:
West 1978 p. 306; Gow 1952 vol. 2 pp. 250–1. The link sometimes made with
the wine of Byblos in Phoenicia (see pp. 96–7) is illusory.

5 *Psíthios oînos*: Eubulus 136; Anaxandrides 73 [*Epitome* 28f]; Dioscorides, *Materia Medica* 5.6.4; Columella, *On Agriculture* 3.2.24; Pliny, *Natural History*
14.80; Scholia on Nicander, *Alexipharmaca* 181 (equating Psithian with
Pramnian); Florentinus [*Geoponica* 5.2.4]. Lambert-Gócs 1990; André 1953.

6 There are now thousands of grape varieties in regular use, though most
drinkers taste the products of only a few, since the majority are grown in very
restricted territories. How many were there in classical times? The question
was outlined briefly in Chapter 2 (p. 48) with a reference to the work on Greek
Crimean vineyards of Janushevich and Nikolaenko 1979; on the complexity of
Roman vine nomenclature see André 1953. The answer may depend on
whether it is believed that cultivated grapes spread from one or a few centres
of early domestication (in which case a gradual increase to the present or
recent number of varieties seems logical) or that they were domesticated
independently from wild grapes in many localities (in which case the number
of varieties may have remained constant, or fallen slightly in recent times as
growers respond to market imperatives by changing to widely-known
varieties). Pliny's remark (*Natural History* 14.20), introducing his survey of
wines, suggests the latter answer may be correct. He refers to the researches
of a fifth-century BC philosopher to whom an early work on agriculture was
attributed: 'Democritus, who alone believed that the varieties of vines were
countable, claimed to know all those of Greece. Others have pronounced them
uncountable and infinite.'

7 Obscure technical terms associated with the process occur in an *Odyssey*
passage (7.122–6). Beside Alcinous' orchard (see p. 77), the poet says, is an
*aloé* (apparently a 'reserved ground': in other early contexts a threshing-floor).
In one part of this there is a *theilópedon* (understood later, evidently correctly,
to have to do with the drying of grapes: see e.g. Dioscorides, *Materia Medica*
1.32, 5.6) in a *leurós* place (*leurós* was understood later to mean 'level': see e.g.
Aeschylus, *Prometheus Bound* 371, 396), which dries in the sun. The *theilópe-*

*don* may be the raised straw matting, or the like, on which the grapes are placed to dry, or it may be a paved area.

8 On Pramnian wine, Meyer 1974. See also Chapter 6 (p. 148 and n. 51), where some later sources are referred to.

9 Darby *et al.* 1977 pp. 597–607; Cerny 1965 vol. 2 pp. 1–7. On Roman Egypt, Rathbone 1983.

10 Based on J. A. Wilson's translation in Pritchard 1969 p. 19.

11 *Epitome of Athenaeus* 34b citing Dio the Academic. Darby *et al.* 1977 pp. 531–3; K. G. Hoglund in Bottéro 1985 p. 40; see also Finet 1974–7.

12 The manuscripts read 'is produced *also* in', as if Chalybonian wine had been made earlier in Persia. That could easily have been assumed from reading the next clause, if one gathered from it that the Persians were transplanting a chosen cultivar from their ancestral lands. But the sentence makes most sense as an example of the commonplace that the Persians selected their luxuries from the produce of their whole empire. Thus the correct reading is probably not *kân* but *en*, as given by Eustathius in his *Commentary on Homer* 1499.64. Strabo, *Geography* 15.3.22 confirms that the Persians got their 'Chalymonian' wine from Syria.

13 *SIG* 22.13; Ezekiel 27.18.

14 The alteration of *Byblios* to *Byblinos*, made by most editors following Musurus 1514, is unjustified. West in his edition of Hesiod's *Works and Days* (1978 p. 306) is right to ignore it.

15 The inscription is Schwyzer 1923 no. 182.a5. Archestratus' phrase is *phoiníkios oînos*. The Ephippus passages are fragments 24 and 8. Both are repeated later by Athenaeus (*Epitome of Athenaeus* 57e; Athenaeus 642e), but the correct reading of the phrase, though it occurs five times, remains doubtful. Once (in fragment 8 as quoted in the *Epitome of Athenaeus* 29d; and in Eustathius, *Commentary on Homer* 1445.48, based on this passage of Athenaeus) it is *phoinikínou*, which if correct would probably mean 'date wine'. Meineke 1858–67 boldly emended the other four occurrences to agree with this. There is no other evidence, apart from the single phrase which Meineke so assiduously multiplied, that date wine (cheap to make where dates grow but not good) was imported to Greece.

16 *Periplus of the Erythraean Sea* 6, 49. Casson 1989 pp. 13–14 n. 11, p. 113.

17 For other testimonies to the text see Davies 1991– p. 104. I have discussed this tantalising fragment at length in Dalby forthcoming (b). Two details should be noted here. The *Epitome*'s gloss on *ápyron*, 'unboiled', might be doubted; but another early source agrees that 'the Spartans boil their wine until it is reduced by a fifth, and use it after four years' (Democritus [*Geoponica* 7.4]). Alcman's 'flower-scented' seems to be a periphrasis for *anthosmías*, wine made with the addition of brine to the must, for which a brief recipe was given by Phaenias of Eresus in the early third century BC (*Epitome of Athenaeus* 31f). The phrase recurs in Xenophanes 1 [Athenaeus 462c].

18 Herodotus, *Histories* 6.60, 7.134; see Berthiaume 1982 pp. 23–7.

19 *Odyssey* 9.39–42; cf. Strabo, *Geography* 7 fragments 43–4a.

20 Archilochus fragment 2 quoted in the *Epitome of Athenaeus* 30f. Isaac in his archaeological survey of the Greek north Aegean settlements (1986 p. 114) has no doubt that Archilochus can be taken literally: 'The passage . . . shows that the Thasians were drinking wine from Ismaros rather than their own.'

21 Such a conclusion does not go well with the common modern assumption that the *Iliad* and *Odyssey* were created in an aristocratic milieu. I discuss this question in Dalby forthcoming (a).

22 C. Roebuck in Boardman and Vaphopoulou-Richardson 1986 p. 82; cf. J. P. Barron ibid. pp. 94–8; T. C. Sarikakis ibid. pp. 122–4.

23 For example Antidotus 4 [*Epitome* 28e].

24 Salviat 1986 is a collection of the ancient evidence on Thasian wine with full and interesting discussion. On the *Geoponica* text see pp. 172–3. Further papers in Empereur and Garlan 1986 are relevant; see also Bon and Bon 1957.

25 No source praises Peparethan wine unambiguously, but the Peparethans themselves were proud of it: at any rate, fifth-century Peparethan coins, which are fairly numerous, bear a bunch of grapes on the obverse.

26 Cf. Eupolis 478; *Suda* and Photius, *Lexicon* s.v. *saprón*.

27 So Platnauer 1964 p. 117; Salviat 1986 p. 173.

28 Demosthenes, *Against Lacritus* 10; Eubulus 123 [*Epitome* 23a]. Gomme and Sandbach 1973 pp. 698–9.

29 Lambert-Gócs 1990 pp. 145–50 with map. Hermippus' editors, Kassel and Austin (1983– vol. 5 p. 600) actually said 'De Magnete nil aliunde compertum habemus'.

30 Philyllius 23 [*Epitome* 31a]; Archestratus 59 [*Epitome* 29b].

31 Hence modern *krasí*, 'wine', is derived from ancient *krâsis*, 'mixing'. Eideneier 1970.

32 Hesiod *Works and Days* 596; Anacreon 11a [Athenaeus 427a].

33 Athenaeus 426b–427c and elsewhere; Plutarch, *Symposium Questions* 3.9, 5.4; Pollux, *Onomasticon* 6.23–5. Athenaeus (426de) and Plutarch did not agree on the meaning of the proverb that both of them quote, 'Drink five or three but never four.' Probably 'five' meant '2:3' and three meant '1:2' (so Plutarch, *Symposium Questions* 3.9): on these terms 'four' is either uninterpretable (so no one could argue with a recommendation to avoid it) or it is Hesiod's '1:3', which is indeed so weak that few other authors recommend it. All these formulas are to be read as 'wine:water'. No one, in texts earlier than the fifth century, spoke of drinking a mixture stronger than 50 per cent wine.

34 Plutarch, *Symposium Questions* 8.9; Tryphon 136 [Athenaeus 640e].

35 Pindar is also the first to hint at the phrase 'second tables'. This is in a more gruesome context, for he is addressing the murdered Pelops: 'At the tables, the second course, they shared out and ate of your flesh' (Pindar, *Olympian* 1.50–2).

36 This may be 'another wine', 'a second wine', as emended by Musurus 1514: if not, the *euphrosyne* 'cheer' that the mixing bowl is full of would seem to be water. The text as translated is unmetrical and some change is certainly necessary.

37 On this passage see Defradas 1962; Herter 1956; Bowra 1953.

38 For 'Thessaly' the manuscripts have 'Italy': the emendation was proposed by Kock (1880–8). Italy is surely wrong and Thessaly is a likely conjecture, being the district of Greece where wheat and cattle were at their best.

 'Pears and fat apples' is a Homeric pun. *Mêlon* meant 'apple' to later Greeks, but in the Homeric epics (they were evidently amused to find) it also meant 'sheep'. Thus the Homeric formula *bóes kaì íphia mêla*, 'cattle and fat sheep', is turned from the animal to the vegetable kingdom by the change of a single word: *apíous kaì íphia mêla*, 'pears and fat apples'. The same joke occurs in Matron's *Attic Dinner* [Athenaeus 137b]; cf. Strato 1 [Athenaeus 382e].

 'Ornaments of the feast' is a phrase used in the *Odyssey* of 'song and dance' (1.152) and 'song and lyre' (21.430): Hermippus uses it instead, still in its traditional place at the end of a hexameter line, to characterise a more concrete detail of after-dinner entertainment. As we have seen, nuts did indeed come to Greece from Asia Minor.

39  Also the 'richly fed sheep from Naxos' and the 'sheep-bearing scattered islands (*Sporádes*)', Pindar fragments 52m.6–8 and 52e.38.

40  Limet 1987; *Bulletin on Sumerian Agriculture, passim*; Bottéro 1985; Thompson 1949; Darby *et al.* 1977; Gelber 1993; Hoffner 1974.

41  The contradiction is manifest in Aeschylus, *Persians* 41–8, where in a poetic catalogue of the Persian army the 'soft-living' Lydians provide some of its more fearsome cohorts. Bearing such a character, Lydia fell into place naturally as putative ancestral homeland of the Etruscans, also seen as degenerate: see e.g. *Periegesis Anonymi* 366.

42  Perfumes: e.g. Xenophanes 3 [Athenaeus 526a]; Xenophon, *Symposium* 2.3–4. Herodotus, *Histories* 1.155.4; Pindar fragment 125 [Athenaeus 635d]; Plato, *Republic* 398d–399c; Critias 6 [Athenaeus 432d].

43  *Paignía* may perhaps include children's games: but it certainly means party games, cf. Herodotus, *Histories* 2.174. Critias said that the game of *kóttabos* had come from Sicily, see p. 108.

44  Athenaeus 516c; *Etymologicum Magnum* 492.48; Achaeus 12–13 [Athenaeus 173c], cf. Aristophanes, *Knights* 343; Menander fragment 397 [Athenaeus 132e, 517a]. An aside in Menander's *False Heracles* suggests some ingredients (fragment 451 [Athenaeus 172a, 644c]).

45  Timocles 39 [*Epitome* 25f]: 'The Chians, no less than the [Sicilians and Sybarites], are attested for cookery. Timocles: "Chians have devised – far better than others – a cuisine." ' For Semonactides of Chios, apparently a well-known cook, see Baton 4 [Athenaeus 662c].

46  But not the billy-goat's (Aristotle, *Study of Animals* 579a9).

47  Is this a recommendation to eat the dogs, as Greenewalt 1976 assumes (in the context of his investigation of puppy sacrifices in sixth-century BC Sardis), or to use them in hunting the hares and foxes? Foxes were certainly eaten, and were at their gastronomic best at this season, having fattened themselves on grapes.

48  Eupolis 191; Aristophanes, *Acharnians* 163–74; Aristophanes, *Peace* 242–54 (an extended joke is based on the recipe for *myttotós*); the Hippocratic text *Places in Man* 47.5 – there, incidentally, *myttotós* is recommended as an ointment for piles; Scholia on Aristophanes, *Peace* 242–54, on *Acharnians* 174, on *Knights* 771; *Epidemics* 2.6.28; Theophrastus, *Study of Plants* 7.4.11.

49  Cratinus 44 [Athenaeus 119b]; Sophocles fragment 503 [Athenaeus 319a].

50  Lombardo 1995.

51  Antiphanes 233 [*Epitome* 27d]; Philemon 79 [Athenaeus 658a–b]; Euripides, *Cyclops* 136; Antiphanes 131 [Athenaeus 402e], from another play called *Cyclops*.

52  Aristophanes fragment 1 [Athenaeus 112e]; Antiphanes 174 [Athenaeus 112c–d]; Poseidippus 31 [Heracleides Criticus].

53  The anachronisms were observed by Athenaeus (217c–e).

54  Epicharmus 56 [Athenaeus 321b, 325f]. *Tainíai* are glossed *zargánai* in the Scholia on Oppian, *Halieutica* 1.100, and *zargánai* is the modern Greek for 'garfish', Belone belone. The treatments recommended by Alan Davidson (1981 p. 57) for garfish recall Mithaecus in some details (though not the cheese, so favoured in ancient Sicilian fish cookery). But this seems to be a red herring: there were other ancient names for garfish with which *tainíai* are not linked, and indeed Epicharmus (56 [Athenaeus 321b, 325f]) distinguishes *tainíai* from *sargînoi*, 'garfish', ancestor of the modern Greek name. *Tainíai* were probably

the thinner and less appetising cépoles, Cepola rubescens or Cepola taenia: so Thompson 1947 p. 258.

Mithaecus is also cited (Athenaeus 282a) along with others as having referred to the *alphestés*, a kind of wrasse, but no recipe is given.

55 This is the title given twice by Athenaeus. *Suda* (s.v. *Míthaikos*) gives the plural form *Opsartytiká* (and says that Mithaecus also wrote *On Hunting* and other works). Plato (*Gorgias* 518b) uses the word *opsopoiía*, and Pollux (*Onomasticon* 6.71) uses *opsopoiiké*, but they do not necessarily intend these words as book titles.

56 *Hépsema* (with a long second *e*) was grape juice concentrated by boiling, a cheaper sweetener than honey. Much later, a less concentrated *hepsetós*, Latin *decoctum*, was distinguished from a more concentrated *hépsema* (with a short second *e*), Latin *defritum* (Diocletian's *Price Edict* 2.15–16). By that time date syrup was available and was cheaper still (ibid. 3.10–12).

57 The elucidation of the phrase is attributed by Athenaeus, with less than his usual precision, to 'the commentators', but Galen confirms it (*Hippocratic Glossary* s.v. *hypósphagma*). For the recipes, Davidson 1981 p. 350.

58 Athenaeus (369b) says that Glaucus uses the term *rápys* where Speusippus, Plato's taxonomist successor, uses *ráphys* for some kind of turnip or radish. The former could be a local Locrian form, loss of aspiration being a feature of that dialect, but speculation must be tempered by uncertainty as to the precise meaning of the word and its possible variations: cf. Galen, *On the Properties of Foods* 2.39.1.

59 Early references to *kándaulos*: a speaker in Aristophanes, *Peace* 123, puns on the word. See also Alexis 178 [Athenaeus 516d]: the speaker, a cook, claims to have invented it; Philemon 63 [Athenaeus 516f]; Menander fragment 397 [Athenaeus 132e, 517a]; Nicostratus 16 [Athenaeus 517a, 664c]. Late fourth century and after: Menander fragment 451 [Athenaeus 172a, 644c]; Euangelus 1 [Athenaeus 644e].

The Lydian origin of *kándaulos* is stated not only by Athenaeus but also by Eustathius, *Commentary on Homer* (1144.15), but that passage must depend on a reading of Athenaeus. *Kandaúles*, a title of Hermes (Hipponax 3a) and Heracles (Hesychius, *Lexicon* s.v. *Kandaúles*) and name or title of a Lydian king (Herodotus, *Histories* 1.7.2; cf. Nicolaus of Damascus, *Histories* 90F47 [*Excerpta de insidiis* 14.4]), was said to be Lydian for 'dog-throttler' by Tzetzes, scholia on the *Khiliádes* (Cramer 1835–7 vol. 3 p. 351 line 7). See further Greenewalt 1976 pp. 52–4 and n. 57.

60 Callimachus fragment 435 [Athenaeus 643e]; Demetrius the Xenodotean cited by the scholia on Aristophanes, *Peace* 123.

61 Wilkins and Hill 1993, 1995.

# 5 SICILIAN TABLES

1 *Hypótrimma* is a kind of sauce. What kind? Perhaps any kind, perhaps something special: there is not enough contemporary evidence. We have only the limited assistance of a Hippocratic text: 'Dishes cooked in *hypotrímmata* are hot and wet [in the dietetic sense], because the ingredients are fatty, fiery, heating and of opposing properties' (*Regimen* 2.56.8). For a clearer indication of the contents of *hypótrimma* one has to look to much later sources. The Byzantine *Etymologicum Magnum* (which at 492.49 states that *karyke* is a kind of *hypótrimma*) calls for 'dates, honey and some other ingredients' (784.9). There is a recipe in the Roman cookery book *Apicius* (1.33): 'Pepper, rosemary,

dried mint, pine kernels, grape juice, *caryota* date, mild cheese, honey, vinegar, *liquamen* [Greek *gáros*], wine, olive oil, *defritum* or *caroenum* [Greek *hépsema* or *hepsetós*, concentrated grape juices].' For more on these Greek-Latin equivalents see Chapter 8 (p. 180). But recipes can change out of all recognition over such long periods. There is no solid evidence, for example, that pepper, rosemary or dried mint were used in Greek cookery of the fourth century BC, or that *caryota* dates had been distinguished as a separate variety (for which see Pliny, *Natural History* 13.44).

'The other' must mean 'the other fresh meat dish'.

Since 'green', in Greek culinary contexts, is always a noun or adjective referring to fresh herbs, 'green' here presumably means 'Cook or serve with fresh herbs.'

'The reverse' is an acceptable answer in context because Greek had two all-inclusive verbs for the methods of cooking: *optân*, 'cook dry', i.e. roast or bake, and *hépsein*, 'cook with liquid', i.e. boil or fry. One of these having been used in the previous instruction, there can be no doubt as to what word is meant by 'the reverse'. Outside the context of a breathless comic dialogue, cooks could be more explicit than this: terms such as *tagenízein*, 'fry in a shallow pan', were available.

2 This was the view of Dobrée (1831–3 vol. 2 p. 314). Dohm (1964 pp. 125–7) supposes that the interlocutors are two cooks. Cf. Nesselrath 1990 p. 300.

3 Compare Menander, *Bad-Tempered Man* with Plato, *Symposium* 175b.

4 Sotades 1.35 [Athenaeus 293e]; Dionysius of Sinope 2.27–33 [Athenaeus 405c].

5 This has been frequently questioned, and has become linked in modern scholars' minds with the question of how many gastronomic poets called Philoxenus lived in the fourth century BC. In most modern editions the real work discussed below is attributed to Philoxenus of Leucas, as if it were, uncomplicatedly, the poem quoted by Plato and as if the lead-in of the *Epitome of Athenaeus* here had more authority than the several lead-ins later in the *Deipnosophists* for which we can read Athenaeus' words: he usually attributes the poem to 'Philoxenus of Cythera', otherwise simply to 'Philoxenus'. No ancient authority lists the glutton Philoxenus of Leucas as an author.

6 Antiphanes 207 [Athenaeus 643d].

7 The best I can do. The original wordplay sets *kákkabon*, 'casserole', against *síttybon*, 'leather tag', a word not found in surviving Greek literature but attested by Cicero, *Letters to Atticus* 4.4a.1, 4.5.3, 4.8.2.

This passage seems to mock the line of Philoxenus (b.7 [Athenaeus 147a]) that begins: 'And first there came in to them not a casserole, darling, but. . . .' The text is faulty at that point, but it is clear that some *mot juste* must have followed, probably a derivative of *lopás*, 'saucepan'.

8 Dalby 1987.

9 If fragments c and d are correctly so ordered. At any rate drinking is not mentioned during the main course, which fragment b appears to cover fully.

10 Archestratus 62 [Athenaeus 101c].

11 For example, Pherecrates 50 [Athenaeus 96b]; Aristophanes fragment 520 [Athenaeus 96c].

12 This passage is often taken as if it were straight praise by Antiphanes. Cf. Nesselrath 1990 p. 250.

13 Degani 1995.

14 According to Athenaeus 337b, the moralist Clearchus of Soli (78), who appears to have disapproved of Archestratus intensely, said that a certain Terpsion had set the gastronomic poet his example.

Clearchus in *On Proverbs* says that Terpsion had been the teacher of Archestratus, being the first to have written a *Gastrología* telling learners what not to eat; Terpsion having improvised the following about tortoise: 'Eat up, or don't eat, the tortoise's meat'.

Athenaeus' translator Gulick (1927–41 pp. 29–31) understands from this passage that *Terpsion* was the first to write a *Gastrología*; and that is certainly the grammatically preferable sense of Athenaeus' sentence. But the context, especially the word *apeskhediakénai*, 'improvised', suggests Clearchus may have meant that *Archestratus* was the first to write a *Gastrología*, merely the germ of the idea having come from the one-line hexameter proverb on food avoidance that was attributed to Terpsion. Clearchus' severe remarks on Archestratus will be quoted on pp. 118–19.

15 Dalby 1995 (on the title of the poem see note 6 there); Wilkins and Hill 1994; Degani 1982; Corrieri 1978–9. The *terminus post quem*, roughly 358 BC, depends on the settlement, abandonment and resettlement of several Sicilian and south Italian cities: for details see Dalby 1995. The date usually given for the poem, around 330 BC, has no authority. Archestratus must be among the earliest authors included in *Supplementum Hellenisticum* (Lloyd-Jones and Parsons 1983).

16 Schmid 1897; Bettini 1979 pp. 55–64; Wilkins and Hill 1994 p. 11.

17 The promise of 'improving one's life' may actually have been made in the opening words of the manual of Philaenis, apparently a matter-of-fact instruction book on relations between the sexes (*P.Oxy.2891*).

18 Martin 1931; Rossi 1983; Lissarrague 1987.

19 Athenaeus caps the story with one cited from Antigonus to the effect that the narrator, the philosopher Persaeus himself, had been known to take a flute-girl home from a party. See, later, Plutarch, *Symposium Questions* 7.7.

20 Degani 1982 p. 38.

21 Printed texts of this fragment say *Kalkhedóni*, 'Calchedon' (opposite Byzantium), an emendation by Schweighäuser: the manuscript of Athenaeus has *Karkhedóni*, 'Carthage'. Byzantium is named, as a second source for the same fish, in the following line. Schweighäuser, followed by Wilkins and Hill (1994 pp. 50–1), considered it unlikely that Archestratus would have visited Carthage, hence his emendation. There was, however, a Greek community there; and, for what the parallel is worth, in the eleven surviving lines of Ennius' *Hedyphagetica* there is a recommendation to buy dogfish on the beach at Clipea, not far to the south-east of Carthage. Against Schweighäuser's emendation, it may be thought unlikely that the terse Archestratus would have bothered to say, what must almost go without saying, that a fish available in Calchedon is also available in Byzantium.

22 References in Dalby 1995. Although Archestratus refers several times to the produce of the Black Sea, no surviving fragment recommends the purchase of fresh food at any Black Sea city. The only possible exception (44 [Athenaeus 307b]) is that he is said to assess the grey mullet of Sinope as second to those of Abdera. But there is probably an error in attribution here. It is the only occasion on which Athenaeus claims to summarise the views of Archestratus in prose – not surprisingly, since they are so quotable and so pithily expressed in their hexameters. The same view on the produce of Abdera and Sinope, in the same words, is elsewhere attributed to the prose writer Dorion [Athenaeus 118c]: that is probably the correct attribution.

23 Lynceus [Athenaeus 285f, 313f]. Brandt 1888; Wilkins and Hill 1994.

24 At this point Linus interrupts himself with a remark on Heracles. Gulick

(1927–41) marks a lacuna, perhaps correctly: one may suggest completing the sentence '... he was the worst, so his customers used to think'. But the audience might have been left to fill in the antithesis for themselves.

The passage does not say, incidentally, that the actor Simus (a real person) had written a book on food or cookery: if he did it has gone unnoticed otherwise. More likely he had been a cook before becoming an actor.

25 For example Euripides fragments 687–91 and the plot of Euripides' *Syleus* as outlined by Philo, *That Every Good Man Is Free* 100–4; Webster 1970 p. 85 and n. 2.

26 Dohm 1964.

27 Lynceus is rather misleadingly categorised as an author of Athenian new comedy because his comedy fragment is all that is found in the standard collections: his other writings remain locked in Athenaeus. He is discussed in Chapter 7.

28 Cratinus 62 [Athenaeus 344e] and 46–7; Aristophanes, *Knights* 1290–9; Epicharmus 34–5 [Athenaeus 235f–236b].

29 Athenaeus 164f–165b; 242f–244a.

30 Carystius [Athenaeus 235e]. Arnott 1968; see Alexis 183 [Athenaeus 421d].

31 Callimachus fragment 434 [Athenaeus 244a].

32 The full oracle (e.g. scholia on Theocritus, *Idyll 14*.48) evaluated Argos and its men higher than these, and the Megarians lower.

33 Most of what follows is based on the most incidental of asides in classical texts. An ambiguity must be signalled in advance. Since varieties can be and often are named after the places from which they originated or spread, the naming of a place in these contexts may leave us uncertain whether exported foods, or the transplanting of varieties, is in question. Harvey 1995 argues, perhaps a little too firmly, that Lydia was only the source of varieties (of onions, figs and chestnuts) and not also an exporter of the foods. His authority Varro (*On Farming* 1.41.5–6) describes the export of dried figs threaded on strings. This may or may not actually explain how the seeds of recently developed varieties reached Italy, as Varro thinks: botanists would be better able to say. But it does certainly describe how dried figs were (and indeed still sometimes are) packed for export.

34 Herodotus, *Histories* 1.66. Mason 1995.

35 Pausanias 2.13; Archestratus 18 [Athenaeus 293f] and citations at Athenaeus 288c. Lambert-Gócs 1990 p. 187.

36 Archestratus 4 [Athenaeus 111f]; Theophrastus fragment 167 [*Epitome 62b*]; Plato Comicus 169 [*Epitome 68b*]; Theophrastus, *Study of Plants* 7.4.2. The radishes of Corinth and Cleonae are restored to the text of Theophrastus from Athenaeus and Pliny. On Corinth cf. Alexis 292 [*Epitome 30f*], context unknown; Diphilus of Sinope 31 [Athenaeus 227d].

37 The correct answers to the speaker's two questions are yes and no, respectively.

38 Herodotus, *Histories* 6.60, 7.134; Berthiaume 1982 pp. 23–7.

39 Theophrastus, *Study of Plants* 7.4.5–6; Androtion [Athenaeus 75d, 82c].

40 Diphilus of Sinope 96 [*Epitome 67d*].

41 Citations at Athenaeus 82a–c; Androtion [Athenaeus 75d]; Archestratus 20, 43, 9, 62 [Athenaeus 295c, 307d, 285b, 101c]; Lynceus [Athenaeus 285f]; Philemon 82 [Athenaeus 288f]; Aristophanes, *Acharnians* 901, *Birds* 76, fragment 521 [Athenaeus 285e]; Archestratus 4, Plato, *Gorgias* 518b and other citations at Athenaeus 111f–112e; Hippolochus [Athenaeus 130d]; Antiphanes 179 [Athenaeus 74e]; Phoenicides 2 [Athenaeus 652d]; Eubulus 18 or Antiphanes [*Epitome 28d*]; Philemon of Aexone [Athenaeus 652e]; Theocritus, *Idyll 1*.147.

42 For example Aristophanes, *Peace* 1005, *Lysistrata* 36, 702; Antiphanes 233 [*Epitome* 27d]; Matron [Athenaeus 135d]. Wilkins and Hill 1994 broach the difficult subject of how the eels migrated to and from Lake Copais.

43 Theophrastus, *Study of Plants* 7.4.2, 7.4.6; Archestratus 4, 14 [Athenaeus 111f, 316a]; Varro, *On Farming* 3.9.6; Heracleides Criticus 23–4; Hermippus 63, 77 [*Epitome* 27e, 29a]; Ephippus 1 [Athenaeus 112f]; Antiphanes 36 [Athenaeus 127b]; Alexis 196 [Athenaeus 127c]; Diocles of Carystus 125 [*Epitome* 59a]; Strattis 64 [*Epitome* 30f]; Aristophanes fragment 334 [*Epitome* 29a].

44 Archestratus 15, 30, 45, 54, 56 [Athenaeus 305e, 328a, 311a, 326d, 92d]; Eubulus 129 [*Epitome* 29a]; Apollodorus [Pliny, *Natural History* 14.76].

45 Hermippus 63 [*Epitome* 27e]; Mnesitheus 30 [*Epitome* 54b]; Varro, *On Farming* 1.41.6; Archestratus 26, 27, 32, 34, 50 [Athenaeus 327d, 301c, 288a, 301f, 304d]; Pindar fragment 106 [*Epitome* 28a]; Phrynichus 73 and Eupolis 271 [*Epitome* 52c–d]; Archilochus 116 [Athenaeus 76b]; Amphis 40 [*Epitome* 30b]; citations at Athenaeus 81a–82c.

Here, as in several other cases, readers must reach their own views on the range of possible contexts and implications that may lie behind the very brief quotations to be found in Athenaeus.

46 Theophrastus, *Study of Plants* 7.4.9.

47 Andrews 1961b p. 243 and his references; Rouanet-Liesenfelt 1992.

48 Archestratus 54, 30, 20, 23, 45, 8 [Athenaeus 326d, 328a, 295c, 310c, 311a, 298e]; Hegesander [Athenaeus 334e]; Galen, *On the Properties of Foods* 3.24.12; Hicesius [Athenaeus 298b].

49 Archestratus 42, 29, 53, 4 [Athenaeus 325d, 320f, 318f, 111f]; Diphilus of Siphnos [*Epitome* 54b]; Theophrastus, *Study of Plants* 7.4.2. The text of Theophrastus is restored from quotations by Athenaeus and Pliny.

50 Theophrastus, *Study of Plants* 7.4.7; Eubulus 18 or Antiphanes [*Epitome* 28d]; Polemon [Athenaeus 372a]; Pindar fragment 52b.25; Strabo, *Geography* 7 fragments 43–4a; Amphis 36 [*Epitome* 30e]; Archestratus 44, 55, 56, 22 [Athenaeus 307b, 324b, 92d, 326f].

51 Archestratus 56, 24, 34, 35, 40, 13 [Athenaeus 92d, 104f, 301f, 278a, 314e, 320b]; Theophrastus fragment 167 [*Epitome* 62b]; Polybius, *Histories* 4.37; *Economics* attributed to Aristotle, 1347b19. Dumont 1976–7; Gallant 1985; Braund 1995.

52 Archestratus 28, 56 [Athenaeus 321e, 92d]; Philyllius 12 [Athenaeus 86e, 92e], the text varying between Mytilene and Methymna; Theophrastus fragment 167 [*Epitome* 62b].

53 Diocles of Carystus 125 [*Epitome* 59a]; Xenocrates [Oribasius, *Medical Collections* 2.58.115]; Xenophon, *Education of Cyrus* 6.2.22; Theophrastus, *Study of Plants* 7.4.9; Pliny, *Natural History* 12.111, 19.104; Varro, *On Farming* 1.41.5–6; Phylotimus 8 [*Epitome* 53f]; Menander fragment 397 [Athenaeus 132e, 517a]; Archestratus 5 [Athenaeus 112b]. Gleason in Hostetter 1994; Harvey 1995; Greenewalt 1976.

54 Dioscorides, *Materia Medica* 1.70.3, 2.9; Varro, *On Farming* 1.41.6; Archestratus 42, 4, 56, 12, 41 [Athenaeus 325d, 111f, 92d, 328b, 320a]; Diphilus of Siphnos [Athenaeus 90d]. Purcell (1995) refers to inscriptions that give information on the organisation of the fish trade at eastern Aegean cities.

55 Archestratus 34, 56, 45–6, 41, 25, 53 [Athenaeus 301f, 92d, 311a, 319d, 320a, 105e, 318f]; Eubulus 18 or Antiphanes [*Epitome* 28d]; Diocles of Carystus 118 [*Epitome* 55b]; Strabo, *Geography* 14.2.21; Dioscorides, *Materia Medica* 2.9; Pliny, *Natural History* 11.32–3, 30.32, 30.45; *Epitome* 30c; Mnesitheus 46 [*Epitome* 32e]; Theophrastus, *Study of Plants* 7.4.7.

56 Lynceus [Athenaeus 285f]; Archestratus 9, 21 [Athenaeus 285b, 286a]; Hermippus 63 [*Epitome* 27e]; Lynceus [Athenaeus 75e]; Aulus Gellius, *Attic Nights* 13.5; Mnesitheus 46 [*Epitome* 32e].

## 6 LEMONS OF THE HESPERIDES

1 On Roman markets see Frayn 1993.

2 Braund 1995. See further Sherratt and Sherratt 1993; Smith 1987.

3 Some have thought it a late incorporation into the story (this was the view of Zenodotus and Aristophanes of Byzantium (Slater 1986 p. 178), according to Eustathius, *Commentary on Homer* 692.21).

4 The Berezan letter (see e.g. Bravo 1974) is evidence of how far into 'barbarian' territory (in this case, the Ukraine) Greek traders actually did penetrate.

5 Alexis 178 [Athenaeus 516e]; Aristophanes, *Wasps* 838; Eubulus 148 [*Epitome* 65c], similar to Ephippus 3 [Athenaeus 370c]; Semonides 23 [Athenaeus 658c]. Aeschylides [Aelian, *Nature of Animals* 16.32], an agricultural writer, explained the flourishing of Cythnian sheep and the quality of their cheese, which sold (at an unknown date) at 90 drachmas per talent weight.

6 Seleucus [Athenaeus 658d]; Hegesippus [Athenaeus 516d]; Galen, *On the Properties of Foods* 3.16.3, *On the Properties of Simples* 10.1.7 [12.272]; Strabo, *Geography* 12.4.7.

7 Pliny, *Natural History* 11.32–3; Apuleius, *Metamorphoses* 1.5. Just as Chian vines could be transplanted to Italy, attempts were made to reproduce Attic honey by transplanting Attic thyme (Pliny, *Natural History* 21.57). As a *reductio ad absurdum*, Trimalchio is seen boasting of importing Attic bees (Petronius, *Satiricon* 38.3).

8 Salviat 1986 pp. 147–50, 181–5 and his references.

9 Alexis 278 [*Epitome* 28e]. For silphium from Carthage cf. Eubulus 18 or Antiphanes [*Epitome* 28d].

10 Miller 1969.

11 A rather free translation intended to convey the force of Theophrastus' statement.

12 Solomon 1995.

13 Cf. Galen, *On Temperaments* 3 [1.682]; Athenaeus 381b; Eubulus 125; Ophelion 3 [*Epitome* 66d]; Theophrastus fragment 166 [*Epitome* 66f]. Steier 1938; Miller 1969 pp. 80–3.

What the pepper was for in Antiphanes (274–5 [*Epitome* 66d]) is unknown. It occurs in a list of flavourings in Alexis (132 [Athenaeus 170a]) as quoted by Pollux, *Onomasticon* 6.65; in Athenaeus' version of the fragment, *séseli*, a kind of hartwort, takes the place of *péperi*. *Séseli*, not used in kitchens later but known as a medicine (Theophrastus, *Study of Plants* 9.15.5), is *lectio difficilior* and it does not seem safe to dismiss it.

The story in Plutarch's *Sulla* (13) does not demonstrate that pepper was normally used in Roman food at Sulla's time. Horace (*Epistles* 2.1.270) implies a classification of pepper with aromatics rather than food spices. But Pliny (*Natural History* 12.29) is familiar with pepper as an ingredient in food, and pepper was much used in later Roman cookery (*Apicius, passim*).

14 Galen, *Health* 4.5 [6.268]; Pliny, *Natural History* 12.26–8; Galen, *On Antidotes* 1.11 [14.55]. Hyman and Hyman 1980.

15 Celsus, *On Medicine* 5.23.3. Mithridates' antidote had fifty-four costly ingredients, according to Pliny (*Natural History* 29.24). Celsus (*On Medicine* 5.23.3) listed only thirty-eight, some of modest price. Elsewhere (23.149) Pliny appears

to undermine the story of the marvellous compound. He mentions a prescription, in the king's own hand, found among his papers, for 'two dry [ripe?] walnuts, two figs, twenty leaves of rue, pounded together with a pinch of salt': if this ensures a whole-day immunity to poison, why spend a king's ransom on the other?

16 'The root of the [pepper] tree is not, as some have thought, what is called *zingiberi* or *zimpiberi*, though that has a similar flavour' (Pliny, *Natural History* 12.28; cf. Galen, *Hippocratic Glossary* s.v. *indikón*).

17 Similarly Galen, *Health* 4.5 [6.271], cf. *On the Properties of Simples* 6.6.2 [11.880].

18 Galen, *Hippocratic Glossary* s.v. *indikón*; Pliny, *Natural History* 12.28. This has sometimes been considered an error: Miller (1969 pp. 53–7, 107–8), however, states that ginger will grow and is commercially grown nowadays in Ethiopia. Its transplanting to east Africa from Indonesia, even at an early date, is easily imaginable since Indian Ocean seamen took fresh ginger, growing in pots, on voyages as a food flavouring.

19 *Gálanga* (laos, lengkuas: Miller 1969 p. 151), a less fiery relative of ginger, grown in south-east Asia, has never been widely known in Mediterranean countries, though it is called for in a recipe for nard in Aetius, *Eight Books of Medicine* 1.131.

20 For other prescriptions, Alexander of Tralles, *On Fevers* 7 [2.92], *Twelve Books of Medicine* 1.17 [2.235]; Aetius, *Eight Books of Medicine* 1.131. In general, Pliny, *Natural History* 12.30. Miller 1969 p. 47.

21 Dioscorides, *Materia Medica* 3.62; Pliny, *Natural History* 20.163; Galen, *On the Properties of Simples* 6.1.28 [11.824]; Eudemus [Galen, *On Antidotes* 2 [14.185]], a poetic theriac for Antiochus Philometor.

22 For example, Diocles of Carystus 87 [Caelius Aurelius, *Acute Illnesses* 3.17]; Hippocratic *Epidemics* 7.1; *On the Nature of Woman* 70. Thompson 1949; Zohary and Hopf 1993 p. 189. Athenaeus quoted references on the subject, but they are lost (*Epitome of Athenaeus* 68b).

23 Galen, *Health* 4.5 [6.265], *Substitutes* [19.733].

24 Herodotus, *Histories* 3.111; Pliny, *Natural History* 12.85–98, etc.; Galen, *To Piso on Theriac* [14.257]; Dioscorides, *Materia Medica* 1.14, 5.39. Casson 1984; Laufer 1918.

25 Dioscorides, *Materia Medica* 5.54, 5.57, 5.59.

As an addendum to this survey of food spices, turmeric is thought to be the spice known to Theophrastus simply as *khrôma*, literally 'pigment' (*On Odours* 31). I know no positive evidence that it was added to food in Greek or Roman cuisine.

26 Strabo, *Geography* 15.2.10; Arrian, *Anabasis* 3.28. The *sílphion* of Strabo is oddly misunderstood by Jones 1917–32 as a reference not to asafoetida but to terebinth resin. See also Strabo, *Geography*, 11.13.7.

27 Columella, *On Agriculture* 12.59.5. Oribasius, *Medical Collections* 12 s.v. *sílphion*. Laufer 1919 pp. 353–62; Dalby 1993b; Saberi 1993.

28 Galen, *On the Properties of Foods* 1.17; Simeon Seth, *On the Properties of Foods* 126; Megasthenes 715F2 [Athenaeus 153e]; Aristobulus 139F35 and other sources cited by Strabo, *Geography* 15.1.18. Sallares 1991 pp. 22–4; Chang in Harris and Hillman 1989.

The *oríndes ártos* cited by Athenaeus [110e] from the *Triptolemus* of the fifth-century BC tragedian Sophocles (fragment 609) seems unlikely to be rice-bread, though some have thought so (e.g. Hesychius, *Lexicon* s.v. *orínden árton*; Liddell and Scott 1925–40 s.v. *oríndes*); Sallares (1991 pp. 22–4) gives a possible reason for its appearance in the play, however. Pollux (*Onomasticon* 6.73) does not make the link with *óryza* and Athenaeus is wisely doubtful of it.

29 Dioscorides, *Materia Medica* 5.54, 5.72; Theophrastus, *Study of Plants* 6.6.5; cf. Athenaeus 682c; Callimachus, *Hymn to Apollo* 83. Zohary and Hopf 1993 pp. 189–90.

30 Hippocratic *Gynaecology* 2.192, *Nature of Woman* 32, 63; Aristophanes, *Thesmophoriazusae* 486; Galen, *On the Properties of Foods* 2.15–16; Pliny, *Natural History* 12.29. Darby *et al.* 1977 p. 716.

31 Pliny, *Natural History* 19.165, 20.187; Galen, *On the Properties of Foods* 3.1.18, *On the Properties of Simples* 7.11.17 [12.62]: it cures wind; *Apicius passim*; Alexander of Tralles, *Eight Books of Medicine* 8.2. Andrews 1941–2 on the identification and the very problematic link with Liguria: the plant is more probably native to south-western Asia.

32 Galen, *On the Properties of Foods* 3.1.18; *Apicius* 7.6.10, etc.; Pliny, *Natural History* 19.164.

33 Thompson 1984; Crawford 1973b, 1979; Merlin 1984; Zohary and Hopf 1993.

34 Palladius, *Agriculture* 4.10.18. Andrews 1961a; E. H. Schafer in Chang 1977 p. 96. Basing his view, presumably, on the work of Luss 1931, Vavilov (1950 p. 27) considered the citron native to India. The long history of citrus fruit by Tolkowsky (1938) is unsound in its use of classical and Near Eastern sources.

35 Theophrastus, *Study of Plants* 1.11.4, *Plant Physiology* 1.11.1, 1.18.5; Dioscorides, *Materia Medica* 1.115.5. From this early usage is borrowed the modern botanical name for the species, Citrus Medica, a name that is sometimes misunderstood.

36 Note that Athenaeus' speaker 'Democritus' doubts the authenticity of this citation from Juba.

The identification has the strange consequence that a fruit of Far Eastern origin is sometimes called *mêlon hesperikón*, 'western apple', a term used not only by Juba but also by the agricultural writer Africanus [*Hippiatrica Cantabrigiensia* 71.15].

Athenaeus' speaker is certain that the fruits brought on stage in the comedies that he quotes by Antiphanes and Eriphus were citrons. We need not be. The link between citrons and the apples of the Hesperides was familiar in Athenaeus' own time. It is probably only that link that suggests the identification to Athenaeus. At the date of these comedies however, the apples of the Hesperides were commonly identified as quinces. For discussion and references to other sources of Roman date that identified citrons with the golden apples of the Hesperides, as did Juba, see Andrews 1961a p. 38.

37 House I.ix.5: Jashemski 1979–93 pp. 25–30, 74–9; Tolkowsky 1938 pp. 100–3; cf. Andrews 1961a pp. 44–5. Some consider that lemons did not reach the Mediterranean until after the Arab conquests (e.g. Zohary and Hopf 1993).

38 Several other citations of Theophrastus *On Plants* by Athenaeus have nothing to do with the text of his surviving botanical works; some are discussed by Sharples and Minter (1983).

This citation by Athenaeus, whatever its authenticity, was no doubt the source of Candolle's (1883 p. 222) statement, rather unfairly criticised by Laufer (1919 p. 539), that Theophrastus knew of the peach. It has been suggested that the fragment is really dealing with the (*káryon*) Persikón, 'walnut' (so Gulick 1927–41 vol. 1 p. 356 note a): the two trees are close relatives, the two nuts both produce an aromatic oil (as mentioned in the fragment), and it is hardly possible to be certain without a fuller context than Athenaeus allows us. He, at any rate, understood it to deal with the peach.

39 Diphilus of Siphnos [Athenaeus 82f]; Galen, *On the Properties of Simples* 7.12.17 [12.76]; Columella, *On Agriculture* 5.10.20, 9.4.3; Gargilius Martialis 2. Schafer in Chang 1977 pp. 93–4; Schafer 1963.

40 Columella, *On Agriculture* 5.10.19, etc.; Dioscorides, *Materia Medica* 1.115.5. Vavilov 1950 pp. 24, 34; Schafer 1963; Zohary and Hopf 1993; Powell 1987; Postgate 1987; Diethart and Kislinger 1992.

Slightly later than Dioscorides' *brekókia* (*Materia Medica* 1.115: given as a Latin word for 'apricot'), Pliny mentions *praecocia* as a kind of peach 'discovered less than thirty years ago and at first sold for a denarius each', *Natural History* 15.40; this again looks right for the apricot. To confuse matters, however, at 16.103 Pliny distinguishes *praecoces* from *armeniaca*, 'apricots'. It is conceivable that there were similarly named early varieties of both peaches and apricots. It is also possible, the fruits being not very different from one another, that between Pliny and his sources some mistake has arisen.

41 Pliny, *Natural History* 15.47; cf. Columella, *On Agriculture* 9.4.3. Zohary and Hopf 1993. It is sometimes said that the species is native to China: the Chinese themselves, however, introduced jujubes from central Asia in the late first millennium AD, having previously known some less good species or varieties (Schafer in Chang 1977 p. 95).

42 *Odyssey* 9.84; Galen, *On the Properties of Foods* 2.38.5. Zohary and Hopf 1993. There are several other candidates for identification with the epic 'lotus' (Herodotus, *Histories* 4.177; see How and Wells 1912 vol. 1 p. 359; Theophrastus, *Study of Plants* 4.3.1–4; *Scylax* 108–10).

43 Theophrastus, *Study of Plants* 4.4.7; Strabo, *Geography* 15.2.10; cf. Arrian, *Anabasis* 3.28. The passage from Theophrastus was copied by Pliny (*Natural History* 12.25), who failed to realise that this unnamed nut was the pistachio, well known by his time and named and described by him elsewhere (e.g. 13.51). Plutarch (*Artaxerxes* 3.2) names the typical Persian food *términthos*. Sancisi-Weerdenburg (1995) rightly criticises such English translations of this term as B. Perrin's 'turpentine wood' – hardly a palatable food! – and argues that terebinth nuts are in question here, and that pistachios were not known, even in Persia, before Alexander's expedition found them in the Bactrian region.

44 For a variant reading see Athenaeus 649d.

45 Poseidonius 87F3 [Athenaeus 649d]. Cf. Dioscorides, *Materia Medica* 1.124; Galen, *On the Properties of Simples* 8.16.21 [12.102]; Pliny, *Natural History* 15.83, 15.91. Zohary and Hopf 1993.

46 Theophrastus, *Study of Plants* 4.2.4; cf. Dioscorides, *Materia Medica* 1.114; Pliny, *Natural History* 15.95; Galen, *On the Properties of Foods* 2.33; *Babylonian Theodicy* 81.

47 To the Romans carob was *siliqua graeca*, 'Greek pod', and fenugreek was *faenum graecum* 'Greek hay', as if both reached Rome by way of Greece. There were other terms: *siliqua syriaca*, 'Syrian pod', may denote carob in Scribonius Largus, *Pharmacopoeia* 121. Colloquially *silicia* and *siliqua* would apparently do for either; cf. Columella, *On Agriculture* 2.10.33; Pliny, *Natural History* 18.140. Hence in the modern dialect of Velletri *sellégoia* means 'carob pod'.

48 Galen, *On the Properties of Foods* 1.24.1, *On the Properties of Simples* 6.19.6 [12.141]; Pliny, *Natural History* 13.9. Renfrew 1973 p. 188; Zohary and Hopf 1993 pp. 116–17.

49 Alexis 128 [Athenaeus 654f]; Diocletian's *Price Edict* 4.39–40; Aristophanes, *Birds* 102; Antiphon fragment 57: see Sommerstein 1987 p. 206; Antiphanes 173 [Athenaeus 655b]; Menodotus of Samos [Athenaeus 655a]; *Epitome of Athenaeus* 58b. Boessneck and Driesch 1981 and 1983; Witteveen 1989.

The price was five denarii apiece according to Varro (*On Farming* 3.6), who said that the orator Q. Hortensius, in the first century BC, was the first Roman to serve peacocks for food. Athenaeus [654d] remarks on the number of them in Roman gardens.

I have not come across a reference in Greek texts to the eating of *meleagrídes*, guinea fowl, sometimes in ancient sources bracketed with peafowl as exotic birds (see e.g. Menodotus of Samos [Athenaeus 655a]; Clytus 490F1 [Athenaeus 655b]). Even if kept principally as curiosities, it would be surprising if they were not occasionally eaten. Romans certainly did eat them (Varro, *On Farming* 3.9.19; Pliny, *Natural History* 10.74).

50 The seven classed wines of Diocletian's time are Picene, Tiburtine, Sabine, Aminean (see n. 52), Saite (the Egyptian one), Sorrentine and Falernian.

51 Dioscorides, *Materia Medica* 5.6.4 'Cretan or *prótropos* or Pramnian'; Pliny, *Natural History* 14.54 'in the Smyrna district near the shrine of the Mother of the Gods'; *Epitome of Athenaeus* 30b–e citing Eparchides and Semus 'from a tall mountain on Icaros' (other non-geographical explanations are also offered); *Suda* s.v. *Prámnios oînos*. Meyer 1974.

52 Varro, *On Farming* 1.2.7; Galen, *Health* 6.5 [6.337], *On the Therapeutic Method* 12.4 [10.833]; Florentinus in *Geoponica* 4.1, 5.17. On *aminnea*, André 1953; on the ambiguity in Horace, Gowers 1993 pp. 171–2.

53 See also Galen, *On Good and Bad Juices* 11 [6.800–3]. There is a problem with the Theran wine of this period. Pollux (*Onomasticon* 6.2) gives the following gloss: 'Theran wine: the wine from Crete.' Koukoulès (1947–55 vol. 5 p. 125: see his references) takes this to mean that Cretan wine was sold with the appellation of Theran. It may be so, though it is interesting that Galen says nothing about it: he was inquisitive enough to have been aware of any such deception and garrulous enough to have said so.

54 *Apicius* 1.2; cf. Pliny, *Natural History* 14.109.

55 Dioscorides, *Materia Medica* 5.28–9; Columella, *On Agriculture* 12.38. A wine sweetened with honey and scented with flowers was made near the Lydian Olympus, according to the *Epitome of Athenaeus* 38f citing Ariston of Ceos.

By myrtle wine I mean the fermented product of a must which had been flavoured with myrtle berries (or similarly other fruits). With most fruits other than grapes – and even with grapes, in less favourable climates – fermentation into wine is only assured if large quantities of a very sweet ingredient are added to the fruit juice. In ancient times this ingredient was either grape must (resulting in fruit wine) or honey (resulting in fruit mead). Sugar is now used.

A different kind of blend is that of fruit juice or other essences with already-fermented wine. This is what is done with the commercially available apple wine, peach wine, etc. of today.

56 Plutarch, *Symposium Questions* 5.3. André 1964; Howes 1950.

# 7 STRYMONIAN EELS

1 Archestratus 8 [Athenaeus 298e]; cf. Antiphanes 104 [Athenaeus 300c]; Hicesius [Athenaeus 298b]. Like nearly all the places mentioned by Archestratus, the Macedonian capital Pella was at that time accessible by sea (Strabo, *Geography* 7 fragment 22).

2 Archestratus 45 [Athenaeus 311a]; Hegesander [Athenaeus 334e]; Galen, *On the Properties of Foods* 3.24.12.

3 Demosthenes, *Third Philippic* 9.31; Hippolochus [Athenaeus 129d]. Borza 1982 p. 16.

4 Hermippus 63 [*Epitome* 27e]; Critias 2 [*Epitome* 28b]; Antiphanes 249 [*Epitome* 47b].

5 Critias 31 [Athenaeus 527a, 663a].

6 Xenophon, *Anabasis* 7.3; Herodotus, *Histories* 5.18–20. The initial response to this demand, as Herodotus narrates it, was: 'Our custom, Persians, is not to do as you do but to separate men from women [or, husbands from wives].' This observation, because of its clever and studied ambiguity, has been found difficult to reconcile with other sources: could Macedonians preach seclusion to 'Orientals'? How and Wells (1912 vol. 2 p. 7) cite Plutarch (*Symposium Questions* 1.1) against Herodotus here: 'The Persians are right, [moralists] say, to do their drinking and dancing together with their concubines and not with their wives'. Macrobius (*Saturnalia* 7.1.3) borrows Plutarch's remark and understands it of the Parthians, who were certainly the contemporary 'Persians' as far as Plutarch was concerned, though whether Plutarch meant the remark to refer to contemporaries or to the Achaemenid Persians is not known.

7 Demosthenes, *On the Embassy* 19.196–8; Aeschines, *On the Embassy* 154–8.

8 Athenaeus 128a citing Lynceus; Plutarch, *Demetrius* 27.

9 Athenaeus 196a; Rice 1983.

10 The narrative was a *Letter to Lynceus*. Translation and commentary in Dalby 1988. Hippolochus (Ullrich 1908–9 vol. 2 pp. 26–8) does not merit an entry in Pauly's *Real-Encyklopädie* (1893–1972) or supplements, possibly because of a suspicion voiced by Martin (1931 p. 160) that the letter is fictional and written by Lynceus.

11 See especially Menander fragment 452.

12 Deep-fried cheese pastries, coated with honey: Cato, *On Agriculture* 80 gives instructions.

13 Dorotheus of Ascalon [Athenaeus 662f]; Machon [Athenaeus 664b].

14 Cf. Epaenetus [Athenaeus 662d]. On Artemidorus see Wentzel 1896.

15 Pollux's definition (*Onomasticon* 6.70) is exactly to the point: '*matylle*: a food that excites thirst; they used it during a drinking party'.

16 Cf. Alexis 208, Philemon 8, 11, all quoted at Athenaeus 663c-f. In satirising the fashion for the dish, the speaker allows his invented word *mattyázete*, 'you have a *mattye*', to sum up the whole occasion. Athenaeus, puzzling out the comic passages that mention the *mattye*, was right to say that the word is used here of 'the practices of revelry . . . as if he meant the whole dinner'. Henderson (1991 pp. 167–8) reads the whole fragment as sexual, the compulsory dish being one or more male members: I am not convinced.

17 Petronius, *Satiricon* 49; Athenaeus 376c.

18 Hippolochus [Athenaeus 128d]; Dalby 1988 n. 10.

19 Hippolochus [Athenaeus 130d]. Lynceus was brother of the historian and tyrant Duris of Samos. A conjecture by Coraes (*mathetás* for *mathetés* at Athenaeus 128a) has turned Duris also into a pupil of Theophrastus (Dalby 1991).

20 Athenaeus 128a. Very little has been written about Lynceus (note Körte's single column 'Lynkeus' in Pauly (1893–1972)) except for incidental mentions in studies of Duris (Dalby 1991). His letters to Poseidippus [Athenaeus 652c] and to Apollodorus talked of food, but in what context is unknown. His letters to Hippolochus described the three Athenian banquets for Hellenistic

monarchs, see p. 154: there are brief fragments of two of them [Athenaeus 100e, 101e].

21 Cf. Athenaeus 228c. The second verse is an alteration of Archestratus 35.1 (cf. Athenaeus 278a). The first and third verses are taken by Ribbeck 1857; Brandt 1888; Lloyd-Jones and Parsons 1983; and Wilkins and Hill 1994 as undoubted quotations of Archestratus (52, 44). As will be seen from the context ('or some other poet'), they may or may not be so; and as can be seen from Lynceus' use of the second verse, they may or may not have been altered to make an apposite phrase. 'Never worthy' is a reminiscence of Hesiod, *Works and Days* 640.

22 Athenaeus 109d, 285e, 647a, 652d and below.

23 Plato, *Symposium* 176 and *passim*; citations at Athenaeus 426b–431f.

24 Lynceus 1 [Athenaeus 131f].

25 And on to Syria, Persia, Media and India. The work of Theophrastus' anonymous informants can be traced through place-names in the 'Index nominum' of Wimmer (1866): Hort (1916–26) did not index place-names. See also Bretzl 1903.

26 Diphilus of Sinope 17 [Athenaeus 132c]; Menander fragment 397 [Athenaeus 132e, 517a].

27 For Samian cakes see also Sopater 4 [Athenaeus 644c]; Cretan cakes, Chrysippus of Tyana [Athenaeus 647f].

28 Bottéro 1985 p. 42.

29 Athenaeus 326e. Kaibel (1887–90 vol. 3 p. 631) believed that the two titles belonged to a single book. In Pauly (1893–1972 s.vv. 'Pamphilus', 'Epaenetus') an anonymous author argues, ignoring the variation in title, that all citations of Iatrocles and Epaenetus came to Athenaeus through Pamphilus.

30 Callimachus fragment 435 [Athenaeus 643e]. But Athenaeus is not quoting Callimachus' *Subject Catalogue* verbatim, and might well not have troubled to include, with this list of obscure authors, the better-known name of one whose work he had already cited and would shortly cite again.

31 Iatrocles [Athenaeus 646a, b, f, 647b]. Orth 1922 col. 2098.
   The *krimnítes* [646a] had been previously mentioned by Archestratus only if we accept Meineke's conjectural emendation of all three manuscripts' *krimmatían*, in Athenaeus' quotation of Archestratus (4 [Athenaeus 111f]). For another possibly connected form see Hesychius, *Lexicon* s.v. *krimnêstis*.
   The Syracusan Epicharmus had previously referred to the *staitítas*, but the source for Athenaeus' brief recipe for this pancake is stated in the manuscript to be not Iatrocles but an unknown Hierocles. It was Pearson who suggested the emendation to Iatrocles: '*Staitítas*, a kind of cake of batter and honey, mentioned by Epicharmus in *Heba's Wedding*. The wet batter is poured on to a frying pan, and honey and sesame and cheese are added, so Hierocles says' [Athenaeus 646b].

32 Anaxippus 1 [Athenaeus 403e].

33 Athenaeus 114a, 647a; *Epitome* 58b. Athenaeus also [105c, 328d] cites Heracleides twice on difficult fish names: one of these is Heracleides' elucidation of a term used by Epicharmus and already disputed. According to Athenaeus (516c) there were two Syracusan cookery writers called Heracleides.

34 Jouanna 1992; Joly 1961.

35 Wellmann 1901; Jaeger 1963. Wellmann dates Diocles early and thus considers the letter to Antigonus spurious. It is preserved in Paul of Aegina's early Byzantine *Practice of Medicine* (1.100) and partly in the *Hippiatrica Berolinensia* 97.5–7. The other letter (fragment 141) is in Oribasius, *Medical Collections*

3.168–9. Diocles is listed by Athenaeus [516c] among authors of books *On Cookery*; an understandable imprecision on his part.

36 *Epitome* 51a; Scarborough 1970.

37 Apollodorus [Pliny, *Natural History* 14.76]. He is not certainly identified with other Apollodori, but see 'Apollodorus (70)' in Pauly 1893–1972 vol. 1 col. 2895.

38 Pliny, *Natural History* 14.73. Athenaeus twice cites Erasistratus' non-culinary works [666a; *Epitome* 46b]. According to an anecdote in Plutarch's *Demetrius* (38), Erasistratus was physician to King Seleucus and solved the emotional problems of the young prince Antiochus. The story is an early version of a widely-known fairy tale.

Pliny's statement as to Lesbian wine cannot be accepted: Lesbian had come to prominence before Erasistratus' time, as we have seen (e.g. Archestratus 59 [*Epitome* 29b]).

39 'The physician Dieuches' was known to Athenaeus only as teacher of Numenius of Heraclea [*Epitome* 5b], whose poem on *Fishing* Athenaeus frequently quotes. On Mnesitheus and Dieuches see Bertier 1972. The dating of Mnesitheus, as of some others mentioned in this section, is quite uncertain: he has sometimes been placed in the early fourth century.

40 Euthydemus is tentatively classed here as a dietician on the basis of the word *eustomakhótaton*, 'highly digestible', quoted from him by Athenaeus [118b]: the term is typical of dietary writing. All but one of Athenaeus' other citations from Euthydemus are of merely lexicographical interest. Nothing is known of his works, therefore, except that in *On Salt Fish* he inserted a set of hexameter verses which he attributed, in spite of what seem obvious anachronisms, to Hesiod. Athenaeus' speaker [116a] conjectures that the verses are by Euthydemus himself.

41 Athenaeus 312a, 309a. Nutton 1995.

42 Athenaeus 328f, 313b.

43 I take it from the last sentence that Epaenetus saw the *myma* (like *mattye*, beside which it is served in Athenaeus' fictional banquet) chiefly as a supper and *sympósion* dish to accompany wine; but that it could also be served as a dinner dish, as an *ópson*, to accompany bread. The text puzzled Schweighäuser (1801–7), whose emendation would produce 'You may also do it with fish.' But I would want a reconsideration of the offal, and a different selection of flavourings, if I were basing this dish on fish.

44 *Epitome* 58b; Athenaeus 88c, 294d, 297c, 304d, 305e, 312b, 371d, 387d, 395f; scholia on Nicander, *Theriaca* 585.

45 Athenaeus 308f, 648b, 113a, 647c. The quotations from Harpocration and Chrysippus incur the ridicule of Athenaeus' pedantic Deipnosophists: see 113d, 648c.

46 The highly educated cook alludes to Euripides, *Orestes* 37 (double inverted commas in the text). Athenaeus' fictional Ulpian was a stickler for classical Greek vocabulary.

47 Columella, *On Agriculture* 12.4.2, 1.1.13; Pliny, *Natural History* 18.22; Varro, *On Farming* 1.10.

48 The word first occurs in Galen, *Handy Remedies* 3 [14.537], a recipe for laxative biscuits. See also Chapter 9, pp. 196–7 and 205.

49 Cato, *On Agriculture* 76, 80. More precisely the borrowing of *placenta* was on the basis of the Greek accusative form *plakoûnta*. On Cato's culinary terminology see Boscherini 1959; Leon 1943.

50 Goujard 1975 pp. 249–51 says simply that these three words are 'emprunté au grec', but there is no evidence of their existence in real Greek.

51 Chrysippus of Tyana [Athenaeus 113a, 647d]. Pliny, *Natural History* 28.105; Isidore, *Etymologies* 20.2.15; Cato, *On Agriculture* 74, 77–8, 80, 82.

52 Dioscorides' work of the same title is here called *Materia Medica*: it survives complete and it deals with the pharmacological and digestive properties of substances that might be used as drugs, as ingredients in drugs, or as elements in the diet. Of Hicesius' work not enough survives to show whether the same title would be appropriate: are the 'materials' that he dealt with exclusively foodstuffs?

53 *Mélinon*, quince or apple perfume, more likely the former: cf. Dioscorides, *Materia Medica* 1.115.3.

54 Information on some of these perfumes comes from Theophrastus, *On Odours*. Additional ingredients are listed for rose fragrance (25). Rose, mother-of-thyme, saffron and gilliflower were made from the flowers, myrtle (*myrsinon*) and meadowsweet from the leaves. Meadowsweet perfume came from Cyprus, the plants that grew in Greece lacking aroma. The best saffron crocuses for perfume grew in Aegina and in Cilicia (27). Another myrtle perfume, *myrtinon*, was made from the fruit (28).

55 Ullmann 1974.

56 Cf. Grant 1995.

57 Nutton 1981, 1995.

# 8 THE IMPERIAL SYNTHESIS

1 Ulpian's violent death: Dio Cassius, *Histories* 80.2 [Xiphilinus 356]. For the date, earlier placed at 228 BC, cf. *P.Oxy.* 2565. On the identification of the real Ulpian with the speaker, an identification which Gulick finally rejected because of this word 'fortunately', see references given by him (1927–41 vol. 1 pp. viii–ix, vol. 7 p. 175). It should be noted that a later scribe who knew nothing of the real Ulpian or at least of his murder could have attempted to improve the logic of the sentence – it is usually counted lucky to die without suffering illness – by substituting *eutykhos*, 'fortunately', for an original *atykhos*, 'by ill fortune'.

2 Cf. Scarborough 1981.

3 It is thus unwise to speak (as does Anderson (1986 p. 80)) of the real personalities included in the *Deipnosophists* as 'the circle of Athenaeus'.

4 *Epitome* 1b–e. For another partial list see Gulick 1927–41 vol. 1 pp. xii–xiv.

5 A fuller outline is in Düring 1936, and a useful table of contents in the edition by Meineke (1858–67). There is a good selective index in vol. 7 of Gulick's edition (1927–41); Gulick's separate index of Greek words is rather thin. Fuller Greek indexes will be found in the editions of Meineke and of Kaibel (1887–90). There is a very handy separate index of authors in Kaibel's edition.

6 Note Zepernick 1921; Nyikos 1941.

7 Athenaeus' literary technique is the subject of a monograph by Mengis 1920; see also Martin 1931 pp. 270–80; and compare Gallardo 1972.

8 Athenaeus' detachment, through dialogue and quotation, from the subjects he writes on and the opinions expressed has to be kept in mind when reading Madeleine Henry's 1992 paper 'The edible woman', much the most challenging recent study of Athenaeus, which aims to characterise him as a pornographer. Not that it disproves her case, which is forcefully argued: he did, after all, write the book.

9 *Epitome* 1a–e; Düring 1936; Desrousseaux 1956 pp. vii–xix.

10 Ullrich 1908–9; Kaibel 1887–90 pp. v–XLI. It must be remembered that this argument concerns the sections of the *Deipnosophists* that survive *in extenso* (74a–700e with some lacunae) and not the lost sections for which, in modern editions, the abridged text of the *Epitome* has been substituted. In the latter, most of the dialogue has indeed been cut away, along with much else.

Kaibel's examples are listed here, with my brief comments in brackets. 80e–81c: it is unusual for a discussion to begin with dietetic citations (but not unique). 81c: a doctor talks about lexicography (not unusual). 134d: the dialogue begins abruptly without scene-setting (possibly a lacuna, more likely perhaps the author's inattention). 277b–c: we are promised a dialogue on fish without precise source references; what follows is precisely referenced and is not a dialogue (abridgement would not explain this). 196a: we were not told where the speech by Masurius, now under way, began (but, unusually, Athenaeus names Masurius as prospective speaker in the first sentence of book V (185a) and we may be expected to infer that his speech begins immediately). 80e: how did Daphnus change the subject to apples? (He is taking up the term 'Delphic apples' that he had mentioned incidentally at 80d.) 85c: who is speaking? (The narrator.) 541a: in a section without dialogue, the text refers to a locality 'among my Alexandrians': who is speaking? (The narrator again.)

One problem cannot be explained away. Kaibel observes that the speaker of 94c–96c, introduced only with *ho mén tis élege*, 'someone said', is not identified until 107a. He says that it turns out to be Cynulcus, which is a misreading of 107a: in fact it turns out to be Ulpian. Here an emendation may be the correct solution. The *tis* could have been added by a copyist who assumed that a name had fallen out of the text. If we omit *tis*, the remaining clause *ho mèn élege*, 'he said', refers correctly to Ulpian who had been named in the previous sentence.

Kaibel's arguments have been widely accepted (e.g. by Gulick (1927–41 vol. 1 p. xvii) and by Desrousseaux (1956 p. xxi–xxiii)). When looked at afresh they do not come across as convincing.

11 Wilson 1962; Dindorf 1870 p. 73.

12 After these losses some manuscript copies of the Marcianus were made: one of them served as the copy text for Musurus' *editio princeps*. On these copies see Dindorf 1870, especially pp. 74–7.

13 The fullest studies of the transmission of the text are Kaibel 1887–90 vol. 1 pp. v–XLI and Desrousseaux 1956 pp. xix–xliii. Desrousseaux, after a long life-time of acquaintance with Athenaeus, here writes informally and somewhat inexplicitly.

14 Kaibel 1883; Aldick 1928.

An ambiguous expression by Gulick (1927–41 vol. 1 p. xvii) has led some to a misunderstanding of the relation between the fuller text and the *Epitome*. They include Caujolle-Zaslawsky (1989): hers is the most recent bibliographical and textual survey of Athenaeus. In spite of what is said in that article, the *Epitome* actually covers the whole of the *Deipnosophists* at about the same level of abridgement: its existence has nothing to do with the loss of books 1–2 and the other lacunae. It is, however, only the passages covering these lacunae that are normally printed: the only edition, the *editio princeps*, of all the rest of the *Epitome* is Peppink's (1937–9).

Cobet (1847 p. 104ff.) and Wilhelm Dindorf (1870, especially p. 79) reached the view that the epitomator worked from the Marcianus manuscript, which in his time would have been complete. Maas, accepting this argument, further argued that the epitomator was the learned and verbose twelfth-century Bishop Eustathius of Thessalonica (Maas 1952 and earlier papers). These views are no longer tenable (cf. Gow 1965 p. 27; Wilson 1983 pp. 201–2; Collard 1969).

15 Hence the doubt over the long survey of Italian wines (Epitome 26c–27d; Nutton 1995) attributed to *ho parà toútoi tôi sophistêi Galenós*, a phrase that must mean something like 'the Galen of our author': how had Athenaeus himself introduced the passage? Is it a quotation from a lost work of Galen, or is it supposed to be spoken by the fictional Galen from his own (i.e. Athenaeus' own) knowledge?

16 Dindorf 1870; Peppink 1936.

17 Peppink 1937–9 vol. 1 pp. IX–XVIII; Erbse 1950 pp. 75–92; Collard 1969.

It is strange that the *Epitome* has never been printed in complete form. The chief variants of the two best manuscripts, those of Paris and Florence, have been published as follows. The first volume of Desrousseaux's projected Budé text of Athenaeus forms an edition and French translation of books 1–2 of the *Epitome* (Desrousseaux 1956). The first part of book 3 is to be found, in a less reliable text, in Kaibel's 1887–90 edition of Athenaeus. The English reader can find a translation of all this in Gulick's Loeb edition (1927–41 vol. 1 pp. 3–319).

Peppink produced the *editio princeps*, and the only edition so far, of the section from the middle of book 3 onwards: Aldick had previously printed a list of variants (Peppink 1937–9; Aldick 1928).

18 This practice confuses scholars unfamiliar with Athenaeus. It must explain why B. P. Reardon, in an important survey of Greek literature of the second and third centuries AD, selects for analysis a passage not of the surviving *Deipnosophists* but of the *Epitome*; from it he shows the desultory nature of a text which, he seems not to realise, is the certain result of Byzantine abridgement (Reardon 1971 pp. 226–7).

19 Desrousseaux 1956 p. xxii.

20 There is an example at 84d. The manuscript reading *kédrion*, 'juniper berry', led to Gulick's desperate translation: 'Phaenias of Eresus offers us the suggestion that possibly the juniper-berry is intended, from *kédros* ("cedar").' In context this is ridiculous, for the topic of conversation is some large exotic fruit brought on to the stage in an Athenian comedy to general admiration.

Where the manuscript reads *kédrion*, however, *Suda* (as observed by Wehrli (1967–9) in his edition of Phaenias) has the reading *kítrion*, 'citron'. There can be no doubt that it is correct, and it is also clear how the textual error would have arisen, since an unreflective copyist might well have argued to himself, without considering the context, that it is *kédrion* rather than *kítrion* that derives from *kédros*. Once the correct reading is adopted, Phaenias, instead of offering a foolish opinion on the comedy scene, is proposing an etymology (very likely the right one) for *kítrion*: 'Phaenias of Eresus gives me this idea: did the citron get its name from *kédros* ("cedar")?'

21 For lists see Aldick 1928 pp. 61–72; Erbse 1950 p. 75 n. 6.

22 Kaibel noted that several of the quotations from Greek authors in Macrobius, *Saturnalia* 5.18–22 had also been quoted by Athenaeus in widely separated passages of book XI of the *Deipnosophists*. His theory was that Macrobius had taken these quotations directly from the *Deipnosophists* – and that his *Deipnosophists* was a more extensive text, offering some of the other Greek quotations given by Macrobius which are not in the *Deipnosophists* as now known (Kaibel 1887–90 vol. 1 pp. XXXVI–XXXVII). Kaibel was so convinced of this that he interpolated two of these extra quotations into the text of his

edition of the *Deipnosophists* (at 475a and 481e), and was followed in this by Gulick (1927–41 vol. 5 pp. 98 n. 1, 134 n. 5). Wissowa observed that Macrobius normally follows a single source in each section of his compilation, and follows it much more consecutively than he would here seem to follow Athenaeus. In view of the many Latin quotations also appearing in this passage of the *Saturnalia*, Wissowa was confident that Macrobius' immediate source was a Latin commentary on Vergil: this might have drawn on Athenaeus among other authorities (Wissowa 1913 pp. 325–32).

23 Kaibel 1887–90 vol. 1 pp. xxi–xxiii. In the following list, upper-case roman numerals represent the existing fifteen-book division; lower-case stand for the alternative thirty-book division. Surviving rubrics indicate that the alternative book vi began at 96d, book viii at 154a, book x at 201b, book xiv at 297c. At the beginning of the existing book IV, following the letter *gamma* ('III') which is the colophon of the preceding book, we find the rubric *Tôn eis L arkhè tou Z* ('Beginning of book vii of the recension in xxx books'), and similar rubrics occur at the beginning of some later books.

24 Pauly 1975 s.v. 'Athenaios 3'; Papenhoff 1954.

25 Kaibel 1887–90; Gulick 1927–41. Peppink (1936) lists many places where Kaibel reports the manuscript incorrectly, as does Gulick in his later volumes, and there are, from my observation, still others. Kaibel was also far too ready to incorporate his own and others' conjectures into his text, not only to remove what appeared to be errors but even to pad out abridged quotations. Gulick, in accordance with the principles of the Loeb Classical Library, in his first two volumes reprinted and translated Kaibel's text quite uncritically; his text became more independent as his work proceeded.

26 Schweighäuser 1801–7.

27 An example (at Athenaeus 115d) is pointed out briefly in Dalby 1990. The speaker Galen, quoting from Diphilus of Siphnos, interrupts himself with a sentence from Philistion of Locri. The quotation from Diphilus is then resumed without warning. Failing knowledge of Athenaeus' methods, and of the unusual technical vocabulary used by Diphilus, it may appear (as it did to Wellmann 1901 in his edition of Philistion) that Diphilus himself is quoting Philistion, and that the latter was the author of the subsequent passage.

28 Athenaeus 376c; Hippolochus [Athenaeus 129b]; Petronius, *Satiricon* 49. Dalby 1988 n. 15.

29 Alföldi-Rosenbaum 1972.

30 Brandt 1927.

31 There is also the assertion in the *Historia Augusta* (*Aelius* 5.9) that Hadrian's adopted son Aelius Verus 'had the erotic books of Ovid, or, as others said, of Apicius, always at his bedside'. Not much can be said for this, even when editors have amended it to remove the implication that *Apicius* is erotic. There is little that is factual in the life of Aelius. The books of *Apicius* as we know them are at least two centuries later than Aelius' time. Thus the text tells us only that someone of the author's time would be considered by him an eccentric voluptuary if he read *Apicius* in bed.

32 Athenaeus 376d; for later Greek citations see Liddell and Scott 1925–40 s.v. *isíkion*. The form given by Latin grammarians, *insicia* (Varro, *On the Latin Language* 5.110), *insicium* (Macrobius, *Saturnalia* 7.8.1: see the discussion there), may be hypercorrect; the suggested etymology does not account for the long second *i*, guaranteed by many derivatives in Romance languages. For *isicium*, 'mince, forcemeat stuffing', the plural form *isicia*, 'meat balls, sausages', and the adjective *isiciatus*, 'stuffed,' see *Apicius* 2.1.1, 2.3.1 and *passim*.

33 *Apicius* 2.4; Varro, *Latin Language* 111; cf. Cicero, *Letters to Friends* 9.16; *Philogelos* 237.

The stress on *á*, coldly ignored by Liddell and Scott 1925–40 but guaranteed by the medieval and modern Greek forms of the word (Koukoulès 1947–55 vol. 5 p. 66) confirms that, although the word has otherwise a perfectly Greek look, it actually originated in Latin which would naturally stress that syllable (Kalleris 1953 p. 693 n. 4).

Information on the modern derivatives will be found in standard works on the individual languages mentioned, but it has not, I believe, so far been brought together. I am grateful here for unpublished information from Johan Mathiesen.

34 For example Aetius, *Eight Books of Medicine* 5.139; Paul of Aegina, *Practice of Medicine* 7.11; Hierophilus, *Dietary Calendar* January.

35 *Apicius* 7.11.8; Damascenus Studites, *Sermons* 14; *Prodromic Poems* 4.62.

36 The origin of the Greek term is Latin *praecox*, 'early, premature', or rather, the Latin neuter plural *praecocia* (Pliny, *Natural History* 15.40). This is also the origin of various Italian dialect words for 'apricot' (Meyer-Lübke 1911 pp. 502–3).

37 Pliny, *Natural History* 15.39; Alexander of Tralles, *On Fevers* 1; Florentinus [*Geoponica* 10.13]; *Suda* s.v. *rodákinon*; Simeon Seth, *On the Properties of Foods*, 89. Kalleris 1953 pp. 707–8.

38 Martial 5.18.3; Galen, *On the Properties of Foods* 2.31.1; Simeon Seth, *On the Properties of Foods* 34. Weber 1989.

39 The common spelling *maioúlion* and the associated explanation 'picked from May to July' is a fine example of folk-etymology.

40 Galen, *To Piso on Theriac* [14.259].

41 Dioscorides, *Materia Medica* 3.52; cf. Galen, *On the Properties of Foods* 2.65. Sallares 1991 pp. 283–7, 470 n. 397; Heywood 1983.

42 Galen, *On the Properties of Foods* 3.11.1, 3.20.2; *Apicius* 7.3.1. Meyer-Lübke 1911 p. 639; Koukoulès 1947–55 vol. 5 p. 56.

43 *Book of the Eparch* 15; *Miracles of Saints Cosmas and Damian* 34.

44 The usually accepted etymology from Sanskrit may be correct but it is pure guesswork.

45 Pollux, *Daily Conversation* 113r; *Apicius* 7.6. For Greek references, Kalleris 1953 p. 692 n. 5; Du Cange 1688 s.v. *kopádi*.

# 9 BISCUITS FROM BYZANTIUM

1 Jeanselme and Oeconomos (especially 1923), approaching the topic from the point of view of medical history, made a pioneering brief survey of the Byzantine diet. Otherwise, scarcely any modern work is concerned purely with Byzantine food and cuisine (I have not seen Cekalova 1989). Scully (1988) provides a useful bibliography on the contemporary food and cuisine of medieval western Europe.

One modern compilation retains unchallenged its place as a guide to primary sources of information on the daily life of Byzantium. The *Vizandinon vios ke politismos* of P. Koukoulès (1947–55; usefully supplemented from papyri of early Byzantine times by Kalleris (1953)) is a five-volume treasury of references from Byzantine texts of all kinds. The use that Koukoulès made of these references is, admittedly, uncritical, and all must be followed up to see what they really say and mean (I hope I have not too often disobeyed my own injunction). On a smaller scale, and based only on saints' lives of the early

Byzantine period, but similar in intention, is a series of papers by Magoulias (for example, 1971, 1976).

There is as yet no such convenient compilation on the social history of the Ottoman Empire. The most useful sources for the present purpose are not the steadily growing mass of economic and financial documents, but the reports of travellers: not only foreign travellers, but also the Turkish Evliya Çelebi, whose vast work is only partly available in translation. In spite of the limitations of perspective in such writings, they provide – as the more factual documents do not – a social context, and a historical and comparative background, to the undoubtedly subjective observations that they offer. A recent book by Angelomatis-Tsougarakis (1990) is a handy and critical guide to the nineteenth-century British travellers, suggesting something of what their authors failed to see.

2 Or than is realised by Teodorsson 1989– , whose commentary on the *Symposium Questions* is weak on social history. He cites parallels from early Greece, from Rome, and from Imperial Greece without apparent awareness of or interest in the contrasts they display.

3 Oribasius, *Medical Collections* 1.1. Schröder 1940; Scarborough 1984 especially pp. 221–4.

4 Sideras 1974.

5 An edition of this accompanying work (sometimes, but without good reason, attributed to Psellus) was printed by Ideler (1841–2 vol. 2 pp. 257–81). For details and references to other editions see Sonderkamp 1984 p. 31.

6 Different linguistic standpoints are demonstrated by authors in *Der kleine Pauly*, 1975, for whom Anthimus' letter is 'linguistically (vulgar Latin; origins of Romance) of great interest' and an author in Scarborough 1984 p. 210 for whom Anthimus is 'almost illiterate': see further Baader 1970.

7 Harig 1967.

8 Oeconomos 1950; Jeanselme 1924; Scarborough 1984 p. xii n. 43.

9 Ideler 1841–2 vol. 1 pp. 213–32; Stannard 1971, 1984; Riddle 1984.

10 Cf. Varro, *On Farming* 1.1.10. Gemoll 1884; Oder 1890–3; Fehrle 1920.

11 I have been unable to consult the first edition of Agapius' *Geoponikón* and can only cite the text from the page numbers of a nineteenth-century Athens stereotype edition published by Saliveros. Alternative references, to the numbered chapters of the first edition, will be found under numerous headwords in Du Cange 1688.

12 Purely scholarly works of late Roman and Byzantine times are sometimes misread as uncomplicated sources for Byzantine society. For example, there are recipes in the lexica of Roman and Byzantine times, from Pollux (*Onomasticon*) and Hesychius to Photius and the *Suda*; there are recipes in the *Scholia on Aristophanes* and in other commentaries. But these recipes date back (so far as a date can be assigned to them at all) to the classical period: so they should, for their purpose is to elucidate what Imperial and Byzantine readers no longer understood. There are recipes for *kándaulos*, for example, in several of these scholarly works (Pollux, *Onomasticon* 6.69; Hesychius, *Lexicon* s.v. *kandaúlos*; *Etymologicum Magnum* 488.53). This does not mean that the Byzantine Greeks regularly ate *kándaulos*. It means the opposite: they had forgotten what *kándaulos* was, and so every annotator of an ancient text in which the term occurred needed to explain it. Surveys of Byzantine life which uncritically incorporate evidence from such sources can be seriously misleading.

13 For the following section many supporting references will be found in Kou-koulès 1947–55 vol. 5 pp. 9–135.

14 Simeon Seth, *On the Properties of Foods* 33; Liutprand, *Embassy* 38; Hierophi-lus, *Dietary Calendar, passim*; *Timarion* 46.

15 Robert 1961–2; Krumbacher 1903.

16 *Prodromic Poems* 3.83, 3.93, 3.280; Theodore Lascaris, *Letters* 54, 82, 83; *Theologakis* 356. Karpozelos 1984 p. 25 n. 60.

17 Cf. *Timarion* 11.

18 Simeon Seth, *On the Properties of Foods* 70; scholia on Nicander, *Alexiphar-maca* 533; Agapius, *Geoponikón* 75; on fruits in general, Kalleris 1953 pp. 703–10.
  Oranges have sometimes been thought to have reached the Mediterranean far earlier. They are identified by some authors on Roman mosaics and wall-paintings, the earliest a Pompeiian mosaic (Tolkowsky 1938 plate xxvi; Andrews 1961a pp. 45–6; Casella 1950 pp. 358, 361). Recently the date has also been set later, after the fall of Constantinople and the establishment of direct maritime trade between Europe and south-east Asia (Zohary and Hopf 1993), but the scholion cited above throws that very low dating into question.

19 Sotion [*Geoponica* 5.28]; Hesychius, *Lexicon* s.v. *thrîa*. Dalby 1989; Baysal 1988.

20 Dioscorides, *Materia Medica* 5.17–18; Oribasius, *Medical Collections* 5.25; Jeanselme and Oeconomos 1923 pp. 158–60; Agapius, *Geoponikón* 50.

21 Agapius, *Geoponikón* 55; cf. Dioscorides, *Materia Medica* 3.75; Galen, *On the Properties of Simples* 7.11.14 [12.61].

22 Simeon Seth, *On the Properties of Foods* 58; *Prodromic Poems* 2.46, 3.149. Koukoulès 1947–55 vol. 5 p. 45.

23 Karpozilos and Kazhdan in Kazhdan 1991 s.vv. 'Bread', 'Diet'; Koukoulès 1947–55 vol. 5 pp. 12–35, 110–21.

24 Michael Italicus, *Letters* 42; Psellus, *Letters* 206; Koukoulès 1947–55 vol. 5 pp. 31–4.

25 Newett's translation (1907 p. 202), slightly altered.

26 Koukoulès 1947–55 vol. 5 pp. 45–6. Liddell and Scott (1925–40) and Miller (1969 p. 3) suggest that the *kómakon* of Theophrastus (*Study of Plants* 9.7.2; cf. Pliny, *Natural History* 12.135, 13.12) may be nutmeg; Hort (1916–26 vol. 2 p. 461) and Andrews (in Jones 1980 p. 501) give the alternative identification *Ailanthus malabarica*.

27 Simeon Seth, *On the Properties of Foods* 96; Pliny, *Natural History* 12.32; Dioscorides, *Materia Medica* 2.104.

28 Jeanselme 1922.

29 *Prodromic Poems* 2.42a, 3.283; William of Rubruck, *Report* 9. Jeanselme and Oeconomos 1923 p. 161 nn. 10, 12; Witteveen 1985.

30 Oribasius, *Medical Collections* 5; cf. Galen, *On Compounding of Drugs, Arranged by Parts of the Body* 6.4 [12.922]. Koukoulès 1947–55 vol. 5 pp. 131–2.

31 Diocletian's *Price Edict* 2.17–19. For a problem over the price of *apsinthâton* see Kalleris 1953 p. 713 and n. 7.

32 But as yet no distilled spirit was present in the lists of ingredients. Kazhdan 1991 s.v. 'Beverages' talks of liqueurs, but perhaps not using the word in its current sense.

33 On the identification see Thiselton-Dyer 1913–14 pp. 202–4.

34 Eideneier 1970.

35 The Romanian name *tamîioara* (literally 'thyme-flavoured') is a calque rather than a borrowing.

36 Lambert-Gócs 1990; references in Koukoulès 1947–55 vol. 5 p. 125 nn. 7, 11.

37 *Prodromic Poems* 3.285–313; Isaac Chumnus, *Letters* 216, 218; Michael Choniates, *Letter* 50; further references in Kazhdan 1991 s.v. 'Wine production'; and
   in Koukoulès 1947–55 vol. 5 pp. 124–7.
38 Ideler 1841–2 vol. 2 p. 194, vol. 1 p. 421.
39 McNeal 1993 p. 161; Farmayan and Daniel 1990 p. 112. Cf. *Timarion* 2, 'there
   was always someone to meet us'; and for an interesting survey of the *caravan-
   serais* and *hans* of nineteenth-century Greece see Angelomatis-Tsougarakis
   1990 pp. 51–6.
40 Suetonius, *Vitellius* 12. Amouretti 1990; Kislinger 1984.
41 Kolias 1984.
42 Du Cange 1688 col. 1095; Du Cange 1678 s.v.; Koukoulès 1947–55 vol. 5
   pp. 29–30; Kahane and Tietze 1958 s.v. Procopius, *Secret History* 6, uses the
   classical term *dípyros ártos* in telling the story of Justin.
43 Du Cange 1688 s.v. *pístos* glosses this *panis genus*, 'a kind of bread'.
44 Karpozelos 1984.
45 Karpozelos 1984 p. 27; Dembinska 1985–6.
46 Browning 1989.
47 Vryonis 1971 p. 493.
48 *Timarion* 2, for example, praises a good meal as *tyrannikós*, 'fit for a (foreign)
   king'.
49 Michael Choniates, *Letter* 19; Newett 1907 p. 194 and n. 66; Garzya 1963
   p. 233.
50 Pliny, *Natural History* 14.124–8; Plutarch, *Symposium Questions* 5.3.
51 *Epitome* 33b; Fronto and Damogeron [*Geoponica* 7.12–13]. Koukoulès 1947–55
   vol. 2 pp. 123–6; Weber 1980 pp. 78–84.
52 Cf. Liutprand, *Embassy* 63. Weber 1980 pp. 85–8, pp. 90–1; Koukoulès 1947–55
   vol. 5 pp. 40–1: on *gáros* see further below.
     English classicists used to liken *gáros* to anchovy sauce, a Greek Byzantinist
   once translated it as caviar. Weber (1980 n. 77) was misled by the former;
   Koukoulès (1947–55 vol. 5 p. 36 n. 1) by the latter. Neither view has any
   merit.
53 Liutprand, *Antapodosis* 5.23; Hierophilus, *Dietary Calendar* March [Paris MS.
   2244]. Jeanselme and Oeconomos 1923 p. 157.
54 I am inclined to think that persistent rumours of the making of *gáros* in
   backwaters of the modern Mediterranean (e.g. Koukoulès 1947–55) are myths:
   I have not yet come across a first-hand report. *Gáros* in Greece generally now
   means the brine in which olives and feta cheese are preserved (Kalleris 1953
   pp. 695–6) – and indeed the principal ingredients of *gáros*-like products, elsewhere in the world, are salt and water.
55 Perry 1988; Heine 1988 p. 55 n. 148; Baudier 1662 p. 66.
56 Galen, *On the Properties of Foods* 3.15.
57 Baudier 1662 p. 65:

> At the end of autumn the Grand Vizier spends some days overseeing
> the manufacture of *pastirma* for the Sultan and Sultanas' consumption.
> Made of the meat of pregnant cows, so that it will be more tender, it is
> salted just as in Christendom venison and pork are salted.... At the
> Palace this product is counted among the luxuries of banquets, while
> Turkish private households, even those of very modest means, also use it.

I do not know whether Baudier wrote from personal observation.
58 Galen, *Notes on Diet in Acute Diseases* [15.455]; *Geoponica* 3.8, it was made
   of 'Alexandrian wheat'. Cf. Koukoulès 1947–55 vol. 5 p. 40.

Bryer 1985 (with references to earlier notes by Perry (1982) and Conran) and 1995 argues strongly that this Greek word derives from Latin *tracta*: Perry had given a Central Asian derivation. I am not convinced by either. Cato's *tracta*, an ingredient in his cake *placenta*, are utterly different from *trakhanás* in their use.

59 McNeal 1993 pp. 84, 92.
60 André 1981 pp. 25–6; Agapius, *Geoponikón* 72.
61 Simeon Seth, *On the Properties of Foods* 85. Agapius, *Geoponikón* 75.
62 Agapius, *Geoponikón* 50, 25, 66. On spinach see Laufer 1919 p. 395.
63 *Ambar* had been among the stocks of the spice and perfume merchants of Byzantine Constantinople (*Book of the Eparch* 10): Freshfield (1938) translates it 'amber', but it is ambergris.
64 Baudier 1662 p. 66; Evliya Çelebi 139, 154.
65 McNeal 1993 p. 104; Salaman 1987 p. 45.
66 This term has not been understood by lexicographers.
67 Dodwell 1819 pp. 155–7. The scene is illustrated in Dodwell's *Views in Greece* (London 1821).
68 Baudier 1662 pp. 65–7.
69 Tournefort 1717 vol. 1 p. 409.
70 Tournefort 1717 vol. 1 p. 89.
71 Angelomatis-Tsougarakis 1990 pp. 179–86.
72 See Baldwin 1984 pp. 43–4 with pp. 15–17 and nn. 38–40.
73 Reading Miles Lambert-Gócs (1990) is almost as enjoyable. Note his list of prominent modern grape varieties (pp. 292–6) and lexicon of ancient Greek terms for taste and aroma (pp. 272–91).
74 Lambert-Gócs 1990 pp. 162–74; Koukoulès 1947–55 vol. 5 p. 123; Michael Choniates, *Letter* 19.
75 Tournefort 1717 vol. 1 pp. 378–9. Salaman 1993. The mastic trees of Chios were noticed in late Byzantine times by Buondelmonti (De Sinner 1824 pp. 111–14).
76 McNeal 1993 p. 121.
77 Galen and others cited by Grant 1995. Vryonis 1971 pp. 489–91 with references; cf. Koukoulès 1947–55 vol. 2 p. 8; Dodwell 1819.
78 On modern Greek food there is much of interest in Rena Salaman's books (e.g. 1987, 1993). Modern Turkish food is covered in detail in the proceedings of the biennial International Food Congresses (e.g. Halici 1988).
79 Cf. Arnott 1975.

# BIBLIOGRAPHY

Aldick, C. (1928) *De Athenaei Dipnosophistarum codicibus etc.*, Münster. Dissertation.

Alföldi-Rosenbaum, E. (1972) 'Apicius de re coquinaria and the Vita Heliogabali' and 'Notes on some birds and fishes of luxury in the Historia Augusta' in *Bonner Historia-Augusta-Colloquium 1970*, ed., J. Straub, Bonn, pp. 5–18.

Amigues, S. (ed.) (1993) Théophraste, *Recherches sur les plantes*, Vol. 3, Paris.

Amouretti, M. C. (1985) 'La transformation des céréales dans les villes, un indicateur méconnu de la personnalité urbaine. L'exemple d'Athènes' in *L'origine des richesses dépensées dans la ville antique*, ed., P. Leveau, Aix-en-Provence.

—— (1986) *Le pain et l'huile dans la Grèce antique*, Besançon.

—— (1990) 'Vin, vinaigre, piquette dans l'antiquité' in *Le vin des historiens*, ed., G. Garrier, Suze-la-Rousse, pp. 75–87.

Anderson, G. (1986) *Philostratus*, London.

André, J. (1953) 'Contribution au vocabulaire de la viticulture: les noms des cépages' in *Revue des études latines*, vol. 30, pp. 126–56.

—— (1964) 'La résine et la poix dans l'antiquité' in *L'antiquité classique*, vol. 33, pp. 86–97.

—— (1981) *L'alimentation et la cuisine à Rome*, 2nd edn, Paris.

Andrews, A. C. (1941) 'The silphium of the ancients' in *Isis*, vol. 33, pp. 232–6.

—— (1941–2) 'Alimentary use of lovage in the classical period' in *Isis*, vol. 33, pp. 514–8.

—— (1942) 'Alimentary use of hoary mustard in the classical period' in *Isis*, vol. 34, pp. 161–2.

—— (1948a) 'Orach as the spinach of the classical period' in *Isis*, vol. 39, pp. 169–79.

—— (1948b) 'Oysters as a food in Greece and Rome' in *Classical journal*, vol. 43, pp. 299–303.

—— (1949a) 'Celery and parsley as foods in the Graeco-Roman period' in *Classical philology*, vol. 44, pp. 91–9.

—— (1949b) 'The carrot as a food in the classical period' in *Classical philology*, vol. 44, pp. 182–96.

—— (1952) 'The opium poppy as food and spice in the classical period' in *Agricultural history*, vol. 26, pp. 152–5.

—— (1956) 'Melons and watermelons in the classical period' in *Osiris*, vol. 12, pp. 368–75.

—— (1958a) 'The mints of the Greeks and Romans and their condimentary use' and 'Thyme as a condiment in the Graeco-Roman era' in *Osiris*, vol. 13, pp. 127–56.

—— (1958b) 'The turnip' and 'The parsnip as food in the classical era' in *Classical philology*, vol. 53, pp. 131–52.

267

—— (1961a) 'Acclimatization of citrus fruits in the Mediterranean region' in *Agricultural history*, vol. 35, no. 1, pp. 35–46.

—— (1961b) 'Hyssop in the classical era' in *Classical philology*, vol. 56, pp. 230–48.

—— (1961c) 'Marjoram as a spice in the classical era' in *Classical philology*, vol. 56, pp. 73–82.

Anfimov, N. V. (1983) in *PAE*, vol. 2, pp. 117–24.

Angelomatis-Tsougarakis, H. (1990) , *The eve of the Greek revival: British travellers' perceptions of early 19th-century Greece*, London.

Arndt, A. (1993) 'Silphium' in *Spicing up the palate: proceedings of the Oxford Symposium on Food and Cookery 1992*, Totnes, pp. 28–35.

Arnott, M. L. (ed.) (1975) *Gastronomy*, The Hague. Includes her 'The breads of Mani', pp. 297–303.

Arnott, W. G. (1968) 'Alexis and the parasite's name' in *Greek, Roman and Byzantine studies*, vol. 9, pp. 161–8.

Baader, G. (1970) , 'Lo sviluppo del linguaggio medico nell'antichità e nel primo medioevo' in *Atene e Roma*, n.s., vol. 15, pp. 1–19.

Baedeker, K. (publisher) (1911) *The Mediterranean*, London.

Bailey, G. (ed.) (1983) *Hunter-gatherer economy in prehistory*, Cambridge. Includes G. Bailey *et al.*, 'Epirus revisited: seasonality and inter-site variations in the Upper Palaeolithic of north-west Greece', pp. 64–78.

Bailey, G. N. *et al.* (1986) 'Palaeolithic investigations at Klithi: preliminary results of the 1984 and 1985 field seasons' in *Annual of the British School at Athens*, vol. 81, pp. 7–35.

Baird, J. R. and Thieret J. W. (1989) 'The medlar (Mespilus germanica, Rosaceae) from antiquity to obscurity' in *Economic botany*, vol. 43, pp. 328–72.

Baldwin, B. (trans.) (1984) *Timarion*, Detroit.

Battaglia, E. (1989) *Artos. Il lessico della panificazione nei papiri greci (Biblioteca di Aevum antiquum*, 2) Milan.

Baudier, M. (1662) 'Histoire générale du Serrail' in *Histoire générale des Turcs, contenant l'Histoire de Chalcocondyle*, trans., B. de Vigenère, Paris, vol. 2.

Baysal, A. (1988) 'Köfte, sarma and dolma in Turkish cuisine' in *Birinci Milleretlerasi Yemek Kongresi = First International Food Congress, Turkey, 25–30 September 1986*, ed., F. Halici, Ankara, pp. 50–65.

Beavis, I. C. (1988) *Insects and other invertebrates in classical antiquity*, Exeter.

Becker, W. A. (1877–8) *Charikles*, new edn by H. Göll, Berlin.

Bedigian, D. and Harlan, J. R. (1986) 'Evidence for cultivation of sesame in the ancient world' in *Economic botany*, vol. 40, pp. 137–54.

Benndorf, O. (1893) *Altgriechisches Brot*, Vienna.

Bergquist, B. (1990) 'Sympotic space: a functional aspect of Greek dining-rooms' in *Sympotica: a symposium on the symposion*, ed., O. Murray, Oxford, pp. 37–65.

Bernad Aramayo, A. A. (1977) 'Las alubias en las culturas mediterráneas. Su expansión' in *Durius*, vol. 5, pp. 225–37.

Bernal, M. (1987– ) *Black Athena: the Afroasiatic roots of classical civilization*, London.

Berthiaume, G. (1982) *Les rôles du mágeiros: étude sur la boucherie, la cuisine et le sacrifice dans la Grèce ancienne*, Leiden.

Bertier, J. (1972) *Mnésithée et Dieuchès*, Leiden.

Besnier, M. (1904) 'Olea, oleum' in *Dictionnaire des antiquités grecques et romaines*, eds, C. Daremberg and E. Saglio (1877–1919) Paris.

—— (1909) 'Sal' and 'Salsamentum' in *Dictionnaire des antiquités grecques et romaines*, eds, C. Daremberg and E. Saglio (1877–1919) Paris.

Bettini, M. (1979) *Studi e noti sul Ennio*, Pisa.

Bilabel, F. (1920) *Opsartytiká und Verwandtes* (*Sitzungsberichte der Heidelberger Akademie der Wissenschaften, Stiftung Heinrich Lanz. Philosophisch-historische Klasse*, 1919, no. 23; *Mitteilungen aus der Heidelberger Papyrussammlung*, no. 1) Heidelberg.

—— (1921) 'Kochbücher' in *Paulys Real-Encyklopädie der classischen Altertumswissenschaft*, new edn by G. Wissowa *et al.* (1893–1972) Stuttgart.

Billiard, R. (1913) *La vigne et le vin dans l'antiquité*, Lyons.

Bisel, S. C. and Angel, J. L. (1985) 'Health and nutrition in Mycenaean Greece: a study in human skeletal remains' in *Contributions to Aegean archaeology: studies in honor of William A. McDonald*, eds, N. C. Wilkie and W. D. E. Coulson, Minneapolis.

Boardman, J. (1975) *Athenian red figure vases: the archaic period*, London.

—— (1976) 'The olive in the Mediterranean: its culture and use' in *The early history of agriculture*, eds, J. Hutchinson *et al.* (*Philosophical transactions of the Royal Society of London. B*, 275) , London, pp. 187–96.

Boardman, J. and Vaphopoulou-Richardson, C. E. (eds), (1986) *Chios*, Oxford.

Bodson, L. (1977) 'Le mouton dans l'antiquité gréco-romaine' in *Ethnozootechnie*, vol. 21, pp. 107–21.

—— (1978) 'Données antiques de zoogéographie. L'expansion des léporidés dans la Méditerranée classique' in *Les naturalistes belges*, vol. 59, pp. 66–81.

Boessneck, J. (1962) 'Die Tierreste aus der Argissa-Magula vom präkeramischen Neolithikum bis zur mittleren Bronzezeit' in V. Milojcic *et al.*, *Die deutschen Ausgrabungen auf der Argissa-Magula in Thessalien*, Bonn, pp. 27–100.

Boessneck, J. and von den Driesch, A. (1981–3) 'Reste exotischer Tiere aus dem Heraion auf Samos' in *Mitteilungen des Deutschen Archäologischen Instituts: Athenische Abteilung*, vols 96 (1981) and 98 (1983) .

Bökönyi, S. (1974) *History of domestic mammals in central and eastern Europe*, Budapest.

Bolens, L. (1987) 'Le haricot vert en Andalousie et en Méditerranée médiévale' in *Al-Qantara*, vol. 8, pp. 65–86. Reprinted in L. Bolens (1990) *L'Andalousie du quotidien au sacré*, Aldershot.

Bommer, S. and Bommer-Lotzin, L. (1961) *Die Gabe der Demeter*, Krailling bei München. Second edition of S. and L. Bommer (1943) *Die Ernährung der Griechen und Römer*, Planegg.

Bon, A.-M. and A. (1957) *Les timbres amphoriques de Thasos* (*Etudes thasiennes*, 4) Paris.

Börker, C. (1983) *Festbankett und griechische Architektur* (*Xenia*, 4) Constance.

Borza, E. N. (1982) 'The natural resources of early Macedonia' in *Philip II, Alexander the Great and the Macedonian heritage*, eds, W. L. Adams and E. N. Borza, Lanham, Maryland, pp. 1–20.

—— (1983) 'The symposium at Alexander's court' in *Arkhea Makedhonia* = *Ancient Macedonia III*, Thessalonica, pp. 45–55.

Boscherini, S. (1959) 'Grecismi nel libro di Catone de agric.' in *Atene e Roma*, vol. 4, pp. 153ff.

Bottéro, J. (1985) 'The cuisine of ancient Mesopotamia' in *Biblical archaeologist*, vol. 48, pp. 36–47.

Bowra, C. M. (1953) 'Xenophanes on songs at feasts' in his *Problems in Greek poetry*, Oxford, pp. 1–14.

Brandt, E. (1927) *Untersuchungen zum römischen Kochbuche* (*Philologus. Supplementband*, 19, no. 3) Leipzig.

Brandt, P. (ed.) (1888) *Corpusculum poesis epicae Graecae ludibundae*, Vol. 1, Leipzig.

Braudel, F. (1966–7) *La Méditerranée et le monde méditerranéenne à l'époque de Philippe II*, 2nd edn, Paris. Available in English: (1973) *The Mediterranean and the Mediterranean world in the age of Philip II*, London.

Braun, T. (1995) 'Barley cakes and emmer bread' in *Food in antiquity*, eds, J. Wilkins *et al.*, Exeter.

Braund, D. (1995) 'Fish from the Black Sea: classical Byzantium and the Greekness of trade' in *Food in antiquity*, eds, J. Wilkins *et al.*, Exeter.

Bravo, B. (1974) 'Une lettre sur plomb de Berezan: colonisation et modes de contact dans le Pont' in *Dialogues d'histoire ancienne* vol. 1 (*Annales littéraires de l'Université de Besançon*, (166) Paris, pp. 110–87.

Brazda, M. K. (1977) *Zur Bedeutung des Apfels in der antiken Kultur*, Bonn. Dissertation.

Bretzl, H. (1903) *Botanische Forschungen des Alexanderzuges*, Leipzig.

Browning, R. (1989) 'Theodore Balsamon's commentary on the canons of the Council in Trullo as a source on everyday life in twelfth-century Byzantium' in *I kathimerini zoi sto Vizantio*, ed., Kh. G. Angelidis, Athens, pp. 421–7.

Bruit, L. (1990) 'The meal at the Hyakinthia: ritual consumption and offering' in *Sympotica: a symposium on the symposion*, ed., O. Murray, Oxford, pp. 162–74.

—— (1995) 'Priestly eating in ancient Greece: parasites and paredroi. An aspect of the ritual consumption of food' in *Food in antiquity*, eds, J.Wilkins *et al.*, Exeter.

Brunet, F. (trans.) (1933–7) *Oeuvres médicales d'Alexandre de Tralles*, Paris.

Bryer, A. A. M. (1979) 'The estates of the empire of Trebizond' in *Arkhion Pontou*, vol. 35, pp. 370–477. Reprinted in A. A. M. Bryer (1980) *The empire of Trebizond and the Pontos*, London.

—— (1985) 'Byzantine porridge' in *Studies in medieval history presented to R. H. C. Davis*, eds, H. Mayr-Harting and R. I. Moore, London, pp. 1–6. Reprinted in A. A. M. Bryer (1988) *Peoples and settlement in Anatolia and the Caucasus*, London.

—— (1995) in *Food in antiquity*, eds, J. Wilkins *et al.*, Exeter.

Buchheit, V. (1960) 'Feigensymbolik im antiken Epigramm' in *Rheinisches Museum*, vol. 103, pp. 200–29.

Buchholz, H.-G. *et al.* (1973) *Jagd und Fischfang* (*Archaeologia Homerica*, 2, chapter J) Göttingen.

Burkert, W. (1966) 'Greek tragedy and sacrificial ritual' in *Greek, Roman and Byzantine studies*, vol. 7, pp. 87–121.

—— (1983) *Homo necans: the anthropology of ancient Greek sacrificial ritual and myth*, Berkeley.

Byrd, A. (1989) 'The Natufian: settlement variability and economic adaptations in the Levant at the end of the Pleistocene' in *Journal of world prehistory*, vol. 3, pp. 159–97.

Campbell, J. K. (1964) *Honour, family and patronage*, Oxford.

Candolle, A. de (1883) *Origine des plantes cultivées*, Paris. Available in English translation: (1886) *Origin of cultivated plants*, London.

Capelle, W. (1954) 'Der Garten des Theophrast' in *Festschrift F. Zucker*, pp. 45–82.

Carroll-Spillecke, M. (1990) *Kepos. Der antike griechische Garten*, Munich.

Casabona, J. (1966) *Recherches sur le vocabulaire des sacrifices en grec*, Aix-en-Provence.

Casaubon, I. (ed.) (1597) Athenaeus, Heidelberg.

—— (1600) *Animadversiones in Athenaei Deipnosophistas*, Lyon.

Casella, D. (1950) 'La frutta nelle pitture pompeiane' in *Pompeiana*, Naples.

Casson, L. (1984) *Ancient trade and society*, Detroit. Includes 'Cinnamon and cassia in the ancient world', pp. 225–46.

—— (trans.) (1989) *The Periplus of the Erythraean Sea*, Princeton.
Casteel, R. (1976) *Fish remains in archaeology and paleo-environmental studies*, London.
Caujolle-Zaslawsky, F. (1989) 'Athenaios de Naucratis' in *Dictionnaire des philosophes antiques*, ed., R. Goulet, Paris, Vol. 1, pp. 644–8.
Cekalova, A. (1989) *Vizantija: byt i nravy*, Sverdlovsk.
Cerny, J. (1965) *Tutankhamun tomb series*, Vol. 2, Oxford.
Chadwick, J. and Baumbach, L. (1963 and 1971) 'The Mycenaean Greek vocabulary' in *Glotta*, vol. 41 (1963) pp. 157–271; vol. 49 (1971) pp. 151–90.
Chamoux, F. (1953) *Cyrène sous la monarchie des Battiades*, Paris.
—— (1985) 'Du silphion' in *Cyrenaica in antiquity*, eds, G. Barker *et al.*, Oxford.
Chang, K. C. (ed.) (1977) *Food in Chinese culture*, New Haven.
Chapot, V. (1916) 'Vinum' in *Dictionnaire des antiquités grecques et romaines*, eds, C. Daremberg and E. Saglio (1877–1919) Paris.
Charles, M. P. (1987) 'Onions, cucumbers and the date palm' in *Bulletin on Sumerian agriculture*, no. 3, pp. 1–21.
Chase, H. (1993a) 'Scents and sensibility' in *Spicing up the palate: proceedings of the Oxford Symposium on Food and Cookery 1992*, Totnes pp. 56–63.
—— (1993b) 'Suspect salep'. Conference preprint: 'Look and feel, Oxford Symposium on Food and Cookery 1993'.
Clark, C. and Haswell, M. (1970) *The economics of subsistence agriculture*, 4th edn, London.
Cobet, C. G. (1847) *Oratio de arte interpretandi grammatices et critices fundamentis innixa primario philologi officio*, Leiden.
Collard, C. (1969) 'Athenaeus, the Epitome, Eustathius and quotations from tragedy' in *Rivista di filologia e di istruzione classica*, vol. 97, pp. 157–79.
Cooper, F. and Morris, S. (1990) 'Dining in round buildings' in *Sympotica: a symposium on the symposion*, ed., O. Murray, Oxford, pp. 66–85.
Corrieri, A. M. (1978–9) in *Museum criticum*, vol. 13–14, pp. 241, 273–87.
Cotte, H. J. (1944) *Poissons et animaux marins au temps de Pline*, Gap.
Cramer, J. A. (ed.) (1835–7) *Anecdota Graeca e codicibus manuscriptis bibliothecarum Oxoniensium*, Oxford.
Crane, E. (1983) *The archaeology of beekeeping*, London.
Crawford, D. J. (1973a) 'Garlic-growing and agricultural specialization in Graeco-Roman Egypt' in *Chronique d'Egypte*, vol. 48, no. 2, pp. 350–63.
—— (1973b) 'The opium poppy: a study in Ptolemaic agriculture' in *Problèmes de la terre en Grèce ancienne*, ed., M. I. Finley, The Hague, pp. 223–51.
—— (1979) 'Food: tradition and change in Hellenistic Egypt' in *World archaeology*, vol. 11, no. 2, pp. 136–46.
Cullen, T. (1984) 'Social implications of ceramic style in the neolithic Peloponnese' in *Ancient technology and modern science*, ed., W. D. Kingery, Columbus, OH, pp. 77–100.
Curtis, R. I. (1991) *Garum and salsamenta: production and commerce in materia medica*, Leiden.
Dalby, A. (trans.) (1987) 'The Banquet of Philoxenus' in *Petits propos culinaires*, no. 26, pp. 28–36.
—— (trans.) (1988) Hippolochus, 'The wedding feast of Caranus the Macedonian' in *Petits propos culinaires*, no. 29, pp. 37–45.
—— (1989) 'On thria' in *Petits propos culinaires*, no. 31 (March) , pp. 56–7.
—— (1990) 'In search of the staple foods of prehistoric and classical Greece' in *Oxford Symposium on Food and Cookery 1989: Staple Foods. Proceedings*, London, pp. 5–23.

—— (1991) 'The curriculum vitae of Duris of Samos' in *Classical quarterly*, n.s., vol. 41, pp. 539–41.

—— (1992) 'Greeks abroad: social organization and food among the Ten Thousand' in *Journal of Hellenic studies*, vol. 112, pp. 16–30.

—— (1993a) 'Food and sexuality in classical Greece' in *Food, culture and history*, vol. 1.

—— (1993b) 'Silphium and asafoetida: evidence from Greek and Roman writers' in *Spicing up the palate: proceedings of the Oxford Symposium on Food and Cookery 1992*, Totnes, pp. 67–72.

—— (1995) 'Archestratus: where and when?' in *Food in antiquity*, eds, J. Wilkins *et al.*, Exeter.

—— (forthcoming (a) 1995) 'The *Iliad*, the *Odyssey* and their audiences' in *Classical Quarterly* (December) .

—— (forthcoming (b)) 'Vintages of Laconia'.

Dalby, L. (1983) *Geisha*, Berkeley.

Darby, W. J. *et al.* (1977) *Food: gift of Osiris*, London.

Daremberg, C. and Saglio, E. (eds) (1877–1919) *Dictionnaire des antiquités grecques et romaines*, Paris.

Darmstädter, E. (1933) 'Ptisana' in *Archeion*, vol. 15, pp. 181–201.

Davidson, A. (1981) *Mediterranean seafood*, 2nd edn, Harmondsworth.

Davidson, J. (1993) 'Fish, sex and revolution at Athens' in *Classical quarterly*, vol. 43, pp. 53–66.

—— (1995) 'Opsophagia: revolutionary eating at Athens' in *Food in antiquity*, eds, J. Wilkins *et al.*, Exeter.

Davies, M. (ed.) (1991– ) *Poetarum melicorum Graecorum fragmenta*, Oxford.

Davies, M. and Kathirithamby, J. (1986) *Greek insects*, London.

Davis, E. M. (1981) 'Palaeoecological studies at Stobi' in *Studies in the antiquities of Stobi*, vol. 3, eds, B. Aleksova and J. Wiseman, Belgrade, pp. 87–94.

Davis, P. H. (ed.) (1965–85) *Flora of Turkey and the East Aegean Islands*, Edinburgh.

De Laet, S. J. (ed.) (1994) *History of humanity*, Vol. 1, Paris.

De Sinner, G. R. L. (ed.) (1824) *Christophori Buondelmontii librum insularum Archipelagi*, Leipzig.

Defradas, J. (1962) 'Le banquet de Xénophane' in *Revue des études grecques*, vol. 75, pp. 344–65.

Degani, E. (1982) 'Appunti di poesia gastronomica greca' in *Prosimetrum e spoudogeloion (Pubblicazioni dell' Instituto di Filologia Classica e Medievale*, 78) , Genoa, pp. 29–54.

—— (1995) 'Problems in Greek gastronomic poetry: on Matro's *Attikon Deipnon*' in *Food in antiquity*, eds, J. Wilkins *et al.*, Exeter.

Delatte, A. (1930) 'Faba Pythagorae cognota' in *Serta Leodiensia*, Liège, pp. 33–57.

Delorme, J. and Roux, Ch. (1987) *Guide illustré de la faune aquatique dans l'art grec*, Juan-les-Pins.

Dembinska, M. (1985–6) 'Diet: a comparison of food consumption between some Eastern and Western monasteries in the 4th-12th c.' in *Byzantion*, vol. 55, pp. 431–62.

—— (1988) 'Methods of meat and fish preservation in the light of archaeological and historical sources' in *Food conservation*, eds, A. Riddervold and A. Ropeid, London, pp. 13–24.

Dennell, R. W. (1978) *Early farming in south Bulgaria from the 6. to the 3. millennia BC*, Oxford.

Dentzer, J.-M. (1969) 'Reliefs au banquet dans l'Asie Mineure du Ve siècle avant J.-C.' in *Revue archéologique*, pp. 195–224.

—— (1970) 'Un nouveau relief du Pirée et le type du banquet attique au Ve siècle avant J.-C.' in *Bulletin de correspondance hellénique*, vol. 94, pp. 67–90.

—— (1971a) 'Aux origines de l'iconographie du banquet couché' in *Revue archéologique*, pp. 215–58.

—— (1971b) 'L'iconographie iranienne du souverain couché' in *Annales archéologiques arabes syriennes*, vol. 21, pp. 39–50.

—— (1982) *Le motif du banquet couché dans le Proche-Orient et le monde grec du VIIe au IVe siècle avant J.-C.*, Rome.

Deonna, W. (1948) *La vie privée des Déliens*, Paris.

Desrousseaux, A. M. (ed.) (1956) Athénée de Naucratis, *Les deipnosophistes. Livres I et II*, Paris.

Detienne, M. and Vernant, J.-P. (eds) (1979) *La cuisine du sacrifice en pays grec*, Paris. Available in English: (1989) *The cuisine of sacrifice among the Greeks*, trans. Paula Wissing, Chicago.

Dickson, J. H. (1978) 'Bronze age mead' in *Antiquity*, vol. 205, pp. 108–13.

Diels, H. (ed.) (1951–2) *Die Fragmente der Vorsokratiker*, 6th edn, Berlin.

Diethart, J. and Kislinger, E. (1992) 'Aprikosen und Pflaumen' in *Jahrbuch der österreichischer Byzantinistik*, vol. 42, pp. 75–8.

Dindorf, W. (1870) 'Ueber die venetianische handschrift des Athenaeus und deren abschriften' in *Philologus*, vol. 30, pp. 73–115.

Dobrée, P. P. (1831–3) *Adversaria*, ed., J. Scholefield, Cambridge.

Dodwell, E. (1819) *A classical and topographical tour through Greece*, London.

Dohm, H. (1964) *Mageiros*, Munich.

Dölger, F. (1922–43) *Ikhthys: das Fisch-Symbol in frühchristlicher Zeit*, Munich.

Doumas, C. (ed.) (1978–80) *Thera and the Aegean world. Papers presented at the Second International Scientific Congress, Santorini, August 1978*, London.

—— (1983) *Thera: Pompeii of the ancient Aegean. Excavations at Akrotiri 1967–79*, London.

Drews, R. (1988) *The coming of the Greeks*, Princeton.

du Cange, C. du Fresne, sieur, (1678) *Glossarium ad scriptores mediae et infimae Latinitatis*, Paris.

—— (1688) *Glossarium ad scriptores mediae et infimae Graecitatis*, Lyon.

Dumont, J. (1976–7) 'La pêche du thon à Byzance à l'époque hellénistique' in *Revue des études anciennes*, vol. 78–9, pp. 96–119.

Dunbabin, K. M. D. (1991) 'Triclinium and stibadium' in *Dining in a classical context*, ed., W. J. Slater, Ann Arbor, pp. 121–48.

Düring, I. (1936) 'De Athenaei Deipnosophistarum indole atque dispositione' in *Apophoreta Gotoburgensia Vilelmo Lundström oblata*, Göteborg, pp. 236ff.

Eideneier, H. (1970) 'Zu krasin' in *Hellenika*, vol. 23, pp. 118–22.

Empereur, J.-Y. and Garlan, Y. (eds) (1986) *Recherches sur les amphores grecques*, (*Bulletin de correspondance hellénique*, supplement 13) Athens.

Engemann, J. (1968) 'Fisch, Fischer, Fischfang' in *Reallexikon für Antike und Christentum*, ed., T. Klauser (1950– ) Stuttgart.

—— (1983) 'Granatapfel' in *Reallexikon für Antike und Christentum*, ed. J. Klauser (1950– ) Stuttgart.

Erbse, H. (1950) *Untersuchungen zu den attizistischen Lexika*, Berlin.

Facciola, S. (1990) *Cornucopia*, Vista, CA.

Farmayan, H. and Daniel, E. L. (trans.) (1990) *A Shi'ite pilgrimage to Mecca: the Safarnâmeh of Mirzâ Mohammad Hosayn Farâhâni*, Austin.

Fehr, B. (1971) *Orientalische und griechische Gelage*, Bonn.

—— (1990) 'Entertainers at the symposium: the akletoi in the archaic period' in *Sympotica: a symposium on the symposion*, ed., O. Murray, pp. 185–95.

Fehrle, E. (1920) *Richtlinien zur Textgestaltung der griechischen Geoponica*, Heidelberg.

Figueira, T. J. (1984) 'Mess contributions and subsistence at Sparta' in *Transactions of the American Philological Association*, vol. 114, pp. 87–109.

Finet, A. (1974–7) 'Le vin à Mari' in *Archiv für Orientforschung*, vol. 25, pp. 122–31.

Follieri, M. (1986) 'Provviste alimentari vegetali in una casa minoica ad Haghia Triada' in *Annuario della Scuola Archeologica di Atene*, vol. 57–8, pp. 165–72.

Folsom, R. S. (1976) *Attic red-figured pottery*, Park Ridge, NJ.

Foucher, L. (1970) 'Note sur l'industrie et le commerce des salsamenta et du garum' in *Actes du 93e Congrès National des Sociétés Savantes, Tours 1968, section d'archéologie*, Paris, pp. 17–21.

Fouqué, F. (1879) *Santorin et ses éruptions*, Paris.

Fournier, E. (1882) 'Cibaria' in *Dictionnaire des antiquités grecques et romaines*, eds, C. Daremberg and E. Saglio (1877–1919) Paris.

Foxhall, L. and Forbes, H. A. (1982) 'Sitometreía: the role of grain as a staple food in classical antiquity' in *Chiron*, vol. 12, pp. 41–90.

Fraenkel, E. (ed.) (1950) Aeschylus, *Agamemnon*, Oxford.

Frayn, J. M. (1979) *Subsistence farming in Roman Italy*, London.

—— (1993) *Markets and fairs in Roman Italy*, Oxford.

Freshfield, E. H. (1938) 'Ordinances of Leo VI (c. 895) from the Book of the Eparch' in his *Roman law in the later Roman Empire*, Cambridge. Reprinted in *To eparkhikon vivlion = The Book of the Eparch = Le livre du préfet*, ed., I. Dujcev (1970) London.

Frickenhaus, A. (1917) 'Griechische Banketthäuser' in *Jahrbuch des Deutschen Archäologischen Institut*, vol. 32, pp. 114–33.

Gallant, T. W. (1985) *A fisherman's tale: an analysis of the potential productivity of fishing in the ancient world*, Gent.

Gallardo, M. D. (1972) 'Los simposios de Luciano, Ateneo, Metodio y Juliano' in *Cuadernos de filología clásica*, vol. 4, pp. 239–96.

Gallo, L. (1989) 'Alimentazione urbana e alimentazione contadina nell' Atene classica' in *Homo edens: regime, rite e pratiche dell'alimentazione nella civittà del Mediterraneo*, eds, O. Longo and P. Scarpi, Verona, pp. 213–30.

Gamble, C. (1986) *The palaeolithic settlement of Europe*, Cambridge.

Garnsey, P. (1988) *Famine and food supply in the Graeco-Roman world*, Cambridge.

Garzya, A. (1963) in *Byzantinische Zeitschrift*, vol. 56, p. 233.

Gelber, J. (1993) 'Bread and beer in fourth millennium Egypt' in *Food and foodways*, vol. 5, no. 3, pp. 255 ff.

Gemoll, W. (1884) *Untersuchungen über die Quellen, der Verfasser und die Abfassungszeit der Geoponica*, Berlin.

Georgiou, H. (1973) 'Aromatics in antiquity and in Minoan Crete: a review and reassessment' in *Kritika khronika*, vol. 25, pp. 441–56 and plates 18–19.

Georgoudi, S. (1974) 'Quelques problèmes de la transhumance dans la Grèce ancienne' in *Revue des études grecques*, vol. 87, pp. 155–85.

Gill, M. A. V. (1985) 'Some observations on representations of marine animals in Minoan art' in *L'iconographie minoenne: actes de la table ronde d'Athènes, 21–22 avril 1983*, eds, P. Darcque and J.-C. Poursat (*Bulletin de correspondance hellénique*, supplement 11) Paris.

Gomme, A. W. and Sandbach, F. W. (1973) *Menander: a commentary*, Oxford.

Goujard, R. (ed. and trans.) (1975) Caton, *De l'agriculture*, Paris.

Gow, A. S. F. (ed.) (1952) Theocritus, Cambridge.

—— (ed.) (1965) Machon, Cambridge.

Gow, A. S. F. and Page, D. L. (eds and trans.) (1968) *The Greek anthology: the Garland of Philip*, Cambridge.

Gow, A. S. F. and Scholfield, A. F. (eds) (1953) Nicander, Cambridge.

Gowers, E. (1993) *The loaded table*, Oxford.

Grant, M. (1995) 'Oribasius and medical dietetics or the three Ps' in *Food in antiquity*, eds, J. Wilkins *et al.*, Exeter.

Greenewalt, C. H. (1976) *Ritual dinners in early historic Sardis*, Berkeley.

Grieve, M. (1931) *A modern herbal*, London.

Grimal, P. and Monod, T. (1952) 'Sur la véritable nature du garum' in *Revue des études anciennes*, vol. 54, pp. 27–38.

Gulick, C. B. (ed. and trans.) (1927–41) Athenaeus, *The deipnosophists*, 7 vols, Cambridge, Mass.

Gunda, B. (1968) 'Bee-hunting in the Carpathian area' in *Acta ethnographica Hungariae*, vol. 17, pp. 1–62.

—— (1983) 'Cultural ecology of old cultivated plants in the Carpathian area' in *Ethnologia Europaea*, vol. 13, no. 2, pp. 146–79.

Hadjisavvas, S. (1992) *Olive oil processing in Cyprus*, Nicosia.

Halici, F. (ed.) (1988) *Birinci milletlerarasi yemek kongresi = First international food congress, Turkey, 25–30 September 1986*, Ankara.

Halstead, P. and Jones, G. (1980) 'Early economy in Thessaly' in *Anthropologika*, vol. 1, pp. 93–117.

Hammer, Ritter J. von (trans.) (1834–50) Evliya Efendi, *Narrative of travels in Europe, Asia and Africa in the seventeenth century*, Vols 1–2i, London.

Hammond, N. G. L. (1976) *Migrations and invasions in Greece and adjacent areas*, Park Ridge, NJ.

Hanfmann, G. M. A. (ed.) (1983) *Sardis from prehistoric to Roman times*, Cambridge, Mass.

Hansen, J. M. (1988) 'Agriculture in the prehistoric Aegean: data versus speculation' in *American journal of archaeology*, vol. 92, pp. 39–52.

—— (1992) 'Franchthi Cave and the beginning of agriculture in Greece and the Aegean' in *Préhistoire de l'agriculture*, ed., P. C. Anderson-Gerfaud, Paris, pp. 231–47.

Harig, G. (1967) 'Von den arabischen Quellen des Symeon Seth' in *Medizinhistorisches Journal*, vol. 2, pp. 248–68.

Harris, D. R. and Hillman, G. C. (eds) (1989) *Foraging and farming: the evolution of plant exploitation*, London.

Harvey, D. (1995) 'Lydian specialities, Croesus' golden baking-woman, and dogs' dinners' in *Food in antiquity*, eds, J. Wilkins *et al.*, Exeter.

Hayley, H. W. (1894) 'The kóttabos kataktós in the light of recent investigations' in *Harvard studies in classical philology*, vol. 5, pp. 73–82.

Heichelheim, F. (1935) 'Sitos' in *Paulys Real-Encyklopädie der classischen Altertumswissenschaft*, supplement (1903– ) , Stuttgart, vol. 6, cols 819–92.

Heine, P. (1988) *Kulinarische Studien*, Wiesbaden.

Helbaek, H. (1961) 'The plant husbandry of Hacilar' in J. Mellaart, *Excavations in Hacilar*, vol. 1, Edinburgh, pp. 189–244.

Henderson, J. (1991) *The maculate muse*, 2nd edn, New York.

Henry, A. S. (1981) 'Invitations to the prytaneion at Athens' in *Antichthon*, vol. 15, pp. 100–10.

—— (1983) *Honours and privileges in Athenian decrees*, Hildesheim.

Henry, M. (1992) 'The edible woman: Athenaeus' concept of the pornographic' in *Pornography and representation in Greece and Rome*, ed., A. Richlin, New York.

Hepper, F. N. (1990) *Pharaoh's flowers*, London.

Herman, G. (1980–1) 'The "friends" of the early Hellenistic rulers: servants or officials?' in *Talanta*, vol. 12–13, pp. 103–49.

Hermann, K. F. and Blümner, H. (1882) *Lehrbuch der griechischen Privatalterthümer* (*K. F. Hermann's Lehrbuch der griechischen Antiquitäten*, 3rd edn, Vol. 4) Freiburg im Breisgau.

Herter, H. (1956) 'Das symposion des Xenophanes' in *Wiener Studien*, vol. 69, pp. 33–48.

Herzog-Hauser, G. (1932) 'Milch' in *Paulys Real-Encyklopädie der classischen Altertumswissenschaft*, new edn by G. Wissowa *et al.* (1893–1972) Stuttgart.

Heywood, V. H. (1983) 'Relationships and evolution in the Daucus carota complex' in *Israel journal of botany*, vol. 32, pp. 51–65.

Higgs, E. S. *et al.* (1967) 'The climate, environment and industries of stone age Greece, part 3' in *Proceedings of the Prehistoric Society*, n.s. vol. 33, pp. 1–30.

Hoffner, H. A. (1974) *Alimenta Hethaeorum*, New Haven.

Hondelmann, W. (1984) 'The lupin: ancient and modern crop plant' in *Theoretical and applied genetics*, vol. 68, pp. 1–9.

Hopf, M. (1962) 'Bericht über die Untersuchung von Samen und Holzkohlenesten von der Argissa-Magula aus den präkeramischen bis mittelbronzezeitlichen Schichten' in V. Milojcic *et al.*, *Die deutschen Ausgrabungen auf der Argissa-Magula in Thessalien*, Bonn.

—— (1964) 'Nutzpflanzen vom Lernäischen Golf' in *Jahrbuch des Römisch-Germanischen Zentralmuseums Mainz*, vol. 11, pp. 1–19.

Höppener, H. (1931) *Halieutica: bijdrage tot de kennis der oudgrieksche visscherij*, Amsterdam.

Hort, Sir Arthur (ed. and trans.) (1916–26) Theophrastus, *Enquiry into plants*, London.

Hostetter, E. (1994) *Lydian architectural terracottas*, Atlanta. Includes K. L. Gleason, 'Display garden: the plants of Lydia', pp. 79–87.

Houghton, W. (1885) 'Notices of fungi in Greek and Latin authors' in *Annals and magazine of natural history*, ser. 5, vol. 5, pp. 22–49.

How, W. W. and Wells, J. (1912) *A commentary on Herodotus*, Oxford.

Howes, F. N. (1950) 'Age old resins of the Mediterranean regions and their uses' in *Economic botany*, vol. 4, pp. 307–16.

Hunter R. L. (ed.) (1983) Eubulus, *The fragments*, Cambridge. The fragment numbering of *Comicorum Atticorum fragmenta*, ed., T. Kock (1880–8) Leipzig is retained.

Hyman, P. and M. (1980) 'Long pepper: a short history' in *Petits propos culinaires*, no. 6, pp. 50–2.

Ideler, I. L. (ed.) (1841–2) *Physici et medici graeci minores*, Berlin.

Isaac, B. (1986) *The Greek settlements in Thrace until the Macedonian conquest*, Leiden.

Isenberg, M. (1975) 'The sale of sacrificial meat' in *Classical philology*, vol. 70, pp. 271–3.

Jackson, P. (trans.) (1990) *The mission of Friar William of Rubruck*, London.

Jacobsen, T. W. (1984) 'Seasonal pastoralism in the neolithic of southern Greece' in *Pots and potters*, ed., P. M. Price, Los Angeles, pp. 27–43.

Jacobsen, T. W. and Farrand, W. R. (1987) *Franchthi Cave and Paralia: maps, plans and sections (Excavations at Franchthi Cave, Greece, 1)*, Bloomington.

Jacoby, F. (ed.) (1923–58) *F Gr Hist: die Fragmente der griechischen Historiker*, Berlin.

Jaeger, W. (1963) *Diokles von Karystos*, 2nd edn, Berlin.

Janko, R. (1981) 'Un 1314: herbal remedies at Pylos' in *Minos*, vol. 17, pp. 30–4.

Janushevich, Z. V. and Nikolaenko, G. M. (1979) 'Fossil remains of cultivated plants in the ancient Tauric Chersonesos' in *Festschrift Maria Hopf*, ed., U. Körber-Grohne, Cologne, pp. 115–34.

Jardé, A. (1925) *Les céréales dans l'antiquité grecque. Production*, Paris.

Jarman, M. R. and Jarman, H. N. (1968) 'The fauna and economy of early Neolithic Knossos' in *Annual of the British School at Athens*, vol. 63, pp. 241–64.

Jashemski, W. F. (1979–93) *The gardens of Pompeii, Herculaneum and the villas destroyed by Vesuvius*, New Rochelle, NY.

Jasny, N. (1944) *The wheats of classical antiquity*, Baltimore.

—— (1950) 'The daily bread of the ancient Greeks and Romans' in *Osiris*, vol. 9, pp. 227–53.

Jeanselme, E. (1922) 'Sels médicamenteux et aromates pris par les byzantins au cours des repas' in *Bulletin de la Société Française d'Histoire Médicale*, vol. 16, pp. 327ff.

—— (1924) 'Les calendriers de régime à l'usage des byzantins et la tradition hippocratique' in *Mélanges offerts à G. Schlumberger*, Paris, pp. 217–33.

Jeanselme, E. and Oeconomos, L. (1923) 'Aliments et recettes culinaires des byzantins' in *Proceedings of the 3rd International Congress of the History of Medicine*, Antwerp, pp. 155–68.

Johnson, M. (1981) 'North Balkan food, past and present' in *Oxford Symposium 1981: national and regional styles of cookery. Proceedings*, London, pp. 122–33.

Joly, R. (1961) *Recherches sur le traité pseudo-hippocratique Du régime*, Paris.

Jones, H. L. (ed. and trans.) (1917–32) *The Geography of Strabo*, Cambridge, Mass.

Jones, W. H. S. (ed. and trans.) (1980) Pliny, *Natural History books XXIV–XXVII*, 2nd edn, Cambridge, Mass. Includes 'Index of plants' revised by A. C. Andrews.

Jouanna, J. (1992) *Hippocrate*, Paris.

Kahane, H., Kahane, R, and Tietze, A. (1958) *The lingua franca in the Levant*, Urbana.

Kaibel, G. (1883) *De Athenaei epitome*, Rostock.

—— (ed.) (1887–90) *Athenaei Naucratitae Deipnosophistarum libros XV*, 3 Vols, Leipzig.

—— (ed.) (1899) *Comicorum Graecorum fragmenta*, Vol. 1, pt 1: *Doriensium comoedia, mimi, phlyaces*, Berlin.

Kalças, E. L. (1974) *Food from the fields*, Smyrna.

Kalleris, I. (1953) ' "Trofe ke pota" is protovizandinous papirous' in *Epetiris Eterias Vizandinon Spoudhon*, vol. 23, pp. 689–715.

Karali-Yannakopoulos, L. (1989) 'Les mollusques de Porto-Lagos' in *Byzantinische Forschungen*, vol. 14, pp. 245–51.

Karpozelos, A. (1984) 'Realia in Byzantine epistolography, X–XII c.' in *Byzantinischer Zeitschrift*, vol. 77, pp. 20–37.

Kassel, R. and Austin, C. (eds) (1983– ) *P C G: Poetae comici Graeci*, Berlin.

Kazhdan, A. *et al.* (eds) (1991) *The Oxford dictionary of Byzantium*, New York. Includes articles on aspects of social history by A. Kazhdan, A. Karpozilos and others.

Keimer, L. (1924) *Die Gartenpflanzen im alten Aegypten*, Hamburg.

Kislev, M. E. (1992) 'Hunting songbirds as a branch of the economy' (in Hebrew) in *New discoveries in ancient agriculture and economy: the 12th congress*, ed., S. Dar, Ramat Gan, pp. 52–9.

Kislinger, E. (1984) 'Phoûska und glékhon' in *Jahrbuch der österreichischen Byzantinistik*, vol. 34, pp. 49–53.

Kock, Th. (ed.) (1880–8) *Comicorum Atticorum fragmenta*, Leipzig.

Kolias, T. (1984) 'Eßgewohnheiten und Verpflegung im byzantinischen Heer' in

*Byzantios. Festschrift für Herbert Hunger zum 70. Geburtstag*, eds, W. Hörandner *et al.*, Vienna, pp. 193–202.

Körte, A. (1927a) 'Lynkeus' in *Paulys Real-Encyklopädie der classischen Altertumswissenschaft*, new edn by G. Wissowa *et al.* (1893–1972) Stuttgart.

—— (1927b) *Aufbau und Ziel von Xenophons Symposion (Bericht über die Verhandlungen der Sächsischen Akademie der Wissenschaften, Philosophisch-historische Klasse*, vol. 79, no. 5) Leipzig.

Koukoulès, F. (1947–55) *Vizandinon vios ke politismos*, Athens.

Kritikos, P. G. and Papadaki, S. P. (1967) 'The history of the poppy and of opium and their expansion in antiquity in the eastern Mediterranean area' in *Bulletin on narcotics*, vol. 19, no. 3, pp. 17–38 and no. 4, pp. 5–10.

Kroll (1919) 'Käse' in *Paulys Real-Encyklopädie der classischen Altertumswissenschaft*, new edn by G. Wissowa *et al.* (1893–1972) Stuttgart.

Kroll, H. (1979) 'Kulturpflanzen aus Dimini' in *Festschrift Maria Hopf*, ed., U. Körber-Grohne, Cologne, pp. 173–89.

—— (1982) 'Kulturpflanzen von Tiryns' in *Archäologischer Anzeiger*, pp. 467–85.

—— (1984) 'Bronze age and iron age agriculture in Kastanas, Macedonia' in *Proceedings of the 6th Symposium of the International Work Group for Palaeoethnobotany, Groningen, 30 May–3 June 1983: plants and ancient man: studies in palaeoethnobotany*, eds, W. van Zeist and W. A. Casparie, Rotterdam, pp. 243–6.

—— (1991) 'Südosteuropa' in *Progress in old world palaeoethnobotany*, ed., W. van Zeist *et al.*, Rotterdam, pp. 179–87.

Krumbacher, K. (1903) 'Das mittelgriechische Fischbuch' in *Sitzungsberichte der philosophisch-historische Klasse der Bayerischen Akademie der Wissenschaften*, no. 3, pp. 345ff.

Kunisch, N. (1989) *Griechische Fischteller: Natur und Bild*, Berlin.

Lacroix, L. (1937) *La faune marine dans la décoration des plats à poissons: étude sur la céramique grecque d'Italie méridionale*, Verviers.

Lambert-Gócs, M. (1990) *The wines of Greece*, London.

Langkavel, B. (1868) *Simeonis Sethi syntagma de alimentorum facultatibus*, Leipzig.

Laufer, B. (1918) 'Malabathron' in *Journal asiatique*, 11th ser., vol. 12, pp. 5–49.

—— (1919) *Sino-Iranica: Chinese contributions to the history of civilization in ancient Iran with special reference to the history of cultivated plants and products (Field Museum of Natural History publication*, no. 201) Chicago.

Leo, F. (1912) *Plautinische Forschungen*, Berlin.

Leon, E. F. (1943) 'Cato's cakes' in *Classical journal*, vol. 38, pp. 216ff.

Lesko, L. H. (1977) *King Tut's wine cellar*, Berkeley.

Lewthwaite, J. (1981) 'Plains tails from the hills: transhumance in Mediterranean archaeology' in *Economic archaeology*, eds, A. Sheridan and G. F. Bailey, Oxford, pp. 57–66.

Liddell, H. G. and Scott, R. (1925–1940) *A Greek–English lexicon*, 9th edn, Oxford.

Limet, H. (1987) 'The cuisine of ancient Sumer' in *Biblical archaeologist*, vol. 50, pp. 132–47.

Lindsell, A. (1936–7) 'Was Theocritus a botanist?' in *Greece and Rome*, vol. 6, pp. 78–93.

Lisitsina, G. N. (1984) 'The Caucasus: a centre of ancient farming in Eurasia' in *Proceedings of the 6th Symposium of the International Work Group for Palaeoethnobotany, Groningen, 30 May–3 June 1983: plants and ancient man: studies in palaeoethnobotany*, eds, W. van Zeist and W. A. Casparie, Rotterdam, pp. 285–92.

Lissarrague, F. (1985) 'La libation: essai de mise au point' in *Image et rituel en Grèce ancienne (Recherches et documents du Centre Thomas More*, vol. 48) , pp. 3–16.

# BIBLIOGRAPHY

—— (1987) *Un flot d'images: une esthétique du banquet grec*, Paris.

Lloyd-Jones, H. and Parsons, P. (eds) (1983) *Supplementum Hellenisticum*, Berlin.

Lombardo, Mario (1995) 'Food and "frontier" in the Greek colonies of south Italy' in *Food in antiquity*, eds, J. Wilkins *et al.*, Exeter.

Long, T. (1986) *Barbarians in Greek comedy*, Carbondale.

Luss, A. I. (1931) 'Pomerantsevye Yaponii i sosednikh stran yugovostochnoi Azii' in *Bulletin of applied botany, genetics and plant breeding*, vol. 26, pp. 141–240.

Maas, P. (1952) 'Verschiedenes zu Eustathios' in *Byzantinische Zeitschrift*, vol. 45, pp. 1–3.

McCartney, E. (1934) 'The couch as a unit of measurement' in *Classical philology*, vol. 29, pp. 30–5.

McNeal, R. A. (ed.) (1993) *Nicholas Biddle in Greece: the journals and letters*, University Park, Pa.

McPhee, I. and Trendall, A. D. (1987) *Greek red-figured fish-plates* (*Antike Kunst. Beiheft* 14) Basel.

—— (1990) 'Addenda to *Greek red-figured fish-plates*' in *Antike Kunst*, vol. 33, pp. 31–51.

Maggiulli, G. (1977) *Nomenclatura micologica latina*, Genoa.

Magoulias, H. J. (1971) 'Bathhouse, inn, tavern, prostitution and the stage as seen in the Lives of the Saints of the sixth and seventh centuries' in *Epetiris Eterias Vizandinon Spoudhon*, vol. 38, pp. 233–52.

—— (1976) 'Trades and crafts in the sixth and seventh centuries as viewed in the Lives of the Saints' in *Byzantinoslavica*, vol. 37, pp. 11–35.

Mallory, J. P. (1989) *In search of the Indo-Europeans: language, archaeology and myth*, London.

Marinatos, N. (1985) 'The function and interpretation of the Theran frescoes' in *L'iconographie minoenne: actes de la table ronde d'Athènes, 21–22 avril 1983*, eds, P. Darcque and J.-C. Poursat (*Bulletin de correspondance hellénique*, supplement 11) Athens.

Martin, J. (1931) *Symposion*, Paderborn.

Mason, I. L. (ed.) (1984) *Evolution of domesticated animals*, London.

Mason, S. (1995) 'Acornutopia?' in *Food in antiquity*, eds, J. Wilkins *et al.*, Exeter.

Mayer, F. G. (1980) 'Carbonised food plants of Pompeii, Herculaneum and the villa at Torre Annunziata' in *Economic botany*, vol. 34, pp. 401–37.

Meineke, A. (ed.) (1858–67) *Athenaei Deipnosophistae*, Leipzig.

Melena, J. L. (1976) 'La producción de plantas aromáticas en Cnoso' in *Estudios clasicos*, vol. 20, pp. 177–90.

—— (1983) 'Olive oil and other sorts of oil in the Mycenaean tablets' in *Minos*, vol. 18, pp. 82–123.

Mengis, K. (1920) *Die schriftstellerische Technik im Sophistenmahl des Athenaios*, Paderborn.

Merlin, M. D. (1984) *On the trail of the ancient opium poppy*, Rutherford, NJ.

Meyer, E. (1974) 'Pramnios, Pramnos, Prámneios oînos' in *Paulys Real-Encyklopädie der classischen Altertumswissenschaft*, supplement (1903– ) Stuttgart, vol. 14.

Meyer, F. G. (1989) 'Food plants identified from carbonized remains at Pompeii and other Vesuvian sites' in *Studia pompeina et classica in honor of Wilhelmina F. Jashemski*, ed. R. I. Curtis, New Rochelle, NY, vol. 1, pp.183–229.

Meyer-Lübke, W. (1911) *Romanisches etymologisches Wörterbuch*, Heidelberg.

Miha-Lambaki, A. (1984) *I dhiatrofi ton arkheon Elinon kata tus arkheous komodhiografus*, Athens. Dissertation.

Miller, J. I. (1969) *The spice trade of the Roman Empire*, Oxford.

Miller, S. G. (1978) *The prytaneion: its function and architectural form*, Berkeley.

Minchin, E. (1987) 'Food fiction and food fact in Homer's Iliad' in *Petits propos culinaires*, no. 25, pp. 42–9.

Moritz, L. A. (1958) *Grain-mills and flour in classical antiquity*, Oxford.

Müller, C. (ed. and trans.) (1855) *Geographi graeci minores*, Paris.

*Multilingual dictionary of fish and fish products* =*Dictionnaire multilingue des poissons et produits de la pêche* (1978) prepared by the Organisation for Economic Co-operation and Development, 2nd edn, Farnham.

Murray, O. (1980) *Early Greece*, London.

—— (1982) 'Symposion and Männerbund' in *Concilium Eirene*, vol. 16, part 1, pp. 47–52.

—— (1983) 'The symposion as social organisation' in *The Greek renaissance of the eighth century B.C. Tradition and innovation*, ed., R. Hägg (*Skrifter utgivna av Svenska Institutet i Athen*, vol. 30), pp. 195–9.

—— (ed.) (1990) *Sympotica: a symposium on the symposion*, Oxford. Includes his 'Sympotic history', pp. 3–13.

Musurus, Marcus (ed.) (1514) Athenaeus, Venice.

Nafissi, M. (1991) *La nascita del kosmos: studi sulla storia e la società di Sparta*, Naples.

Nenquin, J. (1961) *Salt*, Bruges.

Nesselrath, H.-G. (1985) *Lukians Parasitendialog: Untersuchungen und Kommentar*, Berlin.

—— (1990) *Die attische mittlere Komödie*, Berlin.

Newett, M. M. (trans.) (1907) *Canon Pietro Casola's pilgrimage to Jerusalem in the year 1494*, Manchester.

Nutton, V. (ed.) (1981) *Galen: problems and prospects. A collection of papers submitted at the 1979 Cambridge conference*, London.

—— (1995) 'Galen and the traveller's fare' in *Food in antiquity*, eds, J. Wilkins *et al.*, Exeter.

Nyikos, L. (1941) *Athenaeus quo consilio quibusque usus subsidiis Dipnosophistarum libros composuerit*, Basle. Dissertation. Review in: (1943) *Philologische Wochenschrift*, pp. 169–73.

Oder, E. (1890–3) 'Beiträge zur Geschichte der Landwirthschaft bei den Griechen' in *Rheinisches Museum*, vol. 45 (1890) pp. 58–98, 212–22; vol. 48 (1893) pp. 1–40.

Oeconomos, L. (1950) 'Le calendrier de régime d'Hiérophile d'après des manuscrits plus complets que le Parisinus 396' in *Actes du VIe Congrès International d'Etudes Byzantines, Paris, 1948*, Paris, Vol. 1, pp. 169–79.

Olck, F. (1894) 'Apfel' in *Paulys Real-Encyklopädie der classischen Altertumswissenschaft*, new edn by G. Wissowa *et al.* (1893–1972) Stuttgart.

—— (1909) 'Feige' in *Paulys Real-Encyklopädie der classischen Altertumswissenschaft*, new edn by G. Wissowa *et al.* (1893–1972) Stuttgart.

—— (1912) 'Gartenbau' in *Paulys Real-Encyklopädie der classischen Altertumswissenschaft*, new edn by G. Wissowa *et al.* (1893–1972) Stuttgart.

Orth, (1921a) 'Kochkunst' in *Paulys Real-Encyklopädie der classischen Altertumswissenschaft*, new edn by G. Wissowa *et al.* (1893–1972) Stuttgart.

—— (1921b) 'Schaf' in *Paulys Real-Encyklopädie der classischen Altertumswissenschaft*, new edn by G. Wissowa *et al.* (1893–1972) Stuttgart.

—— (1922) 'Kuchen' in *Paulys Real-Encyklopädie der classischen Altertumswissenschaft*, new edn by G. Wissowa *et al.* (1893–1972) Stuttgart.

Osborne, M. J. (1981) 'Entertainment in the prytaneion at Athens' in *Zeitschrift für Papyrologie und Epigraphik*, vol. 41, pp. 153–70.

Osborne, R. (1987) *Classical landscape with figures*, London.

Papenhoff, H. (1954) *Zum Problem der Abhängigkeit der Epitome von der venez. Handschrift des Athenaios*, Göttingen. Dissertation.

(Pauly) (1893–1972) *Paulys Real-Encyklopädie der classischen Altertumswissenschaft*, new edn by G. Wissowa *et al.*, Stuttgart.

(Pauly) (1975) *Der kleine Pauly*, eds, K. Ziegler and W. Sontheimer, Munich.

Payne, S. (1972) 'On the interpretation of bone samples from archaeological sites' in *Papers in economic prehistory*, ed., E. S. Higgs, Cambridge.

Peppink, S. P. (1936) *Observationes in Athenaei Deipnosophistas*, Leiden.

—— (ed.) (1937–9) *Athenaei Dipnosophistarum epitome*, Leiden.

Perpillou, J. L. (1981) 'Vinealia 1. Vignes mycéniennes, homériques, historiques: permanence de formules?' in *Revue de philologie*, 3rd ser., vol. 55, pp. 41–55.

Perry, C. (1982 and 1983) 'What was tracta?' in *Petits propos culinaires*, no. 12, pp. 37–9 and note in no. 14 (1983) pp. 58–9.

—— (1988) 'Medieval Near Eastern rotted condiments' in *Oxford Symposium on Food and Cookery 1987: taste. Proceedings*, London, pp. 169–77.

Phia Sing (1981) *Traditional recipes of Laos, being the manuscript recipe books of the late Phia Sing*, eds, A. and J. Davidson, trans. Phouangphet Vannithone and B. S. Klausner, London.

Platnauer, M. (1964) Aristophanes, *Peace*, Oxford.

Pollard, J. (1977) *Birds in Greek life and myth*, London.

Ponsich, M. and Tarradell, M. (1965) *Garum et industries antiques de salaison dans la Méditerranée Occidentale*, Paris.

Pope, M. H. (1972) 'A divine banquet at Ugarit' in *The use of the Old Testament in the New and other essays: studies in honor of William F. Stinespring*, ed., J. Efird, Durham, NC, 1972, pp. 170–203. Reprinted in M. H. Pope (1994) *Probative pontificating in Ugaritic and Biblical studies*, ed., Mark S. Smith, Münster.

Postgate, J. N. (1987) 'Some vegetables in the Assyrian sources' and 'Notes on fruit in the cuneiform sources' in *Bulletin on Sumerian agriculture*, no. 3.

Powell, M. A. (1987) 'Classical sources and the problem of the apricot' in *Bulletin on Sumerian agriculture*, no. 3, pp. 153–6.

Pritchard, J. B. (trans.) (1969) *Ancient Near Eastern texts relating to the Old Testament*, 3rd edn, Princeton.

Pritchett, W. K. (1971– ) *The Greek state at war*, Berkeley. 1971 printing of vol. 1 entitled *Ancient Greek military practices*, part 1.

Purcell, N. (1995) 'Eating fish: the paradoxes of seafood' in *Food in antiquity*, eds, J. Wilkins *et al.*, Exeter.

Rankin, E. M. (1907) *The rôle of the mágeiroi in the life of the ancient Greeks*, Chicago.

Rathbone, D. (1983) 'Italian wines in Roman Egypt' in *Opus*, vol. 2, no. 1, pp. 81–98.

Reardon, B. P. (1971) *Courants littéraires grecs des IIe et IIIe siècles après J.-C.*, Paris.

D. G. Reder, (1967) 'La culture du palmier dattier en Égypte et en Palestine pendant la période gréco-romaine' in *Ellinisticheskii blizhnii vostok, Vizantiya i Iran, istoriya i filologiya*, eds, V. V. Struve *et al.*, Moscow, pp. 52–5.

Renfrew, C. (1972) *The emergence of civilisation: the Cyclades and the Aegean in the third millennium BC*, London.

—— (1987) *Archaeology and language: the puzzle of Indo-European origins*, London.

Renfrew, C. and Wagstaff, J. M. (eds) (1982) *An island polity: the archaeology of exploitation on Melos*, Cambridge.

Renfrew, C. *et al.* (eds) (1987– ) *Excavations at Sitagroi: a prehistoric village in northeast Greece*, Los Angeles.

Renfrew, J. M. (1971) 'Carbonized seeds and fruits from the funeral pyres of Salamis 6th-5th centuries BC' in V. Karageorghis, *The necropolis of Salamis*, Vol. 2.

—— (1973) *Palaeoethnobotany: the prehistoric food plants of the Near East and Europe*, London.

—— (1979) 'The first farmers in south east Europe' in *Festschrift Maria Hopf*, ed., U. Körber-Grohne, Cologne, pp. 243–65.

—— (1988) 'Food for athletes and gods: a classical diet' in *The archaeology of the Olympics*, ed., W. J. Raschke, Madison, pp. 174–81.

Reynolds, P. J. (1995) 'The food of the prehistoric Celts' in *Food in antiquity*, eds, J. Wilkins *et al.*, Exeter.

Ribbeck, W. (1857) 'Archestratus von Gela' in *Rheinisches Museum*, new series, vol. 11, pp. 200–25.

Rice, E. E. (1983) *The grand procession of Ptolemy Philadelphus*, Oxford.

Richter, W. (1968) *Die Landwirtschaft im homerischen Zeitalter* (*Archaeologia Homerica* 2, chapter H) Göttingen.

—— (1972) 'Ziege' in *Paulys Real-Encyklopädie der classischen Altertumswissenschaft*, new edn by G. Wissowa *et al.* (1893–1972) Stuttgart.

Riddle, J. M. (1984) 'Byzantine commentaries on Dioscorides' in *Symposium on Byzantine medicine*, ed., J. Scarborough (*Dumbarton Oaks papers* 38) Washington, pp. 95–102.

Riley, G. (1993) 'Tainted meat' in *Spicing up the palate: proceedings of the Oxford Symposium on Food and Cookery 1992*, Totnes, pp. 1–6.

Robert, L. (1961–2) 'Sur des lettres d'un métropolite de Phrygie: philologie et réalités' in *Journal des savants* (July–December 1961) pp. 97–166 and (January–June 1962) pp. 5–74.

Rodden, R. J. (1965) 'An early Neolithic village in Greece' in *Scientific American*, vol. 212, no. 4 (April) pp. 82–92.

Rodden, R. J. *et al.* (1962) 'Excavations at the early neolithic site at Nea Nikomedeia, Greek Macedonia' in *Proceedings of the Prehistoric Society*, vol. 28, pp. 267–89.

Rossi, L. E. (1983) 'Il simposio greco arcaico e classico come spettacolo a se stesso' in *Spettacoli conviviali dall' antichità classica alle corti italiane del '400: atti del VII convegno di studio, Viterbo, maggio 1983*, Viterbo, pp. 41–50.

Rouanet-Liesenfelt, A.-M. (1992) 'Les plantes médicinales de Crète à l'époque romaine' in *Cretan studies*, vol. 3, pp. 173–90.

Roux, G. (1973) 'Salles de banquet à Délos' in *Etudes déliennes* (*Bulletin de correspondance hellénique* supplement 1) Athens, pp. 525–54.

Runnels, C. N. and Hansen, J. (1987) 'The olive in the prehistoric Aegean: the evidence for domestication in the early bronze age' in *Oxford journal of archaeology*, vol. 5, pp. 299–308.

Runnels, C. N. and Murray, P. M. (1983) 'Milling in ancient Greece' in *Archaeology*, vol. 36, pp. 62–3, 75.

Saberi, H. (1993) 'Rosewater and asafoetida' in *Spicing up the palate: proceedings of the Oxford Symposium on Food and Cookery 1992*, Totnes, pp. 220–35.

Saint-Denis, E. (1980) 'Éloge du chou' in *Latomus*, vol. 39, pp. 838–49.

Salaman, R. (1987) *Greek island cookery*, London.

—— (1993) 'Down mastic way on Chios' in *Spicing up the palate: proceedings of the Oxford Symposium on Food and Cookery 1992*, Totnes, pp. 236–8.

Sallares, R. (1991) *The ecology of the ancient Greek world*, London.

Salviat, F. (1986) 'Le vin de Thasos: amphores, vin et sources écrites' in *Recherches sur les amphores grecques*, eds, J.-Y. Empereur and Y. Garlan (*Bulletin de correspondance hellénique* supplement 13), Athens, pp. 145–96.

Sancisi-Weerdenburg, H. (1995) 'Persian food: stereotypes and political identity' in *Food in antiquity*, eds, J. Wilkins *et al.*, Exeter.

Sanquer, R. and Galliou, P. (1972) 'Garum, sel et salaisons en Armorique gallo-romaine' in *Gallia*, vol. 70, pp. 199–223.

Scarborough, J. (1970) 'Diphilus of Siphnos and Hellenistic medical dietetics' in *Journal of the history of medicine*, vol. 25, pp. 194–201.

—— (1981) 'The Galenic question' in *Sudhoffs Archiv*, vol. 65, pp. 1–31.

—— (1984) *Symposium on Byzantine medicine* (*Dumbarton Oaks papers* vol. 38) Washington, DC. Includes his 'Introduction' and 'Early Byzantine pharmacology'.

Schafer, E. H. (1963) *The golden peaches of Samarkand*, Berkeley.

Schaps, D. (1977) 'The woman least mentioned: etiquette and women's names' in *Classical quarterly*, n.s., vol. 27 pp. 323–30.

—— (1987) 'Small change in Boeotia' in *Zeitschrift für Papyrologie und Epigraphik*, vol. 69.

Schmid, G. (1897) *De C. Lucilio et Archestrato atque de piscibus qui apud utrumque inveniuntur et apud alios quosdam*, St Petersburg.

Schmitt-Pantel, P. (1980) 'Les repas au prytanée et à la tholos dans l'Athènes classique: sitesis, trophé, misthos: réflexions sur le mode de nourriture démocratique' in *AION. Annali del Seminario di Studi del Mondo Classico*, pp. 55–68.

—— (1985) 'Banquet et cité grecque: quelques questions suscitées par les recherches récentes' in *Mélanges de l'École Française de Rome. Antiquité*, vol. 97, no. 1, pp. 135–58.

—— (1987) 'La cité au banquet', Lyon. Dissertation.

—— (1990) 'Sacrificial meal and symposion: two models of civic institutions in the archaic city?' in *Sympotica: a symposium on the symposion*, ed., O. Murray, Oxford, pp. 14–33.

Schrader, O. *et al.* (1911) V. Hehn, *Kulturpflanzen und Haustiere*, 8th edn, Berlin. Expansion of Hehn's 1883 edition.

Schröder, H. O. (1940) 'Oreibásios' in *Paulys Real-Encyklopädie der classischen Altertumswissenschaft*, supplement (1903– ) Stuttgart, vol. 7.

Schuster, M., (1931) 'Mel' in *Paulys Real-Encyklopädie der classischen Altertumswissenschaft*, new edn by G. Wissowa *et al.* (1893–1972) Stuttgart.

Schweighäuser, J. (1801–7) *Animadversiones in Athenaei Deipnosophistas*, Strasbourg.

Schwyzer, E. (1923) *Dialectorum Graecarum exempla epigraphica potiora*, Leipzig.

Scully, T. (ed.) (1988) *The Viandier of Taillevent*, Ottawa.

Sharples, R. W. and Minter, D. W. (1983) 'Theophrastus on "fungi": inaccurate citations in Athenaeus' in *Journal of Hellenic studies*, vol. 103, pp. 154–6.

Shelmerdine, C. W. (1985) *The perfume industry of Mycenaean Pylos*, Göteborg.

Sherratt, A. G. (1981) 'Plough and pastoralism: aspects of the secondary products revolution' in *Pattern of the past: studies in honour of David L. Clarke*, ed., I. Hodder *et al.*, Cambridge, pp. 261–305.

—— (1983) 'The secondary exploitation of animals in the Old World' in *World archaeology*, vol. 15, pp. 287–316.

Sherratt, S. and A. (1993) The growth of the Mediterranean economy in the early first millennium BC' in *World archaeology*, vol. 24, pp. 361–78.

Sideras, A. (1974) 'Aetius und Oribasius' in *Byzantinische Zeitschrift*, vol. 67, pp. 110–30.

Skydsgaard, J. E. (1988) 'Transhumance in ancient Greece' in *Pastoral economies in classical antiquity*, ed., C. R. Whittaker, (*Proceedings of the Cambridge Philological Society*, supplement 14) Cambridge, pp. 75–86.

Slater, W. J. (ed.) (1986) *Aristophanis Byzantii fragmenta*, Berlin.

—— (ed.) (1991) *Dining in a classical context*, Ann Arbor.

Smith, Thyrza R. (1987) *Mycenaean trade and interaction in the west central Mediterranean 1600–1000 BC*, Oxford.

Snell, B. *et al.* (eds) (1971– ) *Tragicorum Graecorum fragmenta*, Berlin.

Soffer, O. (1989) 'Storage, sedentism and the European palaeolithic record' in *Antiquity*, vol. 63, pp. 719–32.

Solomon, J. (1995) 'The Apician sauce: ius Apicianum' in *Food in antiquity*, eds, J. Wilkins *et al.*, Exeter.

Sommerstein, A. H. (ed.) (1987) Aristophanes, *Birds*, Warminster.

Sonderkamp, J. A. M. (1984) 'Theophanes Nonnus' in *Symposium on Byzantine medicine*, ed., J. Scarborough (*Dumbarton Oaks papers*, 38) , Washington, DC, pp. 29–41.

Sordinas, A. (1969) 'Investigations of the prehistory of Corfu during 1964–1966' in *Balkan studies*, vol. 10, pp. 393–424.

Sparkes, B. (1995) 'A pretty kettle of fish' in *Food in antiquity*, eds, J. Wilkins *et al.*, Exeter.

Stanley, P. V. (1982) 'KN Uc160 and Mycenaean wines' in *American journal of archaeology*, vol. 86, pp. 577–8. Supersedes his 'de-re-u-ko and Mycenaean wines' in: (1981) *American journal of archaeology*, vol. 85, p. 219.

Stannard, J. (1971) 'Byzantine botanical lexicography' in *Episteme*, vol. 5, pp. 168–87.

—— (1984) 'Aspects of Byzantine materia medica' in *Symposium on Byzantine medicine*, ed., J. Scarborough (*Dumbarton Oaks papers*, 38) , Washington, DC, pp. 205–11.

Starr, C. G. (1978) 'An evening with the flute-girls' in *Parola del passato*, vol. 33, pp. 401–10.

Stearn, W. T. (1965) 'The origin and later development of cultivated plants' in *Journal of the Royal Horticultural Society*, vol. 90, pp. 279–341.

Steckerl, F. (1958) *The fragments of Praxagoras of Cos and his school*, Leiden, pp. 108–23.

Steier (1932) 'Minze', 'Mohn', 'Möhre' in *Paulys Real-Encyklopädie der classischen Altertumswissenschaft*, new edn by G. Wissowa *et al.* (1893–1972) Stuttgart.

—— (1938) 'Pfeffer' in *Paulys Real-Encyklopädie der classischen Altertumswissenschaft*, new edn by G. Wissowa *et al.* (1893–1972) Stuttgart.

Stol, M. (1979) *On trees, mountains and millstones in the ancient Near East*, Leiden.

—— (1985) 'Cress and its mustard' in *Jaarbericht van het Voorasiatisch-Egyptisch Gesellschaft Ex Oriente Lux*, vol. 28 (vol. dated 1983–4) pp. 24–32.

—— (1987) 'Garlic, onion, leek' and 'The cucurbitaceae in the cuneiform texts' in *Bulletin on Sumerian agriculture*, no. 3, pp. 57–92.

Teodorsson, S.-T. (1989– ) *A commentary on Plutarch's Table talks*, Gothenburg.

Tepper, Y. (1986) 'The rise and fall of dove-raising' in *Man and land in Eretz Israel in antiquity*, ed., A. Kasher *et al.*, Jerusalem, pp. 170–96.

Thiselton-Dyer, W. (1913–14) 'On some ancient plant-names' in *Journal of philology*, vol. 33, pp. 195–207.

Thompson, D'A. W. (1936) *A glossary of Greek birds*, 2nd edn, London.

—— (1947) *A glossary of Greek fishes*, London.

Thompson, D. B. (1963) *Garden lore of ancient Athens* (*Excavations of the Athenian Agora. Picture book*, no. 8) Princeton.

Thompson, D. J. (1984) 'Agriculture' in *The Cambridge ancient history* Vol. 7, part 1, 2nd edn, Cambridge.

—— (1995) 'Food for Ptolemaic temple workers' in *Food in antiquity*, eds, J. Wilkins *et al.*, Exeter.

Thompson, R. C. (1949) *Dictionary of Assyrian botany*, London.
Tolkowsky, S. (1938) *Hesperides: a history of the culture and use of citrus fruits*, London.
Torrence, R. (1986) *Production and exchange of stone tools: prehistoric obsidian in the Aegean*, Cambridge.
Tournefort, Pitton de (1717) *Relation d'un voyage du Levant fait par ordre du Roy*, Paris.
Trumpf, J. (1960) 'Kydonische Äpfel' in *Hermes*, vol. 88, pp. 14–22.
Tsountas, H. (1908) *E Proistorike akropolis Diminion ke Sesklon*, Athens.
Ullmann, M. (1974) 'Neues zu den diätetischen Schriften des Rufus von Ephesos' in *Medizinhistorisches Journal*, vol. 9, pp. 23–40.
Ullrich, F. (1908–9) 'Entstehung und Entwickelung der Literaturgattung des Symposion' in *Programme des kgl. Neuen Gymnasiums, Würzburg*.
van Andel, Tj. H. and Lianos, N. (1983) 'Prehistoric and historic shorelines of the southern Argolid peninsula' in *International journal of nautical archaeology and underwater exploration*, vol. 12, pp. 303–24.
van Andel, Tj. H. and Runnels, C. N. (1987) *Beyond the Acropolis: a rural Greek past*, Stanford.
—— (1988) 'An essay on the "emergence of civilization" in the Aegean world' in *Antiquity*, vol. 62, pp. 234–47.
van Zeist, W. (1988) 'Some aspects of early neolithic plant husbandry in the Near East' in *Anatolica*, vol. 15, pp. 49–67.
van Zeist, W. and Bottema, S. (1971) 'Plant husbandry in early neolithic Nea Nikomedeia, Greece' in *Acta botanica Neerlandica*, vol. 20, pp. 524–38.
Vatin, C. (1974) 'Jardins et vergers grecs' in *Mélanges helléniques offerts à Georges Daux*, Paris, pp. 345–57.
Vavilov, N. (1950) *The origin, variation, immunity and breeding of cultivated plants* (*Chronica botanica*, 13) Waltham, MA.
Ventris, M. and Chadwick, J. (eds) (1973) *Documents in Mycenaean Greek*, 2nd edn, Cambridge.
Vernant, J. P. *et al.* (1981) *Le sacrifice dans l'antiquité* (*Entretiens sur l'antiquité classique*, 27) Geneva.
Vickers, M. (1990) 'Attic symposia after the Persian wars' in *Sympotica: a symposium on the symposion*, ed., O. Murray, Oxford, pp. 105–21.
Vickery, K. F. (1936) *Food in early Greece*, Urbana.
Vikentiev, V. (1954) 'Le silphium' in *Bulletin de l'Institut d'Egypte*, vol. 37, pp. 123–50.
Vryonis, S. (1971) *The decline of medieval Hellenism in Asia Minor and the process of Islamization from the eleventh through the fifteenth century*, Berkeley.
Wace, A. J. B. and Thompson, M. S. (1914) *The nomads of the Balkans*, London.
Waetzoldt, H. (1987) 'Knoblauch und Zwiebeln nach den Texten des 3. Jt.' in *Bulletin on Sumerian agriculture*, no. 3, pp. 23–56.
Währen, M. (1974) *Brot und Gebäck im alten Griechenland*, Detmold.
Weber, T. (1980) 'Essen und Trinken in Konstantinopel des 10. Jahrhunderts nach den Berichten Liutprands von Cremona' in J. Koder and T. Weber, *Liutprand von Cremona in Konstantinopel*, Vienna, pp. 71–99.
—— (1989) 'Damaskena' in *Zeitschrift der deutschen Palästina-Vereins*, vol. 105, pp. 151–65.
Webster, T. B. L. (1970) *Studies in later Greek comedy*, 2nd edn, Manchester.
Wehrli, F. (ed.) (1967–9) *Die Schule des Aristoteles*, 2nd edn, Basle.
Wellmann, M. (ed.) (1901) *Fragmentsammlung der griechischen Ärzte*, Vol. 1: *Die*

*Fragmente der sikelischen Ärzte Akron, Philistion und des Diokles von Karystos*, Berlin.

Wentzel (1896) 'Artemidoros (31) ' in *Paulys Real-Encyklopädie der classischen Altertumswissenschaft*, new edn by G. Wissowa *et al.* (1893–1972) Stuttgart.

Werlhof (1875) *Das Silphium von Cyrenaica*, Lüneburg.

West, B. and Zhou, Benh-Xiong (1988) 'Did chickens go north? New evidence for domestication' in *Journal of archaeological science*, vol. 15, pp. 515–33.

West, M. L. (ed.) (1978) Hesiod, *Works and days*, Oxford.

—— (1989–92) *Iambi et elegi Graeci*, 2nd edn, Oxford.

White, K. D. (1970) *Roman farming*, London.

Whittaker, C. R. (ed.) (1988) *Pastoral economies in classical antiquity* (*Proceedings of the Cambridge Philological Society* supplement 14) Cambridge.

Wilkins, J. and Hill, S. (1993) 'The flavours of ancient Greece' in *Spicing up the palate: proceedings of the Oxford Symposium on Food and Cookery 1992*, Totnes, pp. 275–9.

—— (trans.) (1994) Archestratus, Totnes.

—— (1995) 'The sources and sauces of Athenaeus' in *Food in antiquity*, eds, J. Wilkins *et al.* Exeter.

Wilkins, J. *et al.* (eds) (1995) *Food in antiquity*, Exeter.

Wilson, N. G. (1962) 'Did Arethas read Athenaeus?' in *Journal of Hellenic studies*, vol. 82, pp. 147–8.

—— (1983) *Scholars of Byzantium*, London.

Wimmer, F. (ed. and trans.) (1866) *Theophrasti Eresii opera quae supersunt omnia*, Paris.

Wissowa, G. (1913) 'Athenaios und Macrobius' in *Nachrichten der königlichen Gesellschaft der Wissenschaften zu Göttingen, Philologisch-historische Klasse*, no. 3, pp. 333ff.

Witteveen, J. (1985) 'Rose sugar and other medieval sweets' in *Petits propos culinaires*, no. 20, pp. 22–8.

—— (1986–7) 'On swans, cranes and herons' in *Petits propos culinaires*, nos 24–6.

—— (1989) 'Peacocks in history' in *Petits propos culinaires*, no. 32, pp. 23–34.

Wüst, E, and Hug, A. (1949) 'Parásitoi (2) ' in *Paulys Real-Encyklopädie der classischen Altertumswissenschaft*, new edn by G. Wissowa *et al.* (1893–1972) Stuttgart.

Wycherley, R. E. (1957) *Literary and epigraphical testimonia* (*The Athenian Agora*, 3) Princeton.

Wylock, M. (1972) 'Les aromates dans les tablettes Ge de Mycènes' in *Studi micenei ed egeo-anatolici*, no. 15, pp. 105–46.

Zahn (1912) 'Garum' in *Paulys Real-Encyklopädie der classischen Altertumswissenschaft*, new edn by G. Wissowa *et al.* (1893–1972) Stuttgart.

Zepernick, K. (1921) 'Die Exzerpte des Athenaeus in den Deipnosophisten und ihre Glaubwürdigkeit' in *Philologus*, n.s. vol. 77, pp. 311–63.

Zhukovskii, P. M. (1933) *Zemledel'cheskaya Turtsiya* =*La Turquie agricole* (Russian with French summary) Moscow.

Ziehen, L. (1949) 'Parasitoi' in *Paulys Real-Encyklopädie der classischen Altertumswissenschaft*, new edn by G. Wissowa *et al.* (1893–1972) Stuttgart.

Zohary, D. and Hopf, M. (1993) *Domestication of plants in the old world*, 2nd edn, Oxford.

Zymbragoudakis, C. (1979) 'The bee and beekeeping in Crete' in *Apiacta*, vol. 14, no. 3, pp. 134–8.

# INDEX OF ANCIENT AND
# MEDIEVAL SOURCES

References to modern editions are given below in two cases: to identify the text numbering system used when systems differ, and to assist those unfamiliar with the texts cited to locate them. It has seemed best to identify the fragments of certain authors by referring, in square brackets, to the text in which they are preserved. As in the text and notes, book titles are generally given in English rather than the conventional Latin. Classicists will not be seriously inconvenienced by these slight variations from their usual practice.

(KA) means that the fragments of this author are as numbered in Kassel and Austin 1983–. A translation of most of these fragments can be found (under slightly different numbers) in *The fragments of Attic comedy*, ed. J. M. Edmonds, Leiden 1957–61, though, in cases where the fragment is preserved by Athenaeus, the translation given by Gulick 1927–41 may make better sense.

Fragment numbers in the form 99F9 refer to *F Gr Hist: die Fragmente der griechischen Historiker*, ed. F. Jacoby, Berlin 1923–58.

Achaeus: 12–13 (Snell *et al.* 1971–): 244
*Acraephia Price List* (see Schaps 1987): 67, 228, 229
Aelian: *Miscellany* 4.9: 215; 2.28: 225; *Nature of Animals* 4.58: 64, 225
Aeschines: *Against Timarchus* 75: 214; *Letter* 5.2: 233; *On the Embassy* 154–8: 255
Aeschylides [Aelian, *Nature of Animals* 16.32]: 250
Aeschylus: *Agamemnon* 1594: 215; *Persians* 41–8: 244; *Prometheus Bound* 371: 241; 396: 241; fragment 179 (Snell *et al.* 1971–): 216; 211: 75, 230; 309: 59
Aetius: *Eight Books of Medicine* 1.131: 251; 5.139: 262
Africanus [*Hippiatrica Cantabrigiensia* 71.15]: 252
Agapius: *Geoponikón* (cf. p. 263 n. 11) 25: 201; 50: 201, 264, 266; 55: 190, 264; 72: 266; 75: 264, 266
Agatharchides of Cnidos 86F15: 225

Alcaeus Comicus 17 (KA): 223, 236
Alcaeus 322 (*Poetarum Lesbiorum fragmenta*, ed. E. Lobel and D. Page. New edn, Oxford 1968): 108
Alciphron 4.13: 148, 225
Alcman 19 (Davies 1991–): 14, 51, 236, 237; 60: 222; 92: 98; 99: 230; 100: 230
Alexander of Tralles: *Eight Books of Medicine* 8.2: 252; *On Fevers* 1: 262; 7: 251; *Twelve Books of Medicine* 1.17: 251
Alexis 32 (KA): 79; 47: 217; 50: 156; 57: 217; 58: 225; 84: 73; 128: 254; 132: 236–8, 250; 138: 72; 140: 122; 149: 217; 167: 217, 232, 238, 239; 168: 240; 172: 89, 214, 241; 177: 214; 178: 245, 250; 179: 232, 236; 183: 248; 192: 73; 196: 249; 208: 255; 259: 214; 275: 78; 278: 101, 250; 292: 248
Alexis, *Samian Annals* [Ath. 540c–d]: 105
Amphis 36 (KA): 249; 40: 249

287

Anacreon 11a (*Poetae melici Graeci*, ed.
D. L. Page, Oxford 1962): 243; 51: 18
Ananius 5 (West 1989–1992): 107, 117,
223, 228, 229
Anaxandrides 31 (KA): 227; 40: 216; 42:
51, 63, 122, 224, 225; 73: 241
Anaxippus 1 (KA): 236, 256
Andocides fragment [Suda s.v. skándix]:
217
Androtion [Ath. 75d]: 248; [Ath. 82c]:
230, 248
Anthimus: *Letter on Diet*: 188, 263
Antidotus 4 (KA): 243
Antigonus [Ath. 607a–e]: 247
Antiphanes 21 (KA): 42; 36: 239, 249;
57: 216; 63: 234; 71: 236; 88: 238;
104: 254; 123: 229; 130: 227, 228; 131:
238; 150: 9; 158: 235; 166: 237; 173:
254; 174: 244; 179: 217, 248; 180: 114;
203: 147, 215; 204: 228; 207: 116, 246;
221: 113; 225: 217; 233: 125, 216, 244,
249; 249: 255; 274–5: 250; 295: 223
Antiphon 1.14–20: 7; fragment 57 (ed.
T. Thalheim, Leipzig 1914): 254
*Apicius* (ed. M. E. Milham, Leipzig
1969) 1.2: 142, 150, 254; 1.13: 142;
1.30: 141; 1.33: 245; 2.1.1: 261; 2.3.1:
261; 2.4: 262; 7.3.1: 182, 262; 7.4: 180;
7.5.2: 221; 7.5.4: 221; 7.6: 262; 7.6.10:
252; 7.11.8: 262
Apollodorus: *Against Neaera* 34: 18,
214, 215
Apollodorus [Pliny, *Natural History*
14.76]: 148, 162, 249, 257
Apollodorus of Athens 244F151: 216
Apollodorus of Carystus 31 (KA): 123
Apollophanes 5 (KA): 232
Apuleius: *Metamorphoses* 1.5: 250
Archedicus 3 (KA): 228
Archestratus 1 (Brandt 1888): 119; 4:
120, 121, 128, 248, 249, 256; 5: 249;
8: 228, 249, 254; 9: 74, 120, 250; 12:
249; 13–14: 228, 249; 15: 227; 16: 228;
18: 228, 248; 19: 228; 20: 118, 152,
248, 249; 21: 228, 250; 22: 228, 237,
249; 23: 69, 227, 249; 24–5: 229, 249;
26–7: 228; 28: 249; 29: 228, 249; 30:
120, 152, 227, 228, 249; 31–2: 228;
33: 229; 34: 227, 228, 249; 35: 249,
256; 36: 228, 236; 37: 71; 38: 76; 40–2:
249; 43: 248; 44: 247, 249, 256; 45:
68, 70, 227, 228, 238, 249, 255; 46: 68,
228, 249; 47: 227; 48–9: 70; 50: 228;

51: 229; 52: 256; 53: 249; 54: 227, 249;
55: 249; 56: 227, 229, 249; 57: 62,
224; 58: 224; 59: 94, 97, 101, 243, 257;
61: 118, 121; 62: 63, 159, 223, 240,
246, 248
Archilochus 2 (West 1989–92): 242; 116:
249
Archippus 23: 228
Aristobulus 139F35: 251
Ariston of Ceos [*Ep.* 38f]: 254
Aristophanes: *Acharnians* 163–74: 244;
164–6: 215, 236; 478: 235; 786–8: 65,
223, 225; 875: 225; 889–94: 228; 901:
248; 1112: 223; 1116–17: 224; 1125:
226; *Assemblywomen* 306–8: 215;
348–9: 213; 468–70: 215; 595: 215;
1119–39: 88, 100; 1169: 225; *Birds*
13–18: 224; 76: 248; 102: 254; 485:
65; 518–19: 61; 529–32: 224; 531–8:
224, 238; 705–7: 63, 225; 959: 223;
1079–85: 224; 1579–90: 224, 238;
*Clouds* 109: 225; 982: 234; *Frogs*
541–8: 18; 549–62: 215; 1369: 226;
*Knights* 42–60: 215; 343: 244; 422:
235; 480: 226; 606: 238; 677: 235;
1164–220: 215; 1171: 239; 1290–9:
248; *Lysistrata* 36: 249; 702: 249; 856:
214; 1061: 239; *Peace* 123: 245; 242–54:
244; 869: 238; 937–1126: 59; 1005:
249; 1017–18: 214; 1109: 61; 1280:
60; *Thesmophoriazusae* 486: 252; 624:
215; *Wasps* 610–12: 15; 612–18: 215;
679: 236; 838: 250; 878: 225, 238;
1208–20: 215; *Wealth* 253: 27; 298:
26; 544: 217; 1004: 239; fragment 1
(KA): 244; 53: 224; 148: 78; 225: 108;
334: 100, 249; 428: 239; 520: 246; 521:
248; 581: 225, 235
Aristophanes of Byzantium (Slater
1986) p. 178: 250
Aristophon 16 (KA): 237
Aristotle: *Economics* 1347b19: 249;
*Politics* 1323a4: 8; *Problems* 925a28:
235; 925a34: 235; *Study of Animals*
488b7: 228; 522a22–b6: 66; 531a8–30:
229; 542a27: 60; 544b12–546b14: 58;
556b7: 224; 562b3–563a4: 225;
569b10–14: 126; 569b25: 228;
579a4–9: 223, 224, 244; 579b6: 224;
607b2: 227; 613b5: 224, 225;
614b1–620b9: 63; 623b16–627b22: 65;
fragment 83 (*Aristotelis qui
ferebantur librorum fragmenta*, ed.

V. Rose, Leipzig 1886): 116; 195: 239; 310: 69; 351: 147
Aristoxenus [Aulus Gellius 4.11]: 90
Arrian, *Anabasis* 3.28: 251, 253
Artemidorus [Ath. 663d–e]: 156
Artemidorus, *Dream Interpretation* (ed. R. Hercher, Leipzig 1864) p. 271: 215
Athenaeus 74a: 231; 74d: 232; 80d: 259; 80e–81c: 230, 259; 81a–82c: 230, 249; 82a–c: 248; 82e–f: 144; 83a–85c: 143, 144; 83c: 177; 84a–c: 144, 145; 84d: 144, 260; 85c–94b: 229; 88c: 257; 92f: 229; 94c–101b: 223, 259; 96d: 261; 96e: 223; 101a: 223; 104c: 229; 105c: 256; 105d: 229; 107a: 259; 108f–116a: 240; 109b: 178; 110e: 252; 111f: 248; 112a–e: 217; 113a: 257; 113d: 257; 115b: 171; 115d: 261; 126a: 233; 128a–c: 255; 131f: 216; 133a: 216; 134d: 259; 138d: 126; 138e–141f: 215, 216; 146c–d: 154; 146e: 213; 154a: 261; 156a–160b: 239; 164f–165b: 248; 170a: 236; 170d: 214; 185a: 259; 196a: 255, 259; 201b: 261; 211a: 168; 217c–e: 244; 228c: 158; 234c–262a: 214; 242f–244a: 248; 245a–c: 215; 277a: 216; 277b–c: 259; 278e: 124; 282a: 245; 282d–e: 229; 284f: 229; 286b: 228; 288c–294c: 228, 248; 294c: 228; 294d: 257; 294e–f: 229; 295b–297c: 227; 297c: 229, 261; 297d: 66; 300d–e: 229; 301e: 227; 304c: 227; 304d: 257; 305e: 257; 305f: 228; 306d: 227, 228; 307b: 247; 308f: 257; 309a: 162, 257; 309b: 228; 310e: 228; 310a: 118, 228; 312a: 162, 257; 312b: 228, 257; 313a: 228; 313b: 257; 314a: 228; 314e: 227; 315a: 228; 315c: 227; 315e: 228; 316a: 229; 319a: 227; 319b: 228; 322b: 228; 323a: 227; 323c: 229; 325c: 228; 326c: 229; 326e: 160, 256; 328a: 228; 328d: 256; 328f: 257; 329d: 168; 330b: 229; 337b: 216, 246; 364b: 217; 366a: 237; 369b: 245; 369a: 235; 369e: 234; 371d: 257; 371e: 235; 372b: 231; 373a: 225; 375b: 220; 376c: 255, 261; 376d: 164, 261; 381b: 250; 384a–c: 224; 387d: 257; 388e: 225; 392a–393c: 224; 394c–395c: 224, 225; 395f: 257; 399d–402b: 223; 426d–e: 243; 426b–431f: 243, 256; 475a: 261; 481e: 261; 516c–d: 111, 240, 244, 256, 257; 516e: 226; 527a:
255; 532d–e: 215; 537f: 168; 540c–d: 105; 541a: 259; 541c: 115; 542f: 226; 613c–614d: 214; 640a–643e: 216; 642e: 242; 643e–649e: 240; 646b: 256; 646e: 226, 240; 647c: 257; 647d: 258; 647e: 141; 648b–c: 257; 649d: 253; 650b: 232; 650c: 230; 651b: 233; 651e: 232; 652a: 233; 652b: 232; 653b: 232; 654c–d: 225, 254; 658e–662d: 9, 214; 660a–e: 214; 663a–f: 255; 666a: 257; 682c: 252; 686c: 168
Athenaeus: *Epitome* (see p. 260 n. 17) 1a–e: 258, 259; 2a: 169; 4e: 117; 5b: 257; 9d: 220; 16b: 61; 25e: 45, 104; 26c–27d: 193, 260; 28d: 97; 30b–e: 254; 30c: 249; 30f: 241; 33b: 265; 34b: 242; 38f: 254; 46b: 257; 50e: 232; 50f: 231; 51a: 257; 51b: 232; 52a–54d: 232, 233; 54e: 239; 55c: 239; 55f: 90; 55c–56a: 217; 56a: 239; 56b: 231; 56d: 235; 57b: 233; 57e: 242; 58b–c: 65, 161, 216, 254, 257; 58d: 235; 58f: 216, 231; 60b–62d: 234, 235; 63d–64f: 234; 64a: 224; 64f–65e: 224; 65f: 216; 66f: 238; 68b: 251; 68f: 235; 70a–71c: 234; 73d: 231
Athenaeus of Attaleia [Oribasius 1.3]: 166, 224
Aulus Gellius 13.5: 250; 18.2.13: 217

Baton 4 (KA): 161, 244
*Batrachomyomachia* 36: 237
Belon: *Observations* (bk and ch. of: Pierre Belon, *Les observations de plusieurs singularitez et choses memorables trouvées en Grèce, Asie, Judée, Egypte, Arabie et autres pays étrangers.* 2nd edn, Paris 1555; Latin translation by C. Clusius, *Petri Bellonii Cenomani plurimorum singularium et memorabilium rerum ... observationes,* Antwerp 1589) 1.4: 193; 1.19: 195; 1.27: 203; 1.59: 196, 201; 1.65: 216; 1.66: 200; 1.75: 200
*Book of the Eparch* (Freshfield 1938) 10: 266; 15: 262; 18: 190; 19: 193, 196
Buondelmonti: *Liber Insularum Archipelagi* (De Sinner 1824) pp. 111–14: 266

Callimachus: *Hymn to Apollo* 83: 252; fragment 69 (ed. R. Pfeiffer, Oxford

1949–53): 108; 250: 85, 236; 434: 248; 435: 241, 245, 256

Callixeinus of Rhodes [Ath. 196a]: 154

Carystius of Pergamum [Ath. 235e]: 248

Cassiodorus: Variae 12.4: 147

Cato: On Agriculture 74: 258; 76: 257; 77–8: 258; 80: 255, 257, 258; 82: 258; 89: 224; 112–13: 87, 148; 119: 231

Celsus: On Medicine 5.23.3: 250

Chares 125F4: 215

Chrysippus of Soli [Ath. 137f]: 217; [Ath. 285d]: 126; [Ath. 335d–e]: 119; [Ath. 373a]: 225

Chrysippus of Tyana [Ath. 113a]: 165, 258; [Ath. 647d]: 141; [Ath. 647f]: 256

Cicero: Letters to Atticus 4.4a.1: 246; 4.5.3: 246; 4.8.2: 246; 9.16: 226

Clearchus of Soli 59 (Wehrli 1967–9): 217; 63: 118; 78: 246; 81: 72, 118; 102: 216

Cleitomachus of Carthage [Ath. 402c]: 58

Clytus 490F1: 254; 490F2: 105, 108

Columella: On Agriculture 1.1.13: 257; 2.9.14–16: 239; 2.10.33: 253; 3.2.24: 241; 5.10.19–20: 253; 9.4.3: 253; 12.4.2: 257; 12.59.5: 251

Comica Adespota 338 (Kock 1880–8): 233

Crates Comicus 1 (KA): 223

Cratinus 44 (KA): 244; 46–7: 248; 49: 64; 62: 248; 154: 228; 175: 126; 195: 101; 279: 65; 312: 75, 230; 363: 237

Cratinus the Younger 1 (KA): 109

Critias 2 (Diels 1951–2): 108, 255; 6: 106, 244; 31: 255

Criton 3 (KA): 216

Damascenus Studites: Sermons 14: 181, 262

Damogeron [Geoponica 7.12–13]: 265

Demetrius of Scepsis [Ath. 91c–d]: 74

Demetrius the Xenodotean [Scholia on Aristophanes, Peace 123]: 245

Democritus [Geoponica 7.4]: 242; [Pliny, Natural History 14.20]: 241

Demosthenes: Against Androtion 22.15: 217; Against Conon 54.4: 215; Against Euergus and Mnesibulus 47.35–8: 2; 47.53–5: 2, 215; 47.60: 2; Against Lacritus 35.10: 101, 243; Against

Meidias 21.79: 213; Olynthiac II 2.19: 214; On the Embassy 19.196–8: 255; Philippic III 9.31: 255

Dicaearchus [Ath. 668d–e]: 108

Didymus [Geoponica 2.33]: 240

Dio Academicus [Ep. 34b]: 242

Dio Cassius 80.2: 258

Dio Chrysostom 7: 1, 214; 7.46: 148; 7.75: 80, 232

Diocles of Carystus 87 (Wellmann 1901): 251; 118: 249; 125: 249; 126: 225, 233; 133: 229; 135: 228; 141: 256; 142: 161; [Paul of Aegina 1.100]: 256

Diocletian's Price Edict (Diokletians Preisedikt, ed. S. Lauffer, Berlin 1971) 2.1–7: 148; 2.15–16: 245; 2.17–19: 264; 3.10–12: 245; 4.21–2: 224; 4.39–40: 254; 5.11: 226; 6.50–3: 233; 6.96: 226

Diodorus Comicus 2 (KA): 227

Diogenes Laertius 8.19: 216; 8.24: 90

Dionysius of Sinope 2 (KA): 118, 246

Diophanes [Geoponica 7.17]: 147

Dioscorides: Materia Medica 1.14: 251; 1.32: 241; 1.34: 238; 1.70: 233, 249; 1.106: 233; 1.114: 253; 1.115: 252, 253, 258; 1.118: 230; 1.124: 253; 1.125: 233; 2.9: 249; 2.96: 225; 2.104: 264; 2.116: 235; 2.129: 85; 2.160: 138; 3.51: 142; 3.52: 262; 3.62: 251; 3.75: 264; 3.80: 140; 3.128: 237; 4.173: 220; 4.188: 237; 5.6: 241, 254; 5.17–18: 190; 5.17–18: 264; 5.18–73: 88; 5.28–9: 254; 5.30: 221; 5.32: 234; 5.34: 150; 5.39: 150; 5.54–9: 251, 252; 5.72: 252

Diphilus of Sinope 17 (KA): 159, 227, 236, 256; 31: 248; 42: 29; 87: 25; 96: 248

Diphilus of Siphnos [Ath. 82f]: 253; [Ath. 90a–92a]: 76, 83, 249; [Ath. 115c]: 261; [Ath. 369e]: 237; [Ath. 371a]: 234; [Ath. 371b]: 234; [Ep. 51b]: 78; [Ep. 54b–c]: 233, 249

Dorion [Ath. 118c]: 247; [Ath. 285a]: 72; [Ath. 297c]: 229; [Ath. 300f]: 72; [Ath. 309a]: 227; [Ath. 337d]: 70

Dorotheus of Ascalon [Ath. 662f]: 255

Dosiadas [Ath. 143a–d]: 216

Duris of Samos 76F35: 215

Empedocles 33 (Diels 1951–2): 226

Epaenetus [Ath. 297c]: 229; [Ath. 662d]: 163, 255; [Ath. 662e]: 232
Eparchides [Ep. 30b–e]: 254
Ephippus 1 (KA): 249; 3: 22, 225, 250; 8: 242; 12: 227, 229; 20: 214; 24: 242; 28: 101
Epicharmus 34–5 (Kaibel 1899): 248; 41–70: 226; 42: 230; 52: 256; 56: 244; 58: 108; 63: 228; 87: 65; 124: 70; 150: 232; 152: 65; 159–61: 234, 237, 238
Epicrates 6 (KA): 216
Epinicus 1 (KA): 241
Erasistratus (M. M. P. G. R. Fuchs, Erasistratea, Berlin 1892) [Ath. 324a]: 110, 162; [Ep. 46c]: 162
Eriphus 3 (KA): 68
Etymologicum Magnum 488.53: 263; 492.48–9: 244, 245; 784.9: 245
Euangelus 1 (KA): 6, 8, 10, 29, 245
Eubulus 18 (KA): 238, 248–50; 35: 83, 234; 48: 232; 60: 9; 74: 225, 232; 101: 224; 109: 228; 117: 217; 120: 224; 121: 241; 123: 101, 243; 125: 250; 129: 249; 136: 241; 148: 216, 225, 250
Eudemus [Galen, On Antidotes 2]: 251
Euphorion 11 (Collectanea Alexandrina, ed. J. U. Powell, Oxford 1925): 230
Euphron 10 (KA): 237
Eupolis 160 (KA): 71; 174: 61, 228, 229; 175: 123; 191: 244; 226: 224; 271: 104, 241, 249; 478: 243
Euripides: Cyclops 136: 244; 397: 214; 544–89: 215; Orestes 37: 257; fragment 562 (Tragicorum Graecorum fragmenta, ed. A. Nauck. 2nd edn, Leipzig 1889): 216; 687–91: 14, 248
Eustathius: Commentary on Homer 692.21: 250; 1144.15: 245; 1445.48: 242; 1499.64: 242
Euthydemus of Athens [Ath. 116a]: 227, 230, 257; [Ath. 118b]: 257
Evliya Çelebi (p. nos of Hammer 1834–50 vol. 1 pt 2) 104–250: 205; 139: 266; 148: 205; 154: 266; 155: 202
Ezekiel 27.13: 97; 27.18: 242

Florentinus [Geoponica 4.1]: 254; [Geoponica 5.2.4]: 241; [Geoponica 5.17]: 254; [Geoponica 6.52]: 80; [Geoponica 7.7]: 150; [Geoponica 8.23]: 100; [Geoponica 10.13]: 262

Fronto [Geoponica 7.12]: 265

Galen: (vol. and p. nos of edn of C. G. Kühn, Leipzig 1821–33, are given in square brackets): Handy Remedies 3 [14.537]: 257; Health 2.12 [6.159]: 241; 4.5 [6.265]: 251; 4.5 [6.268]: 250; 4.5 [6.271]: 251; 6.5 [6.334]: 149; 6.5 [6.337]: 254; Hippocratic Glossary s.v. álphita: 240; bolbós: 234; epimelís: 230; indikón: 251; hypósphagma: 245; Notes on Diet in Acute Diseases [15.455]: 265; On Antidotes 1.11 [14.55]: 250; On Compounding of Drugs [12.922]: 238, 264; On Good and Bad Juices 5 [6.785]: 145; 11 [6.800–3]: 254; On the Properties of Foods (Galeni de sanitate tuenda . . ., ed. K. Koch et al., Leipzig 1923) 1.2.5: 240; 1.3.1–2: 166; 1.10: 240; 1.11.2: 91; 1.13.19: 239; 1.17: 251; 1.18–22: 237, 239; 1.23: 217; 1.24.1: 253; 1.25.2: 217; 2.4–5: 231; 2.11.1: 174; 2.15–16: 252; 2.25: 80; 2.28.1: 232, 233; 2.31.1: 262; 2.33: 146; 2.37.2: 144; 2.38: 43, 80, 232, 253; 2.39.1: 245; 2.44.3: 235; 2.49: 236; 2.50.2: 85; 2.51.5: 236; 2.56: 234; 2.58.2: 233; 2.63: 217; 2.65: 216, 262; 2.68.2: 50, 237; 3.1.6: 61; 3.1.9: 60, 223; 3.1.10: 62; 3.1.11: 60, 223; 3.1.18: 252; 3.2.1: 21, 62; 3.11.1: 262; 3.15: 66, 265; 3.16.3: 250; 3.19.2: 225; 3.20.2: 262; 3.21.1: 166; 3.24.12: 249, 255; 3.32.2: 73; On the Properties of Simples 6.1.28 [11.824]: 251; 6.1.32 [11.826]: 232; 6.4.9 [11.865]: 226; 6.5.4 [11.868–72]: 238; 6.6.2 [11.880]: 251; 6.19.6 [12.141]: 253; 7.1.2 [12.68]: 233; 7.11.14 [12.61]: 264; 7.11.17 [12.62]: 252; 7.12.17 [12.76]: 253; 7.12.18 [12.76]: 145; 7.12.19 [12.77]: 144; 8.15.17 [12.92]: 86; 8.16.21 [12.102]: 253; 8.18.16 [12.123]: 140; 8.19.2 [12.138]: 234; 10.1.7 [12.272]: 226, 250; 11.1.31 [12.353]: 238; 11.1.37 [12.360]: 224; On Temperaments 3 [1.682]: 250; On the Therapeutic Method 12.4 [10.830–4]: 149, 254; Substitutes [19.733]: 251; [19.741] 238; To Piso on Theriac [14.257]: 251
Garcia da Orta: Colóquios: 141
Gargilius Martialis 2: 253

*Geoponica* (*Geoponica sive Cassiani Bassi scholastici de re rustica eclogae*, ed. H. Beckh, Leipzig 1895) 2.33: 240; 2.43: 240; 2.5.4: 235; 3.8: 265; 4.1: 254; 5.17: 254; 5.2.4: 241; 5.28: 264; 6.52: 80; 7.12–13: 265; 7.17: 147; 7.4: 242; 7.7: 150, 151; 8.23: 100; 10.13: 262; 18.19.2: 226; 20.46: 75

Glaucus of Locri [Ath. 324a]: 110, 162; [Ath. 369b]: 245; [Ath. 661e]: 111

Hanno: *Navigation* (Müller 1855): 177
Hegesander [Ath. 334e]: 249, 255; [*Ep.* 44c]: 223
Hegesippus [Ath. 516d]: 250
Hellanicus 4F56: 233
Heracleides of Syracuse [Ath. 114a]: 161; [Ath. 647a]: 161
Heracleides Criticus (F. Pfister, *Die Reisebilder des Herakleides*, Vienna 1951): 249
Hermippus 63 (KA): 81, 104, 105, 108, 117, 127, 228, 233, 238, 239, 249, 250, 255; 75: 234; 77: 100, 249
Herodotus 1.1: 135; 1.7.2: 245; 1.66: 248; 1.94.2: 106; 1.146.3: 21; 1.155.4: 244; 1.160: 223; 1.193.5: 82; 1.193.4: 238; 1.216: 226; 2.36: 239; 2.39.4: 21; 2.174: 244; 3.6: 96; 3.23: 226; 3.111: 251; 3.117.4: 90; 4.35: 215; 4.169: 238; 4.177: 253; 5.18–20: 255; 6.60: 126, 242; 7.134: 126, 242; 9.82.1–3: 124
Hesiod: *Shield of Heracles* 407: 223; *Theogony* 36: 117; *Works and Days* 41: 24, 217, 235; 232–3: 47, 216, 238; 442: 91, 216; 582: 85, 216; 590: 91; 591: 58; 596: 243; 609–14: 96; 640: 256
Hesychius: *Lexicon* s.v. *árton*: 251; *Kandaúles*: 245; *kándaulos*: 263; *krimnêstis*: 256; *mímarkys*: 223; *thrîa*: 264
Hicesius [Ath. 87b]: 229; [Ath. 298b]: 228, 254; [Ath. 320d]: 228; [Ath. 689c]: 165
Hierocles [Ath. 646b]: 256
Hierophilus: *Dietary Calendar* (Ideler 1841–2 vol. 1 pp. 409–29): 188, 192, 262, 264, 265
*Hippiatrica* (*Corpus hippiatricorum graecorum*, ed. E. Oder and C. Hoppe, Leipzig 1924–7): *Berolinensia* 97.5–7: 256; *Cantabrigiensia* 71.15: 252

Hippocrates: *Epidemics* 2.6.28: 244; 7.1: 251; *Gynaecology* 2.192: 252; *Nature of Woman* 32, 63: 252; 70: 251; *On Diseases* 4.34: 238; *Places in Man* 47.5: 244; *Regimen* 2.42.2: 239; 2.45.4: 51; 2.46.3: 61; 2.46.4: 224; 2.47.2: 225; 2.54.8: 237; 2.55.3: 232; 2.56.8: 245; 2.60.3: 215; 3.79.2: 60; 3.82.2: 60; 3.82.2: 223; *Regimen in Acute Diseases* 88: 223
Hippolochus [Ath. 128a–130e]: 27, 85, 155, 157, 160, 179, 223, 224, 237, 248, 255, 261
Hipponax 3a (West 1989–92): 245; 26: 107; 26a: 86; 60: 78, 222; 79: 106; 124: 107; 166: 110
*Historia Augusta* (*Scriptores historiae augustae*, ed. E. Hohl. Rev. edn, Leipzig 1965), Aelius Verus 5.9: 261
Homer: *Iliad* 7.467–75: 95, 99, 134; 11.630: 103; 16.747: 74; 22.501: 61; *Odyssey* 1.140–2: 104; 1.152: 243; 2.338–42: 93; 3.391–2: 90; 3.404–73: 60; 3.441: 223; 3.461–72: 60; 5.72: 222; 5.194–9: 16; 5.432: 72; 6.163: 82; 7.112–21: 77; 7.122–6: 241; 7.127: 83; 7.136–8: 102; 9.21–8: 33; 9.39–42: 242; 9.84: 253; 9.154–65: 223; 9.204–11: 99; 9.218–23: 66, 108; 9.246–9: 66; 9.556–9: 59; 10.242: 80, 89; 11.589–90: 230; 14.10: 39; 14.80–1: 43, 104, 223; 14.407–38: 214; 14.413–56: 59; 15.160–74: 224; 15.455: 135; 16.49–52: 104; 17.213–14: 58; 17.295: 224; 18.6: 11; 19.59–64: 214; 19.536–7: 64; 20.299: 45; 21.430: 243; 24.247: 83; 24.336–44: 230
*Homeric Epigrams* 15.7: 86
*Homeric Hymn to Apollo* 3.51–60: 216; 3.117: 82
*Homeric Hymn to Demeter* 2.209: 85
Horace: *Epistles* 2.1.270: 250; *Odes* 3.21.1: 95; *Satires* 2.8.15: 148; 2.8.88: 224
Hypereides: fragment 68–70 (ed. F. G. Kenyon, Oxford 1907): 216; 205: 3

Iatrocles [Ath. 326e, 646a, 646b, 646f, 647b]: 160, 256
*IG* XII suppl. 347 (*Inscriptiones Graecae*, Berlin 1873–): 136, 238; XIV 643: 214
Isaac Chumnus: *Letters* 216, 218 (J.-F.

Boissonade, *Anecdota nova*, Paris
1844): 265
Isaeus: *On Pyrrhus' Estate* 14: 5
Isidore: *Etymologies* 20.2.15: 258

Juba [Ath. 83b]: 144, 176
Justinian: *Digest* 50.16.205: 232

Knossos tablets Ga415, Ga418, Ga517,
Ga675, Og424: 221; Ga1530,
Ga1532: 222

Leo VI, *Novel* 58: 197
*Life of St Theodore of Syceon* (*Vie de
Théodore de Sykéôn*, ed. A.-J.
Festugière, Brussels 1970) 3, 6: 195
Liutprand: *Antapodosis* 5.23: 265;
*Embassy* 1: 198; 11: 199; 20: 199; 38:
264; 63: 265
Lucian: *Lucius or the Ass* 2–3: 16, 148;
*On Salaried Posts in Great Houses* 26:
216
Lynceus [Ath. 75e]: 159, 250, 232, 256;
[Ath. 100e–f, 101e]: 238, 256; [Ath.
109d]: 158, 178; [Ath. 128a]: 255;
[Ath. 131f]: 122, 227, 256; [Ath.
241e]: 63; [Ath. 245a]: 215; [Ath.
285e–294f]: 118, 158, 228, 229, 247,
248, 250, 256; [Ath. 313f]: 118, 158,
227, 228, 247; [Ath. 330a]: 72; [Ath.
402a]: 62; [Ath. 499c]: 159; [Ath.
583f–585f]: 216; [Ath. 647a]: 256;
[Ath. 652c]: 255; [Ath. 652d]: 232,
256
Lysias: *Against Alcibiades for Desertion*
14.25: 215; *Against Pancleon* 23.6:
226; *Against Simon* 3.6–7: 3, 215

Machon [Ath. 577d–583d]: 7, 216, 217,
223; [Ath. 664b]: 255
Macrobius: *Saturnalia* 5.18–22: 260;
7.1.3: 255; 7.8.1: 261
*Mantissa Proverbiorum* (*Corpus
paroemiographorum Graecorum*, ed.
E. L. A. Leutsch and F. G.
Schneidewin, Göttingen 1839–51,
vol. 2 p. 748) 26: 25
Martial 3.75.4: 237; 5.18.3: 262
Matron [Ath. 134d–137c]: 10, 116, 214,
227, 243, 249
Maximus of Tyre (ed. M. B. Trapp,
Stuttgart 1994), *Dissertation* 17: 110
Megasthenes 715F2: 251

Menander (ed. F. H. Sandbach, Oxford
1972): *Arbitrators* 451–85: 6; *Bad-
Tempered Man* 260–3: 213; 393–401:
59; 401–21: 4; 423–4: 6; 427–518: 215;
430: 4; 447–53: 3, 21, 213; 461–3: 3;
546–51: 122; 563–7: 7; 568–70: 5;
616–19: 4, 5; 644–7: 9; 775: 4; 855–9:
6; 931: 3; 940–9: 6, 214, 241; 950–3:
7, 213; *Samian Woman* 287–92: 9;
fragment (ed. A. Koerte and A.
Thierfelder, vol. 2. 2nd edn, Leipzig
1959) 238: 215; 264: 154, 213; 385:
213; 397: 159, 244, 245, 249, 256; 451:
155, 226, 244, 245; 452: 215, 255; 910:
237
Menodotus of Samos [Ath. 655a]: 254
Michael Choniates: *Letters* 19, 50 (ed.
S. P. Lampros, Athens 1879–80): 265,
266
Michael Italicus: *Letters* 42: 264
*Miracles of Saints Cosmas and Damian*
(L. Deubner, *Kosmas und Damian*,
Leipzig 1907) 2: 181; 34: 262
Mithaecus [Ath. 282a]: 245; [Ath. 325f]:
72, 110
Mnesitheus (Bertier 1972) 28: 239; 30:
233, 249; 46: 249, 250
Moeris: *Attic Glossary* s.v. *ópson*: 216
Molpis [Ath. 141e]: 223, 225
Mycenae tablet Ue 611: 48

Nausicrates 1 (KA): 228
Nicander: *Alexipharmaca* 228: 224;
489–93: 232; *Theriaca* 876–7: 234;
890–1: 146; 909–14: 235; fragment 50:
230; 68: 59; 70: 85, 235; 71: 85, 234,
236; 72: 235; 73: 225; 74: 234; 76–7:
233
Nicander Nucius (ed. J. A. Cramer,
London 1841 [Camden Society]): 23,
153
Nicolaus of Damascus 90F47: 245
Nicostratus 1 (KA): 234; 4: 62, 223; 7:
156; 13: 240; 16: 245
Numenius [Ath. 320d]: 228; [Ath. 326f]:
228

Ophelion 3 (KA): 250
Oribasius: *Medical Collections* 1.1: 263;
2.58: 74, 76, 230, 249; 5.25: 190, 264;
5.33: 192; 12 s.v. *silphion*: 251
Ovid, *Art of Love* 2.415: 237

*P.Cair.Zen.* (*Zenon papyri*, ed. C. C. Edgar, Cairo 1925–31) 59012.48, 59013.24, 59702.22: 233

*P.Oxy.* (*The Oxyrhynchus papyri*) 2565: 258; 2891: 247

Pamphilus [Ath. 326e]: 160, 256

Panini: *Grammar* 6.1.139: 50

Paul of Aegina: *Practice of Medicine* 7.3: 138; 7.11: 262; 1.100: 256

Pausanias 2.13: 248

Paxamus [*Geoponica* 2.43]: 240

Pegolotti, Francisco: *Pratica della Mercatura*: 193

*Periegesis Anonymi* (Müller 1855) 366: 244

*Periplus of the Erythraean Sea* 6: 242; 14: 221, 226; 49: 242

Persaeus 584F4: 119

Petronius: *Satiricon* 8.4, 20.7: 237; 38.3: 250; 49: 255, 261

Phaenias of Eresus (Wehrli 1967–9) 41: 242; 42: 232; 43: 239

Pherecrates 14 (KA): 235; 49: 223; 50: 246; 73: 214; 113: 234; 138: 237; 158: 61, 232; 162: 29; 255: 223

Philaenis [*P.Oxy.* 2891]: 247

Philagrius: *On Soft Drinks* [Oribasius 5.33]: 192

Philemon 8 (KA): 255; 11: 255; 63: 245; 79: 244; 82: 227, 248; 113: 83

Philemon of Aexone [Ath. 652e]: 248

Philistion of Locri (Wellmann 1901) [Ath. 115d]: 261

Philochorus [Ath. 245c]: 215; [*Ep.* 38c]: 216

*Philogelos* 237: 181, 262

Philostratus: *Gymnasticon* 44: 237

Philoxenus: *Banquet* (*Anthologia lyrica graeca*, ed. E. Diehl, 3rd edn, pt 3, Leipzig 1952) a: 115; b: 59, 223; b.1–2: 14; b.7: 246; b.21: 227; b.36: 226; e: 237, 240; *Cyclops or Galatea* (*Dithyrambographi Graeci*, ed. D. F. Sutton, Hildesheim 1989): 217

Philyllius 12 (KA): 249; 23: 100, 101, 243

Phoenicides 2 (KA): 248

Photius: *Lexicon* s.v. *roûn*: 238; *saprón*: 243

Phrynichus 73 (KA): 249

Phylotimus (F. Steckerl, *The fragments of Praxagoras of Cos and his school*,

Leiden 1958, pp. 108–23) 8: 233, 249; 11: 230

Pindar (ed. H. Maehler, Leipzig 1987–9): *Olympians* 1.50–2: 243; 9.48: 94; 13.33: 222; fragment 52b (Paean 2).25: 99, 249; 52e (Paean 5).38: 244; 52m (Paean 12).6–8: 244; 106: 106, 249; 124c: 103; 125: 244

Plato: *Gorgias* 518b: 109, 245, 248; *Laches* 179c: 11; *Letters* 7.326b: 108, 118; *Republic* 372b: 215; 372c: 232, 238; 398d–399c: 244; *Symposium* 175b: 10, 246; 176a–e: 10, 256; 190d: 80; 212c–e: 19

Plato Comicus 71 (KA): 16; 169: 248; 189: 114, 227; 215: 75, 230

Pliny: *Natural History* 10.74: 254; 11.32–3: 249, 250; 11.34: 225; 12.25: 253; 12.28: 138, 251; 12.29: 250, 252; 12.30: 251; 12.32: 264; 12.85–98: 140, 251; 12.111: 249; 12.135: 264; 13.8: 232; 13.9: 253; 13.12: 264; 13.19: 232; 13.44: 246; 13.51: 253; 13.55: 238; 14.20: 241; 14.54: 148, 254; 14.59–72: 147; 14.73–6: 147, 148; 14.80: 241; 14.94: 95; 14.100–12: 87; 14.109: 254; 14.113: 65; 14.124–8: 265; 15.7: 238; 15.39: 262; 15.40: 253, 262; 15.47: 253; 15.80: 48; 15.83: 253; 15.87: 233; 15.91: 146, 253; 15.95: 253; 15.99: 232; 15.102: 231; 16.103: 253; 18.22: 257; 18.140: 253; 18.144: 238; 19.39: 140; 19.67: 231; 19.104: 249; 19.164: 142, 252; 19.165: 252; 19.168: 237; 20.163: 251; 20.187: 252; 21.57: 226, 250; 21.89: 236; 21.90: 237; 21.108: 217; 23.149: 250; 28.105: 258; 29.24: 250; 30.32: 249; 30.45: 249; 31.93: 229; 31.95: 229

Plutarch: *Lives, Artaxerxes* 3.2: 253; *Lives, Demetrius* 27: 255; 38: 257; *Lives, Sulla* 13: 250; *Moralia* 10c: 17; 157f: 217; 158e: 235; 172b: 217; 778d: 123; 915e: 45; *Moralia, Symposium Questions* 1.1: 255; 1.6: 232; 3.9: 243; 4.2: 83; 5.3: 254, 265; 5.4: 243; 5.5: 215; 7.7: 247; 8.9: 103, 137, 144; *Moralia*, fragment 26 (ed. F. H. Sandbach, Leipzig 1967): 216

*Poem on Medicine* (Ideler 1841–2) 1.209: 190

Polemon [Ath. 138e–139c]: 216, 223,

239; [Ath. 372a]: 249; [Ath. 388c]: 224; [Ath. 588c]: 7
Poliochus 2 (KA): 217, 224
Pollux: *Daily Conversation* (ed. A. Boucherie, Paris 1872) 113r: 180, 262; *Onomasticon* (ed. E. Bethe, Leipzig 1900–37) 6.2: 254; 6.23–5: 243; 6.65: 236, 250; 6.69: 263; 6.70–1: 161, 240, 241, 255; 6.73: 252; 6.107: 222; 9.48: 215, 223
Polybius 4.37: 249; 12.3.10: 219; 34.8.1: 68, 227
Polycrates [Ath. 139d–f]: 216
Porphyry: *On Abstinence from Animal Foods* 1.14: 223; 2.25: 223
Poseidippus 31 (KA): 244
Poseidonius 87F3: 253
Procopius: *Secret History* 6: 265
*Prodromic Poems* 2.38–45: 196; 2.42a: 264; 2.46: 264; 3: 198; 3.54: 181; 3.83: 264; 3.93: 264; 3.149: 264; 3.280: 189, 264; 3.283: 264; 3.285–313: 265; 4.49–70: 196; 4.62: 181, 262
Psellus: *Letters* 206 (*Scripta minora*, ed. E. Kurtz and F. Drexl, Milan 1936–41): 264; *On Medicine* (*Poemata*, ed. L. G. Westerink, Stuttgart 1992): 188; *To a Shopkeeper* (*Oratoria minora*, ed. A. R. Littlewood, Leipzig 1985) p. 56: 193
Ptolemy Physcon 234F2a: 225
Pylos tablets Un08 and Un09: 221
Pyrgion [Ath. 143e]: 21

Quintilii [Ath. 649e]: 146

Satyrus [Ath. 541c]: 115
Scholia on: Aristophanes: *Acharnians* 174: 244; 1112: 223; *Knights* 1167: 223; *Peace* 123: 245; 242–54: 244; 869: 237; *Thesmophoriazusae* 624: 215; *Wealth* 253: 217; 298: 217; Dioscorides: *Materia Medica* 2.170: 235; Homer: *Iliad* 16.747: 229; Nicander: *Alexipharmaca* 181: 241; 533: 264; Oppian: *Halieutica* 1.100: 244; Theocritus 9.19: 226; 14.48: 248
Scribonius Largus: *Pharmacopoeia* 111: 238; 113: 238; 121: 253
Scylax (Müller 1855) 108–10: 253
*SIG* (*Sylloge inscr. Gr.* ed. G. Dittenberger, 3rd edn) 22.13: 97, 242
Seleucus [Ath. 658d]: 250

Semonides 23 (West 1989–92): 250
Semus [*Ep.* 30b–e]: 254
Simeon Seth (Langkavel 1868) p. 30: 225; p. 33: 264; p. 34: 262; p. 40: 145; p. 55: 191; p. 58: 264; p. 70: 264; p. 85: 201, 266; p. 89: 262; p. 96: 264; p. 125: 189; p. 126: 251; p. 137: 90
*Sinuhe* (see p. 242 n. 10) 82–4: 96
Solon 38 (*Poetae lyrici Graeci*, ed. T. Bergk. 4th edn, Leipzig 1882; cf. West 1989–92): 239; 39: 87, 238; 40: 232; 41: 238
Sopater 4 (Kaibel 1899): 256; 12: 230
Sophilus 5 (KA): 156, 216, 223
Sophocles: fragment 503 (Snell *et al.* 1971–): 244; 606: 75, 230; 609: 251; 759: 232; 1122: 214
Sophron 24 (Kaibel 1899): 73
Sotades 1 (KA): 228, 246
Sotion [*Geoponica* 5.28]: 264
Speusippus [Ath. 327c]: 228; [Ath. 369b]: 235, 245
Strabo 5.2: 227; 7 fragment 22: 254; 7 fragments 43–44a: 242, 249; 7.6.2: 68; 8.3.14: 235; 11.13.7: 251; 12.4.7: 250; 14.2.21: 249; 15.1.20: 191; 15.2.10: 146, 251, 253; 15.3.11: 96; 15.3.22: 140, 242; 17.3.20: 136
Strato 1 (KA): 243
Strattis 45 (KA): 228; 47: 239; 64: 249; 66: 234, 236; 71: 237
*Suda* s.v. *amphidrómia*: 216; *kítrion*: 260; *Míthaikos*: 245; *Páxamos*: 164; *oînos*: 254; *rodákinon*: 262; *saprón*: 243
Suetonius: *Vitellius* 12: 265
Synesius: *Letters* 106: 140

Tâyan-Kannanâr: *Agam* 149.7–11: 137
Telecleides 1 (KA): 240
Terpsion [Ath. 337b]: 216, 246
Theocritus 1.147: 248; 1.48–9: 223; 2.152: 216; 3.26: 227; 4.34: 240; 5.125: 235; 7.111–15: 218; 7.68: 234; 9.21: 240; 10.4: 234; 10.54: 239; 11.20: 226; 12.3: 230; 13.34: 215; 14.17: 224; 14.18: 216, 217; 16.27–8: 217; 24.45: 232
Theodore Balsamon: *Commentary on Trullo* (*Patrologiae . . . series graeca*, ed. J.-P. Migne, vol. 137, Paris 1865): 197
Theodore Lascaris: *Letters* 54 (ed. N.

Festa, Florence 1898): 264; 82: 264; 83: 264
Theodore Prodromus: *On Diet*: 188
Theodoridas [*Anthologia Palatina* 6.155]: 226
Theognis 467–9: 218; 863–4: 65; 879–84: 98
*Theologakis* p. 356: 264
Theophilus 8 (KA): 60
Theophrastus: *Characters* 20.10: 10; 22.4: 29, 214; *On Odours*: 136; 10: 137; 25–8: 258; 31: 251; *Plant Physiology* 1.11.1: 252; 1.18.5: 252; 1.20.3: 89; 2.5.3: 234, 235; 4.2.1: 233; *Study of Plants* 1.10.7: 234; 1.11.4: 252; 1.12.1: 236; 2.2.5: 230; 3.10.1: 239; 3.13.1–3: 231; 3.14.4: 233; 3.15.1–2: 81, 232, 233; 3.2.1: 232; 3.3.1: 231; 3.3.5: 233; 3.6.1: 231; 3.6.2: 233; 3.8: 239; 4.2.4: 253; 4.3.1–4: 253; 4.4.2: 143, 176, 252; 4.4.7: 146, 233; 4.5.4: 233; 4.8: 221, 233; 4.10.1: 221; 6.3.1–7: 140, 238; 6.4.2: 234; 6.4.7: 236; 6.4.10–11: 234; 6.6.5: 142, 252; 6.7.2: 237; 7.1.2: 221, 234; 7.3.5: 231; 7.4.1: 231, 235; 7.4.2–6: 234, 248, 249; 7.4.7–9: 249; 7.4.11: 244; 7.6.1: 235; 7.7.1–2: 85, 216, 235; 7.11.4: 236; 7.12.1: 217, 236; 7.13.1–4: 217; 8.1: 221, 235; 8.3.2: 239; 8.4.2: 239; 8.4.3: 240; 8.7.3: 217, 235, 239; 9.1.2: 233; 9.1.7: 238; 9.7: 50, 136, 236, 264; 9.12.4: 237; 9.15.5–20.2: 234; 9.15.5: 250; 9.18.3: 237; 9.20.1: 138; fragment 166 (Wimmer 1866): 250; 167: 235, 248, 249; [Ath. 82e]: 144; [*Ep.* 782a]: 103
Theopompus 115F49: 153; 115F62: 128; 115F162: 153; 115F249: 215; 115F276: 100
Thucydides 2.38.2: 217; 4.26.8: 237

*Timarion* (tr. B. Baldwin, Detroit 1984) 2: 265; 4–5: 205; 11: 264; 17: 196; 46: 264
Timocles 25 (KA): 217; 34: 215; 39: 244
Timotheus 1 (KA): 215
Tryphon 117 (ed. A. de Velsen, Berlin 1853): 178, 240; 136: 243
*Typikon of Pantokrator*: 217
Tzetzes: *Scholia on the Khiliádes* 3.351.7 (Cramer 1835–7): 245

Varro: *On Farming* 1.1.10: 263; 1.10: 257; 1.2.7: 254; 1.41.5–6: 248, 249; 3.6.6: 254; 3.9.6: 249; 3.9.19: 254; 3.12.6: 219; 3.16.26: 225; *On the Latin Language* 5.110: 261
Vegetius 1.13: 240
Vinidarius: *Outline Apicius*: 139, 141, 180

*Widsith* (ed. K. Malone, London 1936) 76–8: 193
William of Rubruck (Jackson 1990) 9: 192, 193, 264

Xenocrates: *On Seafood* [Oribasius 2.58.67–125]: 74, 76, 230, 249
Xenophanes 1 (Diels 1951–2): 104, 242; 3: 244; 5: 103; 39: 231
Xenophon: *Anabasis* 2.3.15: 82; 2.4.13: 90; 7.3: 255; 5.4: 216; *Constitution of Sparta* 6.4–5: 217; *Education of Cyrus* 1.2.8: 234; 6.2.22: 249; *Hunting*: 61; 9: 224; 10: 223; *Management* 7.30: 215; *Symposium* 1.11–15: 11; 2.1: 7, 10; 2.3–4: 244

YBC 4644 (see Bottéro 1985): 160

Zenodotus [Eustathius 692.21]: 250

# GREEK INDEX

Where possible, modern Greek, Turkish, English and scientific Latin equivalents have been given for names of foodstuffs.

In revising this index I was able to consult, besides works cited in the notes, Nan Dunbar's edition of Aristophanes' *Birds* (Oxford 1995) and the welcome enlarged edition of Rena Salaman's *Greek Food* (London 1993).

Ádipson, cure for thirst 24

Adráphaxys, modern *khrisolákhano, atrafalís*, Turkish *koyun sarmaşığı*. Orach, Atriplex hortensis 84

Afáka, dwarf chickling 239; *see also* apháke

Aghriokíperi, English galingale 221; *see also* kýpairos

Aghriospanákia, modern *vromókhorto*, Turkish *sirken*. Goosefoot, Fat hen, Chenopodium album 85

Agorá, market place 11, 14, 129

Aigókeras 146; *see also* têlis

Aîra, darnel 91

Aíx, modern *ghídha*, Turkish *keçi*. Goat, Capra spp. 58, 62

Aíx ágrios, wild goat 62

Akaléphe, sea anemone, *see also* kníde 74; modern *tsikhnídha*, Turkish *ısırgan*. Nettle, Urtica spp. 83

Akanthís. Siskin or linnet, Carduelis spp.? 63

Ákherdos, akhrás, modern *aghriakhladhía*, Turkish *ahlat*. Wild pear, Pyrus spinosa, P. elaeagnifolia 39, 80

Ákoron. Yellow flag, Iris pseudacorus 192

Akrís, locust 224

Aktê, elderberry 220

Ákylos, modern *prinári, pournári*,

Turkish *pernar*. Acorn of holm-oak, Quercus ilex 89, 239

Alektryón, cock 65; *see also* órnis

Áleuron, wheat flour 91, 240

Álimon, cure for hunger 24

Álix, fermented fish cake 75

Aloé, grape-drying ground 241

Alópex, modern *alepoú*, Turkish *tilki*. Fox, Vulpes vulpes 62; dogfish 158; *see also* galeós

Alphestés, wrasse 72, 245; *see also* phykís

Alphiton, barley meal 91, 121, 240

Amanítes, modern *manitári*, Turkish *mantar*. Mushroom, Agaricus spp. and others 83

Amárakon, modern *madzouróna*, Turkish *mercanköşk*. Marjoram, Majorana hortensis 237

Ámbar, ambergris 202, 266

Ámes, amétiskos, cakes 91, 240

Amía, modern *palamídha*, Turkish *palamut, torik*. Bonito, Scomberomoridae spp. 70

Ámmi. Ajowan, Trachyspermum ammi 139

Ampelóprason. Allium ampeloprasum 83

Amygdalê, modern *amígdhalo*, Turkish *badem*. Almond, Amygdalus communis 81

Ámylon, starch 240

Ámylos, frumenty 91, 240
Anarítes. Top-shell, Trochocochlea spp.? 73
Anárrinon, modern *aghriosinápi*, Turkish *yabani hardal*. Mustard greens, Brassica arvensis 83
Andrákhne, modern *glistrídha*, Turkish *semiz otu*. Purslane, Portulaca oleracea 84
Andreîon, men's house 21
Andrón, dining room 13, 115
Ánethon, modern *ánithos*, Turkish *dere otu*. Dill, Anethum graveolens 83, 236
Anisâton, anise-flavoured wine 192
Ánison, ánnesos, ánnetos, ánoitton, modern *glikániso*, Turkish *anason*. Aniseed, Pimpinella anisum 85, 236
Antakaîos, modern *stourghióni*, *xirríkhi*, Turkish *mersin balığı*. Sturgeon, Acipenser spp. 68
Anthías, unidentified fish 75, 107, 229
Anthosmías, brine-flavoured wine 95, 242
Ánthryskon, modern *skadzíki*, Turkish *zühre tarağı*, *frenk maydanozu*. Chervil, Anthriscus cerefolium 85, 235; *see also* skándix
Apápe, modern *aghrioradhíki*, Turkish *kara hindiba*. Dandelion, Taraxacum officinale 236
Apháke, modern *afáka*. Dwarf chickling, Lathyrus cicera 89
Aphýdia, aphýe, small fry 72, 74, 120
Ápios, modern *akhládhi*, Turkish *armut*. Pear, Pyrus spp. 79, 243
Apoplýnas, having rinsed 110
Apópyris, annual sacrifice 152
Apsinthâton, apsinthítes, absinthe-flavoured wine 150, 264
Apsínthion, modern *apsithiá*, Turkish *pelin*. Absinthe, wormwood, Artemisia spp. 85
Ápyros, naturally warming 242
Árakos, modern *aghrióvikos*. Bird vetch, cow vetch, crow vetch, Vicia cracca 89, 239
Áriston, lunch 12
Arkeuthís, modern *kédhros*, Turkish *ardıç*. Juniper, Cedrus and Oxycedrus spp. 142
Árktos, modern *arkoúdha*, Turkish *ayı*. Bear, Ursus arctos 62; modern *líra*,

Turkish *ayı istakozu*. Cigale, Scyllarus arctus 74
Áron, modern *fidhókhorto*. Cuckoo-pint, lords-and-ladies, Arum maculatum 85
Ártamos, cook 214
Artoptíkios, a bread 165
Ártos, bread 91
Askolópas. Woodcock, Scolopax rusticola? 63
Aspháragos, modern *sparángi*, Turkish *kuş konmaz, asperj*. Asparagus, Asparagus spp. 83
Asphódelos, modern *sferdhoúkli*, Turkish *ciriş otu*. Asphodel, Asphodelus ramosus 85, 235
Astakós, modern *astakós*, Turkish *istakoz*. Langouste and lobster, Nephropsidae and Palinuridae spp. 229
Atháre, athéra, a broth 91
Atheríne, modern *atherína*, Turkish *gümüş balığı*. Sand-smelt, Atherina spp. 72
Attagâs, modern *taghinári* (Tournefort 1717), Turkish *duraç, turaç*. Francolin, Francolinus francolinus 65
Aulopías, unidentified fish 75, 229

Bálanos. Acorn, Quercus spp. 89, 220, 234
Basilikón *see* káryon
Batís, modern *vatí*, Turkish *vatoz*. Skate, Rajidae spp. 70
Batós, modern *vátos*, Turkish *bögürtlen*. Blackberry, Rubus fruticosus 80
Bátrakhos, modern *vatrakhópsaro*, Turkish *fener balığı*. Angler-fish, monkfish, Lophius spp. 68
Belóne, modern *sarghános, velonídhi*, Turkish *zargana*. Garfish, Belone acus 72
Bembraphýe, a fish dish 72
Bembrás, modern *papalína*, Turkish *çaça*. Sprat, Sprattus sprattus 72
Bíblinos oînos, a wine 95
Blékhon, modern *fliskoúni, glifóni*, Turkish *yarpuz*. Pennyroyal, Mentha pulegium 85
Blíton, modern *vlíto*, Turkish *lita*. Blite, Amaranthus blitum 83
Bolbós, modern *volvós*, Turkish *misk*

soğanı. Grape hyacinth, Muscari comosum 83, 234

Bótrys, modern stafíli, Turkish üzüm. Grape, Vitis vinifera 80

Boúglossos, modern glóssa, Turkish dil. Sole, Dover sole, Solea solea 72

Boúkeras, fenugreek 146; see also têlis

Bouniás, turnip 85; see also gongylís

Boûs, modern vódhi, Turkish inek. Ox, Bos taurus 59

Boútyron, butter 66, 226

Bôx, modern ghópa, Turkish gupa, kupes. Bogue, Boops boops 71

Brábilos, wild plum 78; see also kokkymêlon

Brekókion, prekókkion, modern veríkokko, Turkish kayısı, zerdali. Apricot, Armeniaca vulgaris 145, 181, 253

Brínkos, unidentified fish 75, 229

Brómos, modern vrómi, Turkish yulaf. Oats, Avena sativa 90


Dáktylos, modern khoúrmas, Turkish hurma. Date, Phoenix dactylifera 234

Daûkos, carrot 83, 234; see also staphylînos

Deîpnon, dinner 12, 106

Délphax, porker 59; see also hŷs

Dendrolíbanon, modern dhendrolívano, Turkish biberiye. Rosemary, Rosmarinus officinalis 190

Depsticius, a bread 165

Diosbálanos, sweet chestnut 220, 233; see also kastanaikón

Dípyros ártos, a biscuit 265

Dólikhos, later lovós. Dolichos lablab 90

Dolmádhes, a dish 79, 190

Domáta, Turkish domates. Tomato, Lycopersicon esculentum 201

Dorákinon, peach 182; see also persiké

Dorkás, roe deer 189; see also próx

Drákon, modern dhrákena, Turkish trahunya. Weever, Trachinus spp. 72

Drakóntion, modern dhrakondiá, Turkish yılan yastığı. Edderwort, dragon arum, Dracunculus vulgaris 66

Drûs, oak 220

Drypepés, fully ripe 78

Eídar, relish 104

Eilípous, with rolling gait 223

Eis toûpsa, eis toùs ikhthýas, ek tôn ornéon, sections of the Athenian market 27, 63

Ekhînos, modern akhinós, Turkish deniz kestanesi. Sea urchin, Paracentrotus lividus 74

Ekkoilíxas, having gutted 110

Élaion, modern eliá, Turkish zeytin. Olive, Olea europaea 78

Élaphos, modern eláfi, Turkish ala geyik. Red deer, Cervus elaphus 62

Elelísphakos, modern faskómilo, Turkish adaçayı. Greek sage, Salvia triloba 86

Eleodýtes, waiter 21

Élops, unidentified fish 75, 229

Élymos, foxtail millet 46, 90; see also melíne

Engraulís, modern ghávros, Turkish hamsi. Anchovy, Engraulis encrasicolus 72, 120

Énkhelys, modern khéli, Turkish yılan balığı. Eel, Anguilla anguilla 69

Énkhytos, a cake 156, 165

Epimelís 230; see also hamamelís

Epítyron, olive relish 231

Erébinthos, modern revíthi, Turkish nohut. Chickpea, Cicer arietinum 90

Erigéron, modern martiákos, Turkish kanarya otu. Groundsel, Senecio vulgaris 85

Erýsimon. London-rocket, Sisymbrium irio? 85, 235

Erythrînos, modern lithríni, moúsmouli, Turkish mercan, mandagöz. Pandora, pageot, Pagellus spp. 71, 228

Eskharítes, a bread 91

Étnos, bean soup 90

Euphrosýne, good cheer 243

Eustomakhótatos, very digestible 257

Eúzomon, modern róka, Turkish roka, solobur. Rocket, Eruca sativa 84


Fegós, modern velanídhi, Turkish palamut. Acorn of Valonia oak, Quercus macrolepis 9, 239

Féta, a cheese 190

Froxiliá, elderberry 220


Gála, milk 66, 226

Gálanga, laos 251
Galathenós, suckling 59
Galê, weasel 69
Galeós, modern *skilópsaro, ghaléos,*
Turkish *kedi balığı, köpek balığı.*
Dogfish, Scyliorhinidae, Squalidae,
Trichidae spp. 69
Gáros, fermented fish sauce 25, 75, 164,
199, 200, 229, 265
Gastrología, gourmet writing 119, 247
Gazéli, gazelle 189
Gelabrias, hake 228; *see also* kallarías
Gelotopoiós, joker 11, 214
Gentiané. Gentian, Gentiana spp. 192
Géranos, modern *gheranós,* Turkish
*turna kuşu.* Crane, Megalornis grus
65
Gerokomeîon, old people's home 217
Géron, old 94
Géteion, gethyllís, spring onion? 84,
163
Glanís, modern *glanídhi,* Turkish *yayın
balığı.* Catfish, Parasilurus
Aristotelis 68, 227
Glaúkiskos, unidentified fish 75, 229
Glaûkos. Bluefish, Pomatomus
saltator? 68
Gleûkos, must 89
Glykýs, sweet 25
Gnapheús, unidentified fish 75
Góngros, modern *moungrí,* Turkish
*mığrı.* Conger eel, Conger conger
69, 227
Gongylís, modern *réva,* Turkish
*şalğam.* Turnip, Brassica rapa 85
Groûta, a pudding 192
Gynaikonîtis, yinekonítis, women's
quarters 2, 15

Háles, salt 76
Halikákabon, modern *kerasoúli,*
Turkish *güveyfeneri.* Winter cherry,
Chinese lantern, Physalis alkekengi
80
Hálimon, modern *alimiá,* Turkish *kara
pazı.* Sea orach, Atriplex halimus 84
Hamamelís, crab apple 78
Hedýosmon, modern *dhiósmos,*
Turkish *nane.* Mint, Mentha spp. 83
Hépatos, unidentified fish 228
Hépsein, fry, boil 246
Hépsema, hepsetós, concentrated must
89, 245

Hepsetoí, a fish dish 72
Herakleotikón, hazelnut 233; *see also*
káryon pontikón
Hérpyllos, modern *khamothroúbi,*
Turkish *yabani kekik otu.* Creeping
thyme, Thymus spp. 86
Hestiatórion, temple dining room 215
Hetairá, courtesan 2, 12, 19, 20, 25, 154,
156, 214, 216
Híppos, modern *álogho,* Turkish *at.*
Horse, Equus caballus 61
Híppouros, modern *kinighós.* Dolphin-
fish, Coryphaena hippurus 68, 227
Horaîon, salted tuna 76
Hýaina, unidentified fish 228
Hýdnon, modern *troúfa,* Turkish *yer
mantarı, keme.* Truffle 83
Hydrómeli, mead 65
Hydroposía, water-drinking 197
Hypobinetiônta brómata, lascivious
foods 107
Hypokhoirís, modern *mounarídha,*
Turkish *dağ marulu.* Cat's ear,
Hypochoeris radicata 85
Hypósphagma, a sauce 110, 162
Hypótrimma, a sauce 245
Hŷs, modern *khíros,* Turkish *domuz.*
Pig, Sus scrofa 59
Hŷs, unidentified fish 71, 127, 228
Hýssopos, modern *íssopos,* Turkish
*zufa otu.* Hyssop, Hyssopus
officinalis 85

Ikhthŷs, fish 27
Intibus, endive 182; *see also* kíkhora
Íon, modern *menexés, ghioúli,* Turkish
*menekşe.* Violet, Viola odorata 192
Íops, sardine 72; *see also* bembrás
Ioulís, modern *ghilós,* Turkish *gün
balığı.* Rainbow wrasse, Coris julis
72
Ipnítes, a bread 91
Isíkion, a sausage 164, 180, 261
Iskhás, dried fig 79

Ka-na-ko 51; *see also* knêkos
Ka-ra-ko 51; *see also* blékhon
Kafenío, coffee house 206
Kákkabos, casserole 246
Káktos, cardoon 234; *see also* kinára
Kallarías, modern *bakaliáros,* Turkish
*barlam.* Hake, Gadiidae spp. 72
Kandaúles, divine name 245

Kándaulos, kándylos, a dish 106, 107, 111, 128, 156, 245, 263

Kántharos, modern *skathári*, Turkish *saragoz* (Davidson 1981 p. 89). Griset, Spondyliosoma cantharus 71

Kapeleîon, wine shop 182

Kápparis, modern *káppari*, Turkish *gebre*. Caper, Capparis spinosa 26, 83

Kápros, wild boar 62; *see also* hŷs; unidentified fish 227

Kárabos, modern *karavídha*, Turkish *kerevit*. Langoustine, Dublin Bay prawn, crayfish, Nephrops norvegicus 74, 229

Kárdamon, modern *kárdhamo*, Turkish *tere*. Cress, Lepidium sativum 83

Karís, modern *gharídha*, Turkish *karides*. Prawn, shrimp, Palaemonidae and Penaeidae spp. 74, 229

Karkharías, modern *karkharías*, Turkish *köpek balığı, harhariyas*. Shark, Squaliformes spp. 69, 227

Kárkinos, modern *kávouras*, Turkish *pavurya, yengeç*. Crab, Cancer and Carcinus spp. and others 74

Karó, modern *karnavádhi*, Turkish *karaman kimyonu, keraviye*. Caraway, Carum carvi 142

Karotón, carrot 83, 182; *see also* staphylînos

Karpésion, modern *miristikí*. Valeriana Dioscoridis 192

Karýke, a sauce 106, 128, 156, 245

Karykkopoiós, cook 106

Káryon, káryon basilikón, modern *karídhi*, Turkish *ceviz*. Walnut, Juglans regia 81, 232

Káryon kastanaikón, *see* kastanaikón

Káryon persikón 252; *see also* káryon basilikón

Káryon pontikón, modern *foundoúki*, Turkish *fındık*. Hazelnut, filbert, Corylus spp. 233

Karyóphyllon, gariofilum, modern *gharífalo*, Turkish *karanfil*. Cloves, Syzygium aromaticum 138, 183

Kásia, cinnamon, cassia 140; *see also* kinnámomon

Kastanaikón, modern *kástano*, Turkish *kestane*. Sweet chestnut, Castanea sativa 233

Katákhysma, a sauce 63

Katharós, white [bread] 190

Kaukalís, modern *kafkalíthra*, Turkish *girid sasalı*. Small hartwort, Tordylium apulum 85, 236

Kaulós, silphium stem 86, 87; *see also* sílphion

Kédrion, juniper berry 142, 260; *see also* arkeuthís

Kekarykeuména, spiced dishes 107

Kénkhros, modern *kekhrí*, Turkish *ak darı*. Broomcorn millet, Panicum miliaceum 90

Képhalos, kestreús, modern *kéfalos, gástros*, Turkish *kefal*. Grey mullet, Mugilidae spp. 68, 152, 166

Képphos. Stormy petrel, Hydrobates pelagicus? 63

Kérasos, modern *kerási, víssino*, Turkish *kiraz, vişne*. Cherry, Prunus avium, P. cerasus 78, 231

Keratonía, modern *kharoúpi*, Turkish *keçi boynuzu*. Carob, Ceratonia siliqua 146

Kerkópe, cicada 62; *see also* téttix

Kêryx. Horn-shell, Cerithium vulgatum? 73

Késtra, modern *toúrna, loútsos*, Turkish *turna balığı, iskarmos*. Pike and barracuda, Esox lucius, Sphyraena sphyraena 68

Kestreús, grey mullet 68; *see also* képhalos

Khalkís, pilchard 72; *see also* trikhís

Khamaiaktê, danewort 220

Khamaímelon, modern *khamomíli*, Turkish *tıbbi papatya*. Chamomile, Chamomilla aurea 192

Khelidón, modern *khelidonópsaro*. Flying fish, Exocoetus volitans, Dactylopterus volitans 72

Khéme leía, modern *kipréa*. Smooth venus, Callista chione 73, 229

Khéme trakheîa. Warty venus, Venus verrucosa 73

Khén, modern *khína*, Turkish *kaz*. Goose, Anser anser 64

Khenalópex. Egyptian goose, Chenalopex aegyptiaca? Shelduck, Casarca ferruginea? 65

Khlorís. Greenfinch, Chloris chloris? 63

Khoîros, piglet 59; *see also* hŷs

Khóndros, cracked emmer 91, 240

Khóndrylla, gum succory 236

Khórion, a pudding 66

Khrôma, turmeric 251

Khromís, modern *milokópi*, Turkish *minakop*. Maigre and ombrine, Sciaena spp. 70

Khrysókolla, honey sweets 51

Khrýsophrys, modern *tsípoura*, Turkish *çipura*. Daurade (gilt-head bream), Sparus aurata 71

Ki-ta-no, terebinth resin? 222

Kíkhle, modern *tsíkhla, tsártsara*, Turkish *ardıç kuşu*. Mistle thrush, Turdus viscivorus 63; wrasse 72; *see also* phykís

Kíkhora, modern *andídhi, radhíki*, Turkish *asıl hindiba*. Chicory and endive, Cichorium spp. 83

Kinára, kynára, modern *aghriaginára*, Turkish *kenger*. Cardoon, Cynara spp. 83, 234

Kínklos, modern *sousourádha*, Turkish *kuyruksallayan*. Wagtail, Motacilla spp. 65

Kinnámomon, modern *kanela*, Turkish *tarçın*. Cinnamon and cassia, Cinnamomum spp. and others 140

Kítharos. Guitar-fish, Rhinobatus rhinobatus? 70, 199

Kítrion, modern *kítron*, Turkish *ağaçkavunu*. Citron, Citrus medica 144, 176, 182, 260

Kítta, modern *kíssa*, Turkish *alakarga*. Jay, Garrulus glandarius 63

Klibaníkios, klibanítes, a bread 91, 165, 197

Klíbanos, kríbanos, baking-crock 59, 121, 197, 223

Knêkos, modern *saflanóni, aghriozaforá*, Turkish *aspur, yalancı safran*. Safflower, Carthamus tinctorius 86

Kníde, modern *kalıfídhi, tsiknídha*, Turkish *deniz sakayıkı*. Sea anemone, Anemonia sulcata 74

Ko-ri-ja-da-na, ko-ri-ja-do-no 50; *see also* koríannon

Kobiós, modern *ghoviós*, Turkish *kaya balığı*. Goby, Gobius spp. 72

Kodymalon, quince? 230

Kokhlías, modern *sáliagas*, Turkish *salyangoz*. Snail 62

Kokkymêlon, modern *dhamáskino, korómilo*, Turkish *erik*. Plum, Prunus spp. 78

Kókkyx, modern *kapóni*, Turkish *mazak*. Gurnard and piper, Trigla, Eutrigla spp. 72

Kólax, flatterer 11, 123, 214

Kóllix, a bread 91

Koloiós, modern *kárgha*, Turkish *karga*. Jackdaw, Corvus monedula 63

Kolokýnthe, colocynth 79

Kolymbís, modern *voutiktára*, Turkish *yumurta piçi*. Grebe, dabchick, Podiceps ruficollis 64

Kómakon, modern *moskhokáridho*, Turkish *küçük hindistancevizi*. Nutmeg, Myristica fragrans 264

Komastés, reveller 18

Kômos, drunken revel 18, 153, 156

Kónkhe, modern *méthistra, kidhóni*, Turkish *tarak*. Cockle, Cardiidae spp. 73

Kônos, modern *koukounári*, Turkish *çam fıstığı*. Pine kernel, Pinus spp. 81

Kopádi, copadia, a dish 183, 262

Kopís, Spartan festival 126

Kópsikhos, modern *kótsifas*, Turkish *karatavuk*. Blackbird, Turdus merula 63

Korakînos, modern *skiós*, Turkish *işkine*. Corb, Sciaena umbra 70

Koríannon, modern *kólliandros, kousvarás*, Turkish *kişniş*. Coriander, Coriandrum sativum 85

Kórkhoros. Molokhia, Jew's mallow, Corchorus olitorius 85, 236

Kórydos, modern *katsouliéris*, Turkish *tarla kuşu, toygar*. Crested lark, Galerida cristata 63

Korýphaina, dolphin-fish 227; *see also* híppouros

Kóssyphos, wrasse 72; *see also* phykís

Kóstos. Kuth, Saussurea lappa 192

Kóttabos, a party game 16, 17, 103, 108, 115, *see also* 216 n. 60

Koukkià misiriotiká, 'Egyptian beans', probably Dolichos lablab 218; *see also* dólikhos

Krámbe, modern *lákhano, krámbi*, Turkish *lahana*. Cabbage, Brassica oleracea 83

Kránon, modern *kráni*, Turkish *kızılcık*. Cornel, cornelian cherry, Cornus mas 44, 80

Krasí, wine 193, 243

Krâsis, mixing 243

Kratér, mixing bowl 48, 102, 112

Kreôn prátes, butcher 182

Krêthmon, modern *krítama*, *almiriá*, Turkish *deniz rezenesi*. Samphire, Crithmum maritimum 85

Kríbanos *see* klíbanos

Krímna, cracked barley 91, 240

Krimnêstis, krimnítes, a cake 256

Krithaíe sesamóessa, a broth 86

Krithé, modern *krithári*, Turkish *arpa*. Barley, Hordeum vulgare 90

Krókos, modern *zaforá*, Turkish *safran*. Saffron, Crocus sativus 142

Krómyon, modern *kremmídhi*, Turkish *soğan*. Onion, Allium cepa 84, 103

Kteís, modern *kténi*, Turkish *tarak*. Scallop, Pectinidae spp. 73

Ku-mi-no 50; *see also* kyminon

Ku-pa-ro 221; *see also* kypairos

Kýamos, modern *koukkí*, Turkish *bakla*. Broad bean, faba bean, Vicia faba 90

Kýbion, salted tuna 76

Kydonâton, marmalade 181

Kydónion, modern *kidhóni*, Turkish *ayva*. Quince, Cydonia vulgaris 78, 230

Kykeón, a broth 85, 151, 196

Kýknos, swan 225

Kýminon, modern *kímino*, Turkish *kimyon*. Cumin, Cuminum cyminum 50, 85, 221

Kýminon aithiopikón. Nigella, Nigella sativa 139

Kynára *see* kinára

Kynóglossos, modern *skilóglossa*. Hound's tongue, Cynoglossum officinale 85

Kýon, modern *skylí*, Turkish *köpek*. Dog, Canis familiaris 60

Kýon píon, dogfish 69; *see also* galeós

Kýpairos, English galingale 221

Kyprînos, modern *kiprínos*, Turkish *sazan*. Carp, Cyprinus carpio 68

Lábrax, modern *lavráki*, Turkish *levrek*, *ispendik*. Bass, Dicentrarchus spp. 70

Lagós, modern *laghós*, Turkish *tavşan*. Hare, Lepus spp. 61

Lakáre, bird cherry? 231

Lampsáne, modern *lákhana tou vounoú*. Hoary mustard, Hirschfeldia incana 85

Lápathos, modern *lápatho*, Turkish *labada*. Sorrel and dock, Rumex spp. 85

Látax, wine drop 108

Láthyros, modern *lathoúri*. Grass pea, chickling vetch, Lathyrus spp. 89

Látos, unidentified fish 75, 229

Leía *see* khéme leía

Leióbatos, ray 70; *see also* bátos

Lemóni, Turkish *limon*. Lemon, Citrus limonia 201

Léon, modern *léondas*, Turkish *aslan*. Lion, Panthera leo 62

Lepás, modern *petalídha*, Turkish *deniz kulağı*. Limpet, Patella caerulea 73

Leptokáryon, hazelnut 233; *see also* káryon pontikón

Leurós, level? 241

Ligystikón. Lovage, Levisticum officinale 142

Línon, modern *linón*, Turkish *keten*. Flax, linseed, Linum usitatissimum 85

Lopás, saucepan 246

Lotós, palíouros, modern *melikoukkiá*, *loutós*, *ghrizeliá*, Turkish *aleç*, *sidre*, *nebık*. Hackberry (nettle wood), Celtis australis; Christ's thorn, Zizyphus spina-Christi; Jew's thorn, Z. lotus 41, 80, 81, 145

Loukánikon, a sausage 181

Ma-ra-tu-wo 50; *see also* marathon

Mageireîon, where cooks were hired 11

Mageirikè tékhne, cookery 30

Mágeiros, sacrificer-cook 4, 6, 8, 9, 10, 114, 214

Magýdaris, Cachrys ferulacea 88

Maidonós, parsley 182; *see also* petrosélinon

Maíne [and smarís], modern *ménoula*, *marídha*, Turkish *izmarit*. Picarel and mendole, Spicara spp. 72

Maioúlion, lettuce 262; *see also* thrídax

Makedonikón, parsley 182; *see also* petrosélinon

Makelários, butcher 182

Makrókerkos, 'long-tailed' 237

Makropéperi. Long pepper, Piper longum 137

Malábathron, cassia 140; *see also* kinnámomon

Malákia, soft-bodied sea creatures 72

Márathon, modern *máratho*, Turkish *rezene*. Fennel, Foeniculum vulgare 83

Maroúli, lettuce 182; *see also* thrídax

Mastíkha, mastic-flavoured spirit 207

Mastíkhe, modern *mastíkha*, Turkish *sakız*. Mastic 82; *see also* skhînos

Mattyázein, have a mattye 255

Mattýe, a dish 156, 157, 255, 257

Mâza, barley mash 25, 91, 240

Medikós *see* mêlon; póa

Mékon, modern *afióni*, *paparoúni*, Turkish *afyon çiçegi*, *haşhaş*. Poppy, Papaver spp. 86

Melankóryphos, modern *kalóghiros*, Turkish *baştankara*. Great tit, Parus major 63

Melánouros, modern *melanoúri*, Turkish *melanurya*. Oblade, Oblada melanura 71

Melánthion, love-in-a-mist 139

Meleagrís, guinea fowl 254

Méli, honey 65

Méli kaì gála sýmpakton, melípekton, a dish 66, 226

Melíne. Foxtail millet, Setaria italica 46, 90

Mélinon, quince perfume 258

Melitzána, Turkish *patlican*. Aubergine, Solanum melongena 189

Mêlon, modern *mílo*, Turkish *elma*. Apple, Malus pumila 77, 78, 243

Mêlon armeniakón 145; *see also* brekókion

Mêlon hesperikón 252; *see also* kítrion

Mêlon kydónion *see* kydónion

Mêlon medikón 144, 182; *see also* kítrion

Melopépon, modern *pepóni*, Turkish *kavun*. Musk melon, Cucumis melo 79, 231

Mêon. Spignel, Meum athamanticum 192

Méspilon, modern *méspilo*, Turkish *muşmula*, *beşbıyık*. Medlar, Mespilus germanica 80

Méthy, wine 87, 226

Mi-ta 51; *see also* mínthe

Mimaíkylon, modern *koúmaro*, mamátsulo, Turkish *koca yemiş*. Arbutus berry, Arbutus unedo 80

Mímarkys, a dish 62

Mínthe 83; *see also* hedýosmon

Mízithra, a cheese 190

Molókhe, modern *molókha*, Turkish *ebegümeçi*. Mallow, Malva spp. 83

Monembasiós, malmsey 193

Mórmyros, modern *mourmoúra*, Turkish *çizgili mercan*. Morme (striped bream), Lithognathus mormyrus 71

Móron, modern *moúro*, Turkish *dut*. Mulberry, Morus nigra 80

Mýkes, mushroom 83; *see also* amanítes

Mýllos, unidentified fish 75, 229

Mŷma, a dish 163, 257

Mýraina, modern *smérna*, Turkish *izmirna*. Moray eel, Muraena helena 69, 228

Mýrsinon, myrtle blossom perfume 258

Mýrtinon, myrtle fruit perfume 258

Mýrton, modern *mirtiá*, Turkish *mersin*. Myrtle, Myrtus communis 80, 232

Mŷs, modern *mídhi*, Turkish *midye*. Mussel, Mytilidae spp. 73

Myttotós, a sauce 107, 244

Nâpy, modern *sinápi*, Turkish *hardal*. Mustard, Sinapis alba, Brassica nigra 85

Nárdos agría, modern *ághrios zaboúkos*, Turkish *kedi otu*. Valerian, Valeriana spp. 140

Nárdos keltiké. Valeriana celtica 140

Nárdos syriaké. Syrian nard, Cymbopogon iwarancusa 140

Nardóstakhys. Spikenard, Nardostachys jatamansi 192

Nárke, modern *trighóni*, *nárki*, Turkish *igneli vatoz*. Ray, Dasyatis and Torpedo spp. 70, 228

Nastós, a bread 91

Nebrós, fawn 62

Nerántzi, Turkish *turunç*. Bitter orange, Citrus aurantium 189

Nêssa, modern *pápia*, Turkish *yeşilbaş*. Mallard, Anas platyrhynchos 63

Nêstis, grey mullet 68; *see also* képhalos

Nítron, baking powder 91

Nýmphe, nubile woman 16

Óa, modern *soúrvo*, Turkish *üvez*. Sorb, service berry, Sorbus domestica 80
Oinás, modern *koutoupáni*, Turkish *üveyik*. Stock dove, Columba oenas 64
Oînos, wine 23, 87
Oînos ágrios, vin de pays 192
Oînos khydéos, vin de table 192
Oión, egg 65
Oiotárikhon, botargo 189
Ôkhros, modern *aghriafkós*, Turkish *papulas*. Lathyrus ochrus 25, 89
Ókimon, modern *vasilikós*, Turkish *fesleğen*. Basil, Ocimum basilicum 85
Ólyra, emmer 90; *see also* zeiaí
Ónagros, wild ass 62
Ónos, modern *gháidharos*, Turkish *eşek*. Ass, Equus asinus 60; modern *ghaidhourópsaro*, Turkish *gelincik balığı*. Rockling, Gaidaropsarus mediterraneus 72
Opós, silphium sap, fig sap, rennet 66, 86, 87
Opsárion, fish 24
Opsartysía, cookery 114
Opsartytikón, cookery 30, 110, 241
Ópson, relish 22–4, 27, 59, 103, 216, 257
Optân, bake, roast 246
Órdeilon, hartwort 236
Oríganon, modern *ríghani*, Turkish *kurthelvası*. Oregano, Origanum vulgare 85
Oríndes ártos, a bread 251
Orkhís, orchid, salep, *see also* satyrídion 86, 202
Órmenos, petraîon, modern *aghriosparángia*, Turkish *dikenli acı otu*. Wild asparagus 83, 234
Órnis, modern *kóta*, Turkish *tavuk*. Domestic fowl, Gallus gallus 63, 65
Ornithógala, Turkish *tükürük otu*. Star of Bethlehem, Ornithogalum spp. 85
Órobos, modern *oróvi*, Turkish *burçak*. Bitter vetch, Vicia ervilia 89
Orphós, modern *rofós*, Turkish *orfoz*. Grouper, Epinephelus spp. 70
Órtyx, modern *ortíki*, Turkish *bıldırcın*. Quail, Coturnix coturnix 63
Óryza, modern *rízi*, Turkish *pirinç*. Rice, Oryza sativa 141

Oryzítes plakoûs, a cake 141
Óstreon, modern *strídhi*, Turkish *istiridye*. Oyster, Ostrea edulis 73
Ótion. Ormer, Haliotis tuberculata 73, 226
Otóstyllon, unknown plant 238
Oulaí krithôn, groats 223
Oúzo, anise-flavoured spirit 207
Óxos, vinegar 89
Oxyé, modern *oxiá*, beech 239
Oxýgala, yoghourt? 66, 200
Oxylápathon. Curled dock, Rumex crispus 85

Paián, hymn 16, 17
Paigníon, game 244
Palíouros 40, 80, 81, 145; *see also* lotós
Parasiteîn, dine as guest 11
Parásitos, 'parasite', non-reciprocating guest 2, 11, 28, 123, 154, 216
Parthénion. Knotweed (water pepper), Polygonum spp. 85, 236
Patáta, Turkish *patates*. Potato, Solanum tuberosum 201
Paxamâs, paximádion, paksimat, a biscuit 165, 197, 205
Péganon, modern *apíghanos*, Turkish *sedef otu*. Rue, Ruta graveolens 86
Peleiás, modern *peristéri*, Turkish *yabani kumru*. Rock dove, Columba livia 64, 225
Pelekán, pelican 225
Peloriás, modern *khávaro*, *akhívadha*. Carpet-shell, Venerupis decussata 73, 229
Péperi, modern *pipéri*, Turkish *biber*. Pepper, Piper nigrum 137, 250
Pepón 79; *see also* síkyos pepón
Pérdix, modern *pérdhika*, Turkish *keklik*. Rock partridge, Alectoris graeca 65
Peristerá, modern *peristéri*, *pitsoúni*, Turkish *güvercin*. Domestic pigeon, Columba livia varieties 64, 225
Pérke, modern *pérka*, Turkish *yazılı hanı*. Comber, Serranus spp. 70, 228
Persiké, modern *rodhákino*, Turkish *şeftali*. Peach, Prunus persica 145
Persikón, peach 252; *see also* káryon basilikón
Petraîa, wrasses etc. 71, 288; *see also* phykís
Petraîon, wild asparagus *see* órmenos

Petrosélinon, makedonikón, modern *maidanós*, Turkish *maydanoz*. Parsley, Petroselinum sativum 182

Phágros, modern *fangrí*, Turkish *sinarit*. Pagre, Couch's sea bream, Sparus pagrus 71, 228

Phakê, lentil soup 90

Phakós, modern *fakí*, Turkish *merçimek*. Lentil, Lens culinaris 90

Phalarís, modern *falarídha*, Turkish *sakarmeki, sutavuğu*. Coot, Fulica atra 65

Pháselos, modern *mavromátiko*, Turkish *börülce*. Calavance, Vigna sinensis 90, 239

Phasianós, modern *fasianós*, Turkish *sülün*. Pheasant, Phasianus colchicus 64

Phátta, modern *fássa*, Turkish *tahtalı*. Wood pigeon, ring dove, Columba palumbus 64

Phoiníkios oînos, a wine 242

Phoîniks, date palm 233

Phournákios, a bread 165

Phoûska, cheap wine 85, 89, 196

Phratría, fraternity 12

Phykís, modern *khiloú*, Turkish *lapina*. Wrasse, Labrus, Crenilabrus spp. 72

Phýllon. Tejpat, Cinnamomum tamala 192; also modern *dháfni*, Turkish *defne*, Bay, Laurus nobilis

Píne, modern *pínna*, Turkish *pines*. Fanmussel, Pinna nobilis 73

Písos, modern *bizéli, arakás*, Turkish *bezelye*. Pea, Pisum sativum 90

Pistákion, modern *fistíki*, Turkish *antep fıstığı, şam fıstığı*. Pistachio, Pistacia vera 146

Píston, a broth 197, 265

Plakountopoiikós, cake-making 111

Plakoûs, cake 91, 111, 165

Po-ni-ki-jo, purple 221, 234

Póa mediké, alfalfa, lucerne 238

Pontikón *see* káryon pontikón

Porphyríon. Moorhen, Gallinula chloropus? 63, 224

Pótos, drinking 12, 102, 103, 156

Poulypódeia, little octopuses 72

Poulýpous, modern *khtapódhi*, Turkish *ahtapot*. Octopus, Octopodidae spp. 72

Prámneios oînos, a wine 95, 254

Prasía, garden 83

Práson, modern *práso*, Turkish *prasa, pırasa*. Leek, Allium porrum 83

Prekókkion, *see* brekókion

Próbaton, modern *arní*, Turkish *koyun*. Sheep, Ovis aries 59

Prosphágema, prosphágion, prosfái, relish, cheese 15, 24, 216

Prósphatos, a cheese 190

Prótropon, a wine 96, 149

Próx, dorkás, modern *zarkádhi*, Turkish *karaca*. Roe deer, Capreolus capreolus 62

Prytaneîon, municipal building 12, 13, 215

Psár, modern *psaróni*, Turkish *sığırcık*. Starling, Sturnus spp. 63

Psári, fish 24

Psêtta. Sinistral flatfish, Citharus, Lepidorhombus, Bodus, Arnoglossus spp.? 72

Psíthios oînos, a wine 241

Psomí, bread 190

Ptisáne, a broth 91

Pyós, beestings 66

Pyramís, a cake 160

Pyrgítes, sparrow 189; *see also* strouthós

Pyriáte, yoghourt? 66

Pyrós. Club wheat, Triticum turgidum ssp. compactum (Triticum aestivocompactum) 46, 91, 240

Raphanís, modern *repáni*, Turkish *turp*. Radish, Raphanus sativus 84

Ráphanos. Kale, Brassica oleracea var. acephala 83

Ráphys, rápys, turnip 85, 235, 245; *see also* gongylís

Réngai, kippered herrings 189

Ríne, modern *ángelos*, Turkish *keler balığı*. Angel shark, angel-fish, monkfish, Squatina squatina 69

Rizotómos, herbalist 125

Róa, modern *roídhi*, Turkish *nar*. Pomegranate, Punica granatum 80

Rodákinon, peach 182; *see also* persiké

Rómbos, modern *kalkáni*, Turkish *kalkan*. Brill and turbot, Rhombus spp. 72

Roûs, modern *soumáki*, Turkish *sumak*. Sumach, Rhus coriaria 86, 238

Ryparós, wholemeal 190

Sa-sa-ma 52; *see also* sésamon
Sálpe, modern *sálpa*, Turkish *çitari*, *sarpa*. Saupe, Sarpa salpa 71
Salsíkion, a sausage 181
Sámpsykhon 237; *see also* amárakon
Sapérdes, salt fish 76
Saprías, a wine 101
Saprós, rotten 75, 100
Sargînos 244; *see also* belóne
Sargós, modern *sarghós*, Turkish *karagöz balığı*. Sar, Diplodus sargus 71
Satyrídion, satýrion, modern *salépi*, Turkish salep. Orchis mascula 86, 237
Saûros, modern *savrídhi*, Turkish *istavrit*. Scad, Trachurus spp. 72
Seirà salsikíon, string of sausages 181
Selákhe, cartilaginous fish 69
Sélinon, modern *sélino*, Turkish *kereviz*. Celery, Apium graveolens 83
Semídalis. Durum wheat, Triticum turgidum ssp. durum 91, 239, 240
Sepía, modern *soupiá*, Turkish *mürekkep balığı*, *supya*. Cuttlefish, Sepia officinalis and Sepiolidae spp. 72
Sepídia, little cuttlefish 72
Sepíes hypósphagma, cuttlefish ink 110
Séris 83; *see also* kíkhora
Sesamóeis, sesame-flavoured 86
Sésamon, modern *sisámi*, Turkish *susam*. Sesame, Sesamum indicum 86, 221
Sesamópastos, sesame-sprinkled 86
Sesamótyron, a sweet 86
Séseli, hartwort 236, 250
Síde 126; *see also* róa
Sikýa, modern *fláski*, Turkish *su-kabağı*. Gourd (bottle gourd), Lagenaria vulgaris 79
Síkyos, modern *angoúri*, Turkish *hıyar*. Cucumber, Cucumis sativus 79
Síkyos pepón, modern *karpoúzi*, Turkish *karpuz*. Watermelon, Citrullus lanatus 79
Silígnion, sílignis, modern *stári*, Turkish *buğday*. Bread wheat, Triticum aestivum 240
Sílouros. Sheatfish, Silurus glanis 68
Sílphion, silphium. Sílphion medikón, Asafoetida, Ferula asafoetida 86, 251

Sínon. Stone parsley, Sison amomum 192
Síon, modern *nerosélino*, Turkish *su-kerevizi*. Water parsnip, Sium latifolium 85
Síraion, concentrated must 89
Sisýmbrion, modern *aghriódhiosmos*, Turkish *su-yarpuzu*. Water mint, Mentha aquatica 83
Siteutós, force-fed 224
Sîtos, food, army food supply 22, 23
Síttybos, tag 246
Skándix, modern *aghriokádzika*, Turkish *çoban darağı*. Wild chervil, Venus' comb, Scandix pecten-Veneris 85, 235
Skaren, perhaps same as next 67, 228
Skáros, modern *skáres*, Turkish *iskaroz*. Parrot wrasse, Scarus cretensis 71, 72
Skhînos. Lentisk, Pistacia lentiscus 81
Skhoínanthos. Ginger grass, Cymbopogon schoenanthus 192
Skílla, modern *skilokremídho*, *koutsoúpi*, Turkish *adasoğanı*. Squill, Urginea maritima 85, 190
Skólion, drinking song 17
Skólymos, modern *skólimbros*, *askolímbri*. Golden thistle, Spanish salsify, Scolymus hispanicus 85
Skómbros, modern *skoumbrí*, Turkish *uskumru*. Mackerel, Scomber spp. 71
Skórodon, modern *skórdho*, Turkish *sarmusak*. Garlic, Allium sativum 85, 236
Skórpios, modern *skórpena*, Turkish *iskorpit*. Rascasse, Scorpaena spp. 72
Skriblítes, a cake 165
Smyrneîon, modern *mavrosélino*, *skilosélino*. Alexanders, Smyrnium olusatrum 85
Solén, modern *solína*, Turkish *solinya*. Razor-shell, Solen vagina 73
Sónkos, modern *zokhós*, *galatsídha*, Turkish *süt otu*. Sow-thistle, Sonchus spp. 85
Spaerita, a cake 165
Spanáki, Turkish *ispanak*. Spinach, Spinacia oleracea 84, 201
Spáros, modern *spáros*, Turkish *ispari*. Sparaillon (annular bream), Diplodus annularis 71
Spétsiai, modern *piperiá*, Turkish

*kırmızı biber*. Chilli, Capsicum spp. 201

Sphákos, sage 86; *see also* elelísphakos

Sphoungâton, omelette 181

Sphýraina, pike 68; *see also* késtra

Spínos, modern *spínos*, Turkish *ispinoz*. Chaffinch, Fringilla coelebs 63

Spîra, a cake 165

Splánkhna, vital parts 61

Spodítes, a bread 91

Staitítas, a cake 256

Staktέ, myrrh oil 165

Staphylînos, modern *karóto*, Turkish *havuç*. Carrot, Daucus carota 83, 234

Stibás, semicircle of diners 14

Stróbilos, pine kernel 81; *see also* kônos

Strómbos. Triton, Triton neritea, or whelk? 73, 229

Stroúthion, quince 78; *see also* kydónion

Strouthós, pyrgítes, modern *spourghítis*, Turkish *serçe*. Sparrow, Passer spp. 63

Strýkhnon, modern *stífno*, Turkish *it üzümü*, *köpek üzümü*. Garden nightshade, Solanum nigrum 85, 235

Stýrax, modern *astírakas*, *stourakiá*, Turkish *asilbent*. Benzoin, Styrax benzoin 192

Sykalís. Blackcap or other warblers, Sylviidae spp. 54, 63, 224

Sŷkon, modern *síko*, Turkish *incir*. Fig, Ficus carica 54, 79

Sykotón, liver 182

Sympósion, symposium, drinking party 12, 13, 16–20, 63, 102, 119, 155, 212

Synagrís 228; *see also* synódous

Synanthropeuómena, animals symbiotic with man 60

Synaristôsai, 'Women Lunching Together' 213

Synódous, modern *sinaghrídha*, Turkish *sinarit*. Denté, Dentex spp. 71, 228

Syssítion, communal meal 20

Tabérnion, wine shop 182

Tagenízein, pan-fry 246

Tahôs, modern *paghóni*, Turkish *tavus kuşu*. Peafowl, Pavo cristatus 146

Tainía, modern *tzípoula*. Cépole, Cepola rubescens 72, 110, 244

Tamòn temákhea, having sliced 110

Tárikhos, salt fish 230

Teganítes, pancake 91

Têlis, modern *nikháki*, Turkish *boy otu*. Fenugreek, Trigonella foenum-graecum 146

Tellíne, modern *kokhíli*. Wedge-shell, Donax trunculus 73, 229

Términthos, modern *tsíkoudho*, *kokkorevithiá*, Turkish *çitlembik*. Terebinth, Pistacia terebinthus 81, 253

Téthyon, modern *eliá*, Turkish *deniz yumurtası*. Sea-squirt, Microcosmus sulcatus 74

Téttix, modern *tsítsikas*. Cicada 62

Teuthídia, little squids 72

Teuthís, modern *kalamári*, Turkish *kalamar*. Squid, Loligo vulgaris, Todarodes sagittatus, Alloteuthis media 72

Teûtlon, modern *padzári*, Turkish *pazi*. Chard, beet, Beta vulgaris 83

Theilópedon, grape-drying mat? 241

Therápontes, servants 214

Thérmos, modern *loúpino*, *liboúsi*, *pikrokoukkiá*, Turkish *acı bakla*. Lupin, Lupinus alba 89

Thólos, municipal building 14

Thrídax, modern *maroúli*, Turkish *marul*. Lettuce, Lactuca sativa 83

Thrîon, fig leaf; a dish 79, 156, 189

Thríssa, modern *fríssa*, Turkish *tersi*. Shad, Alosa spp. 72

Thýmbra, modern *throúmbi*, Turkish *girid kekik*. Roman hyssop, Satureja thymbra 86

Thýmon, modern *thimári*, Turkish *kekik*. Cretan thyme, Coridothymus capitatus 86

Thýnnos, modern *tónnos*, Turkish *orkinos*. Tunny, Thunnus, Euthynnus spp. 68

Típhe. Einkorn, Triticum monococcum 90

Tórdylon, hartwort 236

Tragémata, dessert 23

Tragopógon, modern *laghókhorto*, Turkish *yemlik otu*. Salsify (goat's beard), Tragopogon spp. 85

Tragós, traganós, trakhanás, a broth 201, 266

Trapezopoiós, waiter 9, 10, 213, 214

Trígle, modern *barboúni*, *koutsomoúra*,

Turkish *tekir, barbunya*. Red mullet, Mullus spp. 72

Trikhís, modern *fríssa tríkhios, sardhélla*, Turkish *sardalya*. Pilchard, Sardinella spp. 72

Trimmátion, a sauce or salad 69

Trókhilos, modern *vrokhopoúli*, Turkish *yağmur kuşu*. Plover, Charadrius spp. 64

Trygón, modern *trighóni*, Turkish *yusufçuk*. Turtle dove, Streptopelia turtur 64

Tyrós, cheese 66

Tyrotarichus, a dish 66

Vatrakhópsaro, angler-fish 227; *see also* bátrakhos

Vouziá, danewort 220

Xenodokheîon, inn 196

Xerophagía, eating without oil or sauce 197

Xiphías, modern *xifía*, Turkish *kılıç balığı*. Swordfish, Xiphias gladius 68

Yinekonítis, women's part of church 15

Zaboúkos, elderberry 220

Zargánai 244; *see also* belóne

Zeiaí. Emmer, Triticum turgidum ssp. dicoccum 90

Zingíberi, modern *zingíveris*, Turkish *zencefil*. Ginger, Zingiber officinale 138

Zízyphos, modern *tzítzifo*, Turkish *hünnap, çiğde*. Jujube, Zizyphus jujuba 145

# GENERAL INDEX

Abdera 99, 127
absinthe 142, 150, 192
Abydos 128
Acanthus 127
Achaea 136
acorns 24, 43, 47, 89, 125
*Acraephia price list* 67
acrobats 155
Adrianople 197
Aegean island produce 105, 107, 127, 244
Aegeate wine 149
Aegilia 126
Aegium 125
Aelius Verus 261
Aenus 127
Aetius of Amida 188
Aetolia 136
African produce 129
Agapius of Crete 188
Agathon 18
Aghia Triada 36, 219
ajowan 139
Akhillion 43
Akrotiri 36, 38, 43, 47, 52, 75, 219
Alcibiades 20
Alexander, King 15, 143, 152, 154
alexanders 85
Alexandria 191
almonds 38, 43, 81, 104, 105, 115, 209
amber 266
ambergris 202
Ambracia 120, 127
Ambraciot wine 148
Aminean wine 148
Anatolia 77, 79, 81, 145
Anatolius of Berytus 188
anchovy 72

angel shark 69
anise 50, 85, 192, 221
Anthedon 127
Anthimus 188
antidote 138
Antigonus, King 154, 161
Anzabegovo 43
aphrodisiacs 83, 86, 119
Aphrodisiaean wine 149
*Apicius* 179
apples 43, 77, 78, 105, 126, 127, 181, 198, 203
apples of the Hesperides 144
apricots 145, 181, 230
arbutus 43, 80
Arcadia 125
Archestratus 117–21, 158, 159
Argissa Magoula 35, 36, 42, 219
Argos 125
Aristomenes of Athens 171
Aristophanes of Byzantium 58
Aristotle 157, 159
Aristoxenus of Cyrene 59
Ariusian wine 148, 149
Armenia 145
aromatics *see* spices
artichoke 201; *see also* cardoon
asafoetida 87, 140
asparagus 83, 181
asphodel 24, 85
Asprokhaliko 35, 36, 219
ass 36, 37, 60, 62, 156, 189
Assiros 46
Astypalaea 128
Athenaeus 110, 133, 167–79
Athenaeus of Attaleia 166
Athens 26, 27, 63, 120–6, 154, 158; dining customs 1–20

Attica 105
aubergine 189

bachelor's buttons *see* feverfew
baker 106, 109, 128, 190, 205
baking 39, 44–5, 90–1, 246
bananas 209
barley 22, 25, 39, 41, 44–6, 52, 90, 91, 115, 121, 128, 190
basil 82, 85
bass 68, 70, 113, 152
beans (broad bean, faba bean) 46, 90, 218
bear 36, 62
beef *see* ox
bees 47
beet 82, 83
beggars 25
Belon, Pierre 200
benzoin 192
Berezan letter 250
Bergamot mint 235
Bibline wine 95, 100
Biddle, Nicholas 196, 201
bilberry 232
bird-catchers 63
birds 62, 63, 159, 166
biscuit 165, 192, 196, 257
Bithynia 136, 148, 150
black broth 45, 126
Black Sea trade 68, 75–6, 120, 128–9, 189
blackberries 43, 80, 81
blackbird 63, 166
blackcap, beccafico, warbler 63, 157, 166
blite 82, 83
blood 62, 197
bluefish 68, 113, 152
Boeotia 127, 136
boiling 22, 44–5, 65, 246
Bolbe, Lake 152
bonito 70, 128, 158
*Book of the Eparch* 197
botargo 189
brain 22
bread 27, 30, 44, 91, 115, 121, 126, 157, 178, 190, 204
bread wheat 190, 220, 240
bream 71
brine 87, 95, 148
bulb *see* grape hyacinth
butchers 182, 205

butter 65, 89, 204
Byblian wine 96, 97
Byzantium, Constantinople 120, 128, 187–205

cabbage 22, 51, 82, 83
cakes 22, 30, 86, 91, 120, 126, 156, 160, 171
calavance 25, 90, 199
Callias, 4th century 11
Callias, 5th century 154
Calydna 129, 136
Calydon 127
Calypso 15
camel 60
Candia 190, 195, 204
capers 25, 83
Caranus 154
caraway 142, 199, 221
cardamom 180
cardoon 83
Caria 79, 128, 129
carobs 146, 192
carp 43, 68
carpet-shell 73
carrot 83, 182
Carthage 120
Carystus 127
cassia 140
cat's ear 85
Catacecaumenite wine 149
Çatal Hüyük 42
catfish 68
Cato 165
cattle *see* ox
caviar 189, 200, 227
celery 50, 83, 222
Cephallenia 44
Chaerephon 123, 124
chaffinch 22, 63
Chalcedon 128
Chalcis 127
Chalybonian wine 97
chambre 128
chamois 37, 40
chamomile 180, 192
Charax 136
Chares 14
cheese 22, 23, 24, 42, 66, 104, 105, 108, 125, 135, 136, 166, 190, 196, 204, 250
cherries 78
Chersonesus Taurica 48
chervil 25, 85

chestnuts 81, 104, 105, 127, 128, 220
Chevdar 36, 219
Chian wine 95, 100, 147, 148, 193
chicken *see* fowl, domestic
chickpeas 46, 90, 128
chicory 83, 182
chilli 201, 209
Chios 128
Christ's thorn 81, 145
Chrysippus of Tyana 164, 165
chufa 221
cicada 25, 62
cigale 74
Cimolos 127
cinnamon 140, 192
citrons 143, 145, 176, 182, 192, 203
Clazomenean wine 148
Cleonae 125
cloves 138, 192
club (compactum) wheat 46, 90, 220
Cnidian wine 147, 149
Cnidos 128
Coan wine 87, 147, 148
Cochin 137
cockerel *see* fowl, domestic
cockles 37, 73
coffee 205
colocynths 79
comber 70
communal meals 12, 20
conditum 192; *see also* flavoured wine
conger 68, 69, 113, 120, 125
conserves 192
Constantine Porphyrogennetus 164, 188
Constantinople *see* Byzantium
cooks 3, 4, 11, 28, 30, 106, 108, 113, 125, 128, 161, 162, 163, 182, 195, 205, 214
cookery books 109–11, 113–14, 122, 240
cookery in comedy 121
coot 64
Copais, Lake 69, 120, 127
corb 70
coriander 49, 85, 221
Corinth 125
cornels 43, 80
Coron 203
Cos 128, 136; *see also* Coan wine
couches 3, 13, 14
courtesan *see* hetairá in Greek index
courtship 12, 17, 19, 27, 29, 61, 63, 65, 78, 157, 198

crab 74
crane 65
cress 82, 83, 128
Cretan wine 149, 193, 195, 204
Crete 20, 127, 136, 190, 193, 194, 200, 204
Crimea 48, 241
cuckoo-pint 85
cucumber 79, 126, 127, 128, 203
cumin 50, 85
cumin-salt 199
currants 201
cuttlefish 22, 72, 110, 127, 166, 220
Cuzinas 193
Cyclops 26, 108, 109
Cydonia 127
cyperus 180, 221
Cyprus 81, 107
Cyrene 86, 105, 136, 142
Cythnos 136, 250

dancers 7, 10, 119, 153, 155
dandelion 236
danewort 43, 220
darnel 91
date wine 82, 242
dates 47, 82, 105, 203
deer 36–8, 40, 43, 62
Delos 21, 127
Demeter 85, 121
Demetrius Poliorcetes, King 154, 156
dessert 8, 23, 103, 115, 155, 156, 159
didactic poetry 116, 117, 121
Didyma 128
dietetics 161, 191, 193
Dieuches 162
dill 50, 83
Dimini 36, 44, 219
dining clubs 12
dining room *see* andrón and hestiatórion in Greek index
Dio Chrysostom, *Euboean Oration* 1
Diocles of Carystus 161
Diocletian, Emperor 183; *Price Edict* 179
Dionysius the Elder, King 115
Dionysius the Younger, King 115
Dionysus 18, 20, 87, 96, 101, 105, 214
Dioscorides 133, 165, 188
Diphilus of Siphnos 161
Dium 127, 152
dock 85
dog 21, 45, 60, 107, 219

dogfish 69, 113
dolphin-fish 43
dolphins 21
domestication 37–52, 77
dormouse 180
dove 64, 166
dried meat 40, 189
drinking party *see sympósion* in Greek index
duck 44, 63, 199
durum wheat 46, 91

eel 69, 76, 113, 120, 125, 127, 152
eggs 7, 44, 65, 80, 115, 147, 157, 161, 166, 225
Egypt 21, 94, 96, 218, 221
einkorn 40, 90
elderberry 220
elephant 36
Elis 21, 125
emmer 40, 45, 90, 201
endive 83, 182
English galingale 221
Ennius, *Hedyphagetica* 118
Epaenetus 163
Ephesian wine 149
Ephesus 128
Epicharmus 116
Epimenides 24, 85
*Epitome of Athenaeus* 174, 175
Erasistratus of Iulis 162
Eresus 121, 128
Eretria 127
Erythrae 121, 128
Euboea 81, 105, 127
Euboean wine 193
Eumaeus 24, 59, 104
Eustathius of Thessalonica 260
Euthydemus of Athens 162
Evliya Çelebi 197, 205

fairs 204, 205
fan-mussel 73
Farâhâni 196
fast days 197
fat hen *see* goosefoot
fennel 50, 83
fenugreek 25, 146, 165
festivals 6, 12, 20, 21, 26, 101
feverfew 85
fig leaves 79, 107, 189
fig-pecker *see* blackcap

figs 24, 25, 43, 47, 48, 77, 79, 105, 107, 126, 128, 129, 159, 191, 223, 248
filberts 81, 233
fish 23, 24, 27, 43, 66–76, 124–9, 199, 207
fish sauce *see gáros* in Greek index
fish-plates 226
flatfish 72
flatterer *see kólax* in Greek index
flavoured drinks 192, 197
flavoured wine 87, 137, 142, 150, 190, 192, 221
flax 51–2, 85
flour 39, 91
flute-players 6, 9–11, 17–18, 119, 125, 153, 214
flying fish 72
foie gras 64, 182, 224
food avoidances 21–2, 216
food from the wild 26, 43, 80, 81, 85
food storage 36, 39
food terminology 71, 110, 163–5, 179–83
food trade 104–5, 133
fowl, domestic 63, 65, 127, 156, 166, 203
fox 38, 62, 107
francolins 65, 166
Frankhthi 35, 37, 38, 42, 49, 57, 219
fruit 7, 23, 76–82, 142–6
frumenty 91, 192
frying 72, 166, 246
funeral banquets 15

Galen 133, 166, 169
gallinule 224
games 106
Ganitic wine 193
gardens 82
garfish 72, 244
garlic 85, 107, 199, 200
gazelle 189
gentian 180, 192
*Geoponica* 164, 188
gifts 27, 61, 63, 65, 78, 154
gilliflower 165
ginger 138
ginger grass 192
Glaucus of Locri 110, 162
gluttony 60, 108, 122, 153
goat 41, 44, 45, 58, 62, 105, 107, 166
goby 72
golden thistle 24, 85
goose 44, 63, 64

goosefoot 51, 85
gourds 79, 127
grape, vine 23, 43, 47, 53, 77, 80
grape hyacinth 83
grass pea 45, 89
grasshopper 224
grebe 64
greenfinch 63, 166
grey mullet 68, 127, 152, 158, 166
greyfish see bluefish
groundsel 85
grouper 70
grubs 21, 62
gruel 45, 91
guests 7, 10–15, 17, 21, 29, 59, 104, 123, 203
guinea fowl 254
guitar-fish 228
gurnard 72
gypsum 199

Hacilar 36, 43, 219
hackberries 43, 80, 145
Hadrian, Emperor 171
hake 72, 127
hare 27, 37, 38, 43, 61, 107
haricot bean 201, 239
Harpocration of Mendes 164
hartwort 85, 250
hazelnuts 43, 81
heart 22, 61
Hecale 85
hedgehog 21, 62, 224
Hegesippus of Tarentum 111
Hellenistic agriculture 96, 143, 181
Hellespont 105, 107, 128
Heracleides of Syracuse 161
Heracles 14, 122
herbal remedies 221
herbalists 125, 205
herbs 50, 85–6, 127
Hermes 16, 61, 121
Hesiod 117
Hicesius of Smyrna 165
Hierophilus the Sophist 188, 192
Hippolochus 155, 158
hippopotamus 36
Hissarlik 44
Historia Augusta 179
hoary mustard 85
Homeric epic 22, 99; agriculture 76–7, 241–2; gastronomy 104; hospitality 102, 104; trade 134–5

honey 24, 47, 65, 104, 115, 126, 136, 167, 199, 208, 209, 250
horn-shell 38, 73, 128
horse 21, 60, 61
hospitality 2, 21, 29, 102, 104, 126
hound's tongue 85
human flesh 61
hunting 27, 43, 61, 155
Hymettus, Mount 126
hyssop 85

Iasus 128
Iatrocles 160
ibex 37, 39, 40, 43
Icaros 128
ice 202
incense 104, 109
Indian Ocean trade 97
inns 12, 61, 195, 196
invalid foods 141, 189
Io 135
Ionia 107, 110, 111
iris 235
Ismarus 99, 148
Italian wine 147, 148, 193
Italy 108
Ithaca 33

jackdaw 63
jay 63
Jew's mallow see molokhia
jokers 11
jujubes 145
Julian, Emperor 188
juniper 142, 260

Kamares Cave 218
Kastanas 36, 46, 50, 52, 57, 219, 220
Kastritsa 35, 37, 219
Kazanluk 36, 43, 219
kermes-oak 239
kestrel 224
kid 43, 58, 59, 113, 199
kidney bean 239
kidneys 61
kill-off patterns 42, 220
kipper 189
Klithi 35, 37, 219
Knossos 35, 36, 42, 46, 218, 219
knotweed 85, 236
Konitsa 45
kuth 180, 192

Laconia 126; *see also* Sparta
Lais 7
lamb 42, 59, 190
Lamia 154
lamprey 228
Lampsacus 107
langoustine 74, 166
laos 251
lark 63
Lathyrus spp. 25, 45, 89, 239; *see also* grass pea
leek 83, 199
Lemnian wine 206
Lemnos 203
lemons 144, 192, 201, 203
lentil soup 90
lentils 22, 39–45, 90
lentisk 38, 43, 81, 207
Lerna 35, 43, 46, 219
Lesbian wine 97, 100, 101, 136, 149, 162, 193
Lesbos 128
lettuce 82, 83, 126, 182
Leucadian wine 127, 148
libation 16, 61, 104
limpets 43, 73
Linear B 50–2
linseed *see* flax
lion 62
Liutprand of Cremona 198
liver 61, 182
lobster 74
local gastronomy 105, 124–9, 157–60, 193
locust 224
London-rocket 85
long pepper 137
lovage 142
love-in-a-mist 139
lupins 24, 25, 89
luxury 38, 47, 49, 93–109, 152–7, 197
Lydia 106, 110, 128, 248
Lynceus 122, 157–60, 248
Lysimachus 162

Macedonia 14, 62, 152–7
mackerel 71, 105, 200
Magnesia 127
Magnesian wine 99, 101
Mago 164
maigre, meagre 70, 107, 127, 152
mallard *see* duck
mallow 24, 51, 83, 217

malmsey grape 193, 194, 195
Manlian vintage 95
Marathon 126
marjoram 129, 165, 237
markets 27, 125, 128, 133, 158, 204
marmalade 181, 192
Marmariani 36, 50, 219
Maronea 99, 127
marrow 38, 61, 231
mastic 82, 128, 192, 207
mead 65
meadowsweet 165
meagre *see* maigre
meal times 12, 18–20
meat 22, 23, 58–65
Media 143
medlars 80
Megara 126
Meliboea 101
melons 78, 201
Melos 35, 40, 219
men at meals 4–6, 15
Menander 2, 212
Mendaean wine 99, 100, 101, 152
mercenaries 118
Mesopotamia 96
Methymna 128
Middle Comedy 121
migrations 34
Milan 204
Miletus 21, 105, 128
milk 42, 65, 106
milk pudding 66
millet 46, 90, 197
mint 51, 83, 222, 246
Mithaecus 109–10
Mithridates 138
Mnesitheus of Athens 162
Modon 199, 204
molokhia 85, 236
monastic food 197
Monemvasiote wine 193
monkfish 228
moorhen 63
moray 69
morme 71, 158
Mosul 191
mulberries 80, 145
murri 200
muscat grape 193, 195, 204, 206
mushrooms 25, 83
music, musicians 7, 106, 119, 155; *see also* flute-players

muskmelons 52, 145
mussel 73, 127, 128
must 89, 207
mustard 50, 51, 85, 199
mustard greens 83
mutton *see* sheep
Muziris 137
Mycenae 36, 43, 44
Myconian wine 149
myrrh 150, 165
myrtle 80, 115, 150, 165
Mysia 136
Mysian wine 149
Mytilene 71, 128

nard 140
Naxos 95, 104, 105
Nea Nikomedia 36, 42–5, 219
neat wine 103, 193
Nemea 125
Nero, Emperor 140
nettle 83
New Comedy 1–2, 212
Nicaean wine 193
Nicomedian wine 149
nigella 139
nightshade 51, 85
noble rot 101
nostalgia 103
number of guests 14, 115, 118
Numenius of Heraclea 257
nutmeg 190
nuts 7, 23, 25, 81

oats 39, 90
octopus 22, 72, 127, 128, 220
Odysseus 59, 109
Oeneate wine 148
Old Comedy 116
olive oil 49, 66, 89, 203
olives 23, 25, 47, 48, 53, 77, 78, 221
Olynthus 118, 152, 153
omelette 181
onion 84, 103, 127, 128, 199, 203
Opimian vintage 95
opium 52
orach 82, 84
oranges 189, 203, 209, 264
orchards 77
orchid *see* salep
oregano 85, 125, 127
Oretic wine 148
Oribasius 187

ormer 73
ovens 9, 44–5, 53, 109, 120, 128, 204
owl 63
ox 37, 42, 44, 45, 59, 105, 107, 127, 153, 166, 220
ox feet 45, 60
oysters 43, 73, 123, 127

pancakes 166
Paphlagonia 105
parasite *see parásitos* in Greek index
Parium 128
Parmenon of Rhodes 164
parody 117, 121
Paros 127
parrot 224
parsley 182
parsnip 234
partridge 44, 65
pastirma 189, 201
pastry-chef 156
Patras 206
Paul of Aegina 188
Paxamus 164, 196
peaches 144, 181
peafowl 44, 146, 147, 161
pears 25, 39, 43, 77, 79, 80, 105, 127, 192
peas 39–41, 45, 90
pease pudding 190
pelican 225
Pella 120, 127, 152
pennyroyal 51, 85, 196
Peparethan wine 100, 148
pepper 137, 138, 192, 246
peppermint 235
perfumes 23, 49, 52, 103, 106, 115, 125, 129, 136, 137, 221
Periander 25
*Periplus of the Erythraean Sea* 133
Perperine wine 149
Persia, Persian Empire 83, 124, 143, 145, 153, 154
Persian agriculture 97
Petronius, *Satiricon* 167
Phalerum 120, 126
pheasant 44, 63, 64
Philaenis 119
Philagrius 192
Philip, King 153, 154
Philippopolis 199
Philippus, joker 11
philosophers at meals 119

Philoxenus of Cythera 114–16
Philoxenus of Leucas 114, 246
Phliasian wine 125
Phoenicia, Phoenicians 105, 135
Phoenician wine 96, 97
Phrygia 136
Phryne 25
phylloxera 207
Phylotimus 162
picarel 72
pig 37, 38, 42–5, 59, 60, 61, 105, 107,
    156, 157, 166, 179, 199, 220
pigeon 44, 63, 64, 71, 166, 203
pike 43, 68
pilchard 72
pimpernel 236
pine kernels 81
pistachio 146, 219
pita 157, 178, 197
pitch 199
Pliny, *Natural History* 133
plover 64
plums 78, 182, 203
Plutarch 167, 187
poetry at meals 17
Polycrates 105
pomegranates 52, 77, 80, 198
Pompeii 57, 144, 145
poor people's food 24, 80, 85, 89, 93,
    196
poppy 51, 52, 86, 143, 234
pork *see* pig
porridge 45, 91, 127, 156, 197
potato 201
pottery 18, 44, 212
Pramnian wine 95, 100, 101, 148
prawn, shrimp 74, 107, 128, 166
private and public 13
Prodromos 36, 43, 45, 219
prostitutes 7, 10
Psellus 188
Psithian wine 95
Ptolemies, Kings 154
pulses 25, 89, 90
pumpkin 231
purslane 82, 84
Pylos 36
Pythagoras 22, 90

quail 63, 166
quince 165
quinces 78, 129, 165, 181, 192

rabbit 180, 219
radish 25, 84, 125, 127
raisin wine 96, 149
raisins 23, 80, 105, 129, 192
raki 204
rascasse 72, 127
ray 70
razor-shell 73
reclining 14
red mullet 72, 127, 128
rennet 66
Rethymnon 195
retsina 150, 198, 199, 203, 207
rhinoceros 36
Rhizus 101
Rhodes 79, 105, 129, 158
Rhodian wine 129, 193
rice 141, 192, 203, 251
roasting 38, 60, 61, 63, 113, 246
rocket 27, 82, 84
rockling 72
roe 189
Roman agriculture 181
Roman hyssop 82, 86
Roman influence 163–7, 187
roses 25, 165, 192, 202, 205
rosemary 190, 246
rowan 232
rue 82, 86
Rufus of Ephesus 166

sacrifice 3–6, 58–60, 208, 217, 244
safflower 51, 86, 115
saffron 129, 142, 165, 190
sage 86, 180, 234
Salamis 126
salep 82, 86, 202, 205
salsify 85
salt 47, 76, 167
salt fish 27, 76, 105, 156
salt meat 27, 205
Samian wine 193, 204, 206
Samos 105, 128, 147, 158, 159
Samothrace 127
samphire 85
sand-smelt 72
Sarakatsani 15, 34, 37
Sarambus 109
sardine 72
Sardis 57, 60, 81, 128
satyr play 59
satyrion *see* salep
satyrs 19, 87

saupe 71, 128
sausages 61, 181
savory 237; see also Roman hyssop
scad 72, 200
scallop 73, 128
Sciathos 127
Scione 101
Scyros 105
sea anemone 74
sea level 35, 40, 219
sea travel 33, 39–40, 133–6
sea-squirt 74, 128
sea-urchin 43, 74, 83, 123
seasonal diet 161, 191, 192
seasonal foods 71, 107, 118, 158, 166
second tables 23, 103
secondary products revolution 42
Seleucus, King 257
serenade see kômos in Greek index
sesame 51, 52, 86, 115, 221
Sesklo 36, 43, 44, 219
Seuthes, King 153
shad 72
shark 69, 127, 227
sheep 4, 22, 40, 44, 45, 58, 105, 107, 166, 208
shelduck 161
shellfish 67, 73, 76
sherbet 201, 202, 205
shopkeepers 106
shrimp see prawn
shrines, meals at 2–6, 12
Sicily 105, 108, 125, 136
Sicyon 125
Sicyonian wine 149
Sidari 37, 219
Side 126
Silenus 19
silphium 86–7, 105, 136, 140
Simeon Seth, On the Properties of Foods 188
Simonactides of Chios 161
Simus 122
Siren feasts 70
siskin 63
Sitagri 36, 43–4, 47, 219
skate 70, 113
slaves 4–10, 18, 26, 93, 155, 216
sloes 43, 78
small fry 72, 120
Smyrna 79, 100, 128
snails 25, 38, 62, 128
Socrates 20

soldiers' food 91, 196
sole 72
Sophon of Acarnania 161
sorbs 47, 80
sorrel 51, 82, 85
soup 22, 45, 86, 90, 203
sow's womb 61, 157, 159
sow-thistle 85
Spain 136
sparrow 63
Sparta 20, 74, 110, 124, 126, 217
Spartan wine 95, 97
spelt 239
spices 49, 51, 85, 137–42, 190, 191, 221
spignel 192
spikenard 165, 180, 192
spinach 201, 209
spleen 113
spoon sweets 202
sprat 72
squash 231
squid 22, 72, 127, 152, 166, 220
squill 85, 190
staple foods 22, 44–6, 89–93
star of Bethlehem 85
starch 240
starling 63
Stephanus, cook 195
Stobi 57
stone parsley 192
strawberries 43
Strymon, River 152
student food 25, 27, 85
sturgeon 68, 76, 200
succory 236
suckling animals 43, 59, 104, 189
Sufli 36, 48, 219
sugar 191, 192, 203
sumach 86
supper 61, 63, 73, 156
swan 225
sweets 14, 23, 51, 86, 115, 164, 171, 191
swordfish 128
Sybaris 108
Syceon 195
symposium see sympósion in Greek index
Syracuse 108, 116, 159
Syria 141, 145
Syrian wine 96

Tanagra 127
Taras 20

n 201
128, 182, 196, 205

21
ussa 128
192
os 127
127
28
nth 38, 43, 81, 146, 221, 251
an wine 94, 99, 100, 152
os 81, 121, 127, 136
rion 109
re 17, 213
an wine 193
es 121
dore Prodromus 188
odoric, King 188
ophanes Nonnus 188
ophrastus 143, 157, 159
ra see Akrotiri; Therasia
eran wine 149
erasia 36, 43, 50, 219
eseus 85
essalonica 205
essaly 105, 121, 124, 127, 136, 153, 190
race 95, 99, 153
racian Chersonese 136
rush 22, 63, 156, 157, 166
yme 26, 86, 126, 128, 165, 250
iryns 36, 52, 219
t 63
molite wine 148, 149
oasts 6, 29, 157
omato 201, 209
tongue 61
top-shell 73
Torone 69, 127
Toronean wine 152
tortoise 21, 216
transhumance 34, 37, 45, 218
Trebizond 191
Triglian wine 193
tritons 38, 43, 73, 229
Tromilic cheese 136
truffle 83, 125, 128
tunny, tuna 38–9, 53, 68, 76, 107, 113, 128, 166
turbot 72
turmeric 251
turnip 51, 85
turtle 21

Tyndaricus of Sicyon 161
Tyre 97

udder 189
Ulpian 164, 168

valerian 140, 192
Varniote wine 193
vegetables 23, 49, 82–7
vegetarian food 189
venus-shell 73
Vergina 14
vetch, Vicia spp. 25, 39, 41–2, 89
vine leaves 190
vine shoots 80
vinegar 89, 126, 190
vintage 87, 93, 94, 101, 241–2
violet 192
Vlachs 34, 45, 190

wagtail 65
walnuts 43, 81, 115
warbler see blackcap
water 104, 115, 162, 223
water parsnip 85
watermelons 78, 145, 205
wedding 29
wedge-shell 73
weever 72
wheat 22, 42, 44–6, 53, 90, 91, 105, 115, 127, 129
whole animals 157, 179
wild boar 62
wine 23, 47–8, 87, 88, 93–104, 147–51, 193–5, 205
wine dealers 106, 109
wine storage 93, 101
wine tasting 150
wine trade 95–7, 134
wine-mixing 17, 102, 103, 159, 194
winter cherries 80
women: at meals 2–8, 15, 17, 194; social position 13, 213; and wine 8, 101, 194
women's quarters see gynaikonîtis in Greek index
wood-pigeon 22, 64
woodcock 63
wormwood 85; see also absinthe
wrasse 71, 72, 128
wreaths 103, 115, 222

Xenocrates of Aphrodisias 162

Xenophon 153

yellow flag 192

yoghourt 66, 200

Zopyrinus 161